THEORY AT YALE

Sara Guyer and Brian McGrath, series editors

THEORY AT YALE

The Strange Case of Deconstruction in America

+

Marc Redfield

Fordham University Press

New York 2016

Library of Congress Cataloging-in-Publication Data

Redfield, Marc, 1958–
  Theory at Yale : the strange case of deconstruction in America / Marc Redfield.
      pages cm. — (Lit Z)
  Includes bibliographical references and index.
  ISBN 978-0-8232-6866-5 (hardback) — ISBN 978-0-8232-6867-2 (paper)
  1. Deconstruction. 2. Criticism. I. Title.
  PN98.D43R39 2015
  801'.95—dc23

                                                              2015018795

Printed in the United States of America

18 17 16   5 4 3 2 1

First edition

in memory of Helen Tartar

Contents

Introduction: The Strange Case of "Theory"   I

1. Theory, Deconstruction, and the Yale Critics   19

2. Theory and Romantic Lyric: The Case
   of "A slumber did my spirit seal"   62

3. What Remains: Geoffrey Hartman
   and the Shock of Imagination   84

4. Literature, Incorporated: Harold Bloom,
   Theory, and the Canon   103

5. Professing Theory: Paul de Man
   and the Institution of Reading   125

6. Querying, Quarrying: Mark Tansey's
   Paintings of Theory's Grand Canyon   158

Acknowledgments   187

Notes   191

Index   251

THEORY AT YALE

Introduction

The Strange Case of "Theory"

This book is about the event of "theory" in the American academy. The term *theory*—jostled, for reasons to be discussed, by quotation marks that form part of the term itself—refers here primarily to a certain kind of reflection on language and literature that garnered the tag "deconstruction" in the 1970s, and in distorted form became a minor mass-media topic in the 1980s. Both as a media event and, in more complex ways, as an academic one, "theory" was understood to be epitomized by "deconstruction"; and "deconstruction" was in turn understood to be epitomized by the writings, the proper names, and the ambivalently twinned personae of Jacques Derrida and Paul de Man. The reductive force of that dreamlike process of condensation and personification contributes to its historico-cultural and theoretical interest and forms part of what a study of "theory" needs to explain.

This book attempts the double task of respecting the conceptual power of Derrida's and de Man's texts on the one hand and situating the impact of those texts within an institutional and cultural context on the other. I have had to assume some acquaintance with this archive, but have tried to make the discussion accessible to readers of good will whose study of deconstructive theory has been limited. My focus on the primary texts is strategic, in any case. The guiding question here bears on how they were received. Though I am not offering a sociological account of the "theory" phenomenon—and this for essential reasons—my opening chapter will be thinking about "theory" in relation to three broad institutional frames: the structure of the American university, the tradition of public debate about the role of the humanities in the university, and the intersection of theoretical argument with romantic studies in professional academic criticism in the United States. The relevance of that last item becomes clearer if one accepts this book's postulate that a study of "theory" (a study, that is, of the mediatization of theory-as-deconstruction, which, as I note more than once in what follows, is not at all the same as a properly descriptive or historical account of literary theory) encourages one to think not just about the Derrida/de Man couple, but about its temporary embedding in an ensemble of "Yale Critics." The quadrumvirate-plus-one of Harold Bloom, Geoffrey Hartman, J. Hillis Miller, and de Man, with Derrida playing his central role from the margins (since he was of course neither a literary critic nor full-time at Yale), gave a fractured face to "theory" for a little while in the late 1970s and early 1980s. To be sure, this particular representation did not last long, and from the beginning its fractures were on display—the plural noun "Critics" suggests individualized peaks of eminence; and even the thinnest journalistic accounts of the Yale Critics during the years of their media-worthiness usually made a distinction between deconstruction on the one hand and Harold Bloom's theorizing on the other. (The kindred term "Yale School," which suggests a transmissible pedagogy rather than individual performers, has had more referential force and staying power. Though in the early years it sometimes overlapped with the phrase "Yale Critics," it came increasingly to refer to de Manian deconstruction, the only "school" that could be said to have emerged out of the Yale group.) For all sorts of reasons, the notion of the Yale Critics is not one that a conventional history of literary theory would want to spend much time on; but from my particular angle of approach, the cultural and conceptual grammar of this semi-imaginary entity deserves parsing.

This book does not do one or two things that readers might reasonably expect of it. Most obviously, it does not provide a systematic, detailed account of the work of the four Yale Critics. I intend to read slantwise into this archive; the focus, as said, is on the production and reception of a semi-imaginary collective that cannot and should not be taken entirely literally. Embarrassment has always limned serious efforts to write about the Yale Critics. (Are there really only four? Jonathan Arac, Wlad Godzich, and Wallace Martin settle on that number in the preface to their canonizing collection *The Yale Critics: Deconstruction in America*, but not without some awkward sidestepping: after all, "'Deconstruction in America' goes on in many places besides Yale"; furthermore, "there are not just four 'critics' at Yale. Shoshana Felman, for example, works brilliantly within the problem areas that Americans associate with de Man, Hartman, Miller and Bloom."[1]) A more plausible, and indeed, traditional topic will also be slighted here: the similarities and differences between de Man's work and Derrida's. (I have a few things to say on that subject, of course, but I will not be providing an extensive analysis; that would require a differently shaped book.) Another obvious matter for discussion, the collaborationist journalism that de Man wrote as a young man in occupied Belgium, surfaces only sporadically—mainly in connection with my interest in the media uptake of theory. Ortwin de Graef's discovery of the wartime journalism in 1987 and the ferocious debates that followed in 1988–89 have been discussed so widely that I have allowed myself to assume that likely readers of this book will not need much orientation there.[2] Exposition is not the primary task of this study in any case. I have specific comparisons and judgments to make, and, of course, at various points in what follows I describe critical positions, sometimes at length; I shall also be offering swatches of biographical, intellectual, and institutional narrative, particularly in the opening chapter. But those narratives are appendages to an argument that finally has little to do with the Yale Critics as a group, or with individual oeuvres in a traditional sense.

In Chapter 1, I review the production of "Yale" as a metonym for "theory" in the 1970s. This peculiar conjunction, the product of any number of visible contingencies, can remind us for starters of a fact often invoked and less frequently analyzed: the institutional side of the history of literary theory.[3] Since at least the 1940s, most discipline-specific intellectual work has taken place in research universities in the United States and has been enabled, spurred, and in subtle ways informed by the unique structure and size of the American educational system. That pedagogico-scientific system, the development of which forms part of the accomplishment of what is often called late or managerial capitalism, allots only an ever-decreasing fraction of its resources to the humanities; but the humanities play a significant symbolic role in American public discourse about the notion of higher education. In recent decades, that symbolic role may have come to feel particularly meager and hypocritical, but it has a long history and is unlikely to vanish entirely as long as the stratified U.S. educational system persists in anything like its current form. Complaints about university-level instruction in the humanities (which are always in worse shape than they were, always falling down on the job of bequeathing to modern life, research, and pedagogy a sufficiently robust human core) form part of the history of the American university itself. It is in this context that we need to understand the production of "theory" as a U.S. media event: as a spectral phenomenon that received extra oxygen from the fortuitous (and of course almost comically misleading) rhetorical associability of "theory" with Yale, one of the nation's iconic universities. Iconic precisely as a bastion of elite liberal education for the upper and managerial classes, and famous in literary circles as the former home of a Christianizing, conservative strain of New Criticism (to the point that Cleanth Brooks, William K. Wimsatt, and their colleagues had earned the sobriquet "Yale Critics" in the 1950s), Yale

University was an ideal stage on which to discover and denounce a threat to aesthetic education.

The phrase "aesthetic education" may have a somewhat nineteenth-century-sounding ring; but in fact, as we shall review in Chapter 1, twentieth-century debates about American university education have been saturated with Arnoldian rhetoric. No other country in the world supports an equivalent level of talk about "the humanities," or indulges and invests to the same degree in a pastoral idea of "college." Liberal arts colleges and elite universities may compose only a modest fraction of the far-flung American postsecondary educational system, but they garner most of the media attention and inspire an endless stream of books and articles about the crisis of the humanities, the liberal arts, and the university.[4] This is the discursive context within which "theory" became an academic and ultimately a public scandal. The scandal was ushered in, as we shall see, by "the Yale critics" in the mid-1970s, though by the end of the decade its epicenter was contracting to the double figure de Man–Derrida, and above all to de Man—the ultimate personification of theory *as scandal*. That figurative association had already settled firmly into place by the early 1980s, years before the discovery of the wartime journalism. It is therefore necessary to understand the theory-as-deconstruction-as-de-Man phenomenon in relation to cultural and institutional fantasies about aesthetic pedagogy and anxieties about language.

These are, surely not coincidentally, two of the main themes of de Man's late work. Of course, hostile responses to theory have rarely had the patience to examine carefully what theorists actually write or say; yet something about de Man's focus on figurative language made his work vulnerable to a strikingly intense pulse of mediatization. Part of the complexity of the "theory" phenomenon derives from the fact that one is compelled to find ways to explain how it is that "theory" both does and does not do what poorly informed and frequently angry opponents accuse it of doing. The distortion of de Man's critique of aesthetics into melodramatic absurdities—into an effort to "destroy literary studies" and promote "language as a free-floating system of signs," to cite a well-known antitheoretical tract of the era—is not simply an error.[5] Or, better, is not a *simple* error. De Man positioned himself and his work very cunningly in this respect. When, in his programmatic piece "The Resistance to Theory" (1982), he defines theory *as* the resistance to theory (which in turn is "the resistance to the use of language about language . . . to the possibility that language contains factors or functions that cannot be reduced to intuition"), he simultaneously defines theory as "de Manian" theory, and builds in an explanation of the hostile response that this theory inspires.[6] On the one hand, the wild journalistic version will be wrong in demonstrable ways; yet, on the other hand, it will be repeating in a violent, tragicomic idiom a spiral of wincing-away that theory, disclosing itself to itself as the resistance to itself, has pre-performed and predicted. Conceived thus, theory is always already "theory." Put more accurately (and inevitably more densely): de Man conceives of theory as a falsely totalizing, self-fissioning, and non-self-coincident movement of mediation. Theory's own energies cause it to recoil from itself; but in doing so it deconstructs aesthetics as "a phenomenalism of a process of meaning and understanding" (7), and exposes the fallacies of an educational program in which scripted contact with literary texts is taken to promote "the integrity of a social and historical self" (6).

De Man's extraordinary appropriation and reduction of "theory" to his own theory flies in the face of common sense in more ways than one. Even in its earliest openings-up, the discursive terrain called "theory" was heterogeneous, discontinuous, unevenly graded. As a buzzword, *theory* usually meant above all "French theory," but even under the sign of Frenchness, it was divisive and self-dividing; in its opening stages, it threw up a trinity (Lacan, Derrida, Foucault) and a binary opposition (Foucault versus Derrida). By the early 1980s, "theory" was congealing into a canon of texts and invocable proper names, mostly European but not all (Jameson, Fish, Said, Spivak—and for a brief period our Yale Critics). And very soon there were the anthologies, with their smorgasbord of "approaches," of which "deconstruction" was just one, and not by a long shot the freshest or most popular; and when, over the decades, anthologists accorded space to deconstruction, they usually took Derrida as the major figure, which by any ordinary measure he is. In the face of these undisputable facts, can it be that we are proposing to take at face value the de Manian appropriation of theory as the (de Manian) "resistance to theory"? With qualifications, yes—conscious, to be sure, of the multiple ironies of taking such a theory "at face value"; well aware that to do so is necessarily to repeat aspects of a pattern that we will also be trying to analyze; but compelled to pursue this course both by the structure of the "theory" phantasm and by the diagnostic power of de Man's formulation. The dream-logic I invoked at the beginning of this introduction is our topic. In identifying himself with theory, de Man was activating a program that the profession and the wider media were also keying into the system. De Manian theory is the theory of "theory," its author its symbolic emissary.

To a limited extent, similar claims can be made about the work and reception of Jacques Derrida and the curious global fortunes of the term "deconstruction"—a semiotic hypertrophy that plays a central role in the idiom of "theory." But it must also be stressed that Derrida's achievement only partly overlaps with the story I am telling here. Crucial though they were to the American "theory" phenomenon, his writings originated in a different national, linguistic, institutional, and disciplinary context, and already by the early 1970s were being received in numerous discursive, cultural, and geographic frames of reference. The largely American allegorical drama that cast Derrida, Lacan, and Foucault as "French theory" and Derrida and de Man as "high theory" (high theory as the essence of theory as deconstruction-as-theory) was one that French intellectuals, coming from a differently articulated public sphere, were not always able easily to understand.[7] Only once, to my knowledge, did Derrida comment at length on the idiomatic use of the word *theory* that has become normative in the humanities in the United States. In "Some Statements and Truisms about Neologisms, Newisms, Postisms, Parasitisms, and Other Small Seismisms," a paper written for a symposium titled "The States of 'Theory'" that took place at the University of California at Irvine in the spring of 1987, Derrida identified "the word and the concept of 'theory'" as "a purely North American artifact, which only takes on sense from its place of emergence in certain departments of literature in this country."[8] He was prepared to be interested, at least over the space of a few pages, in a term that was so insistently eager to be enclosed in quotation marks. The absence of a metalanguage, he noted, implies a generalization of quotation marks, since no term or idiom can be insulated from citationality or parasitism: "these quotation marks impose themselves at a time when the relationship to all languages, to all codes of tradition, is being deconstructed *as* a totality and *in* its totality to an ever-increasing extent. . . . What is at stake, then, is another writing of the quotation marks themselves, which . . . destabilizes even the opposition between discourse *with* quotation marks and discourse *without* quotation marks, mention and use, and the entire system of associated values; that is, philosophy in its entirely, theory in its entirety" (74, 75). Late in his paper Derrida cites approvingly from de Man's "Resistance to Theory" while maintaining a discreet distance from its arguments and its master-term. He prefers the term *deconstruction*, and he opposes it to a *theory* stripped both of its quotation marks and its de Manian paradoxes ("Deconstruction is neither a theory nor a philosophy" [85]; "Deconstruction resists theory then because it demonstrates the impossibility of closure" [86]; deconstruction "institutes itself neither as a regional theory (for example, of literature) nor as a theory of theories" [87]). It is a pushback moment against de Man, one of several in Derrida's later oeuvre.[9]

Derrida does not explain *why* "the word and concept of 'theory'" should be "a purely North American artifact." In Chapter 1, I offer a brief genealogy of this word and concept, as well as a few reflections, some of which have been sketched, on the institutional and discursive contexts that made "theory" an imaginable byproduct of "certain departments of literature in this country." As regards the word *theory* itself, there are at least three competing meanings to juggle: (1) the normative meaning operative in most modern disciplinary contexts, according to which *theory* means an explanatory hypothesis; (2) the somewhat idiomatic (though, as noted, in the humanities by now normative) meaning that Derrida is commenting on, which demands quotation marks for all the reasons he offers, yet nonetheless refers to a recognizable canon of texts, area of instruction, style of thought, and so on, mainly in literary and cultural fields, though also in sectors of other fields that have been influenced by these developments (media studies, art history, anthropology, law, sociology, etc.), and that has transformed knowledge production across a variety of disciplines; and (3) the hyperidiomatic use of the word that de Man signed and that we shall be retracing, where "theory," pressed to the wall, turns into "deconstruction" and then, pressed harder, turns into "de Manian deconstruction." (Rather than multiply eye-fatiguing quotation marks around the word *theory*, I shall let them recede into invisibility from now on, except when it appears that a bit of extra emphasis is required.) This last use of the word is often signaled in academic discourse by the adjectival compound "high theory," a phrase that suggests that the second and third meanings of *theory* bleed into each other—which in turn suggests that de Man was not indulging in mere self-promotion when he claimed for rhetorical deconstruction a strange, counterintuitive exemplarity.

It is therefore necessary to try to measure the gravitational pull of de Manian rhetorical reading within the emerging force-field of theory in the 1970s, a task that also requires us to assess and leverage de Man's characterization of the "aesthetic" as theory's complicated counterpoint. We shall go over these issues more patiently later in this book, but a synopsis here may be helpful. Earlier I cited de Man defining aesthetics as "a phenomenalism of a process of meaning and understanding." According to that broad definition, aesthetics becomes an inflection of logocentrism, "part of a universal system of philosophy rather than a specific theory" (8). Philosophy, according to this claim, wants to make the impersonal, imperceptible, unmotivated, potentially random differences making up language *present* to consciousness and perception. That desire, de Man implies, may be an irreducible part not just of philosophy but also of our being-in-language. Yet as soon as we begin attending to the rhetorical complexity of linguistic acts—as soon as we begin genuinely to *read*, as de Man puts it—we find that language disarticulates its own aesthetic illusions, by generating structures and processes that cannot be experienced in the mode of perception. Aesthetics, shaken loose from its root meaning of perception (*aesthesis*), would thus be another potential name for theory as the (self-resisting) deconstruction of aesthetics as phenomenalism. In "The Resistance to Theory," this possibility remains somewhat hidden; de Man speaks negatively of the "aesthetic function of language" in contradistinction to language's "rhetorical" dimension, and reserves the honorific term "literariness" for the "autonomous potential of language" (10). Yet literariness leads immediately to "literature" as a peculiar kind of writing that generates aesthetic effects as a byproduct of its deconstruction of aesthetic syntheses:

> Whenever this autonomous potential of language can be revealed by analysis, we are dealing with literariness and in fact with literature as the place where this negative knowledge about the reliability of linguistic utterance is made available. The ensuing foregrounding of material, phenomenal aspects of the signifier creates a strong illusion of aesthetic seduction at the very moment when the actual aesthetic function has been, at the very least, suspended. (10)

As we shall see in more detail in Chapter 5, "literature" is not a particularly stable category for de Man (as the site of literariness, literature is more of a performance or disturbance within a signifying medium than it is a formally or socially marked kind of writing). Yet the aesthetic category of literature inevitably becomes exemplary of literariness as semiotic unrest—a mode of writing that can be incorporated into a humanist or national-aestheticist pedagogy only through ideological obfuscation. Aesthetics makes trouble for itself; and in his late readings of Kant and Hegel's aesthetic writings de Man stresses the point: philosophical systems become vulnerable when they engage aesthetics, provided only that they are rigorous enough to follow out far enough "the critical thrust of aesthetic judgment."[10] For when they do, they disclose linguistic operations indifferent to "truth and falsehood, good and evil, beauty and ugliness, or pleasure and pain" ("Resistance," 10). They uncover the radical instability of the rhetoric of moral betterment that plays such a salient role in the American discourse of the humanities and arts, on the left as well as the right, in the idiom of theoretically inclined cultural critics as well as in that of reactionary cultural warriors.

Here we note another way in which Derrida's work can seem at once central to and slightly askew from the American theory-storm that had de Man at its eye. The category of the aesthetic plays a much less prominent and more traditional role in Derrida's writing than it does in de Man's. It has often and plausibly been claimed that Derrida preserves a certain loyalty to the philosophical tradition he shakes up and displaces, whereas de Man seizes with considerably more overt violence on "technical terms . . . without regard for their established definitions and procedural rules" (as Rodolphe Gasché comments with mingled disapproval and admiration).[11] De Man's emphatic transcoding of the aesthetic is an interpretive move that, in its boldness if nothing else, bears comparison with Jacques Rancière's quite differently pitched characterization of aesthetics as "the distribution of the sensible" that opens political space.[12] Yet, since the generalizing force of de Man's definition of the aesthetic is always in productive tension with specific acts of reading, the universalizing claim remains marked by its scene of production, and it will be my goal, in Chapter 1 and again somewhat differently in Chapter 5, to stress ways in which de Man's work functions as a commentary on the American academic context in which it was being produced.

An analysis of that context that aims at explaining the brief, potent, and phantasmatic isomorphism between "theory" and the "Yale Critics" during the late 1970s encounters as a related question the ambivalent affinity between literary deconstruction and romantic studies. Strong in many literary-historical fields during this era, Yale was without peer in the field of British and comparative romantic literature, thanks above all to Bloom and Hartman's scholarly accomplishments in the 1960s.[13] De Man's appointment in 1970 consolidated Yale's unique standing in this field; and as his model of rhetorical reading gained followers over the next decade, "Yale deconstruction" became visibly affiliated with romantic studies. Even today (and at present writing, the theory-at-Yale conjuration is getting on to being half a century distant), professional romantic literary criticism in the United States remains far more preoccupied with de Man's work than any other academic field is. The persistence of this legacy—a conflicted one, to be sure, that manifests itself sporadically throughout a complex and heterogeneous academic ecosystem—may to some extent be explained in personalized terms as the influence of particular teachers on particular students. But at a certain point, if one is to take the measure of the phenomenon, one needs to move on to institutional and discursive considerations. Several of this book's chapters track intersecting lines of force among the discursive-institutional and conceptual clusters of theory, aesthetics, and romanticism.[14] Romanticism, the era that gave modernity its concepts of revolution and art, has been a persistently hypercathected and contested period and concept in European literary, intellectual, and political history, particularly when aesthetico-political questions or a proximity between literature and philosophy are in play. (It comes as absolutely no surprise, for instance, that Rancière's account of the politics of aesthetics culminates in the romantic era, at which point, according to Rancière, a newly dominant "aesthetic regime of the arts" promises a democratized distribution of the sensible.)[15] A certain aesthetic excess, legible in wildly divergent ways—as escapism; as revolutionary energy; as apocalyptic humanism; as deconstructive rhetorical performance—has remained associable with romantic literature even in the dryly professional-bureaucratic world of American postwar scholarship, not least because of the heavy institutional focus on a small, charged canon: the lyric poetry of a "visionary company."[16] Given the tormented symbiotic relationship between aesthetics and theory, it is thus no accident that one of the high-profile debates about theory in the early 1980s took as its object an iconic romantic lyric, Wordsworth's "A slumber did my spirit seal." After an initial look at the "new lyric studies" of our era, Chapter 2 examines the ability of "A slumber" to generate anxious accounts of textuality and intentionality by examining first J. Hillis Miller's and M. H. Abrams's well-known debate about it, and then Stephen Knapp and Walter Benn Michaels's peculiar use of it in their even better-known position paper "Against Theory" (1982). The theory that Knapp and Michaels are most determinedly "against" is of course, "theory": that is to say, once again and above all, de Manian theory.

I propose to understand the phenomenon of the Yale Critics in terms of the vexed interplay of aesthetics and theory that, as we have seen, became particularly visible in academic romantic studies. What matters is not so much that the Yale Critics were professionally identified as romanticists (with Miller a qualified exception and Derrida, of course, again the odd man out, as the pseudo–"Yale Critic" manifesto *Deconstruction and Criticism* of 1979 made clear), as that, as a collective, they were able to personify aesthetico-theoretical excess.[17] The trope of personification is a major leitmotif in the following chapters; it is a primordial component of the "theory" phenomenon (and a primary trope in the theoretical-rhetorical analysis of that phenomenon). De Man came to *personify* theory. That personification also came doubled: Derrida/de Man. And during the "Yale" floruit, it came redoubled—deconstruction *and* criticism, as both the book's title and Hartman's preface insisted: "Derrida, de Man, and Miller are certainly boa-deconstructors. . . . But Bloom and Hartman are barely deconstructionists. They even write against it on occasion."[18] Earlier in the 1970s, Bloom and Hartman had drawn fire for being excessively mannered, aestheticizing, self-involved critics; they brought that aesthetic jolt to the group during the brief period that the Yale Critics provided a synecdoche for "theory." Something stranger was in store. By the mid-1980s, Harold Bloom was undergoing, or achieving, a personification that was arguably even more remarkable than de Man's. He became a unique figure in the American higher-brow mass media: the critic as genius, who personified the internalization of the Western canon. Bloom was the critic as cyborg—almost as monster, insofar as his ingestion of the canon required preternatural reading speed and memory; but he also stood for the embodiment of an aesthetic judgment that, at once omnivorous and discriminating, knew how to ingest, specifically, *the canon*. By the final decade of the twentieth century, Bloom and de Man had become, respectively, aesthetics and theory, opposed; the fragile covalent bond of the Yale Critics, seemingly, had blown apart into its elements.

I explore Bloom's transformation into this extraordinary public figure in Chapter 4. But I do so in the context of an argument that seeks to enrich our sense of the Yale Critics as a group. Even a phantasm can have a logic, and by stressing the fractured intimacy between aesthetics and theory I have already been suggesting the logic of this one. These scholars obviously had intellectual points of contact that preceded and exceeded their personal friendships or their appointments at Yale. My hope is to be able to push a little beyond generalities—beyond, say, the fact that they tended to be interested in certain authors and texts, and in fundamental questions about literature—and access scatterings of textual density that drag Hartman and Bloom into the orbit of (de Manian) theory.[19] My chapters take differently slanted approaches (once again, I am not offering straightforward *accounts* of any of these critics, though because in Bloom's case we shall be examining the construction of a persona, my chapter will have affinities with the traditional overview of a career or oeuvre). In Chapter 3, a study of Hartman's work focused mainly on *Wordsworth's Poetry* (1964), I examine the oldest archaeological layer of the Yale Critics: their mutual interest in peculiarly nonreferential or apocalyptic aspects of the "romantic imagination." As always de Man's was the strangest take on it, as manifested in his famous essay "The Intentional Structure of the Romantic Image" ("Structure intentionnelle de l'image romantique," 1960), where he entertained the possibility "for consciousness to exist entirely by and for itself, independently of all relationship with the outside world, without being moved by an intent aimed at a part of this world."[20] Hartman (who barely knew de Man at this point except as the author of that essay) pursues his own reading of the independent imagination in his epoch-making book. In the process, he discloses how violent, haunted, and rhetorically complex the Wordsworthian apocalyptic imagination is. Far from being an exaggerated instance of the egoistic sublime or of so-called romantic ideology, it operates on the near side of trauma and seems in its most intense manifestations a nonhuman, even nonanimate force; at such points it has affinities with what de Man was to call "language" in his late work. Hartman's great theme in *Wordsworth's Poetry* is the binding of this force to the phenomenal world. In our present context, the main point to stress is the way in which, some years before the era of theory, this powerful interpretation is both lingering with and warding off questions of the sort that rhetorical reading would later ask.

Chapter 4, as noted, takes up the figure and work of Harold Bloom, in order to explore ways in which Bloom's writing, particularly his critical theorizing during the 1970s, at once entertains and resists deconstructive themes and insights—entertains them more extensively and resists them more anxiously and ambivalently than Bloom's overt position-taking ever admits. Bloom characterizes much of his 1970s work as an agonistic struggle with de Man; that this agon is less stable—less stably an agon—than he would like is not without relevance for an understanding even of his later role as the representative of the Western Canon. In that context, Bloom's scanner-like reading speed and total recall become figures for the impossibility and instability of the figure of literary knowledge that they underwrite. In order to embody the humanities in an age of ever-accelerating technological reproducibility, Bloom has to not just mobilize but exhibit—theatrically display—figures of nonhuman mnemotechnical processes of inscription, storage, and dissemination: processes that Derrida interrogates by way of the trace, and that de Man tropes as language.

In Chapter 5, I turn, finally, to an extended discussion of de Man, the central figure in theory's carpet and in my overall narrative. But since my narrative is set up less to explicate or interpret de Man than to analyze a particular reception-effect, this chapter addresses itself to the sociological critique of de Man that John Guillory mounts in his *Cultural Capital: The Problem of Literary Canon Formation* (1993). It says something about the peculiarity of the de Man phenomenon that Guillory's classic study offers what is so far as I know the *only* sustained, informed, and rigorous negative account of de Manian rhetorical reading that the academy has ever produced. For that reason alone, it deserves close scrutiny; but Guillory's reading of de Man also has the advantage of returning us to the question of the institutional framework within which "theory" happened. Guillory interprets the emergence of a theory canon as symptomatic of a broader crisis in literary instruction: the "moment of theory is determined . . . by a certain defunctioning of the literary curriculum, a crisis in the market value of its cultural capital occasioned by the emergence of a professional-managerial class which no longer requires the (primarily literary) cultural capital of the old bourgeoisie."[21] Rightly taking de Man as the very figure of theory, Guillory sets out to show that de Manian rhetorical reading can be read against its grain as the fully developed symptom of theory's moment.

According to this argument, rhetorical reading reduces the social to the linguistic as part of its unconscious (and defensive) refiguring of "the new social form of intellectual work, the technobureaucratic labor of the new professional-managerial class"—the social truth concealed and relayed by the de Manian pathos of "rigor" (181).

I am a little leery of the idiom of crisis that, throughout most of the twentieth century and into our own, has marked discussions of the humanities in the United States. As noted earlier, my own sense is that versions of liberal education are likely to remain a prestige marker on elite levels of the stratified American university system for the reasonably near-term future. Despite the well-publicized retrenchments of recent years, the overall state of the humanities is too complex for easy summary.[22] No doubt, the cultural capital that even the most elite universities now dispense to their young consumers gets cashed out in a currency different from that circulating in the era of the *Bildungsbürgertum* (not that that old-European fractional class ever existed in the United States); and no doubt part of that currency changeover—a metaphor offered here in recognition of the emphatic monetization of education in recent decades along neoliberal lines—has involved an increasing marginalization of traditional high literary culture in normative higher education.[23] It is surely also the case, as Guillory and many others have argued, that since the early decades of the twentieth century and above all since the Cold War, the American university system has served the credentialing needs of a professional-managerial and technocratic cadre.[24] (The odd media figure of Harold Bloom as the allegorical embodiment of the "Western Canon" can and from certain vantages must be read along such lines, as an instance of literary prestige being consumed *as* entertainment in a post-literary media culture.) But is "theory"—epitomized, as so often when the temperature rises, by de Manian deconstruction—explainable as the distorted reflection of professional-managerial modernity? The results of my critique of Guillory's critique of de Man suggest not. Guillory's powerful but demonstrably aberrant interpretation has the merit of clarifying, against its own intentions, the degree to which de Manian rhetorical reading incorporates into its protocols an ironic remarking of the bureaucratic conditions of its own production, while thematizing the radical instability of language as an aesthetic category. Rhetorical reading, therefore, is not a mere symptom or reflection of techno-bureaucratic social forms, but is rather a self-reflexive critique of the aesthetic work—as well as the deconstructive unworking—that those forms enable.

"Theory" could not have happened as it did outside of the institutional and professional contexts of the late twentieth-century American university.

And if for a moment we relieve the word *theory* of its perverse attachment to de Man, on which I am otherwise insisting here, and return it to its quotidian job of pointing to an alternative or supplemental "canon"—Agamben to Žižek; anthology to syllabus—if, that is, we step back to the second meaning of "theory," as I put it a moment ago: the meaning Derrida was addressing, the meaning we give to this word in daily life in most areas of the humanities, these days—if we do that, we would then certainly want to say that theory impacted and changed those professional contexts in substantive and obvious ways. Viewed from this normative (and necessary) perspective, theory is the nickname of a complex but in many ways massively successful intra- and extra-institutional mutation in professional-academic praxis.[25] As Jonathan Culler comments, "We are ineluctably in theory."[26] Theory is part of the business of the academy, part of the skill set of a professionalized professoriat; and though the contact-points between "theory" in that broad sense, on the one hand, and the administered, technologized world of our current neoliberal order, on the other, deserve the closest scrutiny, it is also important to affirm how many strong, exciting, durable acts of speculation and interpretation have been enabled by the confluence of texts, discourses, and insights to which the term *theory* refers. But a residue of unease remains ground into theory's fabric. The encryptions, symptoms, revenants, and trigger-names of that residue vary, depending on the context (Freud, psychoanalysis, continental philosophy, Derrida), but its most persistent figure is Paul de Man, the allegory and allergen of theory-in-America, who haunts the archive as the figure for theory's half-obliterated, never quite eradicable or forgettable or entirely present-to-itself *event*.[27] That event is also the flash point at which theory becomes "theory": mediatized, hypercathected, disseminated beyond its immediate context. In my final chapter, which serves more as postscript than conclusion, I look closely at two well-known paintings from 1990 by Mark Tansey, *Derrida Queries de Man* and *Constructing the Grand Canyon*. These paintings offer subtle, complex reflections on the strange event of theory in America. They help us resist the lazy thought that theory will always or even usually be better understood inside rather than outside a professional academic cadre. Mediatization is not the equivalent of simplification or degradation. Mass mediatization enables massive patterns of distortion; but as deconstruction emphasizes, mediatization is already at work whenever there is writing, language, representation, or thought. That drift, dissemination, and exposure to loss is precisely what opens up the chance *for* thought. In the mediatization of the theory that theorizes mediatization, Tansey's paintings discover a subject for art.

—+—

It remains, finally, to address briefly one obvious question that my account of this book has not yet answered directly enough. Why this archive, now? Is a dubious collective called the Yale Critics worth remembering and analyzing so very many years later? I would hope for a faint "yes" even from readers who refuse this book's interpretive effort, since historical memory is always worth curating; but, of course, antiquarianism is not the point. As a group and a media phenomenon, the Yale Critics are a relic of history, but the same cannot be said of the cultural tectonics that produced the "theory" tremor. Seismic activity still marks this territory. A strong delayed aftershock is Evelyn Barish's *The Double Life of Paul de Man* (2014), a book that, like David Lehman's much earlier semibiography *Signs of the Times: Deconstruction and the Fall of Paul de Man* (1991), compresses and puts compactly on display the symbolic-sacrificial economy of the discourse of "theory" in America in its most negative and hysterical form. Both these biographies were written from a distance (Lehman is a cultural journalist and poet, Barish a scholar with expertise in nineteenth-century American transcendentalism, and no visible interest or training in literary theory)—it is as though the desire to write a life of Paul de Man is scripted, in our culture, to run counterclockwise to the desire to understand what his theoretical texts are saying. Both biographers approach their subject with an odd blend of anger, fascination, and ignorance—seemingly inexhaustible anger; near-obsessive fascination; an ignorance that can at times seem almost willed, like a strenuous act of faith or courage. Barish frankly admits in her opening pages that she does not understand de Man's professional work.[28] What has driven her, then, to research and write her book over all these years? The answer is peculiar but clear: she has been driven by a desire to disqualify through ad hominem argument *the theory she admits she does not understand.* We are returned to the paradoxes of the resistance to theory, which manifest themselves here in particularly stark form. Barish understands that she does not understand (and, unlike many cultural warriors, is honest enough to say so), yet she also understands that de Manian theory threatens to disturb what we think we understand about understanding. And since she indeed does not understand de Man (or Derrida or Heidegger or any of the other Continental thinkers who show up at various points in her story), she renders this threat in very crude form (e.g.: like "Bataille, Blanchot, and others," de Man "denied language's capacity to communicate" [369]). On the one hand, such statements are absurd; on the other hand, they express an anxiety capable of driving a professor to devote decades to a book about de Man—and of fueling reviews of the book in the most important American media venues (*New York Times, New Yorker, Wall Street Journal, Washington Post*). The reception of Barish's biography makes it clear that to speak of an anxiety elicited by theory is not to speak simply of an author's psychological state. Theory is a strange case, as Sigmund Freud or Sherlock Holmes might judge it (we shall be calling on Holmes, a "theorist" of sorts, at the end of this book). Laced as it is with anxiety, this cultural event resists being cleanly consigned to the past.

Barish's biography and its reception underscore the nonclosure of the "de Man affair" of 1988–89. However severely or generously one ends up judging de Man's behavior as a young man in occupied Belgium during the war, at least one thing is clear: the "affair" that erupted in the United States some forty-five years later belongs entirely to the history of "theory" as a media event. There would have been no media-worthy story at all if de Man had not been the quasi-allegorical figure *for* theory. The scandal had its effects, obliterating de Man in most sectors of the highbrow public sphere behind the toxic, thought-stopping sign of "Nazism";[29] yet the gap between de Man's collaborationist literary journalism during 1941–42 and de Man's professional writing during the 1970s required such violent hermeneutic acts to bridge that even theory's most fervent opponents, I think, have been saddled with the nagging sense that their case was not closed. That, at least, is one way to explain a striking feature of the de Man biographies, which is their unappeasable hunger for more scandal, more occasions for outrage, however petty: anything to confirm that de Man was *bad*. Lehman published a new, expanded edition of his book when he was told that de Man had once been an irresponsible house sitter;[30] Barish, who has dug up a wealth of information about de Man's early life, some of it quite unflattering, "knows only one note, sustained outrage," as a by no means pro-"theory" reviewer of her biography commented.[31] One may grant that the record of de Man's complicated life includes some deplorable decisions, while being struck by the hysterical tone that this by now long-dead literature professor continues to be able to inspire.[32] That tone relays the internal tensions of an ad hominem argument with an allegorical core. In its March 2014 issue, to accompany Carlin Romano's "Deconstructing Paul de Man"—a particularly shrill ad hominem denunciation of de Manian theory inspired by Barish's biography—*The Chronicle Review* published an image of de Man's face defaced with allegorical brandings: "Embezzler," "Anti-Semitic," "Liar," and "Forger" (all four squeezed onto de Man's high forehead); "Bigamist" and "Hustler" (on each cheek); "Fraud" (crammed down the line of the nose); "Nazi Sympathizer" (on the chin).[33] It is a disturbingly violent image. An archaic impulse to dehumanize through defacement has been triggered here,

I think, by the backwash of de Man's allegorical role: every square inch of this face, the face of "theory," is being branded so as to efface its humanness. And de Man is being effaced as a human being out of a desire to *have him give a face to "theory."* The sadistic excess of this image responds to the willfulness of that association; for of course "theory" does not have a face, and cannot have one, except by way of an act of figuration that, as here, can turn violently dehumanizing.

What is it about theory, and de Man, that inspires such aggression? Psychoanalysis tells us that symptoms constitute efforts to bind anxiety. And if de Man is right—and in certain ways he seems to have won his bet about the exemplary function of his own theoretical approach—the anxiety is about language. The allegorical labels inscribed on the image of de Man's face relay a hunger for fixed meanings, for signs as recognizable as faces, for faces as transparent as signs. But signs are not transparent, and faces only seem natural. The image in the *Chronicle* offers an angry version of a trope that de Man saw as constitutive of reading itself: "the endless prosopopoeia by which the dead are made to have a face and a voice which tells the allegory of their demise and allows us to apostrophize them in our turn."[34] De Man's insistent focus on the threat of the unreadable requires us, as we have seen, to attend to aspects of language that are indifferent to meaning, intention, and desire. And that attention to those aspects of language triggers a program of resistance that unspools at a deeper level than that on which our normal distinction between "understanding" and "not understanding" a text resides. Lehman's *Signs of the Times* feeds its fires almost entirely with caricatural versions of the threat of unreadability (e.g., "the idea that all interpretations are misinterpretations, that none should be 'privileged,' that the author's intentions are irrelevant, and that meanings are 'undecidable'" [104]; such wild claims evoke and ward off the more serious problem that interpretative cruxes *can* be "undecidable," and that intentions are enabled by a signifying system that exceeds them). Barish, condemning the theory she does not understand, symptomatically yet also quite rightly identifies its crime as an overweening focus on "the slipperiness of language" (355). The "theory" phenomenon has snowballed down that slippery slope. And if we had to nominate one word as the depth charge for that avalanche, probably our best candidate would be that seemingly innocuous word *language*, which under pressure turns so explosive.

"There is probably no word to be found in the language," de Man claims, "that is as overdetermined, self-evasive, disfigured and disfiguring as 'language'" (13). Derrida often took pains to distinguish deconstruction from linguisticism, as part of his career-long effort to counter the systematic distortion to which his work was subjected;[35] but as I have already suggested, what de Man means by "language" overlaps considerably with Derrida's privileged figures of trace, iterability, *différance*. Derrida used the term "language" in this large sense in *Of Grammatology* (1967) and a few other early writings: "However the topic is considered, the *problem of language* has never been simply one problem among others. But never as much as at present has it invaded, *as such*, the globalization of the most diverse inquiries and the most heterogeneous discourses. . . . The inflation of the sign 'language' is the inflation of the sign itself, absolute inflation, inflation itself."[36] Here, in his book's opening pages, Derrida is working to locate his project within a context that forces us to rethink traditional notions of text and context. The referential grip of that abstract-sounding phrase "inflation itself" becomes clearer when we realize that the natural as well as the human sciences partake of this inflationary movement: "It is also in this sense that the contemporary biologist speaks of writing and program in relation to the most elementary processes of information within the living cell. And finally, whether it has essential limits or not, the entire field covered by the cybernetic program will be the field of writing" (9). "Language" becomes an opaque limit-figure for mnemno-machinal processes that cut across the difference between life and death:

> one could speak of a "liberation of memory," of an externalization always already begun but always larger, of the trace which, beginning from the elementary program of so-called "instinctive" behavior up to the constitution of electronic card-indexes and reading machines, enlarges *différance* and the possibility of putting in reserve: it at once and in the same movement constitutes and effaces so-called conscious subjectivity, its logos, and its theological attributes. (84, translation modified)

The "electronic card-indexes and reading machines" of 1967 have mutated into the vastly more powerful and pervasive reading and writing machines of our era: an era in which the boundaries between machine and organism, writing and voice, animate intent and inanimate pattern, have become more porous than ever. It is hardly surprising that the question of the humanness of language, once posed, should become a flash point in humanistic and literary contexts. Conditioned by deracinating processes toward which they could not help being profoundly ambivalent, American institutions and discourses of aesthetic pedagogy made "theory" into the defining media event of the humanities during the last third of the last century. That event, never entirely real in the first place, has not yet run its course.

1. Theory, Deconstruction, and the Yale Critics

In the opening sentences of an early essay, "Force and Signification" (1963), Jacques Derrida imagines a figurative future beachscape strewn with signs:

> If it recedes one day, leaving behind its works and signs on the shores of our civilization, the structuralist invasion might become a question for the historian of ideas, or perhaps even an object. But the historian would be deceived if he came to this pass: by the very act of considering the structuralist invasion as an object he would forget its meaning and forget that what is at stake, first of all, is an adventure of vision, a conversion of the way of putting questions to any object posed before us, to historical objects—his own—in particular. And, unexpectedly among these, the literary object.[1]

The spent "structuralist invasion" lingers on as works and signs (*oeuvres et signes*); the historian of ideas objectifies this event, so as to know it as a subject knows an object. He thereby forgets the meaning of an invasion that has already invaded him and thought past him—past the Cartesian paradigm of the knowing subject and its world picture. The works and signs are traces of an act that questions how best to question "historical objects"; and as soon as the historian sets out to know such an act as one more such object, he mistakes what it is.

Though Derrida does not say so explicitly, that predicament turns out to motivate the appearance of the "literary object" in the last sentence quoted above. The literary object does not appear on the beach—the flotsam is rather the wrecked record of the structuralist invasion's "unexpected" effort to *read* (among other objects) the literary object—yet it shadows these membra disjecta. For Derrida's essay, a respectful but sharp critique of Jean Rousset's literary-critical study *Forme et signification* (1962), will find that the structuralist critic, like the beachcombing historian, erroneously converts an act into an object. "The force of the work, the force of genius, the force, too, of that which engenders in general, is precisely that which resists geometrical metaphorization and is the proper object of literary criticism" (20). But "a structuralist reading, by its own activity, always presupposes and appeals to the theological simultaneity of the book" (24); it "risks stifling force under form" (26). Its wreckage, washed up on the shore of history, passes a version of that error on to the historian of ideas.

Derrida's parable speaks richly to a would-be historian of theory in America. It does not say that histories of critical thought are impossible or should not be written, or even that they have to move beyond the formalizing mode of a "history of ideas" to be useful (in fact, "by virtue of the essential shadow of the undeclared, the structuralist phenomenon will deserve examination by the historian of ideas" [4]). But it reminds us how easily we slip into remembering such events by forgetting the impact that makes them memorable. The works and signs of an "invasion" solicit narrative; and theory, so frequently caricatured as an invasion from France in American polemics, has often enough been flattened into a history of falsely objectified ideas, dangling one after the other like beads on the string of a homogenous temporal and communicational medium. Admittedly, the historian of theory faces an even more recalcitrant and evanescent historical object than that offered by structuralism (which itself, from the perspective of the historian of theory, becomes an appendage to the history of theory). Whereas "structuralism" names a reasonably identifiable if diverse intellectual movement, "theory" does not. The heterogeneity of the texts to which it makes reference is such that its meaning threatens to wither away. A broad-brush account such as François Cusset's *French Theory* inevitably processes its titular subject into an empty signifier, "no longer designating anything but its own aptitude for dissemination, its sheer power of contamination."[2]

The problem of telling a history of theory, furthermore, goes beyond both the difficulty of resisting the temptation to objectify the act that puts objectification into question, on the one hand, and the challenge of describing a diffuse and diverse phenomenon, on the other. "Theory" never functioned simply as an empty descriptor. The word itself was embarrassing, and often appeared protected by inverted commas, little compulsive flickers of irony; its emptiness came laced with affect and performative effectivity; it met with an intense, complex response, to the point that that response became part of the story about it; it collected itself around a spike of intensity that came to be called "poststructuralism" or "deconstruction." Deconstruction was "high" theory—a phrase implying a pure extract, a sovereign instance. (It is symptomatic that Cusset's generalization is in fact not entirely empty, but bears the signature of a Derridean idiom of "dissemination" and "contamination." This is the basic law of the *discourse of theory*, as I shall be calling it: The more the question of theory is taken to its limit, the more likely it is that the equally charged term "deconstruction" will be in some way invoked.) Histories of theory have rarely failed to register this phantasmatic exemplarity of deconstruction. Hence the near-mythic role accorded the Johns Hopkins conference of 1966, "The Languages of Criticism and Sciences of Man," when, as the story goes, Derrida's critique of structuralism obliterated the structuralist controversy in the United States before it began.[3] From this vantage, the opening parable in "Force and Signification" says more to us now than it did to readers half a century ago. Its metaphor of the receding structuralist wave has become, in retrospect, a proleptic trope for the force of Derrida's writing about force—a figure for the catastrophic origin of "theory."

All of this is a myth, to be sure. A responsible historical examination of the influence of French structuralist thought (let alone European thought overall) on American criticism in the 1960s would produce a diverse and multilayered picture of an intellectually fertile period. Yet at some point—supposing it extended its account into the later 1970s—that history, however sober its intentions, would have to in some way take account of the discourse that by that time had grown up about and around the term "theory".[4] For "theory," used in this idiomatic sense (about which we will of course have to say more later), is always also talk *about* "theory." The quotation marks register not just embarrassment and irony but also citation, iteration, broadcasting: in a word, *mediatization*.[5] If we let the brake slip and abandon our story to the pulse of its internal melodrama, we can have the young Derrida predicting this, too—this spectral hypertrophy of theory—at the beginning of "Force and Signification," in the sentences that follow the ones quoted earlier:

> By way of analogy: the fact that universal thought, in all its domains, by all
> its path-ways and despite all its differences, should be receiving a formidable
> impulse from an anxiety about language—which can only be an anxiety of
> language, within language itself—is a strangely concerted development: and
> it is the nature of a development not to be able to display itself in its entirety
> as a spectacle for the historian, if, by chance, he were to attempt to recognize
> in it the sign of an epoch, the fashion of a season, or the symptom of a crisis.
> Whatever the poverty of our knowledge in this respect, it is certain that the
> question of the sign is of itself more or less, or in any event something other,
> than the sign of the times. To dream of reducing it to the sign of the times is to
> dream of violence. (Ibid.; translation slightly altered)

An "anxiety" about "language" was to become the most insistent motif of the theory phenomenon in the United States in the 1970s and 1980s, expressed in countless denunciations of the "prison house of language"; of poststructuralism as a ridiculous but somehow threatening textualism; of deconstruction as an abandonment of thought and moral being to the play of the signifier. Theory as deconstruction was accused of forgetting force (referential, historical, moral force) by critics who were themselves often very keen to forget the Derridean question of force, to "dream of violence" and reduce "the question of the sign" to "the sign of the times." One critic even remembered to affirm this forgetting: at the end of his book about the desirability of putting an end to theory in America, David Lehman quoted these sentences of Derrida's and defied them, without argument—defied them, that is, as violently as possible—and thereby wrote the fall of theory into the title as well as the subtitle of his widely distributed *Signs of the Times: Deconstruction and the Fall of Paul de Man* (1991).[6]

Our topic in this study is theory and its phantasms. "Theory" refers on the one hand to real and substantial institutional and discursive developments in literary and cultural scholarship in the final decades of the twentieth century, and on the other hand to mythologizing narratives and figurative constellations that partake of and cannot simply be teased apart from that institutional and discursive history. As noted before, I shall be speaking of the *discourse* of theory and of theory's *mediatization*. Particularly in the first case, I shall be leveraging the ambiguity of the genitive phrase (objective or subjective: discourse about theory, or theory's own discourse). *Discourse of theory* thus refers to professional argument (the texts and *prises de position* of a "theory canon"), but also to at least two wilder kinds of talk *about* theory: (1) the mythologizing tropes and narratives that, as noted, appear even within sober professional argument, and that saturate loose talk about theory; and (2) the often quite violent distortions and simplifications that fuel straightforward *resistance* to theory. Texts that fall into that last category offer demonstrably false accounts of the texts and discussions that compose the professional subfield of theory (the "discourse of theory" in the first sense), yet their mistakes are part of what we are interested in here, for programmatic, reiterated mistakes about theory form part of the cultural event of theory. They may in fact be understood as reiterating a pattern already discernible in the original theoretical texts. Such was the moral we drew from Derrida's beachside parable; and of course this is the lesson that Paul de Man famously formalized as the equation of theory with self-resistance ("The resistance to theory is a resistance to the rhetorical or tropological dimension of language. . . . Nothing can overcome the resistance to theory, since theory is itself this resistance").[7]

We have moved inexorably from Derrida to de Man in these opening pages because we have been glossing and repeating the structuring myth of the discourse of theory. From the Derridean overbidding of the structuralist invasion at Johns Hopkins in 1966, to the "fall of Paul de Man" in 1988, the discourse of theory narrates the essence of theory as "deconstruction." The heraldic figure of theory-in-America is the fraternal couple, Derrida and de Man (paired in ambiguous coupling or combat over a linguistic abyss, as in the shrewdly ironic painting by Mark Tansey, *Derrida Queries de Man*, that we shall examine much later in this book). Between 1966 and 1988, Derrida became a figure of global renown, whose thought was often associated (often, it must be said, superficially and overhastily) with the "America" where he lectured regularly but never took a permanent position, yet where his work received particularly intense reception.[8] Derrida introduces our story, and he will be haunting it on every page, though mostly from the wings and margins. For we are turning our gaze toward a mythic place in the landscape of theory, a place with which Derrida is only partly associated: New Haven. As Lehman's title suggests, Paul de Man, even more than Jacques Derrida, came to stand in for or personify high theory—to the point that his "fall" could be the fall of deconstruction itself, the sign of the times. And in between genesis and fall—between the Hopkins conference and the wartime journalism affair—there appears that quite improbable Eden, "Yale." It was in good part through the filter of "a new group of critics centered at Yale," as J. Hillis Miller announced in *The New Republic* in 1975, that theory became identified with deconstruction and that theory-as-deconstruction underwent mediatization over the course of the 1970s.[9] (Miller named Harold Bloom, Geoffrey Hartman, and Paul de Man and included himself by implication; "to this group may be added Jacques Derrida, who now presents a seminar at Yale in the early fall each year.") As noted in the introduction to this book, the notion of the "Yale Critics" as a meaningful ensemble was always somewhat troubled and thin; but the attention it received in the academy during the second half of the decade paved the way for the initial mass-media uptake of "deconstruction" in the 1980s. In the rest of this chapter, I shall go over that history briefly and offer some contextual frames for it before returning to consider in greater detail the phantasmatic role that de Man in particular has played in the discourse of theory.

It is understandable that histories of twentieth-century literary theory rarely grant much notice to the Yale Critics, both because those histories have tended to be histories of ideas, and because there is in any case so much to tell. Such histories usually grant some space to de Man and necessarily a good deal of space to Derrida, but they do so in the context of wider narrative arcs: the career of philosophical speculation from Kant and Hegel through Kierkegaard, Nietzsche, Heidegger, and Levinas; the history of literary and aesthetic speculation from the Schlegels through Sartre, Bataille, and Blanchot; the pathbreaking lectures of Saussure; the Russian Formalists (who, both as the *Opoyaz* group in St. Petersburg, and the Moscow and later Prague circles centered around Roman Jakobson, have a claim to be the first real modern *theorists* of literature); postwar phenomenological, existentialist, Marxist, and structuralist movements in France; the work of Benjamin, Adorno, and the Frankfurt School; psychoanalysis from Freud to Lacan; the (limited) reception of Althusser, Barthes, Deleuze, Derrida, Foucault, Lacan, Lévi-Strauss, and other Continental writers in the United States in the 1960s; the suddenly more visible influence of these and various other mainly French *maître-penseurs*, above all Foucault and Derrida (but also Irigaray, Kristeva, Todorov, Iser, Jauss, and others) in the 1970s; the development of a theory-canon in the 1980s and 1990s no longer quite so centered on French and German proper names (the list by now including Butler, Culler, Felman, Fish, Jameson, Said, Sedgwick, Spivak, Weber, Žižek, and many more); a surge of Anglophone interest in a few more European thinkers in the first decade of the twenty-first century (Agamben, Badiou, Rancière). (I have slanted this fragmentary catalog toward literary studies, broadly conceived; if our main interest were film or cultural studies, it would want to look a little different.) One can then feed this story into an institutional narrative that would detail how, by the end of the twentieth century, "theory" had been sorted and catalogued and packaged for consumption and export in the standard surveys and anthologies, which survey and anthologize "approaches" called narratological, psychoanalytic, deconstructive, Marxist, feminist, new historicist, queer, postcolonial, and so on, often thereby encouraging a sense of historical progress (first there would be deconstruction and French Freud and French feminism, then new historicism, then queer and postcolonial theory, etc.). In all of this, the Yale Critics, as a group, figure barely if at all.

Yet, if we scan the books, journal articles, and reviews published during the period when "theory" was first taking shape as an object for future explainers and anthologists in the American academy, the Yale Critics leap into visibility. They were first named as a group in 1975—and not just by Miller—but the names of the individual critics figure in the record with increasing insistence from the beginning of the decade onward. We may take a moment to review what their professional identities looked like at the beginning of the 1970s, when they were in their early forties (de Man in his early fifties). Bloom, Hartman, and de Man had achieved prominence as romanticists interested in imagination and consciousness in the 1960s; de Man and to some extent Hartman and Miller were also known as interpreters and commentators on European thought. Bloom, well known in his field as a passionate and prolific advocate of the apocalyptic-romantic imagination in the 1960s, achieved a different kind and level of fame with the publication of *The Anxiety of Influence* (1973). Hartman, whose *Wordsworth's Poetry* (1964) had reshaped Wordsworth studies, sealed his reputation as a major critic, theorist, and literary historian with his wide-ranging essay collection, *Beyond Formalism* (1970). De Man's essays in the 1960s had been influential enough to produce an invitation to give the Gauss Lectures at Princeton in 1967; with the publication of "The Rhetoric of Temporality" (1969), the collection *Blindness and Insight* (1971), and the beginning of his project of rhetorical reading (already taking shape in earlier work, but announced forcefully in "Semiology and Rhetoric" [1973]), he had become a major theoretical voice by the early 1970s. Miller, who had published influential books on modern poetry as well as Victorian literature, was known in the 1960s as a phenomenological critic inspired by Georges Poulet and the Geneva school; at the beginning of the 1970s, influenced by Derrida's work and, increasingly, by de Man's, he developed a deconstructive position that he publicized in a sequence of articles and challenging reviews.

By 1972, all four of these critics were at Yale, joined by friendship and overlapping professional interests. Bloom had been kept on at Yale after his graduate work, had received tenure there, and never left. Hartman had also taken his Ph.D. at Yale, but in comparative literature rather than in English; he and Bloom first became friends when they were hired as instructors in English at Yale in 1955.[10] Hartman met de Man briefly at an MLA conference around 1960,[11] but their friendship only began in 1965, when de Man recruited Hartman from the University of Iowa (where Hartman had taken up a tenured position in 1962) to Cornell, where de Man had been hired after finishing his doctorate at Harvard in 1960. In 1967 Hartman returned in triumph to Yale as a full professor in English and Comparative Literature, where he played a substantial role in effecting de Man's appointment to a professorship in French and Comparative Literature in 1970. De Man, who had moved to Johns Hopkins in 1967, taught his first course at Yale (after a year of negotiated leave) in the fall of 1971: a graduate seminar titled "Nietzsche's Theory of Rhetoric" that Hartman and Bloom audited—that was the beginning of the friendship between de Man and Bloom. Miller, the last of the four to move to Yale, joined the English Department there in 1972 after teaching for twenty years at Johns Hopkins. He had met de Man at a colloquium in 1964 and had met Derrida at the fabled Hopkins conference in 1966, though his deep friendship with Derrida developed a little later, when Derrida came back to Hopkins for a short-term teaching visit in 1968.[12] De Man had also met Derrida for the first time at the Hopkins conference. He and Derrida were both working intensely at that point on Rousseau's "Essay on the Origin of Languages," and their meeting forms part of the legend of the conference, for their famous friendship began there. Graduate students from Cornell and Johns Hopkins began attending Derrida's seminars in Paris in the late 1960s, joined by graduate students from Yale after 1970. Derrida made two more short-term visits to Hopkins, in 1971 and 1974; and in the fall of 1975 he began teaching six-week courses at Yale on a renewable short-term contract that de Man was able to arrange under the aegis of the French and Comparative Literature departments: an arrangement that would be renewed, despite increasingly bitter opposition from Yale's philosophy department, until 1986, three years after de Man's death, when at Murray Krieger's invitation Miller and Derrida left Yale for the University of California at Irvine.[13]

Having briefly introduced the leading figures, let me now sketch the context within which these critics became "Yale Critics" during the 1970s. Jonathan Culler reminds us that "normal criticism" in the academic era "is not a practice enclosed within a well-defined paradigm but a shifty or sloppy eclecticism that is always engaged in change."[14] It is good to keep in mind the heterogeneity of the critical record even as one seeks to draw attention to patterns—as when Mark Currie persuasively suggests, in his history of deconstruction in the United States, that "after 1967" an "eclectic configuration" of foreign impulses ("Frye, Levi-Strauss, Jakobson, Barthes, Todorov, Lacan and Derrida," representing "the intrusion into literary studies of methodologies derived from anthropology, linguistics, psychoanalysis and philosophy") was "slowly reduced to establish Derrida as the major influence for the 1970s, and perhaps the most prominent figure in theory up to the present day" (35).[15] Currie also notes that the best way to gain a sense of an era in rapid transition is to focus on journals and journal publications (37), and he does a good job of tracking the uptick of the term "deconstruction" during the first half of the 1970s in the newly founded journals *New Literary History* (founded 1969), *Diacritics* (1971) and *Critical Inquiry* (1974). That is a strategy worth pushing a little further. At the risk of forcing readers though a dull paragraph, but with the idea of recalling the quotidian humble-jumble of journal publication while also making it possible to point out details relevant to our topic, I propose that we examine a core sample, as it were—a content list, with an occasional short gloss—of the opening issues of the most theory-oriented of the new theory journals, *Diacritics*.

Founded by David Grossvogel and colleagues in Romance Studies at Cornell, *Diacritics* set itself a broad mandate to cover developments in French, Hispanic, and Italian modern and avant-garde literature, film, criticism, and philosophy. Issue 1, number 1 (Autumn 1971) featured reviews of important new books on Italian criticism, Freud, the French novel, Gabriel Garcia Marquez, and Jean-Paul Sartre; two essays on Fellini; a review by Angus Fletcher of Bloom's *Ringers in the Tower*; a "work in progress" essay by Tzvetan Todorov; an interview with Lévi-Strauss; and a polemical statement by Foucault that produced in the subsequent issue (Winter 1971), an unpleasant exchange between Michel Foucault and George Steiner that brought the journal public notice. That second issue also contained a review by Philip Lewis of Hartman's *Beyond Formalism*; reviews of books by Michel Butor and Jean Piaget; a review by Stuart Schneiderman of Jacques Lacan's *Ecrits* and Anthony Wilden's *The Language of the Self*; essays on Visconti and Fellini; a review by Sandra Siegel of Bloom's *Yeats*; a "work in progress" essay by Bloom titled "Antithetical Criticism"; and an interview with Ernst Gombrich. Having offered that variously underscored but complete list of the contents of the first two issues, let me now cherry-pick my way through a few more. Issue 2, number 1 (Spring 1972) granted Bloom another "work in progress" section, this time titled "Coleridge: The Anxiety of Influence"; the issue also featured an important review of Derrida's *De la grammatologie* by Alexander Gelley that, as part of its account of Derrida, drew approvingly on de Man's critique of Derrida's reading of Rousseau. Two issues later, volume 2, number 4 (Winter 1972) offered a deconstructive cornucopia: a review by Miller of M. H. Abrams's *Natural Supernaturalism* that constituted one of Miller's first great salvos announcing his turn to deconstruction; a review of *Blindness and Insight* by Angus Fletcher; an essay titled "Prolegomenon to Derrida" by Richard Klein; an interview with Derrida (the first of the two "Positions" interviews carried in *Diacritics*); and, as "work in progress," de Man's essay "Genesis and Genealogy in Nietzsche's *The Birth of Tragedy*." The subsequent issue (Spring 1973) featured the second Derrida interview and included Hartman's review of Bloom's *Anxiety of Influence*. One more item and we are done: volume 3, number 2 (Summer 1973) included an ambitious essay by Richard Klein, "The Blindness of Hyperboles: The Ellipses of Insight" that spent many pages analyzing the impact of Derrida's work on de Man's.[16]

Lists have a tendency to want to go on (especially with de Man's "Semiology and Rhetoric" about to appear in volume 3, number 4); but this one suffices to substantiate Currie's claim about the increasing prominence of "deconstruction" and the increasingly visible characterization, in this

important new high-theory journal in the early 1970s, of de Man and Derrida as intimately entangled rivals. (The word *deconstruction* begins its career
of viral reproduction during these years, along vectors too numerous and
entangled to be worth trying to track here. As is well known, in his early
work Derrida did not put a great deal of stress on this term; after a period of
puzzled resistance to its hyperinflation, he eventually accepted, affirmed and
elaborated it as the name his thought was fated to bear. De Man used the
term *deconstruction* sparingly and very much in his own way to point to local
moments in a text's self-undoing; his favored term for his own project, as we
shall review momentarily, was *rhetorical reading*.) "The articles of the winter
edition of *Diacritics* in 1972 perform a kind of bonding between Derrida and
de Man," Currie comments (40); the construction of the master-trope of
"high theory" is underway. Perhaps most surprising to readers unacquainted
with the era is the visibility of Hartman and above all Bloom in this little
archive. Hartman's essay collections *The Fate of Reading* (1975) and *Criticism
in the Wilderness* (1980) kept him in the public eye (and drew attacks, as
we shall see); and the enormously prolific Bloom, who unlike Hartman
had a consistent and dramatic theoretical story to tell, rivaled Derrida and
de Man for a few years as an avatar of "theory"—a fact that may take an
effort to recall, habituated as we are to Bloom in his post-1980s public role
as the cantankerous regent of the Western Canon. As the *Diacritics* record
shows, however, interest in Bloom's new direction was strong even before
The Anxiety of Influence appeared. That book was followed by a volley of
books: *A Map of Misreading* (1975); *Kabbalah and Criticism* (1975); *Poetry
and Repression* (1976); *Figures of Capable Imagination* (1976); *Wallace Stevens*
(1977). The arcane terminology for which Bloom was famous never knew
much influence in itself (the six "revisionary ratios" or ways of wrestling
a precursor, called clinamen, tessera, kenosis, daemonization, askesis, and
apophrades, each with its own associated trope and psychic defense; that
six-part system then sometimes overlaid with other patterns drawn from
kabbalistic writers); but the twinned idea of the "anxiety of influence" and
of reading as "misreading" became one of the best-known shibboleths of
literary theory.[17] It was unsurprising that Bloom received a chapter in Frank
Lentricchia's *After the New Criticism* (1980), or that he was selected to give
the inaugural Wellek Lecture in critical theory at the University of California at Irvine in 1981. (Wellek Lectures would be given by Derrida in
1984, Miller in 1985, and Hartman in 1992; de Man, who died in December
1983, had been scheduled to give the lecture in 1984.) When Miller wrote
in 1975 in *the New Republic* or again in 1976 in *the Georgia Review* of "a new
group of critics gathered at Yale: Harold Bloom, Paul de Man, Geoffrey

Hartman," he was not in the least exaggerating the prominence of these critics in avant-garde critical debate.[18]

Nor was he alone in promoting the idea of a Yale cohort at this time. In an article published in 1975 in *The Hudson Review* that bequeathed its title to the idiolect of antitheoretical polemic, "The Hermeneutical Mafia, or, After Strange Gods at Yale," William H. Pritchard quotes a line from Richard Poirer's review of Hartman's *The Fate of Reading* that had appeared in the *New York Times Book Review* a few months earlier about a "community enterprise" going on at Yale, and sets out on the attack. Pritchard grants "Paul deMan [*sic*] and J. Hillis Miller" glancing attention as two other "prominent members of that community enterprise" (de Man being "the subtlest analyst and best writer of that community"), but for him Hartman and Bloom are the central figures—and central offenders—of the scandal happening at Yale, and not just, one senses, because he happens to be reviewing their books (Hartman's *The Fate of Reading* and Bloom's *Map of Misreading*).[19] Their offense could be called stylistic, but in a way and to a degree that goes beyond ordinary issues of skill or decorum. We encounter in Pritchard's review early versions of the topoi that went into the making of the "discourse of theory" in its negative mode. "Hartman's abstracting is off-putting because of the style in which it's conducted . . . overreachings in Hartman's style make up *clair-obscurs* that are intensely frustrating"; "the level at which [these essays] operate is refined perhaps beyond not merely of desirable but of civilized practice" (603). And "the playful style has its grim corollary in the unanswerable one"—a phrase Pritchard uses to target a reference of Hartman's to (as Pritchard puts it) "the abominable Hegel and his hermeneutics" (605). Thus Hartman's stylistic overwroughtness—the puns and portmanteaux and the complexly allusive phrasing with which some of his texts experiment during this period—turns out to be inseparable (in a way Pritchard himself does not make clear) from forms of obscurity associated with continental philosophy (and, increasingly, continental "theory"). Here Pritchard turns to Bloom, whose idiosyncratic theoretical terminology makes for an easy target. Pritchard quotes swatches of Bloom at his most turgid (e.g.: "Applying the Lurianic dialectics to my own litany of evasions, one could say that a breaking-of-the-vessels always intervenes between every *primary* (limiting) and every *antithetical* (representing) movement that a latecomer's poem makes in relation to a precursor's text") and goes for the obvious joke: "this common reader, not necessarily to be despised, would more willingly submit to such instruction if it were expressed in English" (608). The common reader, invoked repeatedly by Pritchard, is also the common professor, watching members of an elite clique stroking each other's egos: "Particularly unforgettable are moments in which one of the giants confronts another; I remember an English Institute meeting at Columbia when, in the discussion period following on Bloom's talk, Miller rose to ask a question and was recognized by Bloom in some such terms as 'my great antagonist' (or was it 'mighty opposite'?). At such moments other academics in the room feel kind of humble and kind of proud" (602 n. 2). Pritchard's review suggests that by mid-decade the "Yale Critics" were well on their way to becoming a professional obsession.

This text helps us document a development that runs parallel to the emergence of the "deconstruction-as-theory" equation, with its totemic double figure de Man–Derrida: the hostile characterization of literary theory as elite, obscure, pretentious, and empty, at times almost dangerously decadent ("refined perhaps beyond not merely of desirable but of civilized practice"). Deconstruction had become the favored target of such charges by the end of the decade, but interestingly it was Hartman and Bloom who elicited the most visible attacks of this sort in the mid-1970s. They were charged in particular with an *aesthetic* offense: overblown writing that, as its critics saw it, aspired to literary status. To Bloom goes the dubious honor of being the first Yale Critic—and quite possibly the first American postwar literary critic *tout court*—to be attacked ferociously in a mass-distributed venue. That was by Hilton Kramer in the *New York Times*, on August 21, 1977: the insults were many, but the basic charge was that Bloom's theory of "misreading," expressed in "gluttonous verbiage," constituted an aesthetic as well as ethical and epistemological scandal: "For this new mode of freewheeling misreading places the critic—that is, the truly creative critic, the critic willing to go all the way—beyond the realm of truth and error, beyond all mundane plausibility. It gives him the freedom of his imagination. It makes him—dare one say it?—almost a poet."[20] Gerald Graff made a similar point more carefully in a much-remarked essay, "Fear and Trembling at Yale," in the *American Scholar* in 1977. For Graff, as for Pritchard, Hartman's stylistic excesses if anything edged out Bloom's, but both stood accused of writing opaque, onanistic criticism that conveyed "the self-enclosed feeling of the stream-of-consciousness novel. Criticism should not mean but be. That, of course, is what they used to say about poetry. And much of the fear and trembling among the critics stems from the conviction that criticism, like literature, either cannot our should not be 'about' anything but itself."[21] That Bloom published a gnostic science-fiction novel and Hartman a collection of poetry during this period no doubt added a little more fuel to this fire.[22] In the spring of 1981, Hartman (the only Yale Critic who had an aesthetic interest in pursuing "literary" experiments in anything like Graff's or Kramer's sense, or, for that matter, who had a professional interest in the history of style) responded to his detractors in an article in *the New York Times*, "How Creative Should Literary Criticism Be?" In the era of the "new journalism," the "nonfiction novel," and any number of other generic mix-ups, Hartman protested, "literary criticism has become the last refuge of the neo-classical prohibition against mixed genres"; yet, "The critical essay is prose, above all, is an essay, above all: a literary and experimental work rather than a dogmatic pronouncement. . . . It should not be fobbed off as a secondary activity, as a handmaiden to more 'creative' modes of thinking like poems or novels."[23] By the early 1980s, the debate about whether and in what sense "Yale" avant-garde criticism was (or was trying to be) "literary" was fading away, along with the notion of a group of "Yale Critics." In itself, this debate holds limited interest for us; but as a prominent initial reaction-formation to theory, it opens the question of theory as an "aesthetic" scandal, to which we shall shortly need to return.

At this point, though, having begun sketching an account of the way in which "theory at Yale" was being portrayed from the outside during the 1970s, let me double back to say a word, first about the peculiar visibility of Yale in the American literary-critical universe, and then about the way in which Yale's new (to some, newly exciting, and of course to many, newly bad) eminence was being experienced within the institution's own ecosystem. Although it is always possible to imagine a counterfactual world in which Bloom, de Man, Hartman, and Miller ended up at a different elite university and shocked and intrigued the profession under a different sobriquet, such thought experiments have to struggle against the overdeterminations that lent the metonym "Yale Critics" its jolt of electricity. Senior professors doing strange things with literary texts at this particular university, the nation's second richest and second most famous, were particularly media-worthy. There had been a previous generation of "Yale Critics," of course—the conservative, and for the most part Christian New Critics of the legendary Yale English Department: most famously Cleanth Brooks and William K. Wimsatt, but also Maynard Mack, Louis Martz, and others who had been influenced by the New Critical movement; meanwhile, in the Comparative Literature Department, René Wellek stood for a similar blend of historicism and formalism.[24] Wellek retired in 1972, Brooks in 1975; Wimsatt died unexpectedly in 1974; so the generational gears were shifting noisily in the mid-1970s. As the heretical successors of these scholars, Bloom, de Man, Hartman, and Miller occupied uniquely visible institutional space; and though they would in their turn be tagged as formalists and as "newer" new critics, the contrast with the previous era was sharp.

Within Yale University, these new directions in literary theory were increasingly visible yet sharply localized, and as they came into focus they met increasingly with the hostility one might expect from an institution that, two and a half centuries previously, had been founded as a conservative alternative to Harvard (and had preserved versions of that reputation until the student movement of the late 1960s).[25] Stories about the Yale Critics or the Yale School always need to be prefaced with a statement about the slimness of the institutional footprint that sustained these developments. The "theory" phenomenon left little trace in the English Department, despite Miller's best efforts;[26] its institutional support came almost entirely from (portions of the) the French and Comparative Literature departments (and ran out after de Man's death and Miller's departure: though some junior faculty were able to hold on until the end of the decade, by the early 1990s the university had sloughed off all untenured faculty members who were in any way tainted by "deconstruction"). With that caveat registered, we may tell a two-minute version of the affirmative side of the story. De Man, who served as chair first of French and then of Comparative Literature in the 1970s, and late in the decade was accorded Yale's highest honor, a Sterling professorship, was a skillful navigator of the university's political rapids; this, combined with the intellectual power of the project of "rhetorical reading" that he was developing, meant that certain things did happen: the contract for Derrida was arranged; a few of de Man's graduate students obtained assistant professorships in French, Comparative Literature, and in at least one case even in English; a new team-taught undergraduate course, "Lit Z," was launched by de Man and Hartman in the spring of 1977, which provided, among other things, a training ground for the graduate students who served as TAs for the course and, as part of their duties, gave a guest lecture.[27] More remarkable than these minor institutional accomplishments, however, was the sense that a genuine event—something far out of the ordinary—was occurring. "Literary studies rocked at that time with palpable excitement," Hartman comments in his autobiography *A Scholar's Tale* (2007), recalling how "graduate students and even undergrads flocked to Derrida's lectures" and how "de Man, Hillis Miller, Harold Bloom, and Shoshana Felman, different as they were, generated a buzz that spread beyond their university" (93). Although many theoretical interests were represented at Yale, it is fair to say that the epicenter of the buzz was de Man's seminar, along with Derrida's public lectures and six-week courses.[28] I mentioned earlier that Bloom's friendship with de Man took root while he and Hartman were auditing de Man's first course at Yale: something out of the ordinary is happening when professors are attending not just the odd public lecture but the *seminar* of a colleague. As the 1970s rolled on, auditors from any number of backgrounds and with various motives began sitting in on de Man's and Derrida's courses. Andrzej Warminski recalls "attending a class of de Man's (in the fall of 1974) and having sitting next to me a *very* distinguished and very accomplished literary critic from the French department"; Warminski suspects that many such auditors, particularly those whose comprehension of the material seemed weak, were there simply to try to scope out "this new-fangled thing that had turned the heads of the graduate students."[29] Often enough, both inside and outside Yale, the "theory" phenomenon inspired versions of the resentment one hears in Pritchard's comments; inevitably the circle of initiates or would-be initiates was going to look and function like a clique. Yet those familiar institutional effects had an exceptional cause. One is reminded of Hannah Arendt's famous account of the rumor about Heidegger's seminar: "There exists a teacher; one can learn, perhaps, to think."[30] A rumor of that scale does not often circulate in university settings. Arguably no comparably intense institutional scene of intellectual excitement (and bafflement, and hostility) has existed before or since in the history of academic literary criticism in the United States.

As the 1970s came to a close, the academic public sphere came increasingly, as we have seen, to link de Man with Derrida as the redoubled central figure in the landscape of theory-as-deconstruction, while the notion of a "community enterprise" at Yale, as Richard Poirer had put it, grew increasingly nuanced and thin. With the publication of their ironic nonmanifesto *Deconstruction and Criticism* in 1979, Bloom, de Man, Derrida, Hartman, and Miller simultaneously promoted the notion of a group of "Yale Critics" and undermined the idea of a coherent "school."[31] Miller had already stressed the internal heterogeneity of the "new group of critics centered at Yale" in his articles in 1975; so did Hartman in an equivalent piece in *Critical Inquiry* in 1976 ("Perhaps diversity is one reason why no one can agree on what to name this new group of critics. . . . Do they really have a common program, or is their unity simply that of achieving a 'critical mass' at Yale?").[32] In his preface for the 1979 volume, Hartman wrote that "the critics amicably if not quite convincingly held together by the covers of this book differ considerably in their approach to literature and literary theory," and he contrasted the "boa-deconstructors" de Man, Derrida, and Miller, with himself and Bloom, who "are barely deconstructionists. They even write against it on occasion" (ix). On the one hand, *Deconstruction and Criticism* reinforced the equation between deconstruction and Yale, and that was one way the book was received—as the production of a "Deconstruction Gang," as a hostile review put it.[33] On the other hand, to the extent that the volume amplified the dissonance between Hartman and Bloom and their coauthors (one of Bloom's quips in subsequent years was that everybody else had been "deconstruction" and he had been "criticism"), it recorded the ebbing of the idea of the "Yale Critics" right at its high water mark. "What Harold Bloom is doing in this book I have no idea; he is not a deconstructor," wrote Denis Donoghue in his review of it. "A rabbi, a prophet, he would never let himself be shamed out of the language of self, presence, and voice."[34]

By the time Jonathan Arac, Wlad Godzich, and Wallace Martin published their canonizing essay collection *The Yale Critics*—inevitably subtitled *Deconstruction in America*—in 1983, the group they were examining was unquestionably drifting apart in the professional imagination.[35] Deconstruction in America arguably still meant "Yale," but by the end of the 1970s it really meant Miller and Derrida and de Man.[36] The "Yale" phenomenon is unimaginable without Derrida, who nonetheless also remained slightly to the side of it. The *Deconstruction and Criticism* volume showed that too. Derrida's contribution, "Living On: Borderlines," took split form as a text and a running undernote; he made a few gestures toward the original assignment to write on Percy Shelley's *Triumph of Life*, but as he was to comment in a headnote to the French version of the essay that appeared some years later, this "very artificial rule" had been all the more artificial for *him*.[37] Derrida was of course not a literary critic, let alone a romanticist (we shall take up the romantic-studies context of the "theory at Yale" phenomenon a little later in this chapter), and he was only partly identified with the university he visited only a few weeks in the year. By the end of the decade it had become a common gesture in American academic polemic to contrast Derrida with his American (and specifically Yale) "disciples" who were "domesticating" his radical thought. And, of course, the Derrida phenomenon—the larger story of "deconstruction" as a cultural event in the American academy—continued long after the notion of the Yale Critics had disappeared into the archive (displaced by, among other things, Miller's and Derrida's move to UC Irvine in 1986).

Much more tightly identified with the Yale metonym were Miller and de Man. During his two decades at Johns Hopkins, Miller, under the influence of his senior colleague Georges Poulet, had made his reputation as a phenomenological critic in the tradition of the Geneva School. Persuaded by Derrida's critique of Husserlian phenomenology in the late 1960s, Miller began shifting to a deconstructive position, announcing his changed stance most clearly in a long article on Poulet in 1971, in which he underscored the force of Heidegger's and Derrida's critique of temporality and consciousness as presence.[38] Although Miller did not publish a book during the following decade, his polemical exchanges (above all a multipart exchange with M. H. Abrams to be discussed in the next chapter) and his much-noticed essays on canonical British authors (Wordsworth, Dickens, George Eliot) made him—perhaps for a couple of years in the mid-1970s even more than de Man—the major American representative of deconstruction to the profession at large (that is to say, English departments).[39] In 1980, Vincent B. Leitch published a survey of Miller's deconstructive essays that characterized their author in strikingly grandiose terms: "Miller undermines traditional ideas and beliefs about language, literature, consciousness, and interpretation. In effect, he assumes the role of unrelenting destroyer—or nihilistic magician—who dances demonically upon the broken and scattered fragments of the Western tradition."[40] Different in tone and idiom, Leitch's ambivalently positive apocalyptic imagery shares with Pritchard's, Kramer's, and Graff's negative polemics a willingness to cast the avant-garde criticism coming out of Yale as an aesthetic crisis. If Hartman and Bloom threaten to turn criticism into art, Miller, here, threatens the demise of "the Western tradition" (albeit in a rather vatic mode, as a negative demiurge or artist, a "nihilistic magician").

Increasingly, however, by the end of the 1970s and beginning of the 1980s, "deconstruction at Yale" meant de Man. Here I want to interrupt my historical narrative to provide a brief account of de Man's turn to what he called rhetorical reading, since that proved to be the decisive intellectual moment in the constitution of the discourse and phantasm of theory-as-deconstruction in America. Like Miller and, for that matter, like Derrida, de Man worked his way toward his new position from a background in phenomenological and Heideggerian thought. His developing interest in rhetoric constitutes a particularly complex phase of a highly complex oeuvre, and my intent here is simply to grant a little working specificity to the notion of rhetorical reading, while promising to return to aspects of de Man's work later in this chapter, and at various points throughout this book (most extensively in Chapter 5). The reexamination of rhetoric by Roman Jakobson and other thinkers with links to structuralism in the postwar era, and a surge of interest in Nietzsche—an author de Man was reading intensely during this period—among avant-garde French philosophers in the later 1960s, offers a broad intellectual background for de Man's turn to rhetorical questions.[41] De Man himself on one occasion pointed to "The Rhetoric of Temporality" (1969) as an essay that, with its "deliberate emphasis on rhetorical terminology," augured "a change not only in terminology and in tone but in substance" from his previous work.[42] In that text's most famous sentence, de Man defines the allegorical sign as "the *repetition* . . . of a previous sign with which it can never coincide, since it is of the essence of this previous sign to be pure anteriority" (*BI*, 207, de Man's emphasis). This claim has discreet affinities with Derrida's reconceptualization of Heidegger's critique of temporality as the structure of the trace, insofar as the "present" moment (or sign) turns out to be enabled by a structuring element than can never have been present and therefore remains inaccessible to a phenomenology; but in de Man's case, the critical insight is gained through the examination of a specific linguistic structure. The allegorical sign demands a *reading* that does not map onto a possible *experience*. In his essays from the early 1970s, de Man places ever-greater emphasis on the nonnatural, nonreferential substitutions performed by figures of speech, on the ways in which these linguistic structures disrupt—yet also get confused with—the phenomeno-logical world of consciousness and time, on the impossibility of deciding between literal and figural meaning when faced with a genuine rhetorical crux, yet also the necessity of doing so—for to read is to decide, though to decide is to fall short of reading the text. Nor is the reader "making" these decisions in sovereign fashion, for they are inscribed in the text *as* its rhetorical crux. The text is doing something to the reader rather than vice versa (at the end of this chapter, I shall offer an example of how de Man stages that predicament). Thus de Man's critique, in *Blindness and Insight*, of Derrida's account of Rousseau in *Of Grammatology*—the critique that without much hyperbole may be called *the* primal scene of "deconstruction in America"—stresses the self-deconstructive rhetorical performativity of Rousseau's text: "Accounting for the 'rhetoricity' of its own mode, the text also postulates the necessity of its own misreading. . . . It follows from the rhetorical nature of literary language that the cognitive function resides in the language and not in the subject" ("The Rhetoric of Blindness" [1971], *BI*, 136, 137).[43]

As noted, I shall return to these issues later; at this point let me circle back to my broad historical narrative by reviewing the impact that de Man's project had in its institutional context. If one had to identify a signature "Yale" word during the heyday of the 1970s, the most obvious best bet would be "trope." Bloom's antithetical criticism had acquired a rhetori-cal vocabulary in the wake of de Man's powerful review of *The Anxiety of Influence* (we shall go over that encounter in Chapter 4), so even the "Yale Critic" most dramatically at odds with de Man was arguing his case in the idiom of rhetorical turn and swerve. By the later 1970s, rhetorical reading was becoming indistinguishable both from the practice and from the public image of deconstruction at Yale. Miller adopted a rhetorical idiom early on, stressing, in de Manian fashion, the cognitive force of linguistic structures ("any literary text, with more or less explicitness or clarity, already reads or misreads itself").[44] In 1978, Carol Jacobs, who had studied with de Man at Hopkins, published the first book-length exercise in de Manian rhetorical reading, *The Dissimulating Harmony* (for which de Man wrote a foreword); in 1979 de Man brought out *Allegories of Reading*, and several of his graduate students published rhetorical readings in a special issue of *Studies in Romanticism* titled "The Rhetoric of Romanticism" (for which de Man wrote an introduction); in 1980 Barbara Johnson published her incisive de Man–inflected deconstructive study *The Critical Difference*.[45] From roughly this point onward it seems fair to say that the term "Yale School" was becoming, in idiomatic institutional parlance, a reference to de Manian, rhetorical, or "literary" deconstruction.

I have been scrambling a good deal of information into the last ten pages or so; let me summarize the points most essential to retain. The overall goal has been to document the prominence of the "Yale Critics" in literary-critical argument in the 1970s, particularly 1975–80.[46] Bringing the focus in a bit, we then observe two patterns: (1) the association of "deconstruction" with "Yale," the identification of de Man, Miller, and to some extent Derrida with deconstruction-at-Yale, and the formation of de Man–and–Derrida as the privileged *figure* of deconstruction (a fundamental figure of the discourse of theory that will live on long past the waning of the Yale theme); (2) the prominence of Hartman and Bloom in representations of the "Yale Critics" in the middle 1970s, followed by their gradual peeling off from the deconstruction-at-Yale connection at the end of the decade. (Bloom remained a "theorist" for another couple of years, and then in the mid-1980s started his massive Chelsea House publishing project, dropped out of academic debates, and began to become a national celebrity; we shall examine this phase of his career in connection with his earlier theoretical work in Chapter 4. Hartman remained one of the academy's most prominent critics, able to pass as a "theorist" but recognized above all as a vastly learned and sensitive close reader and literary historian; in the 1980s he began to work increasingly in trauma and Holocaust studies.)[47] I am drawing attention to these rhetorical vectors from the mid-1970s because I want to synchronize them to the question of how and why theory-as-deconstruction-at-Yale underwent mediatization. The term *mediatization* is being used here to blur the line between the oral and written delivery systems of the postwar American academic institution, on the one hand, and the national print media on the other. Vastly different though they are, these systems are not simple opposites, and the peculiar hypertrophy of "deconstruction" in the academy found an echo in the sporadic and limited but nonetheless remarkable uptake of deconstruction in the national news.[48]

Let us now turn briefly to that wider context. Mitchell Stephens cautions wisely against exaggerating the newsworthiness of deconstruction prior to the late 1980s, and suggests that the de Man affair was a watershed moment:

> Between 1973 and 1979, while four of Derrida's own books were being published in English translations and his method was roiling the campuses, the word "deconstruction" never once appeared in the Nexis selection of American magazines and newspapers. By the late 1980s many of those involved with deconstruction could recall having read a few articles in mass-circulation publications that grappled with their work, but they were the same few articles: a feature in *Newsweek* in 1981, a book review in *The New Republic* in 1983, and a profile of the "Yale School" of literary criticism in *The New York Times Magazine* in 1986.

That changed, Stephens emphasizes, after Ortwin de Graef unearthed de Man's wartime writings and the *New York Times* picked up the story: "The resulting story appeared on December 1, 1987, on the front page of the second section of the *Times*, and many other major American newspapers and magazines quickly followed the lead of the *Times*. The de Man scandal even made the chart of the week's top stories in the *New Republic*'s 'Zeitgeist Checklist.'"[49]

Stephens leaves aside a number of relevant mass-circulation articles that, because they do not use the word "deconstruction," fall out of his Nexis search parameters; he also leaves out of his account the various non-university-based, medium-circulation Anglo-American literary journals that, as we have just been recalling, published numerous accounts (usually hostile ones) of deconstruction in the decade before 1987.[50] But if we stay with the three articles in mass-circulation magazines that he mentions we may underscore an obvious and, in this context, interesting fact: two of the three were entirely about "the 'Yale School' of literary criticism," and the third partly was. The 1981 *Newsweek* article, titled "A New Look at Lit Crit," with photos of Derrida, de Man, and (as a representative of the opposition) Alfred Kazin, describes an "all-out war" between "partisans of the humanistic tradition" and "the avatars of a radical approach to writing—called 'deconstruction'—that undermines all the humanists' assumptions about the relationships between author and reader, literature and life"; of course the stronghold of the latter group is Yale ("When Yale's Hartman and his redoubtable colleagues—Paul de Man, J. Hillis Miller and Harold Bloom— took up the banner of deconstruction, they were immediately dubbed by traditionalist critics as Yale's 'Gang of Four'").[51] The 1983 article in *the New Republic*, "Deconstruction in America," has a more professional tone and is our "partial" case: an omnibus review by Robert Alter of several books on deconstruction, it discusses "the Yale Critics" as a group but focuses mainly on Derrida and de Man, and in its closing paragraph distinguishes Bloom, for whom "the life of literature is the enactment of dramatic conflict," from deconstruction.[52] As does Colin Campbell in "The Tyranny of the Yale Critics" in the *New York Times Magazine* in 1986 (Bloom is "not a deconstructor," though "his thought and style are comparably radical"; he is "sage, genius, and comic rolled into one").[53] This belated, full-spread glossy feature granted a suitably splashy end to the "Yale Critics" saga. Later that year Miller and Derrida left for UC Irvine, and a feature in *Newsweek* ("Yale's Insomniac Genius") elevated Bloom to a solitary pinnacle.[54] And at the end of 1987 the de Man affair exploded, taking the mediatization of theory-as-deconstruction to a new level, as Stephens reminds us, but no longer routing it through Yale.

What made deconstruction media-worthy in the United States? The archival record suggests that an answer to that question has to take into account the initial mediatizing of deconstruction through an ensemble of Yale Critics. The shape of the reception of Hartman's and Bloom's work in the mid-1970s alerts us to the degree to which deconstruction was produced and received as an *aesthetic* as well as cognitive and ethical scandal. "Aesthetic" turns out to mean far more than a question of style, and rapidly comes to comprehend cognitive and ethical issues. Deconstruction garnered the attention and kind of attention it did because it was processed as a threat, or at least an insult, to (elite) aesthetic-humanist education—more of a threat or insult, at least according to this barometer, than academic Marxism, or structuralism or semiotics or psychoanalysis or any other theoretical approach possessed of a rebarbative vocabulary. (Fredric Jameson, who had been recruited to the Yale French Department in 1975, wrote *The Political Unconscious* there, and published it to great acclaim in the academy in 1981—but in Jameson's case there was no "Yale" trigger, and no wider media uptake of the sort we have been examining. The degree of media attention that deconstruction has garnered over the years is anomalous.)

The accusations of elitism, self-indulgence, and obscurantism directed at Hartman and Bloom—eventuating in the accusation that they were equating their criticism with poetry—may be read, ironically, as the reverse side of the anger directed at canon revisionists a decade later (by which time Bloom, of course, was beginning to be nationally recognized as the canon's representative), insofar as the aesthetic and moral integrity of literature was proclaimed to be at stake in both cases. Hence the stubborn association in the wider media between "theory" and the "canon wars," the twin public scandals of the humanities in the United States in the last twenty years of the twentieth century. The fact that the critics who sought to open the canon to underrepresented groups were usually as hostile as traditionalists were to "high theory" did not prevent the mythic conjunction of deconstruction and canon destruction from imposing itself in journalistic contexts (any more than the production of apocalyptic scenarios in the right-wing press was impeded by the fact that the stories about theory and canon revision always relied on distorted accounts of events at an extremely small number of elite schools).[55] And that is because deconstruction had by then been construed as the epitome of the kind of theory opposed to the ideal of aesthetic-ethical acculturation that has played a prominent role in the history of twentieth-century American pedagogical discourse. Our understanding of the theory phenomenon in the United States will be enriched if we review the broader cultural and institutional context within which it occurred.

Elsewhere I have written at length on the instabilities and ideological complexities of aesthetics.[56] Aesthetics, as the term will be used here, does not primarily mean a subfield in philosophy or the specialized study of art; it points to the emergence, over the course of the eighteenth and nineteenth centuries, of ideas and institutions of art and the artist, culture and acculturation, that little by little enabled or developed into the manifold of cultural institutions and discourses that shapes present-day middle-class Western lives. Very few people become literary critics, art historians, aestheticians, writers, or artists; but in the developed world for the most part only the most severely damaged, radically isolated, and desperately poor members of the population are functionally unaffected by the institutions and images of aesthetic culture. We take for granted that there should be certain objects called "art" and a particular sort of writing called "literature"; that at least a small degree of contact with these objects and this kind of writing plays an essential role in normative psychic and social development; that in consequence, art, music, and literature classes should form part of primary and secondary mass education, and that either the state or the not-for-profit sector of civil society should fund museums, concert halls, and universities with literature departments. None of these phenomena existed or would have made social or intellectual sense three hundred years ago; some of them, like university-level instruction in literature or art history, only began to make enough sense to come into existence a little more than a century ago. The development of aesthetic discourse forms part of the emergence of consumer capitalism, mass politics, and media technology; it partakes of the vast series of transformations we call modernity, and can be linked to the operations of biopower, governmentality, or, in a more traditionally Marxist analysis, to the interests of the hegemonic bourgeois state. It is culture's "function," according to this argument, to serve the state by forming subjects capable of disinterested reflection, and thus capable of recapitulating the state's universality.[57] Culture produces the consensual grounds for representative democracy (hence the emphasis, in middle-class Victorian political writings, on education as a prerequisite for political enfranchisement). Culture manifests itself at the same time a form of capital, as Pierre Bourdieu has emphasized, unevenly distributed across the social field.[58]

It must also be emphasized, however, that aesthetics as a discourse is by no means homogenous or stable, or simply a ruse of power. Aesthetic discourse not only intersects with many forms of critical and emancipatory thought, politics and practice—some of which, no doubt, feed back all too rapidly into a hegemonic program—but also has an oblique affinity with shock, trauma, jouissance, and other forms of intense experience. One rapid way to bring into focus the deeply unstable character of aesthetic discourse is to mount for inspection the peculiar opprobrium so often attached to the word and concept *aestheticism*. As Forest Pyle remarks, "if there is one thing in the fractured field of what used to be called literary studies that a conservative humanist, a critical Marxist, a rhetorically oriented deconstructive critic, a Levinasian ethicist, and a practitioner of cultural studies can actually agree on, it is likely to be a *rejection* of aestheticism."[59] There is something excessive and disquieting at the heart of aesthetic experience and aesthetic discourse, with the result that the latter, even in its most official and normativizing mode as acculturation, tends to unfold in the idiom of crisis, as we shall see in a moment.

Along the way, however, we may flag a theme that will become more prominent in subsequent chapters: the vexed but palpable affinity between "high theory" and "romanticism" in the American academy. Romanticism developed as a field overburdened with aesthetic concerns, and this has made it exceptionally receptive (as well as resistant) to "theory" in de Man's sense. Split between naming a mode and a period, romanticism has always been prodded to justify itself theoretically and engage with fundamental aesthetic questions (for if not everything written during a romantic era is romantic, what is it to be romantic?).[60] As a period metaphor, romanticism references the era that saw the historical emergence of aesthetics (that is, once again, not just aesthetic theory and not just concepts of artwork and artist, but also notions of acculturation, with all the broad subsequent institutional developments we noted earlier); revolution and reaction (including, as we shall see, the first polemical deployment of the word "theory"); modern political and ideological forms (democracy, human rights, nationalism); the concept of history and historicism. "Romanticism," as David L. Clark notes, "is less a period concept than a volatile discourse at once on and of modernity, and this explains its curious oppositional fluidity, from reactionary to revolutionary, false consciousness to self-consciousness, naïve to ironic, anachronistic to futural."[61] To study romanticism is to study our modernity, yet also—because of the instability of that specular structure—to engage a phenomenon that excites complex gestures of disavowal, repetition, and overinvestment. Even in the bureaucratized, routinized environment of postwar American scholarship, romanticism has the capacity to inspire manifestos, claims, and auto-aggressive denunciations in a way and to a degree encountered much more rarely in other fields of literary specialization. The denunciations in particular have made clear the ease with which romanticism can be associated with a certain aesthetic excess. "Romantic" equals "aesthetic" equals "ideology" in arguments of this type, and much linguistic usage, both colloquial and professional, supports that triple equation (which is not so much an equation as a sort of acceleration: thus the "romantic artist," which is to say the artist *tout court*, easily becomes *too much* an artist; a *romantic* revolution is too revolutionary or insufficiently so; etc.).[62] It is no accident that Pyle's powerful argument for the presence of a disruptive "radical aestheticism" in certain texts—an "auratic fascination" that "voids all that we habitually claim in the aesthetic"—locates such moments specifically within the romantic tradition.[63] And because romanticism's excessive aestheticism is usually condemned in the idiom of some kind of ("romantic") aesthetic humanism, it has always been possible for one critic to call anther critic romantic.[64] Certainly the terms in which T. S. Eliot offered his famous diagnosis of a "dissociation of sensibility" between sound and sense, feeling and thought, that, according to Eliot, began to afflict the British canon in the era of Dryden and Milton and reached its height in the romantic era, could hardly be more stereotypically romantic in its aesthetic ("a thought to Donne, was an experience; it modified his sensibility").[65] No one was better than Eliot at recasting "nineteenth-century literary values in a neoclassical-sounding language," as Louis Menand comments.[66] As Hartman summarizes: "the reaction ... of T. E. Hulme, T. S. Eliot, and the New Humanists appears to us more and more as one within Romanticism."[67] That oneness, however, has always been self-conflicted and self-resisting. Particularly (which is also to say ambivalently) invested in aesthetic questions—including that of its own period-metaphor—romanticism as a field offered a natural context for the aesthetic scandal that the experimental writings of Bloom and Hartman, as we have seen, offered the academy in the 1970s.

Romantic studies, however, form part of academic discourse and take place within an academic institution, and we now need to sketch the specificity of the institution within which "theory" happened. The American university took various forms as it developed in the late nineteenth century, and many of them had little to do directly with the rhetoric of aesthetic acculturation, which, despite certain democratizing emphases, and despite tying into the large developments mentioned earlier, has tended to remain associated with privileged versions of higher education, and has been in constant tension with pragmatic and research-oriented notions of the university mission. In his classic *The Emergence of the American University*, Lawrence Veysey identifies four rival conceptions of higher learning struggling with each other in the mid to late nineteenth century: "mental discipline," "utility," "research," and "liberal culture." Mental discipline was the rationale of the old-style college, focused on the classics and emphasizing routine repetition and memorization (a model that remained in force at American liberal arts colleges through the 1890s and in some cases longer). The new land-grant universities stood for social utility; the research model, imported from Germany, famously found expression with the founding of Johns Hopkins in 1874; the "liberal culture" model eventually won out over old-college traditions at schools like Yale and Princeton, and at colleges like Amherst and Williams that refused to grow the carapace of a university and remained liberal arts colleges.[68] "Liberal culture" is of course a model for undergraduate instruction (as is "mental discipline"); graduate training obeys the research imperative; all of these models claim indirect social utility. Thus a fully idealized concept of the modern university presents research and pedagogy as two sides of the same coin, as in Wilhelm von Humboldt's famous definition of the university's mission as "an unceasing process of inquiry": "The lower levels of education present closed and settled bodies of knowledge. . . . At the higher level, the teacher does not exist for the sake of the student; both teacher and student have their justification in the common pursuit of knowledge [*Wissenschaft*]."[69] The pursuit of scientific truth is inseparable from the education or formation (*Bildung*) of the student, because the pursuit of truth is a process of self-realization: the student matures, the teacher learns, and human knowledge develops and unfolds. And if we understand the pursuit of truth as historical progress, then research is also useful, and the three disparate rationales of the modern university—research, utility, and acculturation—blend into a single pedagogico-scientific mission.

Over the past century it has been part of the job of university spokespeople to invoke versions of this ideal.

In reality, of course, the modern university has always been a fractured entity, perhaps above all within the American system, where research universities consist of disparate parts with sharply different missions: a residential college for undergraduates, a sports industry, a graduate research program, research institutes, professional schools. Statements about the overall purpose of undergraduate education usually blend the claims of acculturation with those of utility. The residential-college tradition, with its campus and dorms and college-culture—a rarity elsewhere in the world, and so central to the American imagining of middle-class postsecondary experience—has somewhat encouraged a rhetoric of acculturation, as has the relegation of professional training (at least in the upper echelons of the U.S. system) to postgraduate degree tracks. Meanwhile, the elective system—another uniquely American institution that positions the undergraduate as a consumer in a marketplace—has generated a century's worth of debate about the respective merits of educational freedom and core requirements. Other features of the American university have pulled strongly in the direction of research: the formalized structure of graduate education; the relatively early and extensive professionalization of a degree-credentialed research professoriat, whose members pursue "careers." There has thus developed in the United States a rich tradition of anxious commentary on the role of the liberal arts, and above all the humanities, in postsecondary instruction. For in the humanities, the conflicting imperatives of a normative American university visibly collide. These disciplines became disciplines as the university attained its modern shape at the end of the nineteenth century; they play a fundamental role in the rhetoric of acculturation, yet also have to conform to the scientific mission of a modern university. As Gerald Graff recounts in his seminal history of English studies in the United States, the conflicting imperatives of research and acculturative pedagogy split literary studies from the start.[70] And since literature, taken in some combination with philosophy and history, has historically served as the exemplary discipline of acculturation, a blend of literature-philosophy-history forms the spine of idealizing pedagogies that set themselves against the fragmentation of knowledge in the techno-scientific university, and promote acculturation as the reintegration of human identity. The famous core curricula and great books experiments in the American tradition, from John Erskine's great books program at Columbia in the 1920s to the most recent iteration of the Harvard "Redbook" in 2013, may draw on a broad Western aesthetic and civic tradition, but they are also very much a specific product of conflicts and possibilities built into the undergraduate portion of the American university system.[71]

With such phenomena in mind, Geoffrey Galt Harpham claims that "in no other nation are the humanities discussed with such urgency or fervor" as in the United States.[72] The mode of that discussion is "perennial crisis" (22); for, as the locus of rhetorical and ideological overinvestment, the humanities can never fail to be failing, and are constantly in need of renewal. Harpham points to the early years of the Cold War as a time when particularly extravagant claims for the humanities were being made. The original Harvard "Redbook," *General Education in a Free Society* (1946), identifies aesthetic culture with the interests of the state in unadorned Arnoldian fashion: "In the view of the Redbook, education serves the interests of the nation by calling out and fortifying those attributes most essential to political, economic, and ideological success. . . . A wartime document, the Redbook defines the humanities as the curricular means by which students could achieve full human being, and links the humanities with national identity and security" (161).[73] The report emphasized the Arnoldian phrase "the whole man," opposing this "normative vision of humanity that education is to serve," as Harpham puts it, to "the partial men of the totalitarian states against which America had just waged war," and calling particularly on literature as the central discipline of a "general education" (156). A similar weaponizing of the humanities characterizes the other reports and public papers that Harpham examines, particularly an ACLA-sponsored report of 1964 that, like the Redbook, invoked Matthew Arnold in order to suggest that the humanities can save humanity itself ("With the fate of mankind hanging in the balance, the commission declared, the United States cannot afford to be 'second best' in the humanities").[74] Absurd though these affirmations sound, they form part of a chain of speech acts that had real institutional effects; Harpham reminds us that "the language in the legislation creating the National Endowment for the Humanities was taken almost directly from this report" (166).[75] The vast expansion of the research capabilities of the American university system during the Cold War benefitted professors in all fields of research, creating jobs, programs and departments (including many comparative literature departments: Cornell's, for instance, which de Man was hired in to help initiate in 1960); improving salaries; reducing teaching loads at elite institutions; and increasing both support for, and therefore also the expectation of, research productivity. Thus the modest funding streams that, in the name of idealized and instrumentalized conceptions of the humanities, went to the humanistic disciplines (along with the more pervasive support that accrued to these disciplines simply by being part of the emerging techno-bureaucratic order) accelerated the very professionalization and specialization of knowledge that the humanities were supposed to ameliorate, if not cure. The "theory" phenomenon and the "canon wars" can be partly explained as twin explosions at the end of that fuse.

Yale University was still primarily associated with strength in the humanities in the public imagination in the 1970s; and before the "theory" shakeup, the humanities were primarily associated with acculturation rather than trouble.[76] Let me close this section with a glance at one of those core-curriculum programs with large aesthetic ambitions that form part of the agitated history of the humanities in the United States: even a quick look can remind us both of the cultural tradition that a name like "Yale" stood for, and of the structural vulnerability of the aesthetic tradition. In 1945, while Harvard was writing its "Redbook" report (most of the proposals of which would be rejected by the Harvard faculty in 1949, in favor of distribution requirements), Yale was founding an honors undergraduate track that came to be known as "Directed Studies." An article in *Time Magazine* in 1951 granted the program a brief moment of national exposure:

> The proper function of the university, wrote [Cardinal] Newman, is "teaching universal knowledge." U.S. universities have not always lived up to that maxim. Under the influence of the Germans, who carried their pursuit of facts for their own sake to the last extreme, the laboratory began to overshadow the classroom, the specialist the student, and the idea that men must become well-rounded human beings before they become specialists was almost forgotten. In a later day, U.S. education fell into the anarchy of free electives, and scattered courses piecemeal before its students to be sampled as their taste or fancy dictated.
>
> Today the return to the teaching of universal knowledge is well under way, and nowhere is it more visible than in the Yale of [President] Whitney Griswold. . . . It is in the experimental Directed Studies program that Yale seems to be searching for the pattern of the future. Here, philosophy is the core about which history, literature and the sciences revolve like planets. Philosophy holds them together, relates them, gives them life in common. It is Yale's boldest attempt to make education whole.[77]

The program's rationale distantly echoes Immanuel Kant's proposal to anchor the "conflict of the faculties" in philosophy—the faculty "whose function is only to look after the interests of science," and which is thus "free to evaluate everything" and able to "lay claim to any teaching, in order to test its truth."[78] In the idiom of American humanities programs, this free exercise of reason is called critical inquiry. Directed Studies was imagined as a conservative, even to some extent a reactionary program insofar as it consciously sought to re-capture, according to the faculty who founded it, "the signal virtue of the old classical curriculum—a community of intellectual experience."[79] But unlike the pre-twentieth-century classical curriculum, which had its problems but also had the relatively clear mission of forming a Christian gentleman, a great books program centers its acculturative mission on the nurturing of critical inquiry—drawing, as the *Time* article indicates, on the nineteenth-century aesthetic-humanist tradition of Newman and Arnold. As another eminent Victorian, John Stuart Mill, put it: "What professional men should carry away with them from a University is not professional knowledge, but what should direct their use of professional knowledge."[80] Daniel Bell, writing in the 1960s about general education as a cure for the university's fragmentation, called this knowledge of knowledge "method."[81] We see that another word for it might be "theory"; and that is in fact one way of understanding the force of that charged term, emerging as it did at the intersection of literature and philosophy in the 1970s. For critical inquiry is a potentially dangerous activity. Dedicated though it is to building up our "best self," aesthetic culture must also endeavor, as Matthew Arnold famously put it, "to see the object as in itself it really is"; those two imperatives do not necessarily coincide.[82] And as Theodor Adorno writes: "When people sense that the intelligibility of traditional works begins to crumble, they get angry."[83]

But why this word "theory"? Here, I think, we need to look a little far-ther back in history, while remaining within a specific Anglo-American linguistic and cultural context. The classical roots of this word are often unearthed: *theoria*, which originally referred to acts of seeing and witnessing, came to mean speculation or contemplation in Platonic and Aristotelian philosophy, and preserved versions of this meaning through the Neoplatonic and scholastic traditions.[84] By the seventeenth century, *theory* had begun acquiring its modern meanings of explanatory hypothesis, system of ideas, or systematic statement of general principles. Of particular interest in the present context is the emergence in English of a negative use of this word (to signify "*mere* hypothesis, speculation, conjecture"): the source appears to be the counterrevolutionary writings of Edmund Burke. The *Oxford English Dictionary* offers as its earliest example of *theory* in this negative sense a phrase from a text of Burke's from 1792; in fact two years previously, in *Reflections on the Revolution in France* (1790) and then in "Thoughts on French Affairs" (1791), Burke had already pressed the words *theory* and *theorist* into service as pejoratives (along with the close synonyms *speculation, speculative, speculator*).

The essence of Jacobinism for Burke was mental overreaching—a criminal lunge at the forbidden tree of knowledge. The French Revolution was "a Revolution of doctrine and theoretick dogma," perpetrated by "men of theory."[85] Burke bequeathed this counterrevolutionary, anti-intellectual, and always potentially Francophobic use of the word to the Anglo-American polemical lexicon.[86] Theory in this sense names an *excess* of reason. This genealogy helps explain why "theory" took off as a nickname for a variety of texts in the 1970s, and why deconstruction became identified as "high theory." Though we still need to examine the deconstructive threat to aesthetic-acculturative ideology in greater detail, it seems clear enough that academic and extra-academic portrayals of deconstruction have consistently characterized it as a hyperrational critique of reason, reason pushed to the breaking point—to the point of madness; and, if formulated carefully, that does in fact describe the risk to which Derrida, like Nietzsche, Freud, and Heidegger before him, exposes thought. The modern university, Derrida writes—I am plucking here one thread from a very large conceptual tapes-try—emerges with the emergence of modern technoscience: "One cannot think the possibility of the modern university, the one that is re-structured in the nineteenth century in all Western countries, without inquiring into that event, the institution of the principle of reason." Yet an abyss lurks in that principle, and those who are truly faithful to reason must try to think reason's excess over itself: "who is more faithful to reason's call, who hears it with a keener ear, who better sees the difference, the one who offers questions in return and tries to think through the possibility of that summons, or the one who does not want to hear any question about the reason of reason?"[87] Deconstruction, Derrida will insist, is not a *theory*, because it interrogates the totalizing force of reason on which theorization depends.[88] Yet this is exactly why deconstruction has been received as the epitome of "theory"—that compulsively quotation-mark-clad nickname that carries a Burkean slur as part of its DNA, ready for activation in hostile contexts. "Theory," of course, also works normatively, ever since the 1970s, as the name for a recognizable (if hard to define) canon of influential texts. But the always potentially ex-plosive and toxic exemplarity of deconstruction in the discourse of theory reminds us that, in this discourse, theory and the resistance to theory resist being cleanly pried apart.

The Anglo-American and Burkean caricature of French thought in par-ticular as hyperrational (and therefore diseased, even irrational) thus helps us take a step toward explaining the name, if not the institution, of this "North American artifact" of "theory" that Derrida found so peculiar. The institutional propagation of theory was enabled, as Jonathan Culler and Gerald Graff, among others, have suggested, by particular characteristics of the American research university: its being staffed by a professional cadre required to produce scholarship; its being organized as a modular department- and field-based organization that tolerates innovation through compartmentalization.[89] And we have just glanced at other aspects of the American university and its discourses that suggest why a mutation in "critical inquiry" that seemed to pose a threat to an ideology of acculturation should trigger the mediatization of this irritant, both within and outside the academy. We have contextualized the remarkable if brief salience of the "Yale Critics" as a phenomenon referrable to a number of coincident factors: the unique visibility of Yale in American literary-critical history; the instability of acculturative ideology; the perception of deconstruction as a peculiarly threatening critique of that ideology. We are headed toward a consideration of that last point—it takes us straight to de Man's affirmation of the critical power of rhetorical reading in "The Resistance to Theory." But before turning to that text I want to examine the governing trope of the discourse of theory: personification.

In the opening pages of his *Literary Theory: A Very Short Introduction* (1997), Jonathan Culler comments wryly that "theory" can often seem to mean little more than "a bunch of (mostly foreign) names; it means Jacques Derrida, Michel Foucault, Luce Irigaray, Jacques Lacan, Judith Butler, Louis Althusser, Gayatri Spivak, for instance."[90] Theory, it has often been observed, brought the star system to the humanities. But that phrase can be a little misleading, since the production of stars in the mass media usually involves the circulation of visual images (above all faces), whereas in the discourse of theory, celebrity is routed primarily through proper names. Visual images do play a secondary role—an artist like Mark Tansey, whose work we shall be examining in this book's final chapter, is able to exploit the fact that the faces of major theorists have informed local areas of visual literacy since the 1980s.[91] But the most consequential and durable characteristic of academic celebrity and of much theoretical discourse is the name. As David R. Shumway remarks: "Thus one finds article after article in which Derrida or Foucault or Barthes or Lacan or Žižek or Althusser or Spivak or Fish or Jameson are cited as markers of truth" (95). Shumway notes the paradox—that a discourse famously identified with putting the sovereign subject in question should be so rhetorically addicted to the author function—and proposes that "the construction of the individual personality has become an epistemological necessity" in the wake of theory's having "called into question the traditional means by which knowledge has been authorized" (97). Yet that is to take a symptom for an explanation. Though perhaps now and then it might be fair

to say that "constructions of individual personality" form part of the performance of theoretical discourse, the identities routinely evoked by the magical
names of the theory canon—these "markers of truth"—are more formulaic
than the word *personality* suggests. We are better off with the rhetorical term
personification. Amanda Anderson has suggested that certain styles of thought
have acquired character traits in argumentative practice in the American
academy (for instance, "pragmatists are accused of being, among other things,
smug, complacent, cynical, blithe, and dismissive");[92] these are discursive
functions that have no necessary connection to the particular "personality" of
an empirical individual. They refer to the individual speaking *as* something
(for instance, as a pragmatist): that is, they compose the stylized attributes of
a personification, operative within the polemical field of a certain kind of
public discourse.

What sort of character speaks as a "theorist"? David Simpson has an
answer to that question: with an eye on the Burkean counterrevolutionary
idiom, he suggests that the 1790s bequeathed to later eras a template of the
theorist as Robespierre: cold, cerebral, ruthless, simultaneously enlightened
and blind, rational and mad (173). Throughout the nineteenth and twentieth
centuries, this personification surfaces repeatedly in hostile Anglo-American
portrayals of the anarchist, the terrorist, the socialist, or communist agitator
(and sometimes the Nazi, though there the "cerebral," "enlightened," and
"rational" part of the mix can surface only if the Nazi is a spy, a cultured
officer, or an evil scientist). The personification is masculine but a little
queer, available for homophobic, Francophobic, and above all anti-Semitic
associations (the theorist is overly clever and sometimes overly cultured;
abstract, unrooted, dangerously international). In the 1970s, elements of this
character system collected around Jacques Derrida and Paul de Man, the
representatives of "theory." As the personification or allegorical representative of theory, the theorist is excessively rational, steely, and passionless.[93] His
charisma—his ability to inspire love—springs from his inhuman power of
analysis and withdrawal; from the icy intelligence that makes him a fantastic
locus of authority, a *sujet supposé savoir*, invulnerable as a corpse, unfoolable
even by death—though of course, in sharply antitheoretical discourse this
cold intelligence must be disqualified *as* intelligence: it is diseased and dis-
honest, producing false results through charismatic trickery, for the sake of
personal aggrandizement.[94] In Derrida's case, a further complication then
ensues, since his texts are so often emotionally charged. Given the codes that
control the reception of theory, the passionate texture of Derrida's writing
will therefore have to be identified as a contradiction, as Rei Terada remarks:
"No one argues that Derrida ignores emotion: themes of desire and loss

suffuse his middle and later work. . . . Still, he is often considered a passionate writer whose ideas cannot fully comprehend his feelings."[95] If not cold as ice, the deconstructionist is "pathologically conflicted," caught in the grip of a pathos that he cannot process. Though it is fair to add that in his later years Derrida became such a visible and visibly complex figure that the stereotypes of the discourse of theory sometimes at least partly failed to dictate the terms of his media representation in the United States. The sneering tone of the obituary for Derrida commissioned by *the New York Times* took a number of readers by surprise, I think, because at the back of their minds they had imagined that his reputation had grown too large to be pinned down by the old Lilliputian codes.[96] But if they knew the codes they knew immediately what was to follow when they saw the headline: "Jacques Derrida, Abstruse Theorist, Dies . . ."[97] *Theorist*, not philosopher, thinker, writer. And the theorist is by definition abstruse.

If Derrida strained and even at times shattered the confines of the allegorical shape of the "theorist," however, in doing so he left behind him the very silhouette of theory: Paul de Man. So much ink has been spilled on de Man's "character"—or fantasies about that character—in the wake of the wartime journalism scandal that it is helpful to return to pre-1987 representations so as to isolate the character motifs that the discourse of theory was constructing out of a handful of well-circulated texts and the most basic biographical information. Positioned very differently from Derrida, de Man was able to become the template for that newly prominent creature, the "theorist": neither quite a philosopher nor quite a literary critic, but something improperly in between. Derrida, for all the complexity of his cultural background, was associable with France, French philosophy, and French institutions; de Man was at once foreign and domestic: both the quintessential European—the polyglot native of a small country suspended between France and Germany—and a naturalized American citizen who had taken his Ph.D. in comparative literature at Harvard and made his career in the U.S. academic system. Because he was *quasi*-foreign, he could serve as the switching-point for a theory that was simultaneously too foreign and too domestic—hyper-European and hyper-American. The discursive vectors of theory and the resistance to theory converge on this figure, whose theory provides the final referent for denunciations of theory as linguisticism, charismatic obscurantism, nihilism, bureaucratic routinization, American Euro-elitism.

The intensity of the academy's identification of de Man with theory forms one of the most remarkable chapters in late twentieth-century American intellectual life. Frank Lentricchia's hyperbolic elaboration of William

Pritchard's figure of the "hermeneutical Mafia" in *After the New Criticism* (1980) is at once peculiar and exemplary:

> Assuming there is a Yale Mafia, then surely there must be a resident Godfather. One is forced to finger Paul de Man, who exhibits qualities that may earn him the role of Don Paolo, *capo di tutti capi*. Reading the prefaces and acknowledgments of Harold Bloom, Geoffrey Hartman, and J. Hillis Miller, one is struck by the tone of respect, even reverence, with which the name of Paul de Man is mentioned. It is not difficult to locate reasons. Bloom's latest thesis about literary history was announced by de Man three years before the appearance of *The Anxiety of Influence*; Hartman's thesis in his book on Wordsworth was anticipated by de Man in an obscure essay; Miller's turn from Poulet to Derrida in an essay on Poulet was not much more than a repetition of de Man's earlier essay on Poulet. . . . In the manner of a don whose power is assured and unquestioned, de Man has found it necessary to speak only sparingly; in comparison to his prolific lieutenants he is almost invisible. . . . He presumes to tell us not only what literature has been but also what it must be. And, somewhat chillingly (perhaps it is best to drop the metaphor of the Godfather at this point), he tells us not what literary critics ought to be doing but what "in fact" they shall be doing.[98]

Thus runs what by the end of the 1970s was becoming the dominant gothic story about the "Yale Critics" and by extension about theory per se: everything returns to de Man, the secret, dark, criminal, paternal source of a thought (or a plot) so powerful that it threatens to write the script for all literary study. Unsurprisingly, the character traits of the theorist are taken to the limit in the rhetorical construction of de Man. The Robespierrean motif of icy rationalism dominates. If Derrida's expressions of passion are imagined as contradictory, de Man's "acknowledgment of emotion is supposed to fit on a molecule," as Terada wittily puts it (7). "Rigor" had practically become his Homeric epithet by the late 1970s; foes admitted he was rigorous, friends praised his rigor. For the personification-system of "theory" is not restricted to negative or journalistic accounts of theory; it saturates the entire field. The descriptive tags that recurred in the tributes to de Man offered by friends, colleagues, and students at his memorial service in early 1984 often had a slightly allegorical feel to them, as though they were not merely descriptive of cherished empirical characteristics of a particular human being, but were objective correlatives of rigor, the physical attributes of an incarnate irony (for "Paul was irony itself")—the blue gaze; the ironic shrug; the luminous, quizzical smile that, in pursuit of truth, could turn into "a glint of steel."[99]

It is of course unsurprising that accounts such as these last, offered as part of what was clearly an intensely felt act of mourning, should blend representation with fantasy; the point is simply to stress the points of congruence between these hagiographic descriptions of de Man and the wilder, often aggressive fantasies about him as a fount of rigor, authority, charisma, and nihilistic excess that circulated in the academy from the late 1970s onward, unconnected to any real personal acquaintance with de Man and often, as in the passage by Lentricchia, not particularly interested in empirically nuanced reportage. The wartime journalism scandal of 1988–89 testified to the force of de Man's quasi-allegorical role in the profession. John Guillory's formulation from 1993 is precise: "The immense symptomatic significance of the *figure* of de Man has been indisputably confirmed by the paroxysm which passed through the entire critical profession in the wake of the revelations concerning de Man's wartime journalism. It would not have been necessary for so many theorists and antitheorists, de Manians and anti-de Manians, to 'respond' to these revelations if *theory itself* were not perceived to be implicated in the figure of de Man."[100] The temptation is always to efface the rhetorical work of personification and imagine an essential link between person and theory. This is what antitheoretical polemic does when it seeks to return theory to the charisma and authority of an individual. De Man, as we have seen, was serving as the limit case for this kind of gesture by the end of the 1970s; this pattern intensified exponentially after the discovery of his wartime writings granted antitheoretical writers an opportunity—an unlooked-for, yet, as we have seen, well-prepared-for opportunity—to condemn theory-as-deconstruction by condemning de Man. The ad hominem argument literalizes personification, effacing the difference between theorist and theory, and at the same time reducing the theorist to a minimal psychic point—a cold center of authority, ambition, ruthlessness. The turn of the screw effected by the wartime journalism scandal adds another layer of petrification: the theorist becomes a quasi-embodiment of guilt, a character so fixated on his wartime journalism that everything he writes, decades later, will constitute an excuse for it, or a covert continuation of it. Reduced to the willfulness of a *person*, theory turns out to involve the reduction of a person to a *personification*.

The fantastic character of ad hominem argumentation on this scale is easily discerned by readers who take thought and texts (let alone psychic life) seriously, since it entails such punishing equations and reductions. But a small version of that gesture—that transformation of an allegorical relationship into an essentializing one—happens every time we invoke a proper name as a mark of authority, making it refer not just to a person but to a body of work as an *identity*. The compulsive functioning of the proper name in the discourse of theory not only indicates the degree to which theory functions as a canon, it suggests the inextricability of theory from the identity politics that theory critiques.[101] If, as Barbara Johnson suggests, "identity politics presupposes that human beings are personifications of their readable traits," then the canon reformers, the reactionaries who oppose them, and the literary theorists who put identity-claims into question and who are opposed by both reformers and reactionaries, are all at some point repeating versions of the same gesture.[102] We are reminded again that wild journalistic mistakes—here, the confusion of theory and multiculturalism, or "deconstruction" and the "canon wars"—cannot simply be quarantined off from the discourse of theory.

This does not mean that there are not degrees of error. And it is possibly the case that rhetorical reading has been resisted with particular ferocity because of the stubbornness with which it seeks to resist the effacement of the rhetoricity of personifications. De Man arguably came to personify "theory" because his theory puts so much direct and indirect pressure on personification as a trope. We shall examine this aspect of de Man's theory a little more fully in Chapter 5, but we can recall here that de Manian rhetorical reading grants "language" a ghostly but insistent agency, to the point that personhood itself becomes an unstable concept. Several of de Man's late essays focus on the trope of prosopopoeia: "the fiction of an apostrophe to an absent, deceased, or voiceless entity, which posits the possibility of the latter's reply and confers upon it the power of speech. Voice assumes mouth, eye, and finally face, a chain that is manifest in the etymology of the trope's name, *prosopon poiein*, to confer a mask or a face (*prosopon*)."[103] The *conferral* of face, or answerable speech, carries with it the latent threat that the face or the power of speech might be an illusion, with no identity or ground under it. In his reading of the "Blessed Babe" passage in Wordsworth's *Prelude*, de Man casts prosopopoeia as a trope with enough totalizing power to construct a world—the infant, in Wordsworth's poem, moves from eye to face to identity, "thus opening the way to a process of totalization which, in the span of a few lines can grow to encompass everything" (*RR,* 91). Yet, a world dependent on linguistic figuration is ultimately fragile and privative. It is no surprise that de Manian theory has incited resistance that itself takes the form of a personification-effect. No other theoretical approach has been declared *dead* as often as deconstruction, especially de Man's variety—and of course to call something dead, one has first to imagine it alive. "What does it mean to treat a theory as an animate being?" Barbara Johnson asks. "More precisely, what does it mean to personify deconstruction as animate only by treating it as dead, giving it life only in the act of taking that life away?" (17). At the very least, it suggests that this theory triggers deep anxieties about language and life, speaking and dying. By allowing language to override the polarity of life and death and acquire uncanny (de)animating power, rhetorical reading attracts to itself—"aberrantly," as de Man would say—the energies of a darkly sublime narrative. This in turn helps explain the remarkable reserves of polemical energy that de Man's name can still unleash, decades later. Dead and buried but never quite gone, this theory has proved both enduringly fascinating and stubbornly unpalatable—far less easy to savor and digest than the various "posthumanisms" now popular in the American academy, which chastise the pretensions of *homo sapiens* while overtly or tacitly preserving those of the *zōon logon echon*.[104] We may now turn to de Man's tightly wound paradox (and personification) of theory as its own resistance to itself, and to the complicated interface between this paradox and the aesthetic ideology it critiques.

De Man's essay "The Resistance to Theory" begins with reflections on the institutional context that produced it, or at least the first version of it: an invitation from the MLA in 1980 to write an introduction to literary theory for a volume titled *Introduction to Scholarship*—the sort of book that owes its existence to the enormous American university system, with its substantial support for graduate training and market for pedagogical aids. Because de Man's essay argued for the impossibility of defining theory, the MLA rejected it: "The Committee rightly judged that this was an inauspicious way to achieve the pedagogical objectives of the volume and commissioned another article. I thought their decision altogether justified" (*RT*, 3). Rejection by the MLA thus becomes the first instance of "resistance" to the theoretical problem of theory in an essay that will track that resistance all the way down to the genome of "theory" itself. De Man's own essay, according to its own argument, will be resisting itself. It is certainly a difficult, at times strange text, like most other texts by de Man, and a close reading of it is beyond my ambition here; we shall pick out a few key motifs.

One of them is the pedagogical theme. In his essay's opening section, de Man defines teaching with characteristic audacity: "Overfacile opinion notwithstanding, teaching is not primarily an intersubjective relationship between people but a cognitive process in which self and other are only tangentially involved. The only teaching worthy of the name is scholarly, not personal" (*RT*, 4). Having defined genuine teaching as the transmission of knowledge, de Man sets up the double question of whether literary theory is teachable, and why the question of its teachability matters. The answer to the first question will be a complicated version of yes and no. "As a controlled reflection on the formation of method, theory rightly proves to be entirely compatible with teaching. . . . A question arises only if a tension develops between methods of understanding and the knowledge which those methods allow one to reach." If so, theory is discovering something that is both dependent on and incompatible with the method on which theory reflects. Theory thus encounters a certain unteachability: "a method that cannot be made to suit the 'truth' of its object can only teach delusion." We may say that a negative knowledge *is* being taught: the knowledge of a delusion (a necessary delusion, insofar as theory only unearths it thanks to reflection on the method that produces it, while remaining incompatible with it). Yet we see that an infernal spiral is at work, since to call this negative knowledge *knowledge* is to imply that one has a stable method for acquiring it, whereas the theoretical reflection on method, according to de Man, is constantly producing (or at least threatening to produce) something *incompatible* with its own procedures. If we could count on that incompatibility, however, we would have acquired knowledge after all—so it seems that de Man, as so often, is ushering us toward a state of suspense: when theory reflects on method, it becomes impossible to know whether or not teaching is possible. This, too, of course, is an aberrant knowledge-claim, one that knows it cannot know what it is doing, *even though* it knows that what it does (or teaches) contradicts what it knows (or teaches). This spiral of self-resistance, however, is not sterile; it does critical work and generates supererogatory resistance. "These uncertainties are manifest in the hostility directed at theory in the name of ethical and aesthetic values, as well as in the recuperative attempts of theoreticians to reassert their own subservience to these values. The most effective of these acts will denounce theory as an obstacle to scholarship and, consequently, to teaching." A reflection on literary theory produces a critique of aesthetic pedagogy, a reaction from critics (including "theoreticians"), and a riposte from the theorist: "For if this is indeed so, then it is better to fail in teaching what should not be taught than to succeed in teaching what is not true" (*RT*, 4).

That strikingly sharp affirmation has a classical pedigree, for it is the watchword of the ironist, Socrates: the untrue *should not* be taught. In this case, no doubt the untrue *will* be taught, however, since theory resists itself so stubbornly; and indeed, by the end of his essay de Man is stressing that the transmission of the illusion of knowledge cannot be prevented: "To the extent however that they are theory, that is to say teachable, generalizable and highly responsive to systematization, rhetorical readings, like the other kinds, still avoid and resist the reading they advocate" (*RT*, 19). An all-too-successful teaching is going to happen; but it would be *better* to fail than to succeed. Thus, an ethical imperative attends (or is generated by) the epistemological quandary. The teaching of rhetorical reading fails to fail as it should, but it has the moral duty of trying to inscribe this problematic into its pedagogy, and thereby resist the program of aesthetic education.

"Theory," in this essay, will mean de Manian theory, of course, by way of a massive gesture of appropriation on de Man's part that nonetheless does no more than mime, as we have seen, an equation constitutive of the discourse of theory in the American academy. But de Man's initial move is of interest. The "ill-defined and somewhat chaotic field" that has come to be called "theory" in the American academy, he tells us, admits of a strikingly narrow conceptual (or indeed, though de Man does not use the word here, theoretical) definition: "The advent of theory, the break that is now so often being deplored and that sets it aside from literary history and literary criticism, occurs with the introduction of linguistic terminology in the metalanguage about literature" (*RT*, 8). The "break" or event of theory as "theory," that is, begins with semiotics and structuralism—with the "structuralist invasion," to recall Derrida's trope. Later in the essay semiotics will be subordinated to rhetoric, but de Man is clear that, in his view, theory first manifests itself as a semiotic impulse ("such events as the application of Saussurian linguistics to literary texts" [*RT*, 8]). By drawing attention to the unmotivated link "between word and thing," semiology makes legible "literariness" as the "autonomous potential of language" (*RT*, 10). Literariness not only produces epistemological unreliability, it voids aesthetic syntheses—though as we noted during our brief discussion of this text in the Introduction, de Man also suggests that literariness simultaneously generates the *illusion* of aesthetic synthesis: "The ensuing foregrounding of material, phenomenal aspects of the signifier creates a strong illusion of aesthetic seduction at the very moment when the actual aesthetic function has been, at the very least, suspended" (ibid.). Aesthetics always involves an assertion of the convergence of phenomenality (that is, the presence and intentional structure of a something-perceived, whether we call that something an object or an image or a meaning) with processes and functions of language. "No one in his right mind will try to grow grapes by the luminosity of the word 'day', but it is very difficult not to conceive of the patterns of one's past and future existence as in accordance with temporal and spatial schemes that belong to fictional narratives and not to the world" (*RT*, 11). This leads de Man to his definition of ideology:

> This does not mean that fictional narratives are not part of the world and of reality: their impact upon the world may well be all too strong for comfort. What we call ideology is precisely the confusion of linguistic with natural reality, of reference with phenomenalism. It follows that, more than any other mode of inquiry, including economics, the linguistics of literariness is a powerful and indispensable tool in the unmasking of ideological aberrations, as well as a determining factor in accounting for their occurrence. (*RT*, 11)

The desire to press literature into a pedagogic role offers a primary instance of ideology in de Man's sense. The allergic reaction to de Man's work by both left- and right-wing critics is unsurprising, for rhetorical reading challenges at its root the acculturative mission that has played such a prominent role in American debates about the university, and that surfaces not just in conservative jeremiads or administrative platitudes, but also in the interminable "calls" for redemptive or engaged criticism that form part of the idiom of informed American literary-critical discussion.[105] The idea that literature might not be "a reliable source of information about anything but its own language" has proved a far more irritating claim than any other that has been advanced by literary and cultural critics. It sparks accusations of nihilism and aestheticism precisely because it interrupts aesthetic discourse on a fundamental level.[106]

What, then, is "language" for de Man—that central category in his thinking that disrupts the aesthetic, exceeds phenomenalization, and, in the final twist of de Man's essay, incites theory to resist itself? For theory is self-resistance because theory seeks to engage language: "The resistance to theory is a resistance to the use of language about language. It is therefore a resistance to language itself or to the possibility that language contains factors or functions that cannot be reduced to intuition" (*RT*, 12–13). It follows that "there is probably no word to be found in the language that is as overdetermined, self-evasive, disfigured and disfiguring as 'language'" (*RT*, 13). Linguistic issues, in de Man's sense, arise whenever one encounters patterns that resist intuitive uptake: "whereas we have traditionally been accustomed to reading literature by analogy with the plastic arts and with music, we now have to recognize the necessity of a non-perceptual, linguistic moment in painting and music, and learn to *read* pictures rather than to imagine meaning" (*RT*, 10). The "linguistic moment" characterizes any medium when semantic effects are being produced by structures irreducible to perception or semanticization or—and here is where the rhetorical turn comes in—grammatical formalization. As soon as the tropological play of the text exceeds grammatical control, *reading* becomes the problem that language raises that cannot be bypassed. Encountered as an aporia of reading, literariness is no longer an abstract matter. It has, de Man suggests, the bite of the "actual." Caught up in reading, we cannot be sure where figuration stops—to what extent, for instance, to return to the governing trope of the discourse of theory, persons can be securely differentiated from figurative projections.

Near the end of "The Resistance to Theory," de Man offers, as an example of a rhetorical residue that would not be grammatically controllable, the title of a romantic poem, "The Fall of Hyperion." According to his dense, and, as one might expect, interesting, strange, and slightly violent reading, the title's genitive construction can be taken either as "Hyperion's Fall" or "Hyperion Falling"; in the first case, "the word 'fall' is plainly figural, and we, as readers, read this fall standing up"; in the second case things are trickier, since the "Fall" no longer refers metaphorically to a distinct (and fictional) past defeat, but evokes "an actual process of falling, regardless of its beginning, its end or the identity of the entity to whom it befalls to be falling." That second option enables a chain of identifications, given that Keats's poem is about "a character who resembles Apollo, not Hyperion"—the character, that is, who should be standing, not falling, and with whom Keats ambiguously identifies. Thus,

> if Hyperion can be Apollo and Apollo can be Keats, then he can also be us and his figural (or symbolic) fall becomes his and our literal falling as well. The difference between the two readings is itself structured like a trope. And it matters a great deal how we read the title, as an exercise not only in semantics, but in what the text actually does to us. Faced with the ineluctable necessity to come to a decision, no grammatical or logical analysis can help us out. Just as Keats had to break off his narrative, the reader has to break off his understanding at the very moment when he is most directly engaged and summoned by the text. One could hardly expect to find solace in this "fearful symmetry" between the author's and the reader's plight since, at this point, the symmetry is no longer formal but an actual trap, and the question no longer "merely" theoretical. (*RT*, 16–17)

De Man is strikingly insistent: something "actually" happens when we encounter the rhetorical element of a text. We read "Fall" literally; that meaning opens onto "an actual process of falling"; and that "actual" process, through the chain of identifications, results in "our literal falling as well." What does *literal* mean here? Or *actual*, for that matter? How do they intersect? *Literalis*: of or belonging to letters or writing; *actualis*: pertaining to action. This literality is performative writing—when we read this literal meaning, reading becomes falling. Or is it that reading becomes falling when we *fail* to read? For de Man offers a further complication. The literal meaning ("Hyperion falling") is in tension with the more familiar and, according to de Man, more reassuring figurative meaning ("Hyperion's fall," where *fall*, as a metaphor for a defeat that has occurred and is now completed, signifies the "recognizable story" of "the defeat of an older by a newer power"). And reading is the impossible necessity of deciding between literal and figural meaning, in the absence of any grammatical or contextual rule or safety net. Thus the "actual trap" of the passage ("trap" is *Fall* in German: a pun de Man leaves latent here but exploits elsewhere) does not consist simply in our reading the literal meaning, but rather in our being unable to read either the literal or the figural meaning without obliterating the true difficulty of this microtext.[107] This is what causes us to have to "break off" our understanding. One pole of the tropological structure in this particular case, however—the literal meaning—*figures* that difficulty. No critic is better at destroying meta-language than de Man, and certainly the last thing we should expect when reading him is a literal meaning that would be stable and reassuring. "Literal" here refers us back to a figurativeness that is the actuality, as breaking-off, of reading. That breaking-off is akin to death: de Man is replaying in miniature here his reading of the "actual occurrence" of interruption in Percy Shelley's *The Triumph of Life*, a poem fragmented by "the actual death and subsequent disfigurement of Shelley's body . . . This mutilated textual model exposes the wound of a fracture that lies hidden in all texts" (*RR*, 120).

The figure for the deadly actuality of that figurativeness is falling (falling, that is, figures the inability to decide the difference between standing and falling). In a dense commentary on several texts of de Man's that tell the story "not just of a figurative fall but also of a very literal falling," Cathy Caruth reminds us of what makes falling different from motion in the abstract: falling implies a force (gravity) and promises an impact. "Those who resist theory in the name of perceptual reality, de Man seems to be arguing, are in fact resisting the force, or impact, of a fall."[108] In our example, the literal meaning "Hyperion Falling" provides the *theme* of de Manian theory while also figuring a *force* or *impact* that is evaded or resisted as soon as that theory is thematized: this force is also an unforce.[109] The theoretical lesson is "the story of why all texts, as texts, can always be said to be falling" (*RT*, 16), but that story is only one of the mutually exclusive alternatives staged by the title of Keats's poem. To learn the theoretical lesson is to break off one's reading of the rhetorical crux. All of this is being unfolded, we should also remind ourselves, from nothing more than a title. It is the title, to be sure, of one of the most famous fragmentary texts in British romanticism; but still: A title is supposed to be merely the proper name or promise of a text, not a text in its own right. De Man's hyperbolic focus on a title may be taken as an ironic illustration of the practical rather than ontological privilege that literature enjoys in de Manian theory. The "rhetorical or tropological dimension of language ... is perhaps more explicitly in the foreground in literature (broadly conceived) than in other verbal manifestations," yet it "can be revealed in any verbal event when it is read textually" (*RT*, 17). De Man's exegesis of the small verbal event of *The Fall of Hyperion* as title, not poem, reads the poem's fragmentary status back into the poem's title, decapitates the poem and inflates the resulting fragment of a fragment into an exemplary reading of our failure to read it.

This example of a counter–aesthetic education, in other words, does not fail to fail; it takes the form a professional, pedagogical explanation of a (portion of a) canonical literary text, and that explanation in turn exemplifies a theory, the exemplary theory of the American academy. That failure to fail is the final lesson, of course: "Nothing can overcome the resistance to theory since theory *is* itself this resistance" (*RT*, 19). Yet things do not simply stay the same either. In seeking to elicit the "no longer merely 'theoretical'" force of an "actual trap," de Man's work stands (or falls) as the event around which the discourse of theory has had to arrange its fantasies. The notion of the Yale Critics helped that discourse do its initial arranging for a number of reasons, as we have seen in this chapter, but perhaps above all because, as Hartman asserted in his preface to *Deconstruction and Criticism*, all of these critics, in their quite different ways, were seeking to address "the importance—or *force*—of literature" (vii, Hartman's italics). The rest of this book will try to document that claim.

2. Theory and Romantic Lyric
The Case of "A slumber did my spirit seal"

During their brief tenure as the public face of "theory," the Yale Critics, as we have seen, made visible a conflicted affinity between theory (as "high theory," which is to say as theory-as-deconstruction), on the one hand, and the academic field of romanticism, on the other. We have also seen that, for various institutional, historical, and literary-historical reasons, romanticism—meaning here above all British and comparative romanticism—has been the literary field most intensely engaged with aesthetic questions in the American academy. Given the lines along which modern aesthetics developed, it is then almost tautological to observe that until relatively recently the academic study of romanticism consistently privileged the study of lyric poetry. "Lyric was finally made one of three fundamental genres during the romantic period," Jonathan Culler summarizes, "when a more vigorous conception of the individual subject made it possible to conceive of lyric as mimetic: mimetic of the experience of the subject."[1] Associated with voice, subjectivity, and intensity of expression and feeling, lyric began to become, in the late eighteenth and early nineteenth century, an available name for the essence of poetry, and ultimately, by extension, literature or literariness itself. If one discounts the difficulties encountered whenever one looks closely at particular contexts and texts, one can track an increasingly normative aesthetic concept of lyric from romantic and nineteenth-century writing through the modernist revolution of Eliot and Pound, and into twentieth-century academic criticism. The most remembered work of I. A. Richards, William Empson, Cleanth Brooks, and W. K. Wimsatt turns on the interpretation of lyric poems, to the point that the centrality of lyric in New Critical scholarship and pedagogy has become a cliché of intellectual history. As young-Turk romanticists, Harold Bloom and Geoffrey Hartman shared at least one thing with the disciples of T. S. Eliot: a commitment to literature as poetry, and to poetry as paradigmatically lyric poetry. That postromantic condition lay deeper than many very stark differences.

Their professional commitment to the study of (romantic, lyric) poetry distinguishes the Yale Critics from the other writers, critics and philosophers who were being marshaled into a theory canon at the end of the 1970s, and who were by and large writing about narrative or nonfictional prose, as a glance at any standard anthology or introduction-to-theory syllabus confirms. The pseudo-manifesto *Deconstruction and Criticism* (1979), with its nominal focus on Shelley, stands out as something of an aberration in the history of theory. Looking back in 1985, Culler was already concerned that recent critical trends had "neglected lyric."[2] Furthermore, recent criticism had failed to produce "a new theory of lyric," for, Culler claimed, lyric poetry was still being theorized by way of the figure of overheard utterance—being conceived of, that is, as a sort of isolated dramatic monologue that requires its reader to infer a context and interpret the speaker's tone, stance and attitude. "This is, roughly, the approach to the lyric expounded and exemplified by the New Criticism, and it remains the only theory of lyric to gain wide currency and influence" (38). To be sure there had been "changes in the study of lyric" by 1985; Culler mentions Bloom and de Man along with several other critics, and lists three exemplary differences he perceives between Brooks's and de Man's readings of the closing lines of Yeats's "Among School Children" ("O body swayed to music, O brightening glance/How can we know the dancer from the dance?"): a shift from speaker to trope; a shift from an organic to a disruptive conception of self-referentiality; and a shift from an affirmative to a skeptical treatment of the poetic symbol. (De Man's reading, it will be recalled, insists on the possibility of reading the poem's final question both rhetorically and literally: two incompatible interpretations of the poem result.)[3] These changes, while they deconstruct an aesthetic notion of lyric, do not, as Culler persuasively suggests, produce a new theory of what the lyric is. In this particular essay Culler does not engage de Man's "Anthropomorphism and Trope in the Lyric," but his point would hold as a gloss on de Man's dramatic derogation of lyric in that text: "The lyric is not a genre, but one name among several to designate the defensive motion of understanding, the possibility of a future hermeneutics."[4] Rhetorical reading does not contribute to the project of poetics. Its interest in genre is derivative of its project of critiquing aestheticizing modes of reading. Lyric, the privileged genre term of postromantic aesthetics, is merely "one name among several" for "the defensive movement of the understanding," or for what de Man in another late essay calls "the phenomenalization of poetic voice."[5]

An interest in calling into question lyric as a genre has surged in recent years under the rubric of "new lyric studies," which has occasioned yet another spectral return of Paul de Man in academic criticism. Virginia Jackson's influential *Dickinson's Misery: A Theory of Lyric Reading* (2005) takes its "notion of 'lyric reading' from de Man's interpretation of the genre."[6] Of course, Jackson is flipping the hand over. Repeating a version of a gesture made familiar by the "new historicist" movement in romantic studies in the 1980s (for the fact that in the American academy everything always has to be "new" does not, of course, protect against repetition), Jackson identifies lyric as a largely twentieth-century abstraction that effaces particularities of genre, context, and communicative performance.[7] The texts of Emily Dickinson offer a particularly dramatic example of an "isolated lyric subject"—"a social, even an historical and cultural abstraction"—being extracted from a "densely woven fabric of social relations" (90). More recently, Jackson's and Yopie Prins's *Lyric Theory Reader* (2014) has sought to document the claim that "the lyricization of poetry is a product of twentieth-century critical thought."[8] In their sharply argumentative introductions to the various sections of the reader, the editors repeatedly point out ways in which the texts they anthologize presuppose or idealize lyric as a genre. No "new" concept of lyric emerges from this critical engagement, or is supposed to: "A resistance to definition may be the best basis for definition of the lyric—and of poetry—that we have" (2).

Yet Jackson and Prins frequently write as though they are feeling that lack of definition as a burden, even a trap. Despite—or because of—Jackson's slant admiration for de Man, they have particularly unsparing words for de Manian deconstruction: "Post-structuralism did not unravel the lyric; instead, post-structuralist critics tended to make the lyric even more of a modern icon than did their predecessors in the twentieth century, since by so doing they could demonstrate the difficulties and hazards, perhaps even the impossibility, of thinking about lyric theory in any other way" (274). It is hard to know what would count as "unraveling" the lyric here, since Jackson and Prins themselves cannot propose styles of unraveling that actually unravel lyric. "Models of the lyric," they admit, are "models we seem to be able to work variations on but keep not giving up" (509); "The theory may be increasingly queer, but the lyric uncannily returns as poetic norm. . . . We have yet to find a critical poetic genre that does not look a lot like the modern lyric reading that did not end when the last century ended" (510). This is hardly surprising, since Jackson and Prins present "the history of lyricization" as "the process of abstracting all verse genres into a larger and ever more capacious idea of poetry," from which no poetics, no matter how avant-garde, can escape (453).[9] Of course, when all else fails one can draw on the reserve of liberal optimism, as Jackson and Prins do in the closing sentences of their introduction to their anthology's final section, after once again confessing that nothing fails like success (or succeeds like failure): "Since [the normative model of the modern lyric] continues to allow so many critics to read across cultures, across periods, across disciplinary divides, and across so many other critical points of departure, it is unlikely that we will give it up anytime soon, though perhaps precisely because so many critics have begun to develop variations on that model, another wind is blowing, and with it the small rain down shall rain" (575). That closing lyrical fillip registers the wishfulness of this appeal to an enlightened future, when the knot that today keeps retangling itself might finally be unraveled for good.

One can perhaps claim, as Rei Terada does in her introduction to a special cluster on lyric published in *PMLA* in 2008, that the ideological charge of lyric has slackened. "It comes as a relief that after years, probably centuries, during which lyric is used as an intensifier, reflecting the assumption that lyrics more than other media are concentrates of culture or consciousness, the current conversation about lyric isn't especially heightened. The lyric zone of electrification is dissipating along with belief in the autonomy of the lyric object and in the specialness of the lyric mode."[10] Even this firmly nominalist account, however, puts stress on the task of "working through lyric," as though therapy—a forbidding of mourning—were still required in order to reach the point where "you don't care whether something is a lyric or not" (198). Not only is there institutional and pedagogical investment in the idea of lyric, but there also seems to be the danger of conceptual relapse: "Lyric studies participates in the renewal of lyric ideology when it suggests that lyric, whether conceived as object, dynamic, or even ruse, is irreplaceably exemplary. . . . The last, benedictory function of lyric is to be the lure that attracts suspicion to aesthetic ideology as such" (198–99). In this context, Terada gives credit to de Man, who was "interested in literature and lyric out of vigilance, because they seem uniquely ideological. But there, too, they only seem so" (199). The seeming seems to linger, however; and in Terada's text, as in Jackson and Prins's, one gets the sense that lyric has achieved a position in our contemporary conceptual architecture that allows its analysis to at least *seem* potentially interminable.

Why should that be? In the present context we have the luxury of not needing to take a position on whether or not a new theory of lyric is necessary or even desirable;[11] but since in this book we are tracing some of the interleavings of aesthetics, romanticism and deconstruction-as-theory, we may pause over the question of why an aestheticized concept of lyric seems to have such a stubborn half-life, and why critics seem to care about this as much as they do. Terada cares about having us *not* care what a lyric is; Jackson and Prins at times *do* seem to care a good deal; and this caring about the repetitive return of lyric will itself seem inscribed in a longer-wave pattern of repetition should one decide that the project of a "new lyric studies" bears an extended family resemblance to many similar projects in postwar academic debate for moving "beyond formalism." A discomfort with the literary object seems built into the academic study of it. Self-abnegation is one of the constitutive gestures of aesthetic discourse; a desire to recapture the "densely woven fabric of social relations," as Jackson puts it, accompanies the deracinating movement of aesthetic formalization ("a social, even an historical and cultural abstraction"). And as soon as the lyric is being represented as *abstracted voice*, metaphors of loss and recovery become unstoppable. One then enters the force field of what de Man rather mischievously describes as "the uneasy combination of funereal monumentality with paranoid fear that characterizes the hermeneutics and the pedagogy of lyric poetry" (RR 259). A more tamely descriptive critic might have said: an uneasy combination of elation, frustration, and moral exhortation; but paranoia and mourning are perhaps the right names for the defenses being mobilized—mobilized less against the abstraction of voice than against the threatened loss of the metaphor of voice itself. That is why de Man, the proper name of the theory that posits the devolvement of voice into trope, returns so visibly in these discussions.[12] For if lyric is voice as figure, then, as Barbara Johnson observes, at stake in a lyric text, no less than in a legal one, is the question, "What is a person?"[13] *Pace* Jackson and Prins, that observation does not of itself make lyric into a "modern icon"; rather, it assumes the task of reading the iconicity with which lyric has been burdened in the modern era.

In this context, the question of what a person and a voice are leads to the question of what a text, an author, an intent, and a meaning are. I noted earlier that most of the texts that ended up in the "theory canon"—a disputable entity, but say: the texts assembled in the *Norton Anthology of Theory and Criticism*—focus on narrative or on nonfictional prose. But even in the *Norton Anthology* there are a handful of exceptions, and of them, two are essays strenuously interested in authorial intent, and centered on Wordsworth's short poem "A slumber did my spirit seal": E. D. Hirsch's "Objective Interpretation" (1960) and Steven Knapp and Walter Benn Michaels's "Against Theory" (1982).[14] And, not included in the *Norton Anthology*, but figuring prominently in the history of the mediatization of "deconstruction in America" that we are retracing in this book, is a famous exchange between J. Hillis Miller and M. H. Abrams in which fundamental hermeneutic and rhetorical questions are routed through "A slumber." In the rest of this chapter, I propose to examine these debates as a way of concretizing the challenge that rhetorical reading poses to aesthetic or lyric ideology. This itinerary leaves in the background certain crucial texts by de Man (most obviously, the essays on Baudelaire and lyric already touched on, but also his reading of the "purloined ribbon" episode in Rousseau's *Confessions*, which is discussed by Knapp and Michaels and about which I shall eventually say a brief word); but those essays, which have been much studied, would require us to thread our way through various primary texts.[15] Whereas if we focus on the polemical crisscross over Wordsworth's short poem, we not only remain within the problematic of "lyric reading"; we also reap the advantage of being able to review an important deconstructive reading by J. Hillis Miller from the "Yale" era.

Wordsworth wrote "A slumber did my spirit seal," along with other famous lyrics and an early draft of *The Prelude*, during a cold, lonely winter in Goslar, a town in the foothills of the Harz mountains in Lower Saxony where Wordsworth and his sister Dorothy had repaired to save money (which they did) and learn German (which they did not). One minor but obviously not wholly nugatory reason why this poem has played a prominent role in theoretical argument is that it is short:

> A slumber did my spirit seal;
> I had no human fears:
> She seemed a thing that could not feel
> The touch of earthly years.
>
> No motion has she now, no force;
> She neither hears nor sees;
> Rolled round in earth's diurnal course,
> With rocks, and stones, and trees.[16]

"A slumber" presents editors with few difficulties. No original manuscript exists (Wordsworth's letter to Coleridge containing the poem has been lost), and Wordsworth's revising of the text over the course of his lifetime was minimal.[17] As an editorial object, at least, the poem pretty much is what it is. As an object of traditional literary-historical scholarship, it begins to become a more complicated entity. The degree to which Wordsworth intended readers to associate this poem with other "Lucy poems" is uncertain; traditional scholarly efforts to trace "Lucy" back to a historical person have had to settle for vague compromises;[18] and though such modest referential difficulties are common enough in literary scholarship, they shade into more disturbing complexities as they edge closer to the central problem, routinely evaded but never definitively repressed or solved—the problem of reading what this kind of enigmatic text (call it, at least for now, a lyric) tells us about reading.

It is easy enough to accept that scholars will never know, nor need to know, whether Wordsworth was thinking of any particular woman or girl while writing these lines (always assuming—and this is an assumption, albeit a strong and reasonable one—that the "she" of lines three, five, and six all refer to a person separate from the narrator, rather than to the "spirit" of line one).[19] It can be a little more disturbing to discover that trained readers have reached opposite conclusions about what the poem means, or what Wordsworth meant his poem to mean. The necessity of judging between competing interpretations forms the context in which this text first became an iconic display text for twentieth-century literary-theoretical debate, in the article mentioned above by E. D. Hirsch (at the time a young romanticist at Yale), "Objective Interpretation."[20] Hirsch counterposed two well-known interpretations of "A slumber" by Cleanth Brooks and F. W. Bateson, sharpening to the point of irreconcilability the differences between the two critics' readings of the poem's last two lines.[21] Bateson interprets "Rolled round in earth's diurnal course,/With rocks, and stones, and trees" as an affirmation that "the pantheistic universe is solidly *one*" (Bateson 34): "Lucy is actually more alive now that she is dead, because she is now a part of the life of Nature and not just a human 'thing'" (Bateson 80–81). Brooks, in contrast, reads these lines as part of the narrator's bitter recognition of the loved one's "utter and horrible inertness" in death (Brooks 736). Hirsch sternly refuses the notion that these divergent readings can be synthesized or otherwise reconciled:

> While Bateson construes a primary emphasis on life and affirmation, Brooks emphasizes deadness and inertness. No amount of manipulation can reconcile these divergent emphases, since one pattern of emphasis irrevocably excludes other patterns, and, since emphasis is always crucial to meaning, the two constructions of meaning rigorously exclude one another. (1,698)[22]

Having set up an interpretive choice (both of these critics offer coherent accounts of the poem, but both cannot be right; interpreters must choose), Hirsch goes on to propose that interpretation ask and seek to answer the question, "What in all probability did the author mean?" Meaning is authorial meaning; and though "no one can establish another's meaning with certainty," the interpreter's goal "is simply this—to show that a given reading is more probable than others," by demonstrating that a given context is more probable than others (1,703).

This commonsensical hermeneutic project, however, suffers a curious twist as Hirsch concludes his essay. He favors Bateson's interpretation because, based on the contextual evidence, in 1799 Wordsworth's "characteristic attitudes are somewhat pantheistic" (1,705). But though Hirsch approves of Bateson's method (interpretation as the construction of probable historical, psychological, and biographical contexts), he concedes "the apparent implausibility of Bateson's reading" (1,706). It is hard to believe, Hirsch admits, that the poem's second stanza is really celebrating "pantheistic magnificence" (Bateson, 33). The correct method produces the less plausible reading.[23] Beginning with one sort of textual aporia—a poem that generates two opposing, mutually destructive interpretations—Hirsch ends up with another sort—a poem that generates an opposition between what Hirsch believes to be correct interpretive theory on the one hand and what Hirsch believes to be plausible interpretive results on the other.[24]

Was "A slumber," then, a bad example for Hirsch to have chosen? If so, what—apart perhaps from an admirable willingness to face up to a difficult case—might have drawn him to this recalcitrant example? Let me leave that question hanging while I pursue a little further the story of literary theory's dalliance with Wordsworth's poem. In 1979—not a bad year to pick as the tipping point when "deconstruction" irreversibly imposed itself as the synonym of "theory" in the American academic imagination[25]—J. Hillis Miller published a reading of "A slumber" that a few years later inspired a much-referenced exchange, as noted above, between Miller and the distinguished romanticist M. H. Abrams.[26] Since in the previous chapter we recalled how tightly identified the "Yale critics" were with romantic studies, this is a good moment to note that, although Miller first made his mark in the academy as a Victorianist with particular strength in Dickens and the nineteenth-century novel, he was a well-known critic of modern poetry, and in the 1970s (that is, as a "Yale critic"), he published influential essays in the field of British romanticism.[27] Indeed, the debate with Abrams—the most famous of Miller's polemical exchanges in the 1970s—had its groundwork laid when Miller published a lengthy review essay of Abrams's *Natural Supernaturalism* (1971), "Tradition and Difference," in *Diacritics* in 1972, to which Abrams eventually replied in the form of a broad position paper, "The Deconstructive Angel," in *Critical Inquiry* in 1977.[28] The Miller-Abrams exchange about "A slumber" represents the culmination of a decade-long argument between prominent critics who had taken on the role of spokes-men for their respective positions.

Miller's "On Edge: The Crossways of Contemporary Criticism" appeared not in a specialized journal but in the *Bulletin of the American Academy of Arts and Sciences*; it belongs to a group of essays that Miller published in the 1970s that use a close reading or a book review (as in the case of the review of Abrams) as an occasion to survey the state of criticism and argue the case for Yale-style rhetorical deconstruction.[29] Of these essays, "On Edge" is particu-larly broad in outlook. Miller begins by remarking the historical contingency of literature departments, and he moves through a range of large historical and social issues—the dominance of electronic media, the increasingly mar-ginal role of literature, and the increasing need for remedial education in expository writing—before turning to the changes in high-level literary study that make up his essay's central subject. "In spite of the bewildering array of possibilities in literary methodology," Miller feels that we can narrow the field to two: "One kind [of methodology] includes all those methods whose presuppositions are in one way or another what I would call 'meta-physical.' The other kind includes those methods which hypothesize that in literature, for reasons which are intrinsic to language itself, metaphysical presuppositions are, necessarily, both affirmed and subverted" (100). The latter is "antimetaphysical or 'deconstructive'": it demonstrates that a text's play of figurative language "leaves an inassimilable residue or remnant of meaning, an unearned increment, so to speak, making a movement of sense beyond any unifying boundaries," leading to "the experience of an aporia or boggling of the mind" (101).

Miller's reading of "A slumber" is thus to serve as an "example" within a context that he could hardly have drawn more broadly.[30] He begins in deliberately traditional fashion by describing the poem as the story of the lyric speaker's acquisition of wisdom through suffering. This story links the first stanza's past tense to the second stanza's present tense: "The speaker has moved across the line from innocence to knowledge through the experience of Lucy's death. . . . The speaker confronts the fact of his own death by confronting the death of another. He speaks as a survivor standing by a grave, a corpse, or a headstone, and his poem takes the form of an epigraph" (103). From this perspective, the second stanza "speaks in the perpetual 'now' of a universal knowledge of death" (104).[31] Even while following out this line of interpretation, Miller renders the state of the speaker's knowledge a little uncertain, since this "male poet" has been left behind by his muse and remains "excluded, unable to break the seal" (105). But the main point is to stress the inadequacy of "the account of [the poem] I have so far given."

Miming the poem's shift from its first to its second stanza, Miller shifts to darker terrain, noting the disappearance of the "I" into impersonal assertions: "It is as though the speaker has lost his selfhood by waking to knowledge. He has become an anonymous impersonal wakefulness, perpetually aware that Lucy is dead and that he is not yet dead. This is the position of the survivor in all Wordsworth's work" (105). If the first interpretation had preserved a speaker speaking "as a survivor standing by a grave" and achieving knowledge (however bleak), the second interpretation reimagines that survival as self-loss—the loss of the ability to convert death into meaning through the death of a surrogate.

At this stage in his reading Miller begins to document "an obscure sexual drama" being enacted in the poem, and does so by bringing in passages from *The Prelude* that reference Wordsworth's mother's death, plus a famous passage from Dorothy Wordsworth's journal about the pleasure of imagining oneself dead. The point is to show that nature, in Wordsworth, vacillates between being a sustaining maternal presence and a violent, deadly paternal force, and that the fantasy of "dying without dying" can be read as a fantasy of "re-establishing the bond that connected [the poet] to . . . maternal nature by way of a surrogate mother, a girl who remains herself both alive and dead" (107). Thus the "touch of earthly years" becomes "both a form of sexual appropriation which leaves the one who is possessed still virgin if she dies young, and at the same time . . . the ultimate dispossession which is death" (107). The overall thrust of his reading is to stress once again the doubleness and ambivalence of the fantasy. The speaker survives but is dispersed like "Lucy" (as Miller is willing to call her); far from being her stable, grieving opposite, the speaker becomes "the displaced representative of both the penetrated and the penetrator, of both Lucy herself and of her unravishing ravisher, nature or death" (108). To the extent that he acquires knowledge, he acquires guilt: "The poet has himself somehow caused Lucy's death by thinking of it" (ibid.). This sequence of unstable, at times violent overdeterminations leads Miller to his dramatic closing gesture, as he expands the poem outward to sky and earth and the horizonal curve of metaphysics: "Lucy's name of course means light. To possess her would be a means of rejoining the lost source of light, the father sun as logos, as head power and font of meaning." But the poem's unstable reversals perform "the loss of the logos, leaving the poet and his words groundless" (109).

It is one of Miller's most daring readings, and Miller himself later seems to have grown a little unsatisfied with the essay; responding in "Postscript 1984" to M. H. Abrams's critique of it, he noted that though he was glad he had written it, he "would not write 'On Edge' in the same way today" (111).

There is something intriguingly wild about the text. Abrams was particularly outraged by Miller's construal of the "obscure sexual drama"—the point at which Miller's essay, in Abrams's view, really starts violating the poem's integrity and heading down a slippery slope toward that final, hyperbolic equation of the sun-logos with Lucy ("a name not mentioned in the poem," as Abrams points out more than once [153]). Miller's reading reminds us that "Yale deconstruction" was not formalism in any ordinary sense. Though Miller retains and even exacerbates the privilege of the literary text, that privilege takes the form of a certain excess over form. The literary text, from the perspective of this approach, is demanding readings that, as Abrams objects, *go too far*. And as Miller's elaborate buildup to his reading indicates, this excess of meaning allows the chosen text to function all the more forcefully (if also, perhaps, unreliably) as an example.[32]

Earlier I posed and deferred the question of what might have attracted Hirsch to "A slumber," and I would now like to loop back to that question, splicing it into the equivalent one that Miller's reading raises. What is it about this poem, apart from its convenient brevity, that elicits from critics the most fundamental questions that theories of reading can raise—and then drives them to extremes? Perhaps being driven to extremes is not an obvious way to describe Hirsch's problem, since his tone is so grimly sober (indeed, Hirsch in 1960 sounds uncannily like de Man in the 1970s, as he balances "A slumber" between Brooks's and Bateson's interpretations in the sentence I quoted earlier: "No amount of manipulation can reconcile these divergent emphases, since one pattern of emphasis irrevocably excludes other patterns, and, since emphasis is always crucial to meaning, the two constructions of meaning rigorously exclude one another" [Hirsch 1698]). But this sobriety, as we noted, generates an aporia at the expense of Hirsch's own method and desire, since his chosen example forces method into conflict with desired result. Miller welcomes such contradictions, but the manic energy of his interpretation raises the suspicion that Miller, too, might not be in control of the text he is rendering exemplary. The appeal of "A slumber" as a theorist's display text is in one way clear: since it appears to narrate the story of a passage from mystification to enlightenment, the poem offers theorists an allegory of their own ambition. In each case (with the exception of the antitheorist Abrams, but I shall return momentarily to note a peculiar feature of his response), the theorist shows that a simple-looking text raises complicated hermeneutic problems. (What is the meaning of being rolled around with rocks and stones and trees? Or, as Walter Benn Michaels pungently puts it, "What is a rock?")[33] In the process, though, all these readers suffer a certain loss of control—rolled round slumberously, as it were, in the act of making an example out of those textual rocks and stones and trees.

Though on the one hand such loss of control is Miller's explicit theme, on the other hand the lyric drama of his interpretation may be read as a defense against his reading's own insight. For it is as a lyric drama that his reading unfolds: in Miller's text, "the speaker" (or "poet") remains center-stage, surviving, even thriving on his loss of selfhood ("He has become an anonymous impersonal wakefulness, perpetually aware that Lucy is dead and that he is not yet dead"). The "obscure sexual drama" grants the speaker a blizzard of roles that have him projecting himself everywhere ("the displaced representative of both the penetrated and the penetrator, of both Lucy herself and of her unravishing ravisher, nature or death"). Miller's reading risks being scripted by a Petrarchan drama of identification and scattering, traces of which are indeed legible in "A slumber"—though very faint traces indeed, since the "she" possesses no body parts, indeed, arguably possesses no *body*: though she may seem a thing in stanza one, all her predications are privative in stanza two, and the only word available to represent what is being rolled round with rocks and stones and trees is, tautologically, "she." "A slumber" evacuates the visual register that supports the fetishistic economy of the Petrarchan mode.[34] *Sealing* replaces seeing. This can be our cue to pause over the privative force of the poem's first line: "A slumber did my spirit seal." Whether we take this to mean that the slumber seals the spirit or the spirit seals the slumber, a sealing (seal: from *signum*, sign) is at work. It inscribes, stamps, closes up, and—if slumber is taken to seal spirit (*spiritus*: breath, wind)—it stifles. Slumber stamps itself onto breath and seals it up; alternatively, breath, acting as an inscriptive force, stamps and seals slumber. Either way, the "I" understandably has no human fears, for in one of these readings the "I" is in a coma, and in the other it does not breathe. From the start Wordsworth's poem marks the possibility that the "I" *has no voice*. The "I" would be a grammatical pronoun cut off from breathing human life, and its "voice," breathless as the dead M. Valdemar's in Poe's story, or, less luridly put, as a personification's, would be radically figurative. Miller's baroque deconstructive reading thematizes radical figuration by pushing lyric reading to the breaking point, but also thereby resists its own insight.

A text that entices theorists to read it as an exemplary parable about reading while slipping out of the theorist's grip generates, as Miller emphasizes, anxieties about boundaries. In his reply to Miller, Abrams couches his opposition to deconstruction as a concern for proper limits. This concern appears repeatedly in the secondary literature on "A slumber" (as a relatively recent interpreter of the poem frankly if perhaps a touch impatiently puts it,

"Somewhere there must be a stop").[35] Abrams's way of couching his objection is to claim that Miller "dissolves the 'unifying boundaries' of the poem
as linguistic entity," thereby merging the text "not only with Wordsworth's
other writings, but into the textuality constituted by all occidental languages
taken together" (153). For Hirsch, the loss of authorial intention as a goal
leads to interpretive wildness; for Abrams—at least in this essay; it is an oddly
formalist position for a literary historian to be taking—the loss of textual
identity as a goal leads to interpretive wildness. An intact textual body is
needed to limit textuality, seal in human spirit, preserve human fears. In his
final paragraphs, Abrams—responding, perhaps, to the uncanny grip of this
hyperexemplary text—takes that figure to a peculiar extreme. Though he is
of course committed to the commonsensical view that authors give shape
to texts (poems are composed of "language which is expressed and ordered
by a human author" [157]), his emphasis falls on personifying the text itself:
"Literature has survived over the millennia. . . . I am reassured, however,
by the stubborn capacity of constructed texts to survive their second-order
deconstruction" (157–58). If Miller personifies the poem's "I" as a survivor,
Abrams more exotically personifies the *poem* as a survivor. In an extravagant
gesture, evocative of the pre-professional days of belles-letters and oratory,
Abrams closes his essay by simply quoting, yet once more, Wordsworth's
poem. "Let's put the text to trial," are his text's final words. There follows
"A slumber," quoted this time not as the prelude to more paraphrase and
analysis, but as the manifestation of the poem itself as its own last word—as
the survivor of all its iterations, untouched by time as a ballad-maiden, pure
as a stone rolled up on a beach, washed by a wave.

That last conceit is not properly mine, of course; it is the fantastic story told
in Steven Knapp and Walter Benn Michael's well-known position paper
"Against Theory" (1982) in order to illustrate a radicalized version of the
Hirschean thesis that all meaning is authorial meaning. "By 'theory,'" the
authors explain, "we mean a special project in literary criticism: the attempt
to govern interpretations of particular texts by appealing to an account of
interpretation in general" (2,460).[36] Two versions of this project exist: positive
(the Hirsch-style effort to obtain a method productive of objective interpretation) and negative (the Miller-style effort to demonstrate that correct
interpretation is impossible—though Knapp and Michaels do not mention
Miller; as noted earlier, and for reasons I shall go over in a moment, they are
interested in refuting one of de Man's moves in his reading of Rousseau's
purloined ribbon). Both positive and negative versions of theory, Knapp and

Michaels declare, "rest on a single mistake, a mistake that is central to the notion of theory per se": that of trying to separate inseparable terms. The "clearest example" of such false separation arises when "authorial intention" is distinguished from "the meaning of texts" (2,461). All meaning is intended meaning, and furthermore "all meaning is in fact the author's meaning" (2,463). Whenever we register meaning, we willy-nilly assume that an author intended it. Even if we know nothing about the author, we assume a fundamental intending-to-speak or *vouloir-dire*: "as soon as we attempt to interpret at all we are already committed to a characterization of the speaker as a speaker of language. We know, in other words, that the speaker intends to speak; otherwise we wouldn't be interpreting" (2,463). By clinging to this rudimentary definition of authorship, Knapp and Michaels can accuse Hirsch of forgetting his own insight. To distinguish between author-based meaning (as in Bateson's approach to "A slumber") and text-based meaning (as in Brooks's approach to "A slumber") is to produce a "theory" of meaning via a false distinction (that is, one falls into the trap of imagining that a formalist like Brooks has actually identified a meaning separate from intention, whereas he has in fact simply inferred a different authorial meaning from that of Bateson, based on different contextual information). For reasons that Knapp and Michaels never quite explain, this false distinction, as they see it, has proved stubborn enough to generate a discursive tradition called "theory": "In debates about intention, the moment of imagining intentionless meaning constitutes the theoretical moment itself" (2,463).

Knapp and Michaels have often been criticized for providing a narrow and abstract definition of theory, with the result that their critique leaves untouched most instances of the kind of writing and thinking that gets nicknamed "theory." But in the present context it will be useful to accept their terms of debate. We are interested in the phantasmatic association of theory with deconstruction; and though, as we shall review in a moment, deconstruction certainly does not "imagine intentionless meaning," deconstruction does indeed explore the dependence of intention and meaning on more archaic structures and processes. Knapp and Michaels have, in a sense, only a technical disagreement with Hirsch, even though their proposed way of fixing his interpretive machine is to scrap it. Their real antagonist is theory-as-deconstruction; and everything we have said up to this point in this book should help explain why the name of their chosen opponent inevitably turns out to be de Man, the avatar of the threatening (or thrilling, depending on one's mood) possibility that language might not be congruent with human desires.

Knapp and Michaels's first move is to establish how "radically counterintuitive" the notion of intentionless meaning is. Since they seek to show this by way of a parable that has considerable rhetorical interest, I must now quote from their text at length. We are headed back to the beach, though probably not the one that we visited at the beginning of Chapter 1, where Derrida's befuddled historian of ideas was trying to glean the washed-up works of structuralism. This beach is more of an American affair, and it involves its errant beachcomber in a considerably more melodramatic epistemological plot:

> Suppose that you're walking along a beach and you come upon a curious
> sequence of squiggles in the sand. You step back a few paces and notice that
> they spell out the following words:
>
>> A slumber did my spirit seal;
>> I had no human fears:
>> She seemed a thing that could not feel
>> The touch of earthly years.
>
> This would seem to be a good case of intentionless meaning: you recognize the
> writing as writing, you understand what the words mean, you may even iden-
> tify them as constituting a rhymed poetic stanza—and all this without knowing
> anything about the author and indeed without needing to connect the words to
> any notion of an author at all. You can do all these things without thinking of
> anyone's intention. But now suppose that, as you stand gazing at this pattern in
> the sand, a wave washes up and recedes, leaving in its wake (written below what
> you now realize was only the first stanza) the following words:
>
>> No motion has she now, no force;
>> She neither hears nor sees;
>> Rolled round in earth's diurnal course,
>> With rocks, and stones, and trees.
>
> One might ask whether the question of intention still seems as irrelevant as it
> did seconds before. You will now, we suspect, feel compelled to explain what
> you have just seen. Are these marks mere accidents, produced by the mechani-
> cal operation of the waves on the sand (through some subtle and unprecedented
> process of erosion, percolation, etc.)? Or is the sea alive and striving to express
> its pantheistic faith? Or has Wordsworth, since his death, become a sort of
> genius of the shore who inhabits the waves and periodically inscribes on the
> sand his elegiac sentiments? You might go on extending the list of explanations
> indefinitely, but you would find, we think, that all the explanations fall into
> two categories. You will either be ascribing these marks to some agent capable

of intentions (the living sea, the haunting Wordsworth, etc.), or you will count them as nonintentional effects of mechanical processes (erosion, percolation, etc.). But in the second case—where the marks now seem to be accidents—will they still seem to be words?

Clearly not. They will merely seem to *resemble* words. You will be amazed, perhaps, that such an astonishing coincidence could occur. Of course, you would have been no less amazed had you decided that the sea or the ghost of Wordsworth was responsible. But it's essential to recognize that in the two cases your amazement would have had two entirely different sources. In one case, you would be amazed by the identity of the author—who would have thought that the sea can write poetry? In the other case, however, in which you accept the hypothesis of natural accident, you're amazed to discover that what you thought was poetry turns out not to be poetry at all. It isn't poetry because it isn't language; that's what it means to call it an accident. (2,464)

Having established what they see as the intuitively obvious difference between language and marks-that-resemble-language, Knapp and Michaels offer a closing scene for their drama in which "you" experience a final revelation:

Suppose, having seen the second stanza wash up on the beach, you have decided that the "poem" is really an accidental effect of erosion, percolation, and so on, and therefore not language at all. What would it now take to change your mind? No theoretical argument will make a difference. But suppose you notice, rising out of the sea some distance from the shore, a small submarine, out of which clamber a half dozen figures in white lab coats. One of them trains his binoculars on the beach and shouts triumphantly, "It worked! It worked! Let's go down and try it again." Presumably, you will now once again change your mind, not because you have a new account of language, meaning, or intention but because you have new evidence of an author. The question of authorship is and always was an empirical question; it has now received a new empirical answer. (2,465)

In a fine commentary on Knapp and Michaels's article, Peggy Kamuf notes and puts pressure on the odd status of the term "author" in this scenario. On the one hand, the answer to the question of who authored these wave-inscribed lines ought to be "Wordsworth"; on the other hand, the whole point of the final movement of Knapp and Michaels's fantastic fable is to provide those little figures in lab coats as an answer to the "empirical" question of authorship.[37] Unless to this fantastic story is added the even more fantastic possibility that the submarine crew members do not know Wordsworth wrote "A slumber," think that they are "composing" a text rather than citing it, and just happen by sheer chance, like monkeys on a typewriter, to have repeated exactly Wordsworth's words, in which case perhaps (if you have developed a generous concept of authorship there on the beach) you would be willing to call them joint-stock "authors" of Wordsworth's poem—unless, or indeed, even *if* all this is imagined, the story about the submarine is *still* a story about "evidence (within a fiction) of a mechanical or technical process for inscribing marks on a distant surface," as Kamuf stresses (6). Formalizing authorship down to intent-to-mean, Knapp and Michaels produce a parable that formalizes intention down to intent-to-inscribe; for the experiment would have worked with any iterable mark—a geometrical figure, or a meaningless squiggle ("meaningless" except as signifying an enacted intent).[38]

Why, then, tell a story about a famous poem? Virginia Jackson suggests a generic reason. Under the conventions of "lyric reading" that, in her view, define lyric as a genre, the question of intention—of what the text means—comes up immediately (more so than if the sea had washed up, say, a sentence from a novel).[39] Kamuf offers a more general diagnosis. Literary texts, unlike squiggles or geometric figures, have authors, and this famous text has a famous author; that fact allows the word "author" to continue to refer both to originary intent *and* to citationality. For what Knapp and Michaels are warding off is the "detachability of words or marks from finite intentions"—a detachability that is nonetheless symptomatically "illustrated and acted out by the fable," with its multiplying authors and ever more amazing scenes of inscription (Kamuf, 8). Kamuf refers us to one of the most powerful conceptual moments of literary theory, Jacques Derrida's account of iterability as composing the possibility of, among other things, communication:

> For a writing to be a writing it must continue to "act" and to be readable even when what is called the author of the writing no longer answers for what he has written, for what he seems to have signed, be it because of a temporary absence, because he is dead, or, more generally, because he has not employed his absolutely actual and present intention or attention, the plenitude of his desire to say what he means, in order to sustain what seems to be written "in his name."[40]

Knapp and Michaels imagine, as we have seen, that "in debates about intention, the moment of imagining intentionless meaning constitutes the theoretical moment itself" (2,463); but in fact the Derridean analysis "*at no time* ... invokes the absence, pure and simple, of intentionality," as Derrida stresses (*Limited Inc*, 56). Iterability is the *condition of possibility* of intentionality, even though it divides intentionality from itself. If one reduces the concept of authorship to an intent-to-mean, and that of authoring to an intent-to-inscribe, the iterability of signification will still produce an unstable oscillation between origination and citation within authorship, as Knapp and Michaels (against their own stated intention) clearly demonstrate.

But why should a *poem* be called upon for this demonstration (a *lyric* poem, as Jackson reminds us to specify), and why *this* lyric poem, "A slumber did my spirit seal"? We have been developing answers to that question throughout this chapter, of course; but before looping back to the themes of voice and figure that we have been exploring, let us follow Kamuf's shrewd Derridean commentary to its conclusion. Wordsworth's exemplary poem, she suggests, "exceeds its frame in a manner that reverses the exemplary relation," such that "the framing fable ... become[s] an example of the mistake exposed by the poem" (11). Thus, in Knapp and Michaels's story, the "encounter with the first stanza unfolds in a state of slumber." (Indeed: Kamuf does not elaborate, but recall that, in the first phase of the fable, "you" are wandering by the seashore, so dazed that you don't recognize some of the most recognizable lines of English verse, and so much on autopilot that you "recognize the writing as writing ... without needing to connect the words to any notion of an author at all.") Then, "with the arrival of the second stanza, this sleepwalker is rudely jolted into wakefulness when the assumption of human presence is unsealed." The second stanza, rolling in on the waves, is supposed to shock "you" into realizing the inseparability of meaning from authorial intention, but Kamuf suggests that this shock is also compulsively figuring "the death of the 'present' speaker" (just as the "I" disappears in the second stanza)—a death inscribed in the iterability that forms the condition of possibility of all signs, and of all intentions-to-signify. Spinning a fantastic story in the name of common sense, the anti-theoretical theorists become ever more trapped in the web of a text that has already scripted them. Kamuf closes her reading with the suggestion that the third episode in the story—the emergence of the submarine—represents an attempt to break the spell. Yet "this third moment, when the fable seems to step outside the poem in order to manipulate its example from a safe distance, resembles nothing so much as a return to the illusion characterized by the first stanza ... the illusion of a continuing presence (of intention) untouched by earthly years when it mistakes a (living) agent for a (dead) author." We need have no human fears. For "the author" has been magically "made to rise out of the sea, resuscitated, not dead, still able to speak and to sign" (13).

—†—

Knapp and Michaels's parable knowingly echoes a similar one in P. D. Juhl's *Interpretation: An Essay in the Philosophy of Literary Criticism* (1980). Like Knapp and Michaels, Juhl seeks to purify Hirsch's position into an axiomatic, arguing that "a statement about the meaning of a work *is* a statement about the author's intention."[41] Also like Knapp and Michaels, Juhl returns to the example of Wordsworth's "A slumber did my spirit seal," and indulges in fantasies of the poem's accidental production. "Now suppose that the poem I have quoted above is not in fact by Wordsworth but has been accidentally typed out by a monkey randomly depressing keys on a typewriter. (Or suppose that we found the lines as marks—on, say, a large rock—produced by water erosion)" (71–72).[42] Knapp and Michaels agree with Juhl except on what they see as one crucial point: they criticize him—as they do all other critics they mention—for falling back into the mistake of imagining intentionless language: "Thus he can argue that when a 'parrot utters the words "Water is pouring down from the sky,"' one can understand that 'the words mean "It is raining"' but deny that the '"parrot said that it is raining."' It is clear that, for Juhl, the words continue to mean even when devoid of intention. . . . Whereas Hirsch thinks we have to add intentions to *literature* in order to determine what a text means, Juhl thinks that adding intention to *language* gives us speech acts" (Knapp and Michaels 2,467, citing Juhl 109).

But as noted earlier, the argument with Juhl or Hirsch is in the end an internecine affair. Knapp and Michaels's most important opponent is Paul de Man, the representative of "theory" against whom "Against Theory" directs itself. The immediate target, as noted earlier, is a passage in the "Excuses" chapter of *Allegories of Reading* in which de Man is discussing a speech act that Rousseau recounts early on in the *Confessions*. Reflecting on a shameful moment when, as a young man working as a servant, he was caught stealing a ribbon and falsely accused another servant, Rousseau suggests at one point that he had in fact uttered that servant's name, "Marion," arbitrarily—it was "*le premier objet qui s'offrit*," the first thing that came to mind. De Man takes that claim seriously and pushes it, because at this point in his reading he is focusing on the rhetorical structure and function of the excuse as a speech act in the text, and if the sound "Marion" is taken to be arbitrary, unintended and meaningless, Rousseau achieves "the most efficaciously performative excuse of all" (*AR* 289). Of course de Man is after bigger game: this peculiar moment in the rhetoric of excusing leads him, by way of passages in the *Fourth Rêverie*, to similar-sounding statements of Rousseau's about fiction, which de Man then gathers into a generalization about textuality. Although "the moment in which the fiction stands free of any signification" is "never allowed to exist as such," without it "no such thing as a text is conceivable" (*AR* 293). We cannot and need not retrace de Man's dense and at times manic reading here; the strangeness of Knapp and Michaels's text suffices unto the day, and their engagement with de Man's text is focused and rapid. "De Man's mistake," they claim, "is to think that the sound 'Marion' remains a signifier even when emptied of all meaning. The fact is that the meaningless noise 'Marion' only *resembles* the signifier 'Marion,' just as accidentally uttering the sound 'Marion' only *resembles* the speech act of naming Marion" (2,469, emphasis in original).

This is the claim on which everything hangs for Knapp and Michaels. The whole point of the wave poem is that it is made of marks that, if no author can be found for them, are not words. What "you" in a state of slumber may take to be words may not be: they may only "*resemble* words" (2,464). Again and again, as they perform their ripostes to various antagonists, Knapp and Michaels reiterate this difference—this supposedly fundamental yet deeply weird difference that their fable produces between language, on the one hand, and something-that-looks-just-like-language-but-isn't, on the other. The constitutive instability of this difference has been explored by Orrin N. C. Wang: "To say that such unintelligible sensation resembles language is rather to situate it within a linguistic dynamic, albeit a radically unstable one." Wang proposes the counterintuitive phrase "sensation of meaning" as a way of thinking about such unstable crossings, when nonmeaning resembles meaning: "the sensation of meaning ... marks the moment when linguistic unintelligibility nevertheless becomes a semantic event and resemblance determines the physical and phenomenal as that event. Occurring linguistically, this action figures the compulsive nature of both physical sensation and semantic meaning, of sense and sense, while frustrating either in its pure form" (101).[43] Wordsworth's poetry often turns on such moments; Wang reminds us of the Boy of Winander episode in the *Prelude* and offers the more sweeping suggestion that the literature we call "romantic" exhibits "a fascination with meaning when only a resemblance of meaning might exist, when intention might be rooted in the uncanny instead of simply the intuitive obviousness of common sense" (104).

It is indeed an uncanny difference, this, between language and language's simulacrum: absolute and yet absolutely invisible, impalpable, and unsecurable. "You" can be fooled—indeed, "you" just were fooled, multiple times (first it was language; then it wasn't; then, thanks to the submarine, it was language again . . .). Surely, on this strange seacoast you remain in danger of being fooled once more. Mistakenly imagining, for instance, that some human agent "authored" wave-generated marks, you might mistakenly read and admire the poem you mistakenly think they compose; you might then mistakenly recite it to others, or even put it into a Norton anthology, where it would then mistakenly be read by others—an incalculable number of others—as a real poem written in real language, about which literary critics can write essays. The result is that neither "you" nor we nor anyone else can know for sure whether or not "Marion" is a signifier, even as we *take* it as a signifier, which is the point of de Man's demonstration, and the unintended moral of Knapp and Michaels's fable. The unreadability of that difference drives Knapp and Michaels to tell an ever more lurid story about it: a story that, in deconstructing itself, reveals what its authors never manage explicitly to explain, which is *why* everyone they write about is constantly recommitting the mistake of "theory" (as they see it) by slipping back into the illusion that intention can be added to (or subtracted from) language. For, of course, in composing their parable Knapp and Michaels necessarily repeat, in the form of denegation, the "mistake" of which they convict everyone else. More fantastically than any of their precursors, they dream of marks that would be *exactly* like language—except that intention has been subtracted, or remains to be added in (by, say, the perception of a submarine with the men in lab coats). Knapp and Michaels are committed to this "mistake" more ferociously than anyone, precisely as a way of imagining themselves safe from the contamination it figures, and which they necessarily repeat.[44] Dreaming of an absolute difference between intentional language and nonintentional marks, they produce a hauntingly unstable doubling of intention and chance, meaning and inscription. "Language," over the course of their narrative, generates its own ghost or replicant as the intention that animates it wavers in and out of existence, while shuttling through variously fantastic figurative agents.

When theorists committed to the preservation of authorial intention imagine extravagant scenarios in which "A slumber did my spirit seal" is written by waves, monkeys, and typewriters—which is to say, natural, animal, and technical nonagents: the ancient, haunting doubles of the "human"— they are responding to the rhetorical instability of the poem. The unbreath-ing "I" figures the possibility that "A slumber" merely *resembles* a lyric. Yet this is also to say that it figures the rhetoricity of voice that makes lyric possible. The seal at the origin both mutes and grants a license to speak—to speak beyond death, as a personification can, thanks to the iterability of signs. "A slumber" makes it impossible to secure the differences that must nonetheless constantly be drawn and redrawn between the living and the inanimate, and between figurative and literal agency. In this the poem may be, as Wang claims, exemplary of romanticism, though in the present context it will suffice to call it exemplary of the affinity between romanticism and "theory" that briefly took center stage with the Yale Critics in the peculiar pageant of theory in America. "A slumber" would then exemplify both the persistence and the ruin of lyric as the "phenomenalization of voice" and the "defensive movement of the understanding," for which lyric is, however, only "one name among several," and another name for which is theory as reading and self-resistance.

3. What Remains
Geoffrey Hartman and the Shock of Imagination

By the time Geoffrey Hartman published *Wordsworth's Poetry* in 1964, the academic field of British romanticism in the American academy had achieved professional, if not conceptual, stability. Over the previous two decades, studies by René Wellek, Northrop Frye, M. H. Abrams, Frank Kermode, Walter Jackson Bate, and Earl Wasserman, to name only some of the most obvious names, had established parameters for a field that was no longer marked by the overt polemics of an earlier era.[1] The New Criticism had lost its avant-garde edge during this period and become part of the critical establishment; indeed, "Yale critics" such as Cleanth Brooks and William K. Wimsatt, motivated by an appreciation for the Coleridgean provenance of their aesthetic and a keen awareness of the complexity of romantic-era poetry, had contributed substantially to the romantic critical archive. The New Critical denigration of romanticism that Harold Bloom (as we shall review in the next chapter) encountered at Yale in the early 1950s was an archaism by the 1960s.[2] The romantic archive, in other words, had achieved the stability of a recognized scholarly domain with an active sense of its own history, which is why essays and books by the aforementioned critics still constitute part of the working library of any professional scholar of British romanticism. In this sense, British romanticism had come of age and become a professional specialty like any other by the mid-1960s.

As we have noted in previous chapters, however, romanticism manifested some peculiarities as a scholarly field. Because of its predominant orientation toward lyric and its focus on a relatively small, highly valorized canon—the poetry of Blake, Wordsworth, Keats, and Shelley—British romantic studies was traversed by highly charged aesthetic terms, questions, and ambitions. The conceptual dyad "imagination" and "nature" played a famously salient role in the secondary literature.[3] Indeed, arguably the most daring critical work of the early 1960s was focusing with peculiar intensity on those two keywords, destabilizing their chiasmic interchange and privileging the former over the latter. In the opening sentences of his book's central "Via Naturaliter Negativa" section, Hartman speaks approvingly of "a very small group" of critics who have "pointed to the deeply paradoxical character of Wordsworth's dealings with nature and suggested that what he calls imagination may be *intrinsically* opposed to nature."[4] His bibliographical note refers us to Harold Bloom's *The Visionary Company* (1961) and to Paul de Man's essay "Structure intentionnelle de l'image romantique" (1960) (*WP*, 350–51). Only in the first case is a personal friendship conceivably tincturing a scholarly *parti pris*. Hartman, as we reviewed earlier in this book, knew Bloom well from their years as junior faculty together at Yale, but in the early 1960s he and de Man had still had little personal contact; their affinity was intellectual.[5]

We are uncovering here the oldest foundation wall of the fragile edifice that became known in subsequent decades as the "Yale Critics." Hartman seems to have read de Man's essay soon after it appeared, and he was impressed; it was probably he who brought it to the attention of Bloom, who was to republish a slightly revised English translation of it in his influential compilation *Romanticism and Consciousness* (1970).[6] And de Man, for his part, was reading Hartman and Bloom appreciatively at this time—especially Hartman. In 1962 de Man published a respectful but critical review of Bloom's *Visionary Company* titled "A New Vitalism," in which he singled out for praise a phrase *not* by Bloom: "'a vision in which the mind knows itself almost without exterior cause or else as no less real, here, no less indestructible than the object of its perception'—an admirable definition of Wordsworth's imagination quoted by Bloom but due to Geoffrey Hartman."[7] (The phrase is from Hartman's dissertation-turned-first-book, *The Unmediated Vision*.)[8] The "definition of the imagination" forms the locus of de Man's argument with Bloom in this review. Bloom, inspired by his reading of Blake (and of Northrop Frye on Blake), characterizes the imagination as an apocalyptic power of humanization. As de Man sees it, Bloom believes—or believes, at any rate, that romantic poets believe—that "the subject, by means of a power called imagination, can transform the natural world into its own mode of being, and thus substitute for a subject-object antithesis an intersubjective relationship between two entities that are no longer estranged from each other" ("A New Vitalism" 93). De Man questions the continuity that he understands Bloom as presupposing between a subject-object antithesis bound up with a natural "world of sensation", on the one hand, and intersubjectivity and "poetic consciousness" on the other (95): "there has to be a discontinuity somewhere, a renunciation, a sacrifice, at any rate a delicate and obscure point in the development that cannot be merely crossed by means of the sheer stamina of a blind *élan vital*" (93). Wordsworth in particular, according to de Man, is being mischaracterized by Bloom as a seeker after "apocalyptic experiences of unity between mind and nature," whereas in fact "no dialogue could ever be possible between man and the profound otherness, the 'it-ness' that is always a part of Wordsworth's nature" (93). The Wordsworthian imagination, in turn, has nothing natural about it—as summed up in the sentence by Hartman that I quoted de Man quoting Bloom quoting.[9]

Behind this critique of Bloom and invocation of Hartman is de Man's apodictic yet, on closer inspection, somewhat cagy affirmation, near the end of "Intentional Structure of the Romantic Image," of "a possibility for consciousness to exist entirely by and for itself, independently of all relationship with the outside world, without being moved by an intent aimed at a part of this world."[10] That possibility, according to de Man, has been forgotten in the subsequent literary tradition; it may be read in, or out of, a few passages in a few early romantic texts—though it seems to be barely legible even there: de Man immediately and rather oddly goes on to admit that none of the texts or images he has been citing (by Rousseau, Hölderlin, Wordsworth) actually exemplify what he has been claiming. "We know very little about the kind of images that such an imagination would produce. . . . The works of the early romantics give us no actual examples, for they are, at most, *underway* toward renewed insights" (77, de Man's italics).[11] This radically autotelic poetic consciousness appears to be legible only as a proleptic trace—as a fragile and by no means certain promise of itself.[12]

What indeed would a consciousness, image, or imagination that "exist[ed] entirely by and for itself" look like—given that it could not "look like" anything, despite the stubbornly visual cast of terms like *image* and *imagination*? The notion of an autotelic, world-transcending imagination would seem to be the distilled essence of what Jerome McGann has so influentially chastised as "romantic ideology"—yet taken seriously and pushed to its limit, as Hartman and de Man were doing during these years, such a notion makes for strange imaginings, for it cannot really be accommodated by the clichés of romantic selfhood. How would a consciousness intent on nothing but itself—consciousness as radical *epoché*, independent of body and lifeworld, reflective in a way unindebted to figures of light, sight, and mirroring—manifest itself, except perhaps as a break or gap within representational language, a rupture like death, though maybe also like the leap of a promise? In the 1960s, Geoffrey Hartman began calling this kind of rupturing force the apocalyptic imagination—apocalyptic in a sense antithetical to the marriage of mind and nature that de Man imputes to Bloom: "By 'apocalyptic' I mean that there is an inner necessity to cast out nature, to extirpate everything apparently external to salvation, everything that might stand between the naked self and God, whatever the risk in this to the self" (*WP*, 49).

Hartman's critical stance with regard to this force is complex. His precocious first book, *The Unmediated Vision*, passionately affirms a slant version of it, represented as the modern poet's "effort to gain pure representation through the direct sensuous intuition of reality" (*UV*, 156). Hartman's argument in *The Unmediated Vision* has a broad family resemblance to a number of other penetrating mid-twentieth-century accounts of post-eighteenth-century literature (for instance, Jean Paulhan's diagnosis in *Les fleurs de Tarbes* [1941] of a modern "terror in letters"—that is, the "terroristic" desire of post-Enlightenment writers to discard the flowers of rhetoric in the name of revolutionary immediacy).[13] Hartman's version of this narrative, however, features a remarkable subplot. His stress on "pure representation" makes the desired encounter with things themselves hard to distinguish from an encounter with the mind itself, with the result that the modern poet's heroic phenomenological quest *zu den Sachen selbst* eventuates in a sense of the sublime independence of the mind. Hence the formulation that we saw de Man admiring ("a vision in which the mind knows itself almost without exterior cause"). *The Unmediated Vision* shares with de Man's (and, for that matter, Bloom's) early work an impulse to override the subject-object antithesis in favor of a transcendental consciousness (the mind *knows* itself).

Over the next decade, Hartman continues to affirm "literature's constant flight from literariness: its wish to dissolve as a medium or, at the very least, to renounce romantic props and to intuit things directly," as he puts it in the preface to *Beyond Formalism* (1970).[14] Meanwhile, he will develop and refine his sense that—especially in Wordsworth's case—the poet's desire to intuit things in themselves is bound up with surges of self-consciousness as imaginative power. Thus, in *Wordsworth's Poetry*, Hartman famously defines the apocalyptic imagination as "*consciousness of self raised to apocalyptic pitch*" (*WP*, 17, Hartman's italics). Yet a telling ambivalence settles around the term *consciousness* in an important transitional text between *The Unmediated Vision* and *Wordsworth's Poetry*, "Romanticism and Anti-Self-Consciousness" (1962), an essay that may be read as an indirect response to de Man's "Structure intentionnelle."[15] Here, consciousness is forcefully, if also in the end ambivalently, separated off from imagination. Referring to well-known statements by Carlyle and Mill about the inhibiting power of self-consciousness, Hartman distinguishes self-consciousness from a mature or redeemed imagination, aligning the aesthetic progression "Nature/Self-Consciousness/Imagination" with the developmental narrative "childhood/adolescence/adulthood" and the theological narrative "Eden/Fall/Redemption" (*BF*, 299, 307). Yet the essay's rhetorical energies exceed its naturalizing and theologizing schemata. Redemption may or may not arrive, and the final sentences of "Romanticism and Anti-Self-Consciousness" are remarkably bleak ("The death of poetry had certainly occurred to the Romantics in idea, and Hegel's prediction of it was simply the overt expression of their own despair. Yet against this despair the greater Romantics staked their art and often their sanity" [*BF*, 310]).[16] As for the maturation narrative, "adolescence" is a misleadingly trivializing middle term, since self-consciousness, in Hartman's account, has nothing to do with mooncalf self-absorption and bears rather on the very possibility of self-knowledge. Because "every increase in consciousness is accompanied by an increase in self-consciousness," nothing less than "the ideal of absolute lucidity" comes into question (*BF*, 299)—and this because self-consciousness is morbid, ravaging, diseased, dangerous, murderous, and corrosive (to adjectivize descriptors that surface in the essay's first two paragraphs).[17] Later in the essay Hartman speaks of "the wound of self" (*BF*, 309).

The "particularly Romantic remedy" for this wound is homeopathic: romantic art "seeks to draw the antidote to self-consciousness from consciousness itself" by achieving an "energy finer than intellectual" (*BF*, 300) and thereby becoming "a means to resist the intelligence intelligently" (*BF*, 302). Appropriately enough, since they have to pass beyond self-consciousness, the romantics "do not give . . . an adequate definition of the concept of art" (ibid.).

> The art of the Romantics, on the other hand, is often in advance of even their best thoughts. Neither a mere increase in sensibility nor a mere widening of self-knowledge constitutes its purpose. The Romantic poets do not exalt consciousness per se. They have recognized it as a kind of death-in-life, as the product of a division in the self. (*BF*, 303)

Since the "best thoughts" of the romantics include the thought that art should be anti-self-conscious, Hartman generates a textual knot that can be read as being at once supportive of and "in advance" of his own theme, insofar as it is hinted here that romantic art, in order to pass from the self-conscious to the imaginative, has to *do* something it cannot *think*, even or especially as the thinking of anti-self-consciousness. That hint of a noncognitive performativity rubs against Hartman's idealizing tropes of recuperation and dialectical return (as maturity, as redemption), and points to the difficulty of "draw[ing] the antidote to self-consciousness from consciousness itself." Furthermore, the hyperbolic figure of consciousness as wound suggests that from the start consciousness is marked by an openness or performativity it cannot control.

Two years later, in *Wordsworth's Poetry*, Hartman, as noted, discards the effort to imagine imagination apart from consciousness. But he retains the structure of resistance that he had elaborated in "Romanticism and Anti-Self-Consciousness" (as the overcoming of consciousness by consciousness). Reunited with consciousness, the imagination now resists *itself*, "hid[ing] itself by overflowing as poetry" (*WP*, 69), because in Wordsworth the essential poetic act consists in the never entirely successful binding of a visionary power—an inherently independent imagination—to the world. By way of an intense communion with his beloved poet, Hartman arrives at his signature theme: the gentling of apocalyptic or visionary energies, modes, genres, imagery.[18] Hartman's hyperbolic rendering of selfhood and self-consciousness in "Romanticism and Anti-Self-Consciousness" looks in retrospect like a displaced working-through of an ambivalence that he will subsequently be able to disclose in Wordsworth.

Why the ambivalence about imagination? And why should its thematization in *Wordsworth's Poetry* seem first to require such an energetic repudiation of self-consciousness? Arguably not just because the sublimely self-conscious, apocalyptic imagination threatens to obliterate "things themselves" insofar as they partake of the natural world. To be sure, the tension between a desire for apocalypse and a care for the world composes the official main theme of *Wordsworth's Poetry*, granting structure to interpretations that are exquisitely attuned to the text and strikingly ahead of their time in their ethical and ecological concerns. Yet the passage in "Romanticism and Anti-Self-Consciousness" that we highlighted hints at a darker sublime insight. If, in the name of consciousness, texts have to do things that the most lucid consciousness cannot know, then it becomes possible to imagine that Hartman's (and Hartman's Wordsworth's) figures of self-consciousness and imagination relay a force that we could call *textual*, insofar as this force—or unforce; this doing as undoing—would exceed self-consciousness as knowledge, or the self as a locus of authority. Self-consciousness might then, rather oddly, turn into something other than itself—turn alien to itself (as "self") in its approach toward that strange state of radical independence that de Man had been trying to imagine in "Structure intentionnelle" and that Hartman, ever since his first book, had been working over and through, with increasing ambivalence and complexity. It is thus no surprise that in *Wordsworth's Poetry* the vicissitudes of the imagination, of its binding, and of the "nature" with which it communes on its circuitous route to humanization, will turn out to be complex. Often enough, this otherworldly or, better, antiworldly imagination can seem another name for a divine soul or spark, an archaic power akin to prophetic or inspired speech and mythopoeic making. Yet now and then the pressure of something uncannier becomes palpable: the wing-brush of a dispersive or repetitive force, like the traces of a death-drive. If consciousness is a wound, one can expect the effort to suture the imagination to the world to be infected by something like a repetition-compulsion. Hartman's ambivalent stance toward the autotelic consciousness that his work, like de Man's, remains attentive to in these years produces readings that are far less securely humanist in orientation than they may at first glance appear to be.

—†—

In *Wordsworth's Poetry*, the imagination's manifestations are disruptive, associated with death, absence, fixation, even trauma.[19] Its deathly power is announced immediately and forcefully. Early on in his book Hartman quotes the great lines in Book 6 of the *Prelude* that interrupt the Simplon Pass narrative:

> Imagination—here the power so called
> Through sad incompetence of human speech,
> That awful Power rose from the mind's abyss
> Like an unfathered vapour that enwraps,
> At once, some lonely traveller. I was lost;
> Halted without an effort to break through. (1850, 6:592–97)[20]

These lines compose the most famous statement of the romantic imagination in English-language literature; de Man had also quoted them (though in the significantly different 1805 version) as his culminating bit of evidence of a romantic consciousness affirming its independence from the sensual world. Hartman will submit them to enduringly influential analysis in the "Via Naturaliter Negativa" section of *Wordsworth's Poetry* (half a century later, professional romanticists still often refer to this section of the Simplon Pass episode as "VI-b" in the wake of that reading). But the first time he quotes the lines Hartman does so in order to pause over the fact that "Wordsworth calls this separate consciousness 'Imagination'":

> It is a strange name to give it. Imagination, we are usually told, vitalizes and animates. Especially the Romantic Imagination. Yet here it stands closer to death than life, at least in its immediate effect. The poet is isolated and immobilized by it: it obscures rather than reveals nature; the light of the senses goes out. Only in its secondary action does it vitalize and animate, and even then not nature but a soul that realizes its individual greatness, a greatness independent of sense and circumstance. A tertiary effect does finally reach nature, when the

soul assured of inner or independent sources of strength goes out from and of itself. (*WP*, 17)

Wordsworth's naming of the Imagination is a singular event in *The Prelude*, spurred by the act of writing itself: "From late January to April, 1804, Wordsworth was intensely engaged in work on *The Prelude*; and, under that pressure of composition, came once, and only once, face to face with his imagination" (*WP*, 61). That face-off, a uniquely direct confrontation, "shakes the foundation of his poem" (*WP*, 48). The death of the poem itself—its literal interruption, but also the ruin of its narrative, the obliteration of its myth—forms part of the shock of this moment, even though—or because—it is the moment of an encounter with poetic power.

In what follows we shall be examining a few of the ways in which Hartman's epochal reading of Wordsworth troubles the notion of the imagination as an integral identity or force. Such aspects of his text tend to brush against the grain of the book's dominant argument. The lesson Hartman draws from his first consideration of the VI-b lines establishes the identification of imagination with self-consciousness. This is the affirmation I quoted earlier, given here in fuller form: "The supervening consciousness, which Wordsworth names Imagination in Prelude VI, and which also halts the mental traveller in the Highlands, is *consciousness of self raised to apocalyptic pitch*" (*WP*, 17, Hartman's italics). Yet, as in his essay "Romanticism and Anti-Self-Consciousness," Hartman's discussion of the imagination here near the beginning of *Wordsworth's Poetry* opens questions that it refuses to answer explicitly. If the imagination "stands closer to death than life," might there be something about the imagination that resists figuration as self-consciousness? Or—as we interpreted the text "Romanticism and Anti-Self-Consciousness" as hinting, somewhat in its own despite—might self-consciousness be a trope that paradoxically leads to, or conceals, a kind of self-loss? Wordsworth speaks after all of a vapor and of being lost; only in a secondary beat will he address himself as other ("But to my conscious soul I now can say—/'I recognize thy glory'" [6:598–99]). The idea of imagination as unselfconscious inspiration is nothing if not conventional; but to be at once halted and lost (and one can read the line forcefully: "'I' was lost," the "I" was lost) is a figure of a different order. The halting creates the possibility of a face-off, a specular encounter, and thence self-consciousness. But the getting-lost comes first, and the semicolon that end-stops the "I was lost" forms a pause that can be semanticized and dramatized only after the line break ("Halted . . ."). Hartman would presumably read the semicolon's pause as akin to all those other pauses in Wordsworth's poetry, those little breath-catches, annunciations of death that so often arrive with a haunting gentleness, like the silence that composes "a gentle shock of mild surprise" for the Boy of Winander. Gentled though it is, the shock remains inaccessible to consciousness (the scene sinks unawares into the Boy's mind; nature "forms the child the more deeply as her action is less consciously present to him" [WP, 19]). If shock forms part of the manifestation of the imagination, might consciousness then be thinkable not as equivalent to or identical with the imagination but as (or *also* as) a reaction formation to it?[21] Might the hyperbolic condemnation of "self-consciousness" and the idealization of the otherness of imagination in "Romanticism and Anti-Self-Consciousness" be a kind of working-through that enabled Hartman to approach his subject more rigorously?

Numerous strands of Hartman's reading suggest as much. To be sure, death has everything to do with self-consciousness. As Hartman puts it in an essay published a couple of years after *Wordsworth's Poetry*, "Consciousness must be paid for, and the usual wages are sacrifice and death" (BF, 55). The halted traveler, that emblematically self-conscious figure, is halted by his own epitaph. His self-awareness is the "awareness of irremediable loss" (WP, 161). So it is with the narrator who stands mute, a full half-hour at the Boy of Winander's grave: "the survivor contemplates his own buried childhood" (WP, 21). The structure of self-consciousness requires a death; but this death must be a sacrifice, the death of an other that can stand in for the death of the self. Self-consciousness, for all its withering strength, is thus always a fragile achievement, marked and enabled by a death that it does not really possess and cannot entirely internalize. Wordsworth's quietly resonant stanza breaks in poems such as "There was a Boy" or "A slumber did my spirit seal," like the semicolon after the phrase "I was lost" in VI-b, may therefore be read as gentle shocks provocative of but irreducible to consciousness, at least in the ordinary sense we grant the term *consciousness*—shocks that we as readers of Wordsworth absorb in turn, as pauses that make us hang listening, and that at once elicit and resist our interpretive skill.

—⊢—

In its pastoral manifestation, the imagination, in *Wordsworth's Poetry*, is called surmise. A classical rhetorical figure that "becomes a genre in the Romantic period" (WP, 11), surmise enters Hartman's text as an echo from Milton's *Lycidas*: "For so to interpose a little ease,/Let our frail thoughts dally with false surmise" (lines 152–53). Surmise, which wards off death and discontinuity, cannot dally forever; its own death has been announced from the outset, and Hartman's initial discussion of it attends appreciatively to its penseroso coloring. In the meantime—while waiting on the apocalypse—surmise entertains the Wordsworthian master-theme of nature. "Nature" in *Wordsworth's Poetry*, as in Wordsworth's poetry, is a richly polyvalent term.[22] Usually it means "rural nature, the abiding presences of mountain, lake, and field under the influence of the changing seasons," as Hartman puts it in a retrospective essay;[23] but it can mean organic continuity or development in a quite figurative sense (thus Wordsworth in October 1792 "still considers [the French Revolution] a work of nature"; later he realizes that it "may be a work of the apocalyptic imagination" [*WP*, 244, 245]). It encompasses heavily mortgaged private property (Michael's fields, rather idealistically rendered: "the human imagination . . . cannot be renewed unless it has a nature to blend with, not any nature but land as free and old as the hills" [*WP*, 262]). Above all, however, nature is a personification, lightly handled though constantly put on and worn, and this despite the fact that Wordsworth may also be said to have desired "to liberate nature from human shape" (*WP*, 289). Nature, however, must function as the pedagogical agent in a story, leading the poet as Virgil does Dante toward the Beatrice of the humanized imagination. Hartman knowingly follows his poet in dallying with this surmise. In its finest moments this strategy yields a subtle dialectic: "Were we to give [each type of avoidance] a collective name it would coincide with what the mature poet calls Nature. His Nature is in opposition to the idea of a single or fixed or intransitive place of power" (*WP*, 86). Nature is deflection, indirection: the detour of a trope that allows a little time for surmise, and thereby a remedy for, or at least a defense against, traumatic shock, including that of the visionary imagination.[24]

When Wordsworth's providential myth endures the crisis posed by his brother John Wordsworth's death in 1805, Hartman notes a threat to "the possibility of surmise itself, especially concerning a sympathetic nature, one that participates in the growth and destiny of the human soul" (*WP*, 287). And as Hartman tells the story of the older Wordsworth taking his distance both from "idealizing impulse" and "apocalyptic intimation," Hartman, too, allows surmise to fade away. "The presence of a Sympathetic Nature, which is the one superstition for which he had kept his respect, for it is vital not only to poetry but also to human development, being a necessary illusion in the growth of the mind, this too is falling away. . . . Though Wordsworth no longer dallies with surmise, he cannot entirely forego apocalyptic fancies, or the opposite (if more generous) error which attributes to nature a vital and continuous role in the maturing of the mind" (*WP*, 330–31). Hartman's newly skeptical idiom mirrors his poet's increased caution: the Wordsworthian myth of nature is now "superstition," "illusion," "error"; even the imagination has degenerated into a faculty that produces "apocalyptic fancies." It is a passing scene in Hartman's book, but this momentary dwindling of the book's great theme intimates that the imagination, like nature and like poetry, is mortal.[25] At another point, Hartman says as much. He is explicating "The Thorn": "that wretched thorn is a symbol of the emergent self conserving its being despite everything (including its own strength, its mass of knotted joints) that conspires to bury it. So man must outlive his own imagination, then nature that beguiled it, then the world that betrays it and him forever" (*WP*, 147). Everything passes away, at least at this moment in the book, except for a self/man/thorn that lives on past apocalypse: a mass of knotted joints that has forgotten how to die.

That in turn, though, feels like a compelling figure for a mortal but unstoppable imagination, as we have encountered it in Hartman's book. For, to reprise our question, what would an imagination radically unindebted to the sensory world look like? Like an unfathered vapor, runs one answer; but those uncanny, damaged remainders in the Wordsworthian landscape, like the thorn, the discharged soldier or the leechgatherer, offer figures less of the avoidance of apocalypse than a strange outliving of it.[26] What if imagination, after unveiling itself as self-consciousness, had to go on past such revelation—to go on in halting fashion past or under or alongside the "halted traveler" moment—precisely because the apocalyptic imagination cannot properly figure its own radical cutting-away of the world, any more than self-consciousness can catch up with its own death? The self-resistance that Hartman locates in Wordsworth's imagination, an imagination that reveals itself in hiding and hides itself in unconcealing, is the narrative version of a difference within, a figurative crux. The imagination, as its name implies, may need to realize itself phenomenally in order to be itself; yet no realization suffices, and, as a force that *also* needs to be irreducible to phenomenal manifestation, the imagination moves on, deathward, toward no *determinable* death.[27] The Wordsworthian sublime at its most darkly thrilling harnesses these energies:

> o'er my thoughts
> There hung a darkness, call it solitude
> Or blank desertion. No familiar shapes
> Remained, no pleasant images of trees,
> Of sea or sky, no colours of green fields;
> But huge and mighty forms, that do not live
> Like living men, moved slowly through the mind
> By day, and were a trouble to my dreams. (1850, 1:393−400)

We are of course simply repeating in a more gothic key Hartman's own insight. "Wordsworth's greatest lyrics are acts of a living mind open to the terror of discontinuity" (*WP*, 268). Like his poet and for the same ethical reasons, Hartman gentles his own model and his own reading practices. One sign of this gentling is the underreporting of disruptive cuts and shocks in Wordsworth's intensely imagined scenes. Hartman pushes back more than a little, for instance, against the suddenness with which the Snowdon vision strikes. The narrator, panting upward, emerges out of the mist that has "girt [him] round" into a vision that first approaches with naturalistic gradualism, then falls "like a flash":

> When at my feet the ground appeared to brighten,
> And with a step or two seemed brighter still;
> Nor was time given to ask or learn the cause,
> For instantly a light upon the turf
> Fell like a flash ... (1850, 14:35–39)

There follows the sublime spectacle of moon and firmament and "silent sea of hoary mist," with hills heaving out of it; of "solid vapours" mimicking "headlands, tongues, and promontory shapes" that usurp upon the ocean, and are riven by a rift, "a fixed, abysmal, gloomy, breathing-place," out of which mounts the "roar of waters, torrents, streams/Innumerable, roaring with one voice!" (14:42, 46, 58–60). Partly because he is interested in the tension between eye and ear, but also, I think, because he is turning slightly away from the temporal rupture that scores this scene, Hartman is led to an oddly fussy objection: how can the narrator not have begun hearing the roar of waters earlier? "For the voices, if we examine the vision closely, cannot be sudden except psychologically. . . . If he does not hear the stream of sound, which must have been there all along, it is because his senses were fixed by an obsessively visual image" (*WP*, 185) Such strenuous interpretations, which risk looking like an effort to improve on a poem, are rare; but not infrequently in *Wordsworth's Poetry* one feels that the violence and, at times, inhuman strangeness of Wordsworth's poetic world is being slightly muffled in favor of themes that both poet and critic very much wish to affirm.

Another coping mechanism may be read in, or out of, the myths that Hartman leverages as hermeneutic frames at various points in his work— Perseus; Philomela; and, centrally in *Wordsworth's Poetry*, the Akedah.[28] These are all stories of cutting. It is as though a certain violence is being displaced to the margins of the interpretation. The Akedah is of course the story of a cut threatened, suspended, and safely redirected (from Isaac to the ram); and the brilliance of Hartman's emphatic but quite laconic mobilization of this story is to repeat this pattern of "apocalypse avoided" in his use of it: focusing entirely on its redemptive moral, the "marriage of imagination with nature" (*WP*, 225), he lets the hovering knife, unspoken condition of such binding, recede to the story's frame.

—+—

The theme of cutting and the structural motif of a redirection from middle to ends make up the crucial components of Hartman's theoretical recasting of the Philomela myth in his important essay "The Voice of the Shuttle: Language from the Point of View of Literature" (1969, reprinted a year later in *Beyond Formalism*). The essay takes its title from a fragmentary Greek phrase, *hē tēs kerkídos phonē*, known to us only because Aristotle quotes it in the *Poetics* (1454b37), attributing it to a play of Sophocles, now lost. "Voice of the shuttle" figuratively describes Philomela's overcoming of the mutilation she has suffered at the hands of her brother-in-law Tereus, who had raped her and cut out her tongue, but who had not counted on her ability to weave a picture of her story into a tapestry that she was able to convey to her sister, Procne. Hartman's interest in the story has a strong ethical component that would become visible in later years (his 1989 essay "The Philomela Project" addresses itself to "restitutive criticism," "the restoration of voice to inarticulate people").[29] But in "The Voice of the Shuttle" he focuses mainly on a rhetorical problem: what gives this phrase its power—its literary strength? How do poetic metaphors draw meaning from narratives while leaving them behind? "The phrase would not be effective without the story, yet its focus is so sharp that a few words seem to yield not simply the structure of one story but that of all stories insofar as they are telltales" (*BF*, 337). Hartman unpacks the two metonymies: "voice": a substitution of effect for cause (the tapestry is the cause); "shuttle": part for whole and cause for effect (the tapestry is the effect):

> "Voice" stands for the pictorial legend of the tapestry by a metonymic substitution of effect for cause. We say similarly if less dramatically that a book "speaks" to us. "Shuttle" stands for the weaver's instrument by the synecdochal substitution of part for whole, but it also contains a metonymy which names the productive cause instead of the product. Thus we have, in the first term (voice), a substitution of effect for cause, and in the second (shuttle), of cause for effect. By this double metonymy the distance between cause and effect in an ordinary chain of events is significantly increased, and the termini of this chain are over-specified at the expense of intermediate points. What this etiologic distancing means is not clear from the expression taken out of context. You and I, who

know the story, appreciate the cause winning through, and Philomela's "voice" being restored; but by itself the phrase simply disturbs our sense of causality and guides us, if it guides us at all, to a hint of supernatural rather than human agency. (*BF*, 338)

"The power of the phrase," Hartman concludes, "lies in its elision of middle terms and overspecification of end terms." An overstrong frame with a missing middle, this bit of figurative language is "archetypal"; it exemplifies the figural tension that makes language literary. At one point Hartman offers a psychological gloss reminiscent of eighteenth-century theories of the sublime: "the strength of the end terms depends on our seeing the elided members of the chain (e.g., the full relation of Tereus and Philomela); the more clearly we see them, the stronger the metaphor which collapses that chain, makes a mental bang, and speeds the mind by freeing it from overelaboration and the toil of consecutiveness" (*BF*, 339). But the structure rather than the psychology of the "elision of middle terms and overspecification of end terms" is what mainly holds Hartman's attention over a range of examples from Milton, Stevens, Sophocles, Hopkins, Dickinson, and many other writers, and through a variety of tropes and figures involving pauses, jumps, and cuts (juncture, tmesis, the pun, rhyme, enjambment, hendiadys). The suggestion is that all poetically effective "figures of speech may be characterized by overspecified ends and indeterminate middles" (*BF*, 339).[30] Poetic language originates in and derives its energies from a cut; and the Philomela myth reminds us that this cut can be a literal wound. "We have art, said Nietzsche, so as not to die of the truth" (*BF*, 351).

Hartman's overspecified end terms suggestively resemble the minimal but charged figures of fixed difference that Neil Hertz discovers in sublime scenarios. Hertz calls them "end of the line" figures; they enable the sublime turn—that energizing moment in which a subject, threatened with dispersal, finds an image to identify with.[31] As the "middle" disappears, a figure of fixed difference halts the traveler. The light of sense goes out; a sense of consciousness is renewed; imaginative shock becomes apocalyptic self-consciousness. And we can now add: the voice of the shuttle speaks. That is a stranger formulation because a more obviously rhetorical one. The double metonymy is a personification that on the one hand does the work of self-consciousness—speaking of itself beyond death—yet on the other hand seems the very model of a mechanical process, with voice emerging not just out of death and the mutilation of voice, but also—for this too belongs to the resonance of the figure—out of the clacking reiteration of a shuttle on its loom. That would be something like the persistence of imagination we were considering earlier—imagination imagined as an uncanny remainder, over and above the restitution of consciousness and voice. Voice, in the Philomela story, is a radical catachresis, and the figure "voice of the shuttle" is a personification, a displacement of the power to speak onto an inanimate object.[32] It is the trope of personification, engendered out of the double metonymy, that provides what Hartman calls a "hint of supernatural rather than human agency" here (BF, 338). At such moments, a nonnatural, nonhuman, and not-quite-animate spectrality can seem at work in acts of personification, as things "that do not live like living men" take on a ghostly life and linguistic presence, moving through the mind.

Thus, to the extent that Hartman's analysis restores voice to Philomela by granting voice to voice's technical, visual, external supplement, the analysis may be said simultaneously to remember and conceal the violence, mutilation, and muteness around which the narrative turns.[33] Hartman proffers the Philomela story as a myth about "the alliance of craft (cunning) and craft (art)," which is surely right; but his claim that the story affirms "that truth will out, that human consciousness will triumph" (BF, 337) feels in some tension with the myth itself.[34] Truth, perhaps, comes to light, but only in order to wreak violence without end: Procne, reunited with Philomela, kills her son Itys and feeds him to his father Tereus; the sisters then become birds—swallow and nightingale—as does Tereus, who, in the form of a hoopoe, pursues them eternally. As in so many Greek myths, the family implodes so savagely that its members lose their human identity. (And one fine detail gets lost in translation: in the Greek versions of the myth, Philomela becomes not the nightingale but the swallow, *chelidōn*, a bird associable with the twittering, *chelidonizein*, of barbarians. Her voice, scored by ineffaceable loss, never quite becomes song.)[35] Hartman's essay remains vibrantly poised between an acknowledgement of the deep connections between art and trauma, and an affirmation of art's human purpose that never descends into complacency. It is no accident that his exemplary texts in "The Voice of the Shuttle"—lines by Milton, Hopkins, Dickinson, Nelly Sachs—evoke violence, suffering, silence, and death. Well before the 1970s, all the issues that Hartman was to engage in his debates with deconstruction and French psychoanalysis were already circulating in his readings. "There is always something that violates us, deprives our voice, and compels art toward an aesthetics of silence" (BF, 235).[36]

Speaking past or beyond a cut: from his early writings to his later work on Holocaust testimony, Hartman has accepted, resisted, and lived with the ambivalence of that phrase. On the one hand, the cut: an irreparable, endlessly reopening wound; on the other hand, the speaking-past or beyond: an access to literary power that is also (therefore) a speaking-*past*, an address without guarantees to an other who can never be mastered, assimilated, known—an address without address that is audible in the quiet passivity of Wordsworthian exclamation (Behold! O listen!). Poetic speaking is transcendent (*transcendere*: to overstep, pass over) to the extent that it is uncertainly restorative. Only in the uncertainty of its suspended promise can it fall short or go beyond pretending to heal what cannot be healed. "Literature, I surmise," Hartman writes in the last chapter of *Saving the Text* (and the word "surmise" itself, calling up the "false surmise" of pastoral dallying in "Lycidas," complicates the texture of the speculation), "moves us beyond the fallacious hope that words can heal without also wounding" (122–23). Ultimately, "The Voice of the Shuttle" suggests that literary language obtains echoing power in and through the radical figurativeness of the voice with which it speaks or calls: a figurativeness that undermines aesthetic complacency and links literary power to a restitutive movement that is ethical precisely because it is uninsurable.

What Hartman calls the "Philomela project" of "restitutive criticism"—the restoration of voice to inarticulate people—"must endure the same constitutive ambivalence." The stakes in today's world, he emphasizes, are not low; this "visionary or utopian" task of giving voice "even if there is no voice" must avoid the "essentialist, and at worst racial, slogans that have bedeviled an era of catastrophic nationalism" by preventing restitution from becoming "restitutive pathos" ("The Philomela Project," 170–72). Hartman's effort to think through the paradoxes of restitution becomes most visible in his writings on Holocaust testimony and on the attempt of the Fortunoff Video Archive project to "criticize the image through the image,"[37] writings that affirm video's ability to do testimonial work in a spiritually and tech-nologically ravaged world.[38] And Hartman's affirmation of video testimony is only superficially distant from his investment in Wordsworth's poetry. In her wide-ranging interview with Hartman, an interview that circles repeat-edly around the Boy of Winander and the "gentle shock of mild surprise" he suffers, Cathy Caruth observes that, in Hartman's argument, "a violent imposition often ends up numbing the psyche, so that in fact by making [the imposition] less violent one paradoxically allows for more of a shock." Similarly, "the less direct mode of the video testimony would seem . . . to permit more of a sense of events to enter, without the hypnotic or numbing quality of direct visual representation" (Caruth 311–12).

Hartman does not discuss Wordsworth in "The Voice of the Shuttle," but in the "Retrospect" that he wrote for the 1971 reissue of *Wordsworth's Poetry*, he clearly had his recent essay in mind. His interpretation of "Strange fits of passion" in the "Retrospect" describes this lyrical ballad's minimalist narrative as a fragile middle: "Because imagination leaps over time . . . the narrative movement stalls and tends to collapse almost as soon as begun. This means, structurally, that the poem's middle—the narrative proper—barely keeps beginning and end apart as they converge" (*WP*, xix–xx). Hartman then recalls the even more pronounced patterning of "A slumber did my spirit seal," where all that is left is "two stanzas as poles of the vanished narrative, and the center a blank." Those two poles "are related, clearly, to 'imagination' and 'nature,' to 'romance' and 'realism.' Yet they veer, converge, or cross. You fall, in Wordsworth, from the abyss of ideality (stanza one of 'A slumber') to the abyss of temporality (stanza two), or vice versa. You never remain *in* nature or *in* imagination" (*WP*, xx). Hartman thus points to a minimal narrative— but a fundamental one: that of a "fall"—spanning the narrative void and composing the poem itself as creative errancy. The terms "imagination" and "nature" do not matter greatly at this particular point in Hartman's text; they are names for the pressure points that enable transferential movement. That movement, however—the fragile middling movement of surmise, of life, error and delay—is more easily characterizable as linguistic or imaginative than human or intentional. The consciousness that emerges in "Strange fits of passion" (a gentle parody of apocalyptic self-consciousness: "'O mercy!' to myself I cried"), is precipitated out of strangely non-intentional processes: "At the climax, there is no consciousness intervening between horse and moon: a horse climbs on by itself toward a bright moon. The only way to interpret this ghostliness (or depersonalization) is to suppose that the sense of self has been elided" (*WP*, 24).

What if that tropic movement were reduced further, to an even more minimal shuttling? In conclusion I would like to look briefly at Hartman's reading of *The Ruined Cottage*, the poem in which "the great Wordsworthian myth of Nature" first manifests itself (*WP*, 136). Hartman's seminal study of the manuscript history of this poem shows the poet overcoming a quasi-traumatic experience of place through the construction of distancing mechanisms. In the opening lines of the earliest extant fragment (known as "Incipient Madness"), the narrator encounters a "hut" in which "all was still and dark":

Only within the ruin I beheld
At a small distance, on the dusky ground,
A broken pane which glitter'd in the moon
And seemed akin to life. ("Incipient Madness" 4–7)[39]

The narrator finds that his "sickly heart had tied itself/Even to this speck of glass" (12–13). From this strange, grieving, obsessive experience of what Hartman describes as "the spot syndrome in a form approaching the intensity of madness" (*WP*, 136), the narrator is delivered in successive versions thanks to the intervention of mediating figures. The pane of glass disappears, its place taken by another haunting figure ("four naked walls/That stared upon each other"),[40] but this time the narrator is able to look away—or at least "look round"—and discover a way out:

> I found a ruined house, four naked walls
> That stared upon each other. I looked round
> And near the door I saw an aged Man,
> Alone and stretched upon the cottage bench;
> An iron-pointed staff lay at his side.
> With instantaneous joy I recognized
> That pride of nature and of lowly life
> The venerable Armytage, a friend
> As dear to me as is the setting sun. (*The Ruined Cottage*, D MS, 31–39)

The potentially freezing shock carried in the simple encounter-formula "I found" rhymes away to "I looked round"; the inhuman stare becomes a human look; the uncanny walls acquire a Man and a bench; and though traces of shock arguably remain legible in the gothic suddenness with which the narrator conjures up a hyperbolically dear friend in this disastrous space, Hartman is surely right to see the production of this figure as the solution to Wordsworth's narrative problem. The peddler, Armytage, who provides Wordsworth's "first portrait of the growth of a mind" (*WP*, 135), tells the story of Margaret, who was once bound to this crumbling spot by "a spectral hope," as Hartman, drawing attention to the doubling and redoubling of characters, puts it. "The tale of Margaret has the same locus (an adherence to a specific place) as the poet's original experience, and her hope is as disproportionate to what it half creates as that original speck of glass to Wordsworth's 'sickly heart'" (*WP*, 138).[41] But the distance achieved through reflection and mediation permits a humanizing narrative to emerge. The narrator frees himself from the fixation of place by deploying a sequence of "human filters," as Hartman calls them:

> The result is a spectrum bounded at one side by the apocalyptic imagination and at the other by an alien nature. Their joint symbol is the naked, self-staring ruin. The middle ground of the spectrum, however, is occupied by

the pedlar and his attitude toward nature, and there, "All things shall speak of Man." Human filters are made to intervene between the strange imagination and its strange object: poet → pedlar → (Margaret → Cottage) → the ruin. The theme of the completed poem is the humanized imagination, and the manuscripts of the poem show how Wordsworth's imagination humanizes itself within an act of confrontation as pure as it can be. Ultimately, poet and pedlar still stare at a ruin which stares at itself. (*WP*, 140)

Hartman's extraordinary identification with his beloved poet allows him to relay Wordsworthian ambivalence like no one else; and though earlier in this paragraph, which closes his chapter on *The Ruined Cottage*, he had strongly affirmed the great humanist theme ("the true subject of the poem is the perfected mind of man facing a still imperfect world. . . . Wordsworth separates his imagination from nature without abandoning nature, then remarries the two without abandoning imagination"), the momentum of his closing reflection takes him back to those staring walls and to a more nuanced statement. The phrase "human filters" darkens a little when we stare at it (what is the human, if the human is a filtering device?). The "middle ground of the spectrum" generated by this filtering system, the locus of humanist affirmation ("All things shall speak of Man"), suffers the fragility of the middle, pressed between overcharged ends; and here the ends have joined in an uncanny dead-end. The twin poles of the Wordsworthian world, "apocalyptic imagination" and "alien nature," collapse into a "joint symbol": the "naked, self-staring ruin."

Staring is not the same as seeing: a corpse can stare. (The word *stare* returns to Germanic and Indo-European roots meaning "rigid.") The light of sense does not so much go out in this uncanny figure as modulate into a disastrous radiance that renders illegible the difference between human and nonhuman, living and nonliving, apocalyptic imagination and alien nature. These barely undifferentiated walls that stare upon each other may be interpreted as an allegory of self-consciousness reduced to sheer figure: to the reflexive movement of a prosopopoeia without external props, unliving and undead, barely face-giving, a blind staring at staring. The pure consciousness that de Man seeks to imagine in "The Intentional Structure of the Romantic Image" finds a material correlative here. Hartman shows us Wordsworth attaining such imaginings yet also measuring their cost.

4. Literature, Incorporated
Harold Bloom, Theory, and the Canon

At the beginning of this book, we focused on the "Yale Critics" in an effort to come to grips with the phantasmatic dimension of the institutional and discursive development called "theory" in the American academy and media. In this chapter and the next, I offer case studies of the two most polarizing and dramatically contrastable members of the Yale quadrumvirate, Harold Bloom and Paul de Man. The case of Harold Bloom is unique in the annals of theory, and for that matter in the history of the modern academy. For a few years he occupied a prominent position in the American theory maelstrom as the intimate, internecine opponent of de Man and Derrida; then, during the mid-1980s, he lost professional visibility in the academy while acceding to the seemingly quite different role that he has played ever since in the national media: that of the antitheoretical, antiprofessional champion of the Western Canon, whose nearly superhuman powers of reading and retention allow him to embody (and underwrite and market) the literary tradition for a postliterate age. This Bloom, the "Yiddisher Doctor Johnson" whose books on Shakespeare, genius and the canon show up in airports, and whose Chelsea House volumes fill yards of shelf space, is at least as remarkable a figure as the theoretician of influence whose gnomic texts for awhile spurred critical discussion in journals like *Diacritics*. Bloom's voyage from one end to the other of the discursive galaxy of theory makes his story seem to divide in two, like a conversion narrative; but instead of seeing these two phases or roles as fundamentally opposed, I propose to tease out their affinities. We thereby stand to obtain a richer sense of Bloom's career—of the characteristics of mind and text that allowed this theorist of influence to become the mass-mediated mediator of the canon—while gaining another perspective from which to think about the mediatization of "theory." For the production of Bloom as the representative of the canon in the American media intriguingly mirrors the production of de Man as the representative of theory. In both cases a dramatic act of personification produced an icon for something manifestly irreducible to a person or personality. These two icons function as antitheses in the cultural landscape; yet, both as mediatized icon and as theorist, Bloom turns out upon inspection to be a more ambivalent figure than his position-taking allows for. A close look at the case of Harold Bloom confirms that aesthetic and theoretical discourse entwine in complex, unstable ways.

––––+––––

The story is familiar from the many interviews and feature articles: in a tough East Bronx neighborhood there was a bookish boy who grew up speaking Yiddish and who learned English largely on his own as a child by reading poetry, as early as five or six ("I didn't read children's literature until I was an undergraduate"); who at around ten years old "picked up a copy of the *Collected Poems* of Hart Crane in the Bronx Library. I still remember when I lit upon the page with the extraordinary trope, 'O Thou steeled Cognizance whose leap commits/The agile precincts of the lark's return.' I was just swept away by it, by the Marlovian rhetoric. I still have the flavor of that book in me."[1] A few years later, a scholarship took the young prodigy to Cornell, where he studied with M. H. Abrams; in 1951, at the age of twenty-one, he began graduate study at Yale.

A decade earlier the Yale English Department had refused on openly anti-Semitic grounds to hire Lionel Trilling, and some of that atmosphere lingered.[2] The department was dominated by its iconic New Critics—the first "Yale Critics"—almost all of whom were political conservatives and devout Christians. (The chair of the English department was singled out for praise by William F. Buckley in the book with which he made his name as a young conservative firebrand in 1951, *God and Man at Yale*.)[3] The romantic poets were not favored: "Despite pioneering work by Northrop Frye and Meyer Abrams," as Geoffrey Hartman comments, recalling his and Bloom's earliest years at Yale, "the Romantics were hardly a prestigious field except for editing projects; the academic stock market among Anglophiles was still busy devaluing them in favor of the metaphysical poets, eighteenth-century neoclassicism, and the attempt of T. S. Eliot and fellow Modernists to claim that heritage."[4] Harold Bloom prospected his way through this alien, genteel world with remarkably little compromise. He wrote a dissertation on Shelley and Martin Buber and was hired as an instructor in 1955; some years later he was given tenure against all odds, presumably on the strength of his already extraordinary productivity and his "genius," as it would often be called.[5] This genius manifested itself most prominently as a nearly superhuman power of intake and recall. Bloom, the young self-proclaimed champion of Anglo-American romanticism and arbiter of modern American poetry (passionate advocate of Stevens, Crane, Ashbery, Bishop, Ammons, Merrill), could "recite from memory the entire body of English romantic verse of the nineteenth century."[6] Indeed, he could recite from memory a good deal more than that, as first the many anecdotes and then, after he grew famous, the many interviews inevitably stressed:

> I can, for instance, I think, recite any line or passage or even vast work of poetry that I've ever cared for. I can recite Milton's *Paradise Lost* from beginning to end, like running off a tape, simply because it is for me a major aesthetic experience. I can recite most of Blake from beginning to end, I can recite most of the Hebrew Bible from beginning to end, I can recite most of Spenser's *Faerie Queene* from beginning to end. By the time I was ten or eleven, I was totally addicted to reading poetry, and I can recite nearly any lyric poem in the language I ever cared for. I think I have all of Yeats and Stevens and Hart Crane and you name it by heart.[7]

Bloom's preternatural memory is the one subject that almost never fails to come up in stories about him, with his reading speed a close second and his prodigious output (which perhaps seems somewhat less magical) a distant third.

Stories about Bloom that are long enough to be portraits of the author usually organize Bloom's writing life into phases. First there was the commitment to romantic poetry and the romantic imagination, as materialized in a sequence of academic books from *Shelley's Mythmaking* (1959) to *The Ringers in the Tower* (1971). Then came the decade of Bloom as "Yale Critic," gloomy theorist of influence: a phase of his writing that is supposed to have been triggered by a dream of being smothered—"a vision of an enormous stifling angel" (Taylor 56)—that Bloom suffered in 1967 and wrote out as a gnomic fragment, "The Covering Cherub," which grew into the book he will always be remembered by, *The Anxiety of Influence* (1973). There followed in rapid succession a suite of "theory of influence" books: *A Map of Misreading* (1975), *Kabbalah and Criticism* (1975), *Poetry and Repression* (1976), *Figures of Capable Imagination* (1976), and *Wallace Stevens: The Poems of Our Climate* (1977); this period of intense theoretical speculation tapered off after *Agon: Towards a Theory of Revisionism* (1982) and *The Breaking of the Vessels* (1982). Then came the MacArthur "genius" grant in 1985, the gigantic Chelsea House publishing project, and a new level of public attention. With *Ruin the Sacred Truths* (1989) and *The Book of J* (1990), the latter a national bestseller, Bloom became widely known as a writer on religion (the subject of numerous subsequent books); and with *The Western Canon* (1994) he became the nationally recognized representative, even as we shall see the quasi-allegorical embodiment, of the "canon" during the heyday of the "canon wars." That fin-de-siècle media bonfire has smoldered on dully ever since (as has the related conflagration over "theory") in right-wing (and at times mainstream) cultural venues; and Bloom's public persona, though less visible than it was in the 1990s, has not changed significantly over the intervening years, unless one feels that his role as repository of universal literary knowledge has been slightly overshadowed by his hyperbolic bardolatry, first widely publicized in *The Western Canon* (1994) and emphasized in *Shakespeare: The Invention of the Human* (1998) and other writings. I propose to begin with a look at Bloom's representation in the national media and work backwards, since a review of his mass-mediated role as the genius of the canon stands to offer us a fresh angle from which to consider his writings on influence during the 1970s.

As we recalled in Chapter 1, the so-called canon wars loom large in late twentieth-century media representations of university-level literary instruction. In at least that limited sense the canon wars are inseparable from the scandal of "theory," however little truck those seeking to expand the canon may have wanted with deconstruction (or indeed, at times, with any sort of theoretical reflection). We have noted that a degree of stylized worrying about the state of the humanities has a long history in the United States, for reasons having partly to do with the diversity, size, and structure of the U.S. system of mass higher education. In the 1980s and 1990s, that hortatory tradition found intensified expression in a cycle of media attention shaped by a number of developments specific to the later twentieth century: the increasingly technological orientation of increasingly corporation-like universities; the diversification of university populations and prominence of themes of cultural diversity in classrooms and journals; the emergence of variously labeled, variously interleaved and antagonistic discursive developments such as theory, cultural studies, gender and queer studies, identity politics, debates about the canon, and so forth; and the well-funded production, by mainstream media sources and neoconservative foundations, of a specter of multicultural, anti-aesthetic anarchy threatening the teaching of the humanities. It is possible to knit together some of these developments into a narrative about deep structural transformations in the social order: in the next chapter we are going to consider John Guillory's claim that the "canon debate signifies nothing less than a crisis in the form of cultural capital we call literature," literature being understood to name "the cultural capital of the old bourgeoisie, a form of capital increasingly marginal to the social function of the present educational system."[8] One symptom of that crisis, according to

Guillory, was the emergence of an alternative canon of texts labeled "theory" in the 1970s; other symptoms, presumably, would include the aggressive rejection of the category of the aesthetic by advocates of "cultural studies" in the 1980s and 1990s, and the corresponding backlash by middlebrow cultural journalists and conservative academics.

It is in this context that Harold Bloom became what he still is today: not quite a public intellectual of the traditional sort—he is too eccentric and professorial for that—but a public figure who stands for the possibility that literary culture in its totality (as a "canon") can be internalized and mastered. This persona, which, as we have seen, has root systems leading back to the earliest years of Bloom's professional life, entered the national media with the publication of David Lehman's 1986 *Newsweek* article "Yale's Insomniac Genius." Lehman's piece was written a few months after Bloom had received his MacArthur and taken on the Chelsea House publishing venture.[9] Its opening paragraph reads as follows:

> Harold Bloom looks a lot like Zero Mostel and sounds rather like a sorrowful dandy, a combination of an Old Testament prophet and Oscar Wilde. An indefatigable monologist in a rumpled suit, he reclines in his favorite armchair at the New Haven suite of offices he calls his "factory" for producing literary criticism. The term is apt: Bloom, a professor at Yale University, is editing and writing introductions for five series of critical anthologies comprising no less than 800 separate volumes. His subject—the whole of literature. His model— Samuel Johnson's "Lives of the Poets." The task might daunt a lesser mortal, but leaves Bloom unfazed and rather excited. This is, after all, a man who blithely claims he can read and absorb up to 1,000 pages an hour. A man whose memory is legendary: "I think I have by heart every line of poetry that I like that I've ever read," he says, offering to illustrate with swatches of "The Faerie Queene" and "Paradise Lost."[10]

Lehman dwells on the speed with which Bloom reads and writes, but like most journalists who interview Bloom—and, as noted earlier, like most of Bloom's teachers, students and colleagues—he is particularly fascinated and awed by Bloom's preternatural memory:

> How does he manage to do it all? . . . Bloom's scandalously rapid reading rate helps, of course, and his memory serves as his touchstone: "I've always made it a principle that if I cannot remember it, I won't quote it." Yale colleagues confirm his astonishing powers of verbatim recall. "When I was a student," he says, "I would get a bit drunk and recite Hart Crane's 'The Bridge' frontwards, then backwards, quite like a tape recorder running wild."

An accompanying photo shows Bloom surrounded by books, his arm draped over a stack of Chelsea House volumes. Behind him, on the shelves, sits "the whole of literature"; before him, substituting for his midsection and more or less rhyming with the mass of his head, are the books about books that the genius's internalization of the canon authorizes.

Neither Bloom's pose nor the visual puns it sets in motion are particularly surprising, of course; given the tenor of the article, it would be odd if Bloom were *not* being photographed with books. Yet, in some magazine photos of Bloom from the canon-wars era, this is in fact what happens: the books drop into the background or even disappear, with the result that the teasing equivalence between Bloom's body and the canon becomes all the more emphatic—as though the books had been devoured literally enough to *become* the body. (I am going to have to ask readers to bear with unsubstantiated descriptions of these photographs; anyone interested can easily find them in the archive.) The 1994 report in *Time*, for instance, on the publication of *The Western Canon* (entitled "Hurrah for Dead White Males!"), offers its readers a full-body shot of Bloom in his New York apartment, sitting on a twin bed, with bookshelves relegated to the background. The critic's black-clad stomach anchors the composition, while his open thighs, spread arms, and weary eyes and mouth offer a vulnerable but imposing body to the camera's gaze.[11] In another article from this period, Adam Begley's "Colossus among Critics: Harold Bloom" in the *New York Times Magazine* (1994) the accompanying photos are headshots. The subtitle of Begley's piece reads, "Everything about him is outsized"—and indeed, one of the headshots is offered in full-page size. In both pictures, Bloom is shown camping it up, holding his head in his hands or shading his eyes: the Western Canon, beset by resentniks, is suffering a corporeal and theatrical headache. Such, in any case, is the interpretation with which Begley flirts as he begins his article:

> In early summer, I paid two visits to Harold Bloom, the eminent literary critic famous for his prodigious intellectual energy. On both occasions he seemed intent on staging a deathbed scene. Collapsed on a reclining armchair, brow furrowed, mouth sour, the 64-year-old Bloom looked worse than pained. "The battle is lost," he whispered. "These resentniks have destroyed the canon." Enfeebled despite his generous bulk, he summoned the stamina for some impressive elegiac flourishes. . . . Once with a tragic sigh, he breathed, "I am weary unto death."
>
> Literature is dying and so, ipso facto, is Harold Bloom. Or could it be the other way around?[12]

Goaded on by Bloom, Begley repeatedly toys with the extravagant, not-seriously-meant-of-course fantasy that the headshots encourage: Bloom, having internalized all of literature, has become literature's incorporate representative.[13]

A similarly comic association is encouraged by the full-page, full-body shot by John Hamilton that introduces John Taylor's post–*Book of J* profile of Bloom in a 1990 issue of *New York* magazine, "Bloom's Day: Hanging Out with the Reigning Genius of Literary Criticism." Bloom is sprawled in his easy chair, and the camera angle is strangely high. We look down on a book-surrounded body, uncertain whether Bloom is exhibiting himself or whether the camera is excavating him: his vulnerability is also an aggressive claim on our gaze. The scattered books rhyme with the body's sprawl, suggesting a potential for chaos, yet at the same time offering us the consoling pleasures of metaphor: to the degree that one can imagine the books and the body resembling each other, their scatteredness recomposes into a modest sort of aesthetic form. I am remarking here a figurative equivalence that these feature articles repeatedly insist on themselves. Larissa MacFarquhar's "The Prophet of Decline: Harold Bloom's Influential Anxieties," published in *The New Yorker* on September 30, 2002, comes graced with a luminous headshot of Bloom by Richard Avedon, and it vigorously recycles more than a decade's worth of journalistic commonplaces about the genius and his body:

> He has memorized a large proportion of canonical poetry written in English; once, when drunk, as an undergraduate at Cornell, he recited Hart Crane's long poem "The Bridge" backward, word by word. He claims that in his youth he read a thousand pages an hour. Bloom has had poems inside him for so long that he doesn't really read them anymore. They are not a series of lines following one after the other—they exist in him all at once. He has swallowed them whole.

A few sentences later, MacFarquhar translates Bloom's face into a grotesquely phallic anti-Petrarchan catalogue ("Bloom's face is a cluster of big, swollen, sensing instruments: a heroic nose, nostrils dilating; plump, colossal lips; a giant's heavy eyes . . ."), a description that descends, inevitably, toward the stomach and its canonical contents: "His stomach is prodigious, like a great cathedral, in which all the uncountable poems and plays that he has swallowed roil and commingle with his own passions."[14]

It is a sheerly contingent fact that a literary critic with a phenomenal memory and a turn for dramatic self-presentation should also possess what Bloom genially calls a "Falstaffian body"; but it is the function of ideologies to invest contingencies with significance, and I think we may take these

photographs and articles as symptomatic expressions of the instabilities besetting the notion of the "canon."[15] And although this (intentionally or
unintentionally) parodic rhetoric of embodiment represents a new phase in
Bloom's reception and is in certain ways specific to his transformation into
a media celebrity, Bloom's earlier academic and quasi-public identities had
prepared him uniquely for this role. His uncanny powers of memory, his
productive energy, and his commitment to aesthetic judgment and dramatic
acts of canonization—rescuing the romantics from T. S. Eliot; advocating
for a certain sublime strain of American poetry—shaped from the start his
idiosyncratic academic career. The canon wars produced a context in which
an increasingly public personality called "Bloom"—the precipitate of three
or four decades of scholarship, journalism, and academic anecdote—could
become a visible token of canonical literary history. And it is precisely *because*
the canon had become a questionable idea in the public discourse of the
time that it elicited such figuration. To the extent that they playfully treat
Bloom as an allegorical figure for the canon, these journalists emphasize the
bodiliness of the critic's body—its size, its vulnerability, its potential unrul-
iness—as a way of half-seriously entertaining the fantasy that "the Western
canon" is sufficiently organic to be headachy, wounded, mortal.[16] For the
human body is an ineradicable but unstable trope in aesthetic discourse: if
the image of the body is humanity's "principle of unity," as Jacques Lacan
suggests, it is also the figure of this unity's disruption.[17] The canon submits
to a fantasy of embodiment because it is being seen as an uncertain corpus,
its edges crumbling off into the even more amorphous and unmanageably
vast ocean of "all of literature" (and nothing makes this more obvious than
when the canon is represented as a list, even or especially a list as capacious
as the notorious three-thousand title one offered as *The Western Canon*'s
appendix).[18]

The delight with which these journalists write about or photograph
Bloom, therefore, has about it the headiness but also the uncertainty and
aggressivity of imaginary totalizations; and we may advance a little further
in our interpretation of these scenes if we ask after the ways in which they
construct Bloom as the canon's "genius." As genius, Bloom has in principle
read everything and, even more crucially, judged everything. The first of
these feats is the most obviously impossible of the two, since even a Harold
Bloom will never finish reading and internalizing the archive; the second
is in fact the one that matters, since aesthetic judgment is what, over time,
generates a canon (aesthetically conceived). To memorize a poem is not
necessarily to understand or appreciate it (Hegel tells us that "it is well
known that one knows a text by heart only when one no longer associates

any meaning with the words").[19] Bloom insists on the aesthetic character of his memory, as in the remark quoted earlier ("I can recite Milton's *Paradise Lost* from beginning to end, like running off a tape, simply because it is for me a major aesthetic experience").[20] His memory is not "photographic" but rather "auditory and aesthetic"; he internalizes not texts but voices, voices that call to him and claim him.

Yet Bloom's authority as judge tends rhetorically, in these articles, to refer itself to his sheer ability to read and remember. He is the genius as cyborg, possessed of such an uncanny, even monstrous ability to scan and store data that only the tape recorder and the computer provide adequate metaphors.[21] Bloom, whose relationship to reproductive technologies is minimal and negative in many ways (he claims never to have used a typewriter, let alone a computer), favors the tape recorder; he gives it pride of place in his story about reciting Hart Crane backward ("like a tape recorder running wild"), and he turns to this simile even when, as in the earlier citation from Taylor's article ("like running off a tape"), he is emphasizing his memory's aesthetic character.[22] The tape recorder is Bloom's and everyone else's privileged figure for how he activates or retrieves data, and perhaps implicitly also for how he stores it (the tapes wait inside him as it were, a giant, canon-sized archive of them, each one waiting to be spooled and played). But what figure would do justice to how the information gets registered or inscribed in the first place? One's temptation is to invoke as a simile a high-speed scanner (1,000 pages per hour!), as I did a moment ago;[23] but Bloom, as we have seen, dislikes tropes of photographic uptake, preferring to minimize the mediating role of writing, print, the external sign. (Asked by Antonio Weiss whether he has ever made notes for teaching: "I have never made a note in my life. How could I? I have internalized the text.") For further help we may turn to his work on influence in the 1970s, which is about how texts take possession of a reader-listener. But as we go we may note that even the tape recorder, with its hint that poetry *speaks* to Bloom, has already smuggled a bit of deconstructive contraband into the phantasmatics of canon-embodiment. The tape recorder preserves voice, but it does so thanks to a process of inscription that breaks with the imagined self-presence of voice and transforms voice into writing—or, better, exposes and exploits the "writing," the iterability and self-difference, that inheres in voice and makes it possible: as recorded voice, Hart Crane can always, in a moment of inebriation, be played backward, because his voice endures only in and as the possibility of being grafted, spliced, overdubbed, and played elsewhere. The insistence of this trope testifies to the Derridean specter that haunts Bloom's incorporation of the canon. Despite itself, the canon-embodying aesthetic is forced to have recourse to the figure of an inscription performed by a machine utterly indifferent, as all machines are, to the meaning or beauty of what it records.

—+—

As we return to the 1970s, it will help to retrace the main lines of Paul de Man's extraordinary review of *The Anxiety of Influence*, not just because my overall project involves measuring the gravitational field cast by de Man in such contexts, but also because this review exerted a specific and very visible pull on Bloom's subsequent writing about poetic influence. De Man's review also allows us to loop back to the idea of the autonomous imagination that, as we saw in Chapter 3, preoccupied de Man, Bloom, and Hartman in the 1960s to the point of giving them a sense of a shared project. By the time *The Anxiety of Influence* appeared in 1973, de Man had developed the principles and idiom of rhetorical reading; and in his review he looks back at Bloom's former affirmation of "the absolute power of the imagination" and judges the new theme of influence-anxiety to be in some ways regressive.[24] Bloom's previous work had struggled to think the romantic imagination "beyond the mind-nature dialectic" as "an autonomous power that develops according to its own laws into areas where the category of nature no longer operates. . . . It is extremely difficult to describe this power, for the impact of the tradition on post-romantic poetry and criticism is so overriding that it has once and for all determined the rhetoric and the terminology available to us, thus making it necessary to assert the inadequacy of a conceptual language by means of the very language that is being rejected." Bloom's response to this difficulty, according to de Man, had been "to reach out for a definition of the imagination by means of near-extravagant overstatement." But Bloom's hyperbolic affirmations of a nonnatural imagination were "still being stated in the very language they attempt[ed] to supersede: a naturalistic language of desire, possession, and power." This tension led Bloom to displace a theoretical problem (how to conceive of a nonnatural imagination) onto a historical narrative organized by weighted oppositions (early vs. late, original vs. derivative). "Thus the failure to name the imagination for what it is becomes a temporal predicament in which the latecomer is forever overshadowed by his precursor. . . . In some respects this is a step backward. Just when we were about to free poetic language from the constraints of natural reference, we return to a scheme which, for all its generality, is still clearly a relapse into a psychological naturalism."

These remarks are of interest partly because they hint that de Man saw his own turn to rhetorical reading as a displaced development of the strange thought of a consciousness "exist[ing] entirely by and for itself" that he had cagily posited in "Intentional Structure of the Romantic Image" (1960), and that, as we saw in the previous chapter, Hartman tracks a version of through Wordsworth's poetry. Viewed through the lens of rhetorical reading, nonnatural consciousness or imagination becomes a figure for the nonphenomenal force of language. And in the second half of his short review of Bloom—one of the most stunning ten-page performances in the history of modern criticism—de Man takes Bloom down that rhetorical road, transposing *The Anxiety of Influence* into a de Manian–deconstructive key:

> Behind the arbitrariness of the psychological plot, one feels that the book deals with something else, that it is an oblique version of something much closer to literary problems, much closer to the poetic "imagination" that Bloom tried in vain to define in a vaguely existential terminology. . . . We can forget about the temporal scheme and about the pathos of the oedipal son; underneath, the book deals with the difficulty or, rather, the impossibility of reading and, by inference, with the indeterminacy of literary meaning. If we are willing to set aside the trappings of psychology, Bloom's essay has much to say on the encounter between latecomer and precursor as a displaced version of the paradigmatic encounter between reader and text. (273)

For "to say that literature is based on influence is to say that it is intertextual. And intertextual relationships necessarily contain a moment that is interpretive. In order to be literally productive the encounter implies a reading" (273). That moment of reading (necessary *and* necessarily erroneous, because any reading worthy of the name must aim at totalization) is what Bloom calls "misprision." Despite its strong temporal emphasis, Bloom's taxonomic account of misprision is grounded in patterns of substitution (his "revisionary ratios"). "And," de Man insists, "from the moment we begin to deal with substitutive systems, we are governed by linguistic rather than by natural or psychological models: one can always substitute one word for another but one cannot, by a mere act of will, substitute night for day or bliss for gloom" (274). Therefore, Bloom's six exotically named revisionary ratios can be recoded as tropes (*clinamen* names troping in general, or irony; *tessera* is synecdoche; *kenosis*, metonymy; *daemonization*, hyperbole; *askesis*, metaphor; *apophrades*, metalepsis).[25]

> What is achieved by thus translating back from a subject-centered vocabulary of intent and desire to a more linguistic technology? If we admit that the term "influence" is itself a metaphor that dramatizes a linguistic structure into a diachronic narrative, then it follows that Bloom's categories of misreading not only operate between authors, but also between the various texts of a single author

or, within a given text, between the different parts, down to each particular chapter, paragraph, sentence, and, finally, down to the interplay between literal and figurative meaning within a single word or grammatical sign. (276)

And "even more important," the translation into a rhetorical idiom makes it conceivable "that the affective appeal of text could just as well be the result of a linguistic structure as its cause"—which does not mean that "meaning [is] shown to be centered in a linguistic property instead of centered in a subject" but rather that "the very scheme of things based on such terms as cause, effect, center, and meaning is put in question" (276).

There in a nutshell is the claim and challenge of rhetorical reading. Bloom certainly never went along with any of those conclusions; but he incorporated de Man's suggested rhetorical terms into his system in his next book, *A Map of Misreading* (1975), which is dedicated to de Man and which Bloom much later described as having been "provoked" by that "brilliant polemical review."[26] Hyperbolically laudatory references to de Man punctuate Bloom's writing in the mid-1970s. *A Map of Misreading* announces the appearance of "a new mythic being—clearly implied by Paul de Man in particular—the reader as Overman, the *Überleser*" (*Map* 5); similarly, in *Wallace Stevens: The Poems of Our Climate*, de Manian deconstruction becomes "Over-Reading, or the reading of an Over-Man," and de Man receives Bloom's "reverence" as an "advanced critical consciousness, the most rigorous and scrupulous in the field today."[27] All the while, during these years—the fleeting glory years of the "Yale Critics"—Bloom labors to answer the challenge of deconstruction as represented by de Man and Derrida. I shall not follow out his counterarguments in detail, since Bloom's metalanguage changes somewhat from book to book; it will suffice to highlight a few main points.[28]

The Oedipal struggle, in Bloom's theory, as Bloom and others have often pointed out, "is nothing but a *parable*."[29] Influence, belatedness, and anxiety are not psychological notions in Bloom (his theory is not concerned with the poet's feelings). Nor does influence in Bloom's sense have anything to do with "verbal resemblances" (*Map* 19) or with "the transmission of images or ideas"[30] (though in practice, as Paul Fry notes, Bloom's most persuasive demonstrations of influence tend to rely on verbal echo and allusion).[31] Influence is rather "a figuration for poetry itself" because "there are *no* texts, but only relationships *between* texts" (*Map*, 71, 5, Bloom's emphases).[32] If influence is intertextuality, however, it is intertextuality as, on the one hand, an agon among selves trapped in time, and, on the other, as a dynamic interplay of tropes that are also psychic defenses. The self here, is not an empirical or psychological self, but is rather the "*the poet in a poet*, or the aboriginal poetic self" (*Anxiety* 11).[33] Bloom has also called this essence "neither self nor language but the utterance, within a tradition of uttering, of the image or lie of voice, where voice is neither self nor language, but rather spark or *pneuma* as opposed to self, and act made one with word (*davhar*) rather than word referring only to another word (*logos*)."[34] The twist in the middle of that last quotation is essential to Bloom's thought and typical of his style: the *lie* of voice—and then a cascade of valorized terms from Gnostic and kabbalistic tradition (spark, *pneuma*, act-made-one-with-word), all of which are versions of this lie. Everything is defense, trope, lie; the poetic will, which drives the system, is itself a defense or trope or lie against time, death, and literal meaning. We touch here on what Bloom rightly recognized as a crucial difference between himself and de Man. Whereas de Man affirmed that "no theory of poetry is possible without a truly epistemological moment when the literary text is considered from the perspective of its truth or falsehood" (de Man 272), Bloom denied the necessity of the epistemological moment, since lying goes all the way down. And since lying goes all the way down, what matters is (rhetoric as) persuasion: "We believe the lies we want to believe because they help us survive. . . . Deconstruction touches its limit because it cannot admit such a question. For the deconstructive critic, a trope is a figure of knowing and not a figure of willing" (*Wallace Stevens* 387). Of course Bloom is ready to stress: *figure* of willing, since the will is a lie—a lie that we will to believe. "It is a theory of literature that is literary to the core," Elizabeth Bruss concludes near the end of her elegant and unsparing study of Bloom.[35] She means that as a criticism—as a way of driving home "how fragile the theoretical impulse is" in Bloom (295). "For Bloom, certain errors are indispensable, worth any error to preserve, even if preserving them involves a confession of their unreality. Thus, in the process of saving the self, Bloom is willing to incur enormous losses. Self-knowledge and self-reliance are shored up, but at the cost of making them necessary fictions" (328). And not only that: Bloom's hyperaestheticism in fact represses rather than overcomes the epistemological moment, for his affirmation of the generality of trope generates a host of terms that may be called lies but are granted truth-functionality by being removed (if ambivalently or paradoxically) from the grip of linguistic displacement.[36] To claim that one has *chosen* to believe is simply to kick the problem a step further down the line.

But perhaps there is another way in which Bloom's writing can be thought of as "literary to the core." I suggested earlier that Bloom's theory of influence addresses the question we asked earlier about Bloom's famous memory: how do texts get inside us? Or more specifically, inside *him*? Through a kind of call, runs one answer; through a kind of catastrophe, runs another—supposing we are willing to imagine Bloom being claimed by poetry as he imagines poets are. Poets become poets thanks to a "scene of instruction" that Bloom aligns with the Freudian theory of a primal scene:

> Freud's Primal Scene takes place in the beginning, when an infant sees his parents in the act of love, without in any way understanding that sight. Memory, according to Freud, holds on to the image of copulation until the child, between the ages of three and five, creates the Primal Scene fantasy, which is an Oedipal reverie. One of my former students, Cathy Caruth, caught me in making this same error, so that in my literary transformation of Freud into the Primal Scene of Instruction, I referred to such a Primal Scene as being at once oral and written. I would clarify this now by saying that the "oral" scene is the topos or Primal Scene proper, the negative moment of being influenced, a perpetually lost origin, while the "written" scene is the trope or Primal Scene fantasy. This means, in my terms, that in a poem a topos or rhetorical commonplace is *where* something can be *known*, but a trope or inventive turning is *when* something is desired or *willed*. Poems, as I have written often, are verbal utterances that cannot be regarded as being simply linguistic entities, because they manifest their will to utter *within* traditions of uttering, and as soon as you will that "within," your mode is discursive and topological as well as linguistic and tropological. As a Primal Scene, the Scene of Instruction is a Scene of Voicing; only when fantasized or troped does it become a Scene of Writing. (*The Breaking of the Vessels*, 60–61, Bloom's italics)

The future poet's (or, as we shall be troping here, influence-critic's) catastrophic yet productive encounter is "oral" because, according to Bloom, the poem-as-will must express itself in and through utterance (which prevents the poem from being a "simply linguistic" entity); writing comes later, as the Primal Scene fantasy, produced by the poet willing himself as poet. But the glancing argument with Derrida is overridden by the interesting way Bloom characterizes that "oral" moment of "seeing," as the "former student" whom Bloom credits here, Cathy Caruth, went on to point out in an article published shortly after *The Breaking of the Vessels* appeared:

> The "lostness" of the ["oral" Primal] scene, which is also its "primal" quality, is implicit in the radical negativity of the words "without *in any way* understanding." Such a seeing-without-knowing elides consciousness, as it were, in bypassing perception and imprinting itself on memory. This odd elision is the striking characteristic as well of Freud's early description of trauma. . . .
> The catastrophic nature of trauma (as discussed in the *Project*) is connected, as Laplanche notes, with the impossibility of locating it historically.[37]

Teasing out similarities between Bloom's writing about catastrophe and Freud's writing about trauma, Caruth notes the "odd temporal structure" of trauma—since the trauma's meaning cannot be located in either of its two constitutive moments, the moment of marking or the moment of return or re-marking—and observes that Freud emphasizes "the non-perceptual nature of the first 'seeing' by the use of the term 'memory-trace'" (1,294): "The priority of the first scene with regard to the second scene is not that of a perception with regard to its memory, but rather of a 'trace' with regard to a perception, the two having no simple temporal relation" (1,295). When Bloom acknowledges the "primal scene of instruction" to be radically *lost*, the scene's orality becomes legible as a trope for an immemorial writing. Bloom's theory of creation through catastrophe thereby becomes an extended reiteration and disavowal of the nonphenomenal *inscription* of meaning as memory—a gigantic, unacknowledged commentary, one could say, on the trope of Bloom-as-tape recorder that we examined earlier.

And if Bloom's recourse to the Freudian primal scene and its visual register ("an infant *sees* his parents in the act of love") half-acknowledges that a moment of *reading* opens the possibility of his aesthetic-mechanical memory (as opposed to simply "hearing," in a "Scene of Voicing," the precursor's voice on that figurative tape recorder), his rumination on the primal scene's "orality," however inadequate as theoretical argument, holds interest as a trope.[38] Earlier I quoted one of the authors of a feature article about Bloom, Larissa MacFarquhar, fantasizing about how Bloom has ingested the canon: "Bloom has had poems inside him for so long that he doesn't really read them anymore. They are not a series of lines following one after the other—they exist in him all at once. He has swallowed them whole." For all the willfulness of this fantasy of incorporation—the base-fantasy, as we have seen, of Bloom as Genius of the Canon in the 1990s—*swallowing* is a provocative inflection of the oral trope. Along with its obvious aggressivity, it hints at a certain passivity, a violence suffered (for one can be forced to swallow; indeed, fundamentally one is *always* forced to swallow: "At ten to twelve years of age, I read for the lustres, in Emerson's phrase. These seemed to memorize themselves in me" [*Anatomy* 4].) Aesthetic internalization then comes to resemble the kind of taking-in that psychoanalysts call incorporation: a "literal" ingestion in the sense that the incorporated other refuses symbolic substitutes, resists the work of mourning, and remains other—an encrypted, cherished alienness within.[39] One may then hypothesize that Bloom's pathos-laden style relays a denial or foreclosure of loss—loss as the quasi-traumatic internalization of aesthetic text ("poetry") as ineffaceable inscription. One can go further:

one can imagine the repetitive, modular, compulsive character of Bloom's writing—his gravitation toward proper names, his lack of interest in style and genre, his habit of quoting chunks of text and moving on—as the work of a powerful mechanical memory that is indistinguishable from a powerful process of incorporation and fixation. "[Poems] are not a series of lines following one after the other—they exist in him all at once." Readers of Bloom throughout his long career (particularly those who find his style irritating) have sometimes intuited as much. In the words of an ambivalent reviewer of *The Visionary Company* (a reviewer who clearly either knew or knew of the fabulous young prodigy who had memorized the romantic canon): "One gets the impression that all these works are simultaneously present to the author's consciousness at any given moment—and that he is incapable of forgetting. . . . In his fits of total recall Mr. Bloom appears to throw on the page hot slabs of melded relationships rather than paragraphs."[40] Bruss, writing about Bloom's style, similarly hints that in Bloom a state of being-possessed or being-fixated is finding expression as "a continuous recirculation of swatches of Wittgenstein and Freud, Vico and Kenneth Burke, Nietzsche, de Man, and Derrida, that float, unmoored and anonymous, among Bloom's own recurrent pet phrases (antithetical, central man, severe, ephebe, covering cherub), which themselves turn out to be derived from Yeats, Blake, Emerson, and Stevens" (355–56). Literary to the core, then: literary in a melancholy, manic, and certainly also at times darkly comic key.[41]

$$+$$

Academic writing on Bloom has been sparse since the mid-1980s, but Agata Bielik-Robson's impressive recent monograph *The Saving Lie: Harold Bloom and Deconstruction* (2011) testifies that that the "theory at Yale" phenomenon of the 1970s is still capable of inspiring strong critical writing. I want to consider her book briefly before concluding this chapter, since her study offers us the chance to review the tensions composing Bloom's theoretical speculations by way of a text committed to a painstaking and rigorous defense of Bloom's position. Bielik-Robson reargues Bloom's case for him against Derrida and de Man, convinced as she is of its ongoing significance; she aims to restage a "missed encounter" and recover for our consideration a line of unjustly forgotten argument (4). Her name for Bloom's position is "antithetical vitalism," a stance that she assimilates to Jewish tradition and opposes to a thanotropic philosophical tradition. Having "almost nothing in common with the philosophical type of vitalism," antithetical vitalism is agonistic and antinatural. It is "manifest most of all in the ubiquitous blessing of more life, *l'chaim*, and offers a peculiar vision of life in constant quarrel with itself: *life against life*" (5). Whereas the Western philosophical tradition from Plato to Hegel, Heidegger and Derrida "derives the power of negativity from the confrontation of life with, in Hegel's words, 'death, the absolute master,' which appears as the main agent of dynamics and change," the Jewish vitalist tradition "avoids the idolization of death and locates the primary source of negativity in the vital agon between two manifestations of life: on the one hand, the natural life, which is reconciled with the cyclic and seasonal rhythm of nature—and on the other, the non-natural, intensified life, which wants to break out of the 'oceanic' cycle of becoming and perishing and establish its own dominion on a 'dry open land'" (5). The theme or topic of anti-naturalistic vitalism is without question a major motif in Bloom's work, from his early affirmation of the anti-natural romantic imagination, to his theorization of influence-anxiety ("the anxiety caused by a desire for a fuller, more intense 'blessed life'" [6]) and his writings on the Hebrew Bible, Gnosticism, and the "American religion."[42] Bielik-Robson writes as a faithful but decisive interpreter, ready to part Bloom from "his frequently misleading self-commentaries" when she sees fit (22), and prepared from the start to admit that she is privileging certain aspects of his work over others. The Harold Bloom that interests her is the antithetical vitalist whose "scattered criticism of philosophy as the science of lethal truths" culminates in the 1970s in "the most important agon in his intellectual biography: the war he wages against deconstruction" (26). All of which is to say that her interpretation is a productive misprision of Bloom that holds particular interest in the present context; we may therefore enter briefly into an agonistic struggle with her reading.

As her title indicates, Bielik-Robson's central task is to focus on and endorse Bloom's affirmative identification of life with lying. Lying against time and death is what saves us—perhaps. Salvation is necessarily ambiguous under such conditions, and Bielik-Robson's tone, like Bloom's, is frequently dark. Still, the whole point is to affirm the lie: "A strangely conscious, chosen lie, determined to break through the ranks of the oppressive hopeless truth; an attitude that, in opposition to a naïve illusion, is thoroughly disenchanted, yet not disappointed. How can this complex state of mind be achieved and maintained?" (18–19). Bielik-Robson's question, already sagging under the stress of its own internal tensions, generates more questions. How can a *lie* be known as such and affirmed without projecting a truth (an "oppressive hopeless truth") against which one is heroically lying? Is antithetical criticism in essence a spiritual exercise ("achieving and maintaining" a "state of mind"?) And if we are to perform that exercise efficaciously, will we also need to lie against the knowledge that we are lying, following out a spiral of romantic irony? At what point might we need to pass from believing that we are lying to believing our own lie? Can we be sure of keeping a truthful tally of these lies as they circulate and, like the effaced coins in Nietzsche's "On Truth and Lie," turn into the currency of truth?[43] Later, as we shall see, Bielik-Robson will need to speak of faith, the lie believed—and she has already sketched a scenario in which the "willing error" that opposes "the deadening truth" is "supported by a powerful *fantasy*" of immortality that "defensively veils [the] traumatic core" of that truth (10). The saving lie is supposed to be the heroic act of a Gnostic pneumatic spark; but to the extent that the lie has to be *known* as a lie, it constantly runs the danger of dwindling into a spiritual technique or psychological trick—a trick that, worse yet, can never be sure it is working, unless it is working so well that it does not know what it is doing.

Lying is a linguistic performance; like Bloom, Bielik-Robson emphasizes not just what the lie does but what it is. The lie is a trope. Bloom, drawing on Freud but also on a long and diffuse tradition, identifies figuration with eros and literal meaning with death: "Literal meaning equals anteriority equals an earlier state of things equals death equals literal meaning. Only one escape is possible from such a formula, and it is a simpler formula: Eros equals figurative meaning."[44] Eros is error: Bielik-Robson nicely puns this to "Erros" (10). Vitalistic precisely in its "stubborn refusal to accept death in any way" (55), the poetic self *is* deviation or error; it is lie as desire as defense as figuration. Yet that very pronouncement must also be understood as a lie or act of faith, for the identification of literal meaning with death is a *figurative* identification (as the reiterated verb "equals" in Bloom's formula half-stresses and half-conceals).[45] Paradoxically, this figurative equation works to return figuration to the "vicious thanatic . . . trope of truth" that Bielik-Robson associates with the philosophical tradition (and, oddly but symptomatically, above all with deconstruction) (9). Life, understood as a Freudian circuit of delay and deferral, ends in death, but figuration does not end in literal meaning (except figuratively). To identify figuration with life and literal meaning with death is to orient figurative language toward an inescapable truth—a truth against which figuration lies but to which it must finally succumb (fighting every step of the way). It is thus in fact Bloom and Bielik-Robson and the "party of Erros" who need to equate death with truth and truth with death. On that figurative equation hangs the no less figurative equation between trope and psychic defense, and the entire rationale, power and pathos of antithetical vitalism.

The pressure of that conundrum leaves ripples in the texture of this finely intelligent book. We hear again and again of what Bloom "must" say ("for otherwise all his project would be doomed" [180]). Differences must be maintained, borders policed; now and then the clichés of the resistance to theory erupt into the text ("anything as serious as pain or suffering would merely slow down the swiftness of [Derrida's] masterly play" [94]). The most interesting symptom comes late—very near the end of the book— as Bielik-Robson unexpectedly allows de Man's review of *The Anxiety of Influence* to return, as it were, from the dead to haunt her concluding pages. Despite her extensive demonstrations of the inadequacy of deconstruction in general and de Man in particular (including this particular text of de Man's [83–84]), it turns out that de Man has made an "important point" about Bloom's "gloomy naturalist reductionism": "Indeed, Bloom's 'psychological naturalism' . . . puts in jeopardy the whole project of Bloom's agonistic, antithetical, and antinaturalistic vitalism, which, as we claimed through all this book, constitutes his greatest theoretical invention. The specter of naturalism, therefore, has to be chased away if we are to save what is most precious about Bloom's 'theory of life.'" The recurrent problem of chasing away that specter takes Bielik-Robson back to the vexed question of the epistemological status of the saving lie:

> This aporia leads to another poignant question, also brought about by
> de Man's critical remarks that one simply cannot avoid epistemology forever:
> what *is*, after all, the epistemological status of Bloom's artful lies? . . . For if
> Bloom doesn't lie that the poet's only weapon is "lying against time," then
> *what is the true nature of those lies*: literal or rhetorical? (308, emphasis in the
> original)

No answer can prevent the return of that epistemological question, just as no affirmation of the lie can keep from flapping on the hook of its own performance. Salvation will require an act of faith. "Nature, therefore, cannot be fought on her own grounds: it can only be fought against by a lie which— narcissistically, errotically—believes in its own creative power to wander away from its origins and establish the alternative realm of the non-natural" (315). Remaining true to Bloom, Bielik-Robson reminds us how fragile the compound of faith and knowledge is in antithetical criticism. Not so much despite as because of the impressive intelligence and learning of this study, one obtains from it a sharp sense of why Bloom moved on in the 1980s, letting speculation and struggle cede to phrase-making and mockery—the impatient, grand gestures of the genius of the Western canon.

———

I am a comic critic, and all I get are serious reviews.

Harold Bloom to Imre Salusinszky

This survey of Bloom's writing and persona suggests not just that aesthetic experience can resemble shock—a theme in philosophical aesthetics from Plato to Adorno—but that a memory keyed to shocklike aesthetic experience will display traits of a repetition compulsion, as though the cherished text were equally a wound.[46] ("I've come to understand that the quality of memorability and inevitability that I assumed came from intense pleasure may actually have come from a kind of pain.")[47] I should stress that I am not claiming to describe the actual psychic economy at work in the human being Harold Bloom; the effort here has been to read the composite text of his performance as media figure and influence-theorist. According to that text, the genius-critic's power to store and consciously to retrieve aesthetic text ("the canon")—a power so overwhelming that it demands to be described by analogy with a recording technology—also manifests itself as a melancholy attachment. The cherished text is also always the lost object; its inscription on the mind is the missed experience that makes the text present to memory. That nonsubjective moment of inscription then gets overlaid with figures of voice and ear (the "oral" scene of voicing; the "auditory and aesthetic" memory), which eventuate as identity and proper name, and finally become the valorized proper names that animate Bloom's prose. Bloom's text thus makes legible a radically figurative process of personification that at once undermines and underwrites his own personification in the media as the Genius of the Canon.

But it is appropriate that a literary character like Bloom be allowed to inhabit a more exciting sort of story, or be allowed to tell one; so, by way of conclusion, let me draw attention to an intriguing moment in the Bloom corpus that occurs not in an essay but in an interview he accorded Imre Salusinszky in November 1985. About halfway through the interview, Bloom launches into a polemic—yet once more—against critics who fault him for writing socially irrelevant criticism. He accuses his accusers of self-righteousness and *ressentiment*, and he affirms the "solitary pleasure" of the act of criticism; at a certain point, however, this solitary pleasure yields to an anecdote involving two critics and two bodies:

> The best critic and best human being I've known in my life was my dear friend Paul de Man. "The trouble with you, Harold," he would say with a smile, cupping my head in his hands, and looking at me with an affection that

always made me want to weep, "is that you are crazy: you do not believe in the 'troot.'" I would look at him, shake my head sadly, and say:

"No, I do not believe in the 'troot' because there is no 'troot,' dear Paul.

"There is no method: there is only yourself, and you are highly idiosyncratic.

"And you clone, my dear: I dislike what you do as a teacher, because your students are as alike as two peas in a pod."[48]

Short versions of this exchange appear many times in Bloom's writing— it is his de Man sound-bite: a little act of memory, mourning, and self-affirmation that he has never stopped performing—but this particular version has intriguing elaborations.[49] When, many years ago, I first read the second sentence in this extract, I blinked and read again to confirm that in this remarkable scene—all the more remarkable if, like myself, you have a distant memory of glimpsing from afar these august professors having a decorous coffee together, in New Haven in the late 1970s—yes, de Man is cupping *Bloom's* head, not his own head, in his, de Man's hands.[50] The scene is bizarre, a little grotesque—and comic, and oddly sweet; and it tempts absurd questions: How are the rest of their bodies disposed? How long does the gesture last? Is de Man, for instance, still cupping Bloom's head when it begins shaking sadly? During the Bloomian admonishment? Does the tenderness of de Man's gaze ever waver; does his smile narrow or broaden as he undergoes Bloom's tender chastisement? The storyteller is having his fun, and, with flamboyant self-consciousness, has given his characters the identifying marks they sport in many another academic anecdote featuring de Man or Bloom ("the troot"; "my dear"). In that sense, like all good gossip, it is a highly encoded subliterary story, and we may pause over it a moment longer.

As in a painting by Mark Tansey or a "Yale Critics for Beginners" comic, Bloom and de Man are wrestling. Theirs is a rigged match, of course, and at first glance the antithetical critic, the theorist of agon who is staging this agon for us and for his interlocutor, seems to control all the moves. He rebukes the conceptual rhetorician—the "highly idiosyncratic" but sinful man who has fallen into the error of truth, and who, blind to his own idiosyncrasy, destroys that of his students. The conceptual rhetorician "clones." Bloom's slightly peculiar intransitive use of the verb grants an extra touch of surreality to this dramatic dialogue. Are there actually more than two figures in this scene of instruction? Is Bloom wrestling with a deManic multiplicity, whose name is legion? That would suit the pathos and self-aggrandizement of the narrative, to be sure—and yet this cloning power complicates the other's idiosyncrasy and loveable humanity, troubles the scene's specular structure, and ironizes Bloom's moral. What does it mean to be "only yourself" if the self—the "best human being I've known in my life," at that—has such terrible powers of reproduction? And if de Man's students themselves have nothing but their idiosyncratic selves, through what process do they become pod people, "two peas in a pod"—a twoness at odds with the seemingly more stable twoness of de Man and Bloom with which we began?

Consider one other peculiarity in this little anecdote: the overbalanced, or underweighted, distribution of pathos. Under the affectionate gaze of the beloved other, Bloom wants to weep. He feels himself loved, overloved. In the next chapter we are going to be examining John Guillory's shrewd characterization of de Manian charisma as the effect of a master's apparent indifference to the love his disciples offer him. Here things seem reversed, at least for a moment: the master, de Man, gives love superabundantly—and receives a lesson to boot. Yet it is Bloom, the lesson-giver, who holds back tears. He is not the master's master after all. It is still de Man—Bloom's de Man, to be sure: the de Man of this little fantasy—who runs the show, because, reaching out to cup Bloom's head, he offers love without caring whether or not he is loved back. That is the excess of love that brings Bloom close to tears. He will never be able to repay this gift. Giving or withholding love, the master, de Man, retains the power of his indifference; this is to say that his selfhood, though ungovernably multiple in its self-replication, is also more singular and whole, more unified than Bloom's. It is Bloom who tells this story, who summons his friend from the grave, puts him right and lays him to rest; yet Bloom's very need to perform such gestures makes him the needy one. He can never win.

And who would know this better than Bloom? "Wrestling Jacob could triumph, because his Adversary was the Everliving, but even the strongest poets must grapple with phantoms" (*Map*, 17). The specter always returns. Yet if Bloom can never win, he has nonetheless told a winning story that ironizes, even burlesques its own sentimentality, indulges in love, personifies and thus wards off a threat, while gently parodying the specular, agonistic, obsessed thematics of Bloom's own theoretical plot. The comic and erotic excesses of this fantasy, in other words, both undermine and reenact its announced moral. Selfhood turns uncertain, but the flamboyant storyteller reaffirms his identity through the very narrative overload that calls into question his authority. The satisfactions of gloominess and aggressive burlesque are not dissimilar. And we may understand the pathos and the narrative and figurative excess of Bloom's theories of agon and influence as serving just such a double role—providing him, that is, with a way to evoke, enjoy, and contradict the anonymity, instability, and inscriptive force that makes literary passion memorable.

5. Professing Theory
Paul de Man and the Institution of Reading

Over the course of this book, we have been inching toward the polarizing figure at the symbolic heart of the "theory" phenomenon, Paul de Man; and in this chapter I shall finally engage directly and at length not so much de Man's work—which has received abundant and sometimes excellent commentary over the years—as a dense and interesting moment in the history of de Man's reception.[1] To discuss the reception of a text, however, is also to explain one's understanding of the text, since the truth-claim of a theory can be deferred but not avoided; the same holds, of course, when one is reading a text that reads a text that reads other texts, and so on down the line. The pages that follow offer a sustained, at times slow-crawl interpretation and evaluation of John Guillory's interpretation and evaluation of de Man in his classic study, *Cultural Capital: The Problem of Literary Canon Formation* (1993), and that effort will involve a substantive (if necessarily limited) unpacking of de Man's theoretical statement.[2] In the years that have passed since Guillory's book appeared, his critique of de Man has become famous enough to be invoked across a remarkable range of academic venues and genres when de Manian deconstruction is being debunked and a leavening of scholarly authority is desired.[3] Guillory's reputation as a formidable critic of de Man is unquestionably deserved. Nowhere else, so far as I know, in the extensive archive of critical writing on deconstruction will one find a comparably informed and closely argued negative account of de Manian rhetorical reading, backed up by knowledgeable engagement with a wide range of de Man's texts. It is one of the peculiarities of de Man's reception that, despite (or perhaps because of) the sulfurous passion his work has so often elicited, sharply disputative criticism of his work has often tended to be local—focused on a point of interpretation—or highly abstract, or scatter-shot. On its merits alone, Guillory's argument deserves careful consideration; but there are at least two other reasons why his reading holds interest in the present context.[4] In the first place, it offers an interesting counterpart to the journalistic antideconstructive writing that we evoked at the beginning of this book. There, the challenge was to explain how critics can be "right" (in the sense of being right to be anxious) about texts they manifestly do not understand; here, the challenge is to explain the vitiating recurrence of antitheoretical stereotypes within vibrantly intelligent critical prose. For Guillory's brilliant interpretation of de Man speaks with a voice that we may characterize, without exaggeration or malice, as an *institutional* voice. Yet— and this is the second reason why his work repays study here—his argument, brushed backward, will allow us to read the degree to which de Man was a theorist *of* institutionalization and institution. The sociological argument of *Cultural Capital* returns us to the question of theory's institutional condition of possibility. We shall see that Guillory's chapter on de Man is driven by his book's aesthetic agenda, and that it offers us a finely symptomatic example of aesthetic-institutional resistance to theory; yet its strenuous reduction of de Manian theory to sociological symptom releases a truth that more conventional accounts of de Man are likely to overlook.

—+—

Let me first recall Guillory's overall project and draw attention to some of his argument's vectors and fault-lines. *Cultural Capital*'s fundamental proposition is twofold: first, that the "canon debate" has been "misconceived from the start," and second, that this misconceived debate symptomatically registers a "crisis in literary study" (vii). The debate is misconceived insofar as it reduces the problem of canon formation to a question of representation, falsely rendering symbolic representation in the canon analogous to political representation in a polity. Such a representational notion of the canon makes the canon into "a hypothetical *image* of social diversity," and this politics of the image renders invisible the institution within which canon-formation actually occurs—"the school, and the institutional forms of syllabus and curriculum" (vii). Furthermore, it hampers a critical inquiry into the category of "literature" itself. Literature is a form of "cultural capital," and it is the school's function to regulate and distribute cultural capital, and thereby reproduce the inequities of the social order.[5] Here we encounter, as the book's main thesis, the "crisis in literary study":

> The overarching project of the present study is an inquiry into just this crisis, one which attempts to explain why the category of literature has come to seem institutionally dysfunctional, a circumstance which I will related to the emergence of a technically trained "New Class" or "professional-managerial class."

> To put this thesis in its briefest form, the category of "literature" names the
> cultural capital of the old bourgeoisie, a form of capital increasingly marginal to
> the social function of the present educational system. (x)

Over five meaty chapters, *Cultural Capital* seeks to make good this claim.
Chapter 1 directly engages the canon debate and its shortcomings, emphasizing that mimetic notions of the canon as mirror of social diversity efface the
true sociological role of the school by way of a quasi-sociological conception
of literature as "expressive of the author's *experience*. . . . The author returns
in the critique of the canon, not as the genius, but as the representative of a
social identity" (10). What the school is really about is access to literacy in
the sense of "the systematic regulation of reading and writing," which is "a
question of the distribution of cultural goods rather than the representation
of cultural images" (18); it is in this way that the school reproduces unequal
social relations. And what literature is really about is "linguistic differentia-
tion as a social fact" (64): Literature is the production of a (socially) marked
language within (written forms of) the vernacular. The decline of literary
study in the schools in the late twentieth century responds to the fact that
language marked "literary" no longer functions as "the privileged agent of
ideological subjection."[6]

Chapters 2–4 make up a section Guillory calls "Case Studies," and
compose a broadly historical trajectory with three focal points: the historical origins of the modern category of "literature"; the mid-twentieth-
century professionalization of literary criticism as close reading; and the late
twentieth-century doubling of the literary by the "theory" canon. Chapter 2
reads Gray's *Elegy* as an exemplary "'translation' of classical literacy into an
anthology of quotable vernacular phrases" (x), and thus as a vehicle for examining the emergence of "literature"; under this lens, literature is revealed
as "the discursive category devised to accommodate vernacular works in the
schools" (87). Chapter 3 focuses on the New Critical revision of the canon:
according to Guillory, the technique of close reading produced for the university a new kind of literary language, and thus a new articulation of social
distinction, by way of which "the cultural capital of literature" could be "set
against a 'mass culture' which at once reveres and neglects the monuments
of High Culture" (xii).

Chapter 4, "Literature after Theory," is the de Man chapter we shall
be engaging at length. Here Guillory argues that the "moment of theory
is determined . . . by a certain defunctioning of the literary curriculum, a
crisis in the market value of its cultural capital occasioned by the emergence
of a professional-managerial class which no longer requires the (primarily

literary) cultural capital of the old bourgeoisie" (xii); symptoms of this crisis include the appearance of an alternative "canon" of theoretical texts, and above all—for reasons to be discussed—the exemplary phenomenon of de Manian rhetorical reading.

The final chapter, "The Discourse of Value: From Adam Smith to Barbara Herrnstein Smith," is set off from the rest of the book by also being "Part Three: Aesthetics." In this section, Guillory takes issue with pragmatists such as Barbara Herrnstein Smith who negate aesthetic specificity by discovering "use value" in art, thereby conflating economic and aesthetic "value." In response, Guillory offers a history of the notion of value: he rehearses the origins of modern aesthetics in eighteenth-century political economy, arguing that Pierre Bourdieu's description of "the emergence of aesthetic production as a 'relatively autonomous' field of cultural activity in the eighteenth century" offers a less reductive and more historically attentive approach to aesthetics than the neopragmatist reduction of value to use. He concludes with a ringing endorsement of aesthetic judgment, and with a utopian "thought experiment" that imagines the "transformation of cultural capital into pure 'symbolic distinction'" (339):

> Even were such an [idealized] educational system no longer to regulate access to cultural capital in the grotesquely unequal way it presently does, cultural producers would still compete to have their products read, studied, looked at, heard, lived in, sung, worn, and would still accumulate cultural capital in the form of "prestige" or fame. But social distinctions reinstated on such an aesthetic basis would have to be expressed in social relations as distinctions in "life-style," in other words as a vast enlargement of the field of aesthetic judgment. . . . The point is not to make judgment disappear but to reform the conditions of its practice. If there is no way out of the game of culture, then, even when cultural capital is the only kind of capital, there may be another kind of game, with less dire consequences for the losers, an *aesthetic* game. Socializing the means of production and consumption would be the condition of an aestheticism unbound, not its overcoming. But of course, this is only a thought experiment. (339, 340)

Cultural Capital thus concludes with a fantasy about an Aesthetic State, hedged about with signs of fictionality (as, we may note, such aesthetic-political imaginings traditionally are, from Friedrich Schiller onward: "But does such a State of Aesthetic Semblance really exist? . . . As a realized fact, we are likely to find it, like the pure Church and the pure Republic, only in some few chosen circles").[7]

This brief recapitulation of a rich book allows, I hope, enough of a sense of its overall project to allow us to understand Guillory's interest in confronting the work of Paul de Man. *Cultural Capital* offers food for thought and debate along many lines, many of which cannot be pursued here. It is doubtless the case that, ever since the demise of the classical curriculum in the late nineteenth century, the American university has had as its main task, along with knowledge production, the credentialing of a professional-managerial and technical class, particularly in the wake of the massive expansion of the university system during the Cold War. I think one can plausibly follow Guillory in pointing to a disinvestment in literature as cultural capital, though this is a complicated matter since, as I have noted before in this book, a rhetoric of acculturation continues to do work in elite institutional contexts. Some of Guillory's formulations in *Cultural Capital* draw too sharp a contrast between high and "mass" culture; and in more recent writings he has proposed finer-grained accounts of various aspects of the structure and history of the American higher educational system. Elite levels of that very stratified system provide a kind of acculturation that draws on elements of traditional high culture, precisely by way of marketing their product *as* elite; Guillory writes of a "culture of professionalism" or "culture lite" that translates in limited ways into "social capital" in the higher levels of the American class system.[8] The quite limited but strikingly stubborn persistence of the humanities major on a national level over the past decades speaks to the social importance of a certain kind of attenuated ("middlebrow") literary capital in our era. One would also want to register the diffusion of that cultural capital in the mass-cultural mode of allusion, citation, simplification, parody, revision, and so on, as part of what Fredric Jameson famously identifies as the folding of "aesthetic production . . . into commodity production generally."[9] I leave these interesting issues aside, but to some extent they tangle into the large question of the role of aesthetic discourses and practices in modernity: a question that we have encountered repeatedly in this book, and one that Guillory's book is also working to engage.

The category of the aesthetic figures significantly in Guillory's study, as my summary of his book's closing chapter indicated. Though on the one hand "there is no realm of pure aesthetic experience," on the other hand there is a "*specificity*" of aesthetic experience that is not contingent upon its 'purity'" (336). That claim is one I would endorse; the question is whether Guillory is able entirely to mean what he says here. Pressuring this difference between the pure and the specific, Peggy Kamuf, in her 1995 review of *Cultural Capital*, wonders whether a certain purity is not being smuggled through the sociological customs-house, and whether Guillory's utopian conclusion does not ultimately promise "a relation that is no-relation . . . a specificity

and a property of 'the cultural' without the admixture or contamination of
'the economic' . . . a reclaimed, integral humanities curriculum able to pose
itself independently of the technical training required by the 'professional-
managerial class'" (62). Kamuf argues—and from a different angle we shall be
confirming her diagnosis in the pages that follow—that Guillory's project is
driven by a desire to "'reimagine' the object of literary study as nontechnical,
autonomous, or specifically aesthetic" (69), and that in consequence he needs
to expel the specter of deconstruction, which has "from the beginning and
without reprieve, insisted on the *technicity* of the idea, on the iterability of
the proper, on the divisibility of any mark of division, and therefore on the
necessary contamination of any posed or supposed purity" (64). As Kamuf
emphasizes, iterability, according to the Derridean analysis, is what makes
language, culture, literature, and for that matter life itself possible; and since
iterability as "the possibility of a certain exteriority, or difference" enables
and constitutes institutional space and institutionality per se, deconstruction
can never be "simply *against* institutions as such" (67). Guillory's repression
of the quasi-concept of iterability causes the anti-institutional, antitechnical
idealism that he chastises and expels as "deconstruction" to return within
his own discourse—perhaps most dramatically as his concluding "thought
experiment" of an aestheticized society in which cultural capital has been
decisively disentangled from economic and political capital, and in which
citizens accumulate cultural capital as "'prestige' or fame" as part of an "aesthetic game" without economic or political consequence. One can sharpen
Kamuf's point: this utopia puts on display an aestheticism that, in an ironic
reversal of Guillory's earlier affirmation, is *pure* (insofar as it is framed away
from material consequence) but not *specific* (insofar as it is "unbound"). The
frame of the game (the socialized system of "production and consumption")
must be impermeable, immune to contamination from its superstructure,
if it is to shelter its individualistic and competitive player-citizens within a
purely symbolic economy. Could any artistic practice worthy of the name
tolerate such aesthetic purity (even in and as fiction)? What reserves of violence would be required to keep this symbolic order imagining itself pure—
unscathed, unhaunted by risk and finitude, sealed off from its own death
drive? As with all renderings of an Aesthetic State, the risk-free zone turns
dystopic or illusory with a flick of the finger, not because of any ambiguity in
the humane impulse behind this thought experiment, but because aesthetic
discourse comes with a certain acknowledgment of iterability—of technicity,
risk, and finitude—built into its idealizing momentum. Yet, as we reviewed
in Chapter 1, redemptive affirmations of aesthetic pedagogy and experience
play a remarkably prominent role in the rhetoric of higher education in the

United States, and it is small wonder that *Cultural Capital*, as an eloquent and intelligent text well within the broad Arnoldian tradition, has known such uncomplicated success within the professional bureaucracy it chastises.

We may now turn to Guillory's confrontation with the thought, figure, and legacy of de Man. Kamuf, whose main concern is to dispute Guillory's strategic conflation of "deconstruction" with "de Man," offers little help here; indeed, one gains the impression that she feels it necessary to rekey the discussion to a Derridean idiom if deconstruction is to stand revealed as a thinking of institutionalization.[10] But to ignore Guillory's engagement with de Manian theory is to ignore the heart of his book. Guillory is a powerful writer at all times—allowing oneself to be borne up and along by his rolling, organ-toned prose is one of the regular pleasures of reading him—and, in his long, passionate chapter on de Man (the longest chapter in the book), his writing, while losing none of its eloquence, achieves a new level of intensity and aggressivity. We approach here what a phenomenologically minded critic would call *Cultural Capital*'s imaginative center and origin: the spur or irritant or trauma around which the text grew.

Guillory's chapter on de Man begins with a legible if perhaps not entirely conscious effort to account for its own passion, for its first step is to identify de Man as a symptomatic figure, a stand-in for "theory" per se. He suggests—rightly, in my opinion, of course—that, however erroneous it may seem at first glance, the journalistic equation between "theory" and "deconstruction" merits serious consideration as a *symptom*—as does the concomitant association of the name "de Man" with "deconstruction" as "theory":

> The immense symptomatic significance of the *figure* of de Man has been
> indisputably confirmed by the paroxysm which passed through the entire
> critical profession in the wake of the revelations concerning de Man's war-
> time journalism. It would not have been necessary for so many theorists and
> antitheorists, de Manians and anti-de Manians, to "respond" to these revelations
> if *theory itself* were not perceived to be implicated in the figure of de Man. The
> easy condemnation in the media of theory along with de Man only confirmed
> a symbolic equation already present in the professional imaginary. A symptom-
> atic reading of the de Manian corpus will elucidate this equation along the axis
> of imaginary identification: theory-deconstruction-de Man. (Guillory 178–79)

Noting that de Man's essay "The Resistance to Theory" offers a (de Manian, theoretical) version of the same "imaginary" sequence of identifications (theory as deconstruction as rhetorical reading), Guillory sets out to characterize de Manian theory as the essence of the symptom, as it were—and as the effect of a sociological cause. The argument pursues a triple movement. In a first move, Guillory reworks and develops the link between de Man and theory by arguing that theory "objectif[ies] the charisma of the master teacher as a methodology" (179). Theory, in other words, "is" the transference—the transfer of the transference from the master onto the master's theory, which is in fact what the master desires. In the second phase of the argument Guillory shifts attention to the theory itself, arguing that "the equation of literature with rhetoric" constitutes an ideology that has as its rationale an institutional defense of literature: "Literary theory as a version of rhetoricism defends literature from its half-perceived and half-acknowledged social marginality" (180). This second phase also involves an argument that characterizes theory's "rhetoricism" as a covertly theme-driven enterprise: rhetorical reading is a "linguistic determinism" driven by a master-theme of "determined indeterminacy" (230). Finally, in a third and finely synthetic move, Guillory argues that deconstruction offers an "imaginary reduction of the social to an instance of the linguistic" (237). Rhetorical reading's "thematic of fate" becomes the "rigor of methodology" (231), which, as the pathos of rigor—the cathexis of boredom itself—functions as an unconscious recapitulation of contemporary "conditions of institutional life" (245). That is, "the adjustment of critical practice to new socioinstitutional conditions of literary pedagogy is registered symptomatically within theory by its tendency to model the intellectual work of the theorist on the new social form of intellectual work, the technobureaucratic labor of the new professional-managerial class" (181). Theory is thus revealed to be a symptom of, and a defense against, the increasing marginality of literary culture, and the increasing bureaucratization of the professoriat. Theory reinvigorates the ideology of professionalism by reasserting charismatic authority in a technobureaucratic context, which is why, Guillory claims, de Man's disciples imagine their master to be "outside" the institution, and teaching a doctrine subversive of the institution. As Guillory summarizes near the end of his chapter, de Manian theory

> registers at the heart of its terminology the historical moment of the fusion of the university teacher's autonomous "professional activity" with the technobureaucratic organization of intellectual labor. Within the larger discourse of "theory," rhetorical reading has the important symptomatic function of figuring a rapprochement with the institutional conditions of criticism, by acknowledg-

ing the loss of intellectual autonomy as a theory of linguistic determinism—at
the same time that autonomy is continually reinvested in the figure of the
master theorist. But this is an autonomy which exists only on the imaginary
outside of the institution, as an "anti-institutional" charisma. (259)

It is a brilliant argument, and, in its wide-ranging acquaintance with de Man's
texts, an impressively detailed one. For once a critic hostile to de Man has
had the requisite obsessive energy to read through de Man's work, as well as
the talent to displace it forcefully. As noted earlier, I know of no comparably
impressive attempt to dominate (and thus, in the end, annihilate) de Manian
theory. It will thus be well worth the effort to retrace our steps more slowly
now, so as to begin the work of evaluating the claims and interpretations
making up this argument.

Guillory's account of de Manian charisma and de Manian discipleship,
while not entirely unprecedented and ultimately not without its limitations,
is in many respects very powerful.[11] All pedagogy activates transferential relationships, but de Man's ability to inspire love and emulation—an *excess*
of transference—is part of the record (which is also to say the legend or
phantasmatics) of his reception. The question is what to make of this phenomenon. Guillory's description of the skewed love between disciple and
master and of the disciple's transference of the transference onto the theory
of the master could hardly be bettered, so long as we judge that the lexicon
of mastery and discipleship serves our understanding of the situation. It is all
there: the charisma of the master, whose professed indifference to the disciple's love causes the disciple to work endlessly for the master's ever-withheld
recognition; the disciple's transfer of the transference onto the theory that
the master embodies, to the point that the disciple imitates the master "at
the micro-level of style" (199); the master's investment in this transfer, which
allows pedagogy to survive as doctrine; the extra spin put on all these ma-
neuvers by a theory that, even more stringently than psychoanalysis, identifies transference with resistance. (For de Man, as we recalled in Chapter 1,
theory, in its very transferability or teachability, *is* its own resistance to itself:
resistance inheres both in the movement of theoretical thought from the
specificity of a reading to the generality of a conceptual claim, and in the
personifying dynamic whereby intersubjective relations come to substitute
for linguistic ones. Both master and disciple, according to this account, move
within endless loops of resistance.) The arguments of *Cultural Capital* have
not often been engaged by deconstructive critics, with the exception of
Kamuf; but it is of interest that in at least one case a putative de Man "disciple," Thomas Pepper, has testified to the force of this section of Guillory's

text, confessing that "it is astonishing for me to see many of the insights it took me years to glean from closer readings of de Man's text presented by Guillory in the thick description of an institutional context." Indeed, Pepper then goes on to displace some aggression onto the fantasized figures of *other* disciples who haven't submitted to Guillory's discipline: "Unfortunately, his work has remained unread by those whose predicament is best described in it."[12] This is the sort of thing de Manians often say about de Man himself ("his work has remained unread," particularly by "those whose predicament is best described in it"); and if for a brief moment Guillory comes to resemble or even replace de Man in Pepper's discourse, one must at the very least credit Guillory's analysis with the power necessary to reimpose a mild version of the very phenomenon it studies and seeks to demystify.

And if power, as that formulation hints, is not necessarily purchasable without loss of knowledge, one has reason to ask whether Guillory's study of the "transference of the transference onto theory" can really claim to have mastered its object of study. There are, as I have said, limits to his approach. Though Guillory notes in passing that transferential effects can happen at a distance, he focuses his account entirely on the seminar, and on the kind of transference that most lends itself to being characterized (which is really to say, denounced) as "discipleship." The graduate student who loves the teacher, and by extension the teacher's texts and the texts the teacher loves, is the governing paradigm of "influence" here. The result is that Guillory on the one hand writes very well (if very aggressively) about a certain kind of student that de Man is famous for producing—the graduate student who imitates the teacher's style, writes repeatedly about the bits of Rousseau or Wordsworth or Kant that de Man himself wrote about, and so on—and on the other hand has little or nothing to say about more mediated forms of theory's transmission, or about the wider ripples caused by the impact of de Manian thought.[13] Why Guillory has limited his focus in this way is not hard to apprehend. This is the first installment of a polemic that sets out to reduce the content of de Manian theory to the charisma of its teacher, thereby restricting the reach of this theory to a certain place and time and a highly defined pedagogical context. To adapt one of Guillory's favored turns of phrase we may say that he thus commits himself to an *imaginary reduction to the seminar* of the pedagogico-scientific institutions in and through which theory is replicated and disseminated. His analysis forecloses the larger context of de Man's reception—and that of "theory" itself; for however much one might agree with Guillory that de Man has phantasmatically embodied theory for the professoriate, theory—even as "deconstruction"—is of course not *simply* equivalent to de Manian rhetorical reading. The considerable and diffuse, if erratic influence of Jacques Derrida's work on the academy has obviously *not* travelled primarily by way of the seminar. De Man's association with the seminar is powerful, and deserves scrupulous analysis, but it is in the end an imaginary association, and forms part of the phantasmatics of a "de Man effect" that it has been one of my main objects in this book to try to situate and analyze.

"No legacy without transference," Derrida proposes;[14] and indeed, Guillory's imaginary reduction of theory's dissemination to the seminar is itself our first and largest clue that his analysis is itself being distorted by the transferential effect it describes. I have characterized the writing in this chapter as passionate, and I shall in a moment begin tracking some telling distortions; for the moment let us simply register the more trivial observation that, in this chapter, citations from de Man salt Guillory's prose with a readiness of reference that many a "disciple" might envy—to the point that a quotation from "Semiology and Rhetoric" is even given the last word, directing and capping the chapter's closing sentence ("One may predict, without resorting to prophecy, that such reconceptualization will become 'the task of literary criticism in the coming years'" [Guillory 265]).[15] One need not be a critic of particularly deconstructive or psychoanalytic stripe to feel that such strenuous wrestling with a "master," in conjunction with an analysis that gets a good deal of rhetorical mileage out of relegating the master's students to the anonymity of "disciplehood" (a fratricidal fantasy all the more satisfying when one recalls that many of these "disciples" were Guillory's graduate school and junior faculty colleagues at Yale), tends to cast the agonist as, in Guillory's own words, a "disciple who struggles heretically with the master" (a kind of discipleship, he adds, "I will not discuss here") (198–99). But if Guillory "knows," as we say, his own Oedipal predicament, that knowledge is complicated by the negative-transferential passion with which he denies knowledge to others—to the other disciples, of course, who in this account are little more than bright-eyed dupes, but above all to the master himself. That is the whole point of this section of the chapter, and the locus of its most startling distortions.

Guillory's project throughout is to roll de Man up backward: systematically to reverse the thrust of his texts and thereby render "theory" a symptom—an effect of processes beyond theory's self-knowledge, which is to say beyond the theory *qua* theory. If de Manian theory subordinates the theorist to an impersonal linguistic imperative, Guillory will reverse the poles and discover the theorist in advance of the theory, just as he will eventually discover the institution in advance of the theorist. The charisma-and-discipleship phase of the argument, therefore, as noted above, sets out to reduce theory to the person of Paul de Man. On the one hand—I shall come back to this ambiguity—Guillory's project is not to "disprove the argument of deconstruction" but merely to study the "symptomatology of the de Manian oeuvre" (179); on the other hand, he is seeking to destroy the claims of that oeuvre, and it thus becomes all-important to show that the oeuvre, as symptom, is blind. He thus faces the fantastic task of showing that de Man is blind to the transference. Working his way around de Man's claim in "The Resistance to Theory" that "teaching is not primarily an intersubjective relationship between people but a cognitive process in which self and other are only tangentially involved" (RT, 4), Guillory suggests that de Man "forecloses" the psychoanalytical, adding with a telling abruptness that "if psychoanalytic terms nevertheless pervade [de Man's] essay," this "results from the threatening public prestige of psychoanalysis" (191). It is a sign of weakness to come. The actual argument deserves more attention than I can accord it here—Guillory is proposing that de Man's notion of the self is phenomenological rather than psychoanalytic, that his transfer of the cognitive function from the self to language shunts aside the properly psychoanalytic notion of the subject, and that his displacement of psychoanalytic terms into rhetorical ones actually works to "preserve the phenomenological self of self-reflection" (194). That argument is, I believe, wrong (language, in de Man, is not centered in self-reflection: it is torn apart at its origin by the divergence between its performative and cognitive dimensions), but it is an argument worth having. But that flashing moment of sociologico-personalistic reduction (*public* prestige? of *psychoanalysis*?) registers the extremity of Guillory's need to evacuate de Man's text of self-knowledge. De Man's blindness to the transference needs to be total, uncontaminated by even glimmers of insight: "What de Man has no patience for at all, not even the patience to name, is the notion of transference" (193). "The one analytic concept which cannot be named within this displaced terminology is transference itself, which orchestrates the severance of affect from agency" (194). "The doctrinal insight into the 'linguistic predicament' needs to be read at every moment as symptomatically blind to the *necessary* relation between theory and discipleship" (207).

The problem Guillory faces is that de Man's texts talk about transference constantly. This is, after all, a theory that sets out to say something about figurative language—and "transference," whatever else it means, irreducibly means figuration: the "movement" of figurative transfer. Out of that linguistic black hole (or *mythologie blanche*) spiral any number of narrative lines in de Man's work that address the kind of phenomena Guillory has in mind. De Manian theory is certainly well equipped to explain such phenomena as the master's charisma, the "transfer of the transference onto theory," and the loving obsessiveness of discipleship. The pseudo-dialectic of *Allegories of Reading* derives such phenomena from the predicament of reading that the theory theorizes: the deconstruction of referential systems of language generates the "deconstructive passion of a subject" as an illusory center of authority (199). This master-subject is precisely the revered object of fantasy, the *sujet supposé savoir*, that Guillory has analyzed; he is

> as far beyond pleasure and pain as he is beyond good and evil, or, for that
> matter, beyond strength and weakness. His consciousness is neither happy nor
> unhappy, nor does he possess any power. He remains, however, a center of au-
> thority to the extent that the very destructiveness of his ascetic reading testifies
> to the validity of his interpretation (*AR*, 173–74).

This is, perhaps, merely a dry moment in an allegory of reading (soon to be devoured in the next beat of the reading); but elsewhere de Man's allegories undergo vivid narrative embodiment. One thinks of the ephebe in Kleist's *Marionettentheater*, whose gracefulness is "not an end in itself, but a device to impress the teacher":

> What the young man is ashamed of is not his lack of grace but the exposure
> of his desire for self-recognition. As for the teacher's motives in accepting to
> enter into these displacements of identity, they are even more suspect than those
> of the younger person, to the precise extent that sadism is morally and socially
> more suspect than masochism. Socrates (or, for that matter, Winckelmann)
> certainly had it coming to him. (*RR*, 278)

Or the tricky remarks on institutional and generational succession in the "Introduction" to the special issue of *Studies in Romanticism*, or in the foreword to Carol Jacobs's *The Dissimulating Harmony*.[16] My object here is not to read and do justice to these various texts, but simply to provide a bit of documentary backing for the observation that de Man understood the "linguistic" as possessed of inescapable, if also unreliable, referential and performative force. If for de Man it is possible "that the entire construction of drives, substitutions, repressions, and representations, is the aberrant, metaphorical correlative of the absolute randomness of language" (*AR*, 299), this does not mean that we ever leave drives, substitutions, repressions and representations behind. It is actually hard to think of a critic who is *more* alive to the finer shades of complicity, desire, guilt, ruthlessness, and so on than de Man; whatever else one thinks of his analysis of Rousseau's purloining of the ribbon, it is certainly not a reading easily accusable of psychological naiveté.

Guillory's account of de Man and the transference culminates in a truly strange attempt to strip de Man's discourse of its self-irony. He quotes de Man's comments on Bakhtin's seductiveness in "Dialogue and Dialogism," which I reproduce here:

> the circulation of more or less clandestine class or seminar notes by initiated disciples or, even more symptomatic, the rumored (and often confirmed) existence of unpublished manuscripts made available only to an enterprising or privileged researcher and which will decisively seal one mode of interpretation at the expense of all rival modes—at least until one of the rivals will, in his turn, discover the real or imaginary counter-manuscript on which to base his counterclaim. What in the context of our topic interests us primarily in this situation is that it is bound to engender a community tied together by the common task of decrypting the repressed message hidden in the public utterance. As the sole retainers of an esoteric knowledge, this community is bound to be small, self-selective, and likely to consider itself a chosen elite. (*RT*, 108; cited in Guillory 206–07)

And here is Guillory's commentary: "De Man's contempt for Bakhtinian discipleship is so completely without irony as to constitute the purest form of negation, a simulacrum of irony." One hardly knows what to do with such a straining claim; as in the following sentence, in which we are told that de Man is "merely venting a contempt for discipleship as imitation" in this passage (207), one's attention is forced away from the peculiarities of the primary text by those of the secondary one.

It is not enough, of course, to reduce the theory to a person, a charismatic master, since the master's blindness signifies his subordination to forces beyond his control. The critique will have to move on. It is not yet done with him, however—it will never be done with him: the momentum of personification demands that he be credited with a certain knowledge and a range of intentions (generally negative ones, of course). We have seen Guillory's de Man displacing Freudian terminology because of "the threatening public prestige of psychoanalysis"; later de Man's critique of aesthetic ideology will be said to represent a last-ditch attempt "to preempt the second wave of 'left' reaction to deconstruction" (239). What makes Guillory's book exceptional is that such comments—subsociological in their eagerness to return phenomena to the cunning and fear of an individual—pop up within tenacious, sophisticated arguments far more ambitious in scope than the personifications to which they have recourse. It is this blend of finesse and brutality that we shall need to interpret if we are to develop Guillory's analysis into something closer to a genuine reading of de Man's relation to the pedagogical institution.

The theorist and his theory, as said, will have to yield authority to historical and sociological narrative. Yet, for these reductions or substitutions really to be able to occur, the theory will have to be decertified as theory. Such is the ambiguity of symptomatic reading that I noted earlier. Theory must be shown to be *wrong*, for otherwise the critique will lose its traction: theory, after all, can be ahistorical, elitist, taught by a charismatic master, propagated by blind disciples, akin to bureaucratic styles of work, etc., and still be truth incarnate. The reduction of the theory to the theorist or to sociological reality remains willful so long as the theory itself remains untouched. The encounter can be delayed but not avoided, and Guillory does his best, in this section of his chapter, to prove theory wrong. His occasional protestations to the contrary ("the indistinction of style and doctrine ... falls short of invalidating the doctrine's truth" [202]; "it is not my intention to prove that such a reduction [of rhetoric to trope] is not possible, only that it has not been demonstrated" [218]; "I shall not be concerned directly with the validity of [de Man's] reading [of Proust]" [221]) form part of an ongoing rhetorical strategy, which intends to empty de Manian discourse of its authority by insisting on that discourse's symptomatic status. But the epistemological question lurks, and Guillory addresses it as he seeks to reduce rhetorical reading to thematic narrative.

I shall therefore have little to say about the first half of this section of the chapter, in which Guillory offers an interesting and informed account of the history of rhetoric, and of the emergence of the discursive categories of literature in the eighteenth century, and linguistics in the twentieth. His purpose here is of course to historicize de Man's interest in rhetoric and literature, suggest de Man's unawareness of the historicity of these discourses, and thereby once again insist on the theory/theorist's blindness ("his theorizing of rhetoric elides the historical conditions that produced the category of the literary out of the very obsolescence of poetics and rhetorics in the school system" [214]). Later I shall gloss one error in this section—Guillory's claim that de Man conflates "the referentially disruptive trope with the Saussurian signifier" (211)—and I shall also come back to the question of what the notions of "literature" and "literariness" mean in de Man. But for the moment let us pass to the claim that "the rhetorical terminology in de Man" is "a covert thematic" (221).

It is a crucial claim: ultimately everything hangs on it, and Guillory offers here his most sustained, patient, and careful engagement with a de Manian text. He chooses as his object de Man's reading of Proust in *Allegories of*

Reading. I shall take the liberty of assuming broad familiarity with de Man's interpretation (which is distributed between Chapter 1 and Chapter 3 of *Allegories*), though of course it will be necessary to do at least some pacing over this well-trodden ground. Guillory focuses on de Man's reading of Marcel reading—reading in his room; here is the passage from Proust's *A la recherche*, in de Man's translation:

> I had stretched out on my bed, with a book, in my room which sheltered, tremblingly, its transparent and fragile coolness from the afternoon sun, behind the almost closed blinds through which a glimmer of daylight had nevertheless managed to push its yellow wings, remaining motionless between the wood and the glass, in a corner, poised like a butterfly. It was hardly light enough to read, and the sensation of the light's splendor was given me only by the noise of Camus ... hammering dusty crates; resounding in the sonorous atmosphere that is peculiar to hot weather, they seemed to spark off scarlet stars; and also by the flies executing their little concert, the chamber music of summer: evocative not in the manner of a human tune that, heard perchance during the summer, afterwards reminds you of it but connected to summer by a more necessary link: born from beautiful days, resurrecting only when they return, containing some of their essence, it does not only awaken their image in our memory; it guarantees their return, their actual persistent, unmediated presence.
>
> The dark coolness of my room related to the full sunlight of the street as the shadow relates to the ray of light, that is to say it was just as luminous and it gave my imagination the total spectacle of the summer, whereas my senses, if I had been on a walk, could only have enjoyed it in fragments; it matched my repose which (thanks to the adventures told by my book and stirring my tranquility) supported like the quiet of a motionless hand in the middle of a running brook the shock and motion of a torrent of activity. (translated and cited in *AR*, 13–14)

De Man famously associates this passage's theme of synesthetic totalization with metaphor, and then argues that the passage ultimately deconstructs its own aesthetic vision by exposing the vision's reliance on, or exposure to, a contingency that de Man associates with metonymy:

> [Proust's passage] contrasts two ways of evoking the natural experience of summer and unambiguously states its preference for one of these ways over the other: the "necessary link" that unites the buzzing of the flies to the summer makes it a much more effective symbol than the tune heard "perchance" during the summer. The preference is expressed by means of a distinction that corresponds to the difference between metaphor and metonymy, necessity and

> chance being a legitimate way to distinguish between analogy and contiguity. The inference of identity and totality that is constitutive of metaphor is lacking in the purely relational metonymic contact: an element of truth is involved in taking Achilles for a lion but none in taking Mr. Ford for a motor car. (*AR*, 14)

The "purely relational metonymic contact," however, turns out to underlie and undermine the metaphorical totalization because, de Man argues, the metaphor "torrent of activity" is in fact doubly metonymic: first because, since it is a cliché, "the coupling of the two terms is not governed by the 'necessary link' of resemblance . . . but dictated by a mere habit of proximity," and second, because "the reanimation of the numbed figure takes place by means of a statement, ('running brook') which happens to be close to it, without however this proximity being determined by a necessity that would exist on the level of transcendental meaning" (*AR*, 66).

Guillory remarks the binary oppositions that seem to line up in de Man's analysis (metaphor vs. metonymy, necessity vs. contiguity) and then asks his leading question: "What if the role assigned to the Jakobsonian tropes were determined from the first by the concepts of necessity and contingency, and tropes were being employed simply as the 'technical' rhetorical names for these thematic notions?" (224). What if, that is, the deconstruction were really being directed by its desire for the pathos of "contingency," for the reassurance, self-aggrandizement, and pedagogical effectivity of an ever-reiterated lesson of self-loss in language? Guillory leans heavily on de Man's idiosyncratic use of rhetorical terminology. The metaphor "does not look at first glance like a metaphor at all since the music of the flies does not substitute for summer in its absence. The music is not *like* the summer; it is as much a part of the summer as the quality of the light, or renewed vegetation" (224). The relationship is one of association rather than analogy, and of part (the flies) for whole (the summer). Guillory notes that de Man has in fact had to call the trope of the flies a synecdoche, and append a footnote admitting that "classical rhetoric generally classifies synecdoche as metonymy." However, "the relationship between part and whole can be understood metaphorically, as is the case, for example, in the organic meta-phors dear to Goethe. Synecdoche is one of the borderline figures that create an ambivalent zone between metaphor and metonymy" (*AR*, 63). For Guillory this means that "it is simply at de Man's own discretion whether to assimilate synecdoche to metonymy or metaphor, and the grounds for the choice have little to do with how tropes actually work. Synecdoche is moved across the border into the domain of metaphor only because the concepts of identity, totality, and necessity have already been imputed to metaphor as its defining attributes" (225). And if what de Man calls metaphor is a vexing issue, what he calls metonymy is even more so, since "torrent of activity" is on the face of it a metaphor. It is reanimated by its proximity to the "running brook," but, Guillory objects, "*there is no metonymy*, unless the actual syntax of the sentence, without which no sentence could exist, is being conflated with the trope of metonymy" (226). Because the Proust passage "contrasts not a metaphor and a metonymy but a metonymy (or synecdoche) 'understood' as a metaphor and a metaphor 'understood' as a metonymy," Guillory concludes that "what de Man called the 'metafigural' level of the text was never anything other than a preexistent thematic, now superimposed upon the figural language of the text." The names of the tropes are indeed important, but only, or precisely, as red herrings: "they permit the methodology to advertise itself as rigorously rhetorical or nonthematic, and therefore to displace its thematic to the unconscious of its own terminology" (227).

Guillory is certainly right to point out that de Man reads the text of rhetoric violently—as violently as he does any other text, which is where things get complicated and interesting, for de Man's violent readings have a way of never quite settling down into the willful or (merely) mistaken, though they can certainly also be very strange.[17] So let us, yet once more, go over the Proust passage, its tropes, and de Man's reading of them. One point must be stressed at the outset: *pace* Guillory, rhetorical reading does not—cannot—characterize itself as simply "nonthematic." As de Man noted in a 1972 revision of his 1967 Gauss lecture on Wordsworth, "reading," as he understands it, "means that the thematic element remains taken into consideration." A merely structural analysis of a text, however exhaustive and rigorous, would fall short of a *reading*: "we look for the delicate area where the thematic, semantic field, and the rhetorical structures begin to interfere with each other, begin to engage each other" (*RCC*, 200). The theme of metaphor as necessary link comes directly from Proust's text as well as indirectly from the metaphysical tradition on which that text draws. As Proust's narrator comments near the end of *A la recherche*: "One can list indefinitely in a description all the objects that figured in the place described, but the truth will begin only when the writer takes two different objects, establishes their relationship, the analogue in the world of art of the unique relation created in the world of science by the laws of causality, and encloses them in the necessary rings (*anneaux nécessaires*) of a beautiful style. Indeed, just as in life, it begins at the moment when, by bringing together a quality shared by two sensations, he draws out their common essence by uniting them with each other, in order to protect them from the contingencies of time, in a metaphor."[18] The sentence is quoted and analyzed in Gérard Genette's classic essay "Métonymie chez Proust" (1972), the text with and against which de Man is writing. Genette studies "the role of metonymy *in metaphor*" in Proust, the way in which "the projection of an analogical rapport on a relation of contiguity" forms "a fundamental tendency of Proustian writing and imagination."[19] Genette proposes that resemblance acquires authenticity in Proust through spatiotemporal relationships (a church spire resembles a fish because the town is by the sea); de Man pries that symbiosis apart. Since Proust is not reporting but imagining, the authenticity of the spatiotemporal world is specious except as an aesthetic effect, brought in to underwrite the necessity and totality that Proust associates thematically with metaphor. A rhetorical reading, pushing the text past its literal statement while remaining within the logic of the text, can thus associate metonymy with what Proust calls above "the contingencies of time." The music of the flies is a synecdoche of summer (Genette comments that "natural" metaphors in Proust "are in fact typically synecdochic substitutions" [58]); the point for the rhetorical reading is that this synecdoche is thematized by the text as an instance of a "necessary link" as opposed to the human tune heard "perchance." (The association of flies with summer may be metonymic, but it is *natural*, like the association of heat with summer.)[20]

As for the "torrent of activity," it is of course a ("dead") metaphor, and the question is whether de Man is justified in sticking onto the deadness of the metaphor and the proximity of the brook the rhetorical label "metonymy." Let us zoom in a bit. In the Proust passage, according to de Man, the figurative recuperation of "the total spectacle of summer" by way of the music of the flies does not suffice to complete the reversal such that "the inwardness of the sheltered reader" would "acquire the power of a concrete action" and shed the guilt of illicit solitude (*AR*, 63, 64). That happens by way of the metaphorical transfer of coolness and warmth, repose and action. Repose supports activity like a reposing hand in a current. The persuasiveness of that analogy, however (according to de Man) depends entirely on the "torrent" that (helped along by an available pun on "*torride*" [66]) imports the necessary heat into the cool room—heat being associated with the outside and with action. As is his wont, de Man casts the scene as one of seduction ("Heat is therefore inscribed in the text in an underhand, secretive manner"), and his mode of breaking the spell is to insist on figurative relationships that he calls "metonymic" because they function through contiguity rather than property transfer or shared meaning.

De Man's is a forcing reading, to be sure. But though the Jakobsonian heritage weighs heavily here, as Guillory says, it need not propel us all the way down to "the actual syntax of the sentence, without which no sentence could exist." Proximity or contiguity is a rhetorical device among others; any writer of modest ability, let alone Proust, attends to various sorts of associations and cross-pollinations (I have just attended to *s* and double-*s* sounds). That is an elementary point, but de Man's suspicion that inherently arbitrary linguistic structures might be generating thematic or metaphysical associations is not. Relations of contiguity are open to themes of contingency (we may grant the repetition of *s*-sounds ornamental value, but if we suspect that this repetition is determining a statement making a cognitive claim, we might feel cheated, just as we might if, while reading an aesthetically ambitious rhymed poem, we feel the distorting pressure of a rhyming dictionary). Rhetorical reading thematizes contingency, but the possibility raised by the association of associative linguistic pattern with inessentiality or contingency is that *thematization* runs deeper than *theme*—that the making of meaning involves processes that have no link to meaning. Philosophy's foundational quarrel with rhetoric quarrels precisely with this possibility. "Reading is a praxis that thematizes its own thesis about the impossibility of thematization and this makes it unavoidable, though hardly legitimate, for allegories to be interpreted in thematic terms" (*AR*, 209). Thus, what the rhetorical reading *does* is never quite in line with what it *says*, even though such a nonconvergence of saying and doing *is* what it says. Theory, as the thematization of the figural displacement of theme, resists its theme by thematizing it.[21]

Is "metonymy" a justifiable thematic name in this context for mechanical, nonthematic linguistic elements? Within limits, yes. My own opinion, though, is that de Man himself found the terminology of the Proust essay unsatisfactory. He did not build any of his other early-1970s essays so squarely over the Jakobsonian metaphor-metonymy divide, and said very little about metonymy over the subsequent decade; the metaphor-metonymy binary opposition, I think, soon came to seem to him misleadingly totalizing, no matter how violently one spun and shook it. It is intrinsic to de Man's methodology to devour its own metalanguage, but some terms and oppositions proved more useful to him than others. Over the course of the 1970s, de Manian rhetorical reading developed along lines of thought opened most forcefully in an essay he wrote about the same time as the Proust essay, "Theory of Metaphor in Rousseau's *Second Discourse*," which became Chapter 7 of *Allegories of Reading*, the first in the sequence of Rousseau chapters making up the second half of the book.[22] I can do no more than point toward this dense (and much commented upon) reading of Rousseau's fantasy of a primitive man's encounter with another primitive man, whom he fears and thus perceives and names as a "giant"; we recall that de Man argues that metaphor, according to this particular "allegory of reading," obliterates its own precondition: radical uncertainty. The other primitive man may or may not be dangerous; this is undecidable; "the metaphor [i.e., 'giant'] is blind, not because it distorts objective data, but because it presents as certain what is, in fact, a mere possibility" (*AR*, 151). In becoming a figure, the figure disfigures itself, generating a stable difference between literal and figurative meanings by foreclosing the truly figural, if impossible, "state of suspended meaning" out of which it originated. What de Man means by rhetoric presses in a sense beyond what we ordinarily think of as "language," since the rhetorical reading generates as its allegory of the reading predicament a story about the constitutive (and thus also deconstitutive) activity *of* language as it comes into being—for that is the point of the Rousseau fable that de Man is reading: Rousseau is claiming that "the first language must have been figurative (*figuré*)," and is illustrating his claim with the story of the primitive man calling another primitive man a "giant," a metaphor that precedes its literal meaning, "man," which gets generated later. Language thereby ceases to be merely an object in the world, a constituted entity we can learn or use or study; though such uses of language are on their own terms perfectly necessary and legitimate, they are *uses* that presuppose that language "is." Yet language "is" only in its relation to that which it "is not." Its being is constantly in question: torn and virtualized, propped on the radical otherness of not-language; it is ahead of, behind, beside and beyond itself, more and less than itself. It must refer (here, to that otherness called "giant"), yet it cannot guarantee its referential purchase. "All discourse *has to be* referential but can never signify its actual referent" (*AR*, 160, de Man's emphasis). Language is radically figurative because it demands, yet renders impossible, a decision as to the referential status of figure (including above all the figure called "language"). That decision, which must but cannot be made (and is therefore not a "decision" performed by an already-constituted subject), is the text-producing error that de Man calls reading. Reading unfolds as an allegory of figure that mistakes itself as a story about an object (hence de Man's mobile and violent hyperobjectifications of language terms) and becomes thematic and universalizing.

We see that the skewed, pseudo-dialectic of reading, as de Man narrates it, grants language a phantasmal agency. The metaphor "giant" blindly forgets itself; language, in imposing itself, effaces its own radical figurativeness. The trope of prosopopoeia—the making or giving of mask or face—comes into disruptive contact with what de Man calls the positing power of language. Language *occurs*: "The positing power of language is both entirely arbitrary, in having a strength that cannot be reduced to necessity, and entirely inexorable in that there is no alternative to it. It stands beyond the polarities of chance and determination and can therefore not be part of a temporal sequence of events" (*RR*, 116). Only "after" language has happened, nonintentionally and nonmeaningfully, can there be intention and meaning; the happening becomes a hallucinatory "giant" that, forgetting itself, becomes "man" the name-giver. Through prosopopoeia, "man" acquires a face (and is therefore always in danger of having it disappear, or turn hallucinogenic or monstrous). Guillory does not discuss these strange and powerful figurative narratives, and seems to have misunderstood the sense of de Man's recourse to an Austinian notion of the performative and a Fichtean idiom of positing or positionality, for he represents de Man as privileging cognition over persuasion: "In the metanarrative of deconstruction, tropes are said to have seductive powers of persuasion but never fail, by virtue of their cognitive dimension, to deconstruct their own persuasive performances" (219). But de Man's fundamental point is that the cognitive functioning of language is out of sync with its performativity: "Language posits and language means (since it articulates), but language cannot posit meaning; it can only reiterate (or reflect) it in its reconfirmed falsehood" (*RR*, 117–18).

The uncanny narrative of language as event generates another difficult topic and term in de Man's late work: linguistic "materiality." By now, many an essay has addressed itself to the question of what de Man means by "materiality"; clearly, this is a concept or semiconcept that attentive readers have been able to describe in various ways.[23] What the word surely does *not* mean for de Man, however, is a materialism that "reconstruct[s] contingency as another kind of necessity, one that is not metaphysical but *physical*, a determinate indeterminacy in which the process of signification is subject to the random causality of chance" (Guillory 228, his emphasis). It is of note that Guillory launches this claim at de Man from a considerable distance; fortified by his close, hard reading of de Man on Proust, he does not even glance at, let alone examine carefully, any of the relevant texts. We have reached a site of resistance where interpretative labor cedes to stark misrepresentation. For whatever materiality means in de Man, it does not simply mean physical presence. De Man used the words *materiality* or *materialism* rather rarely, and almost always in conjunction with the words *form*, *inscription*, and *letter*. In "Hypogram and Inscription," he writes of the "materiality of an inscription" (*RT*, 51), and has a few similar phrases in the two late essays on Hegel (e.g., *AI*, 102, 108–9); in the two Kant essays, arguing that "radical formalism . . . is what is called materialism" (*AI*, 128), he uncovers a "formal materialism" at the heart of aesthetic judgment (*AI*, 83), and subsequently refers to the "materiality of the letter" (*AI*, 90). Let us gloss that last phrase briefly. As

Saussure showed, there is no such thing as a letter in purely phenomenal terms—as an unmediated presence-to-self of a perception. A letter can be read (as opposed to ink on paper being seen) only because of its constitutive difference from other letters (I may write my "I" quite variously, so long as something distinguishes it from "J," "i," "l," etc.). When Kant's text, in de Man's reading, crumbles into letters, it is crumbling into minimal units of form—form as the product of difference and iterability. A letter requires and could be said to prop itself on a perceptible and physically material element, but as letter it is neither the physicality of ink nor the molecules or atoms of physical reality.

We have brushed up against instances of de Man–style materiality in previous chapters, for instance at the end of Chapter 3, when Wordsworth's self-consciousness devolves into staring walls in *The Ruined Cottage*. Those walls could be said to figure the sheer "form" of "seeing seeing" (or rather: staring at staring) in the absence of a subject or an understanding or a meaning. At such points we approach what Orrin Wang, over the course of an extended meditation on de Manian materiality, summarizes as "the meaningless imposition of meaning," when an uncanny figure opens "non-meaning's resemblance to meaning";[24] one may also speak of an irruption within the text of a moment in which exchange or substitution—the work of trope—breaks down (the staring walls are what remains when metaphors for self-consciousness exhaust themselves). In Chapter 3 I wrote of a "prosopopoeia without external props"—a trope of face-giving reduced to a minimum as blank, staring wall-faces, frozen beyond narrative or tropological recovery: the end of the line for a narrator who will recover narrative only by turning away. To the extent that this figure refuses exchange and address and performs a break in the text, one might wish to echo de Man's famous assertion about Kant's landscape in "Phenomenality and Materiality in Kant": "The only word that comes to mind is that of a *material* vision" (*AI*, 82). Derrida's formula for the quasi-concept of materiality in de Man, much cited by scholars who work in this area, is "a materiality without materialism and even perhaps without matter."[25] That may be a frustratingly cautious formulation, but it is far more accurate than Guillory's claim that de Man invests "the word as material object" with "the same numinous agency evacuated from the subject" (229).[26]

Neither the natural object nor the "word as material object" (in the mode of being accessible to the senses—as, say, marks on paper perceived *as* a word) is what de Man means by materiality, as even a brief look at one of his texts can confirm.[27] Without getting into the complications of de Man's reading, in "Hypogram and Inscription," of Michael Riffaterre's reading of (among other texts) Victor Hugo's poem "Ecrit sur la vitre d'une fenêtre flamande," we may glance at the end of that essay:

> Every detail as well as every general proposition in [Hugo's] text is fantastic except for the assertion, in the title, that it is *écrit*, written. . . . The materiality (as distinct from the phenomenality) that is thus revealed, the unseen "cristal" whose existence thus becomes a certain *there* and a certain *then* which can become a *here* and a *now* in the reading "now" taking place, is not the materiality of the mind or of time or of the carillon [which are all personifications in Hugo's poem]—none of which exist, except in the figure of prosopopeia—but the materiality of an inscription. (*RT*, 51)

Scratches on a pane of glass, like ink marks on paper, can be perceived as phenomena, but to the extent that they are *read* they are being supported not just by a literal pane of glass (that would be the "physical" materiality Guillory has in mind) but by what de Man tropes here as an "unseen 'cristal,'" a glass beyond seeing: the *inscription* as the self-difference and iterability that, bound up with yet irreducible to the physical reality that contributes to the inscription's finitude and vulnerability, allows these words to be read "here" and "now," a here and a now that are always, in their actual and potential reiterations, other and elsewhere.

—+—

We have reached a point in our analysis where it becomes possible to offer some general observations. Surveying the trajectory of Guillory's argument, we may substantiate the claim I made in my introductory remarks about the *institutional* flavor of Guillory's critique. If his portrait of a de Man flinching at shadows, glued to the publicity barometer, anxiously manipulating his disciples and venting contempt in his essays sounds over-emphatically keyed to the stereotypes of antitheoretical discourse, this is congruent with the overall project of the chapter. All of the tools Guillory employs to retrofit de Manian theory into a symptom of the marginalization of the humanities in the new technobureaucratic world are familiar; they are the clichés of the resistance to theory, animated by the skill and passion of a first-rate polemicist. These commonplaces, as we saw in Chapter 1, emerged from the moment "theory" began to undergo mediatization in the 1970s. De Man invented his theory to defend elite literature; to gain personal prestige; to corrupt the young. He watered down aspects of Continental thought in order to obey "the agenda of a specifically American apparatus" (Guillory 238). At least his theory's unhappy success was soon followed by its "waning" (255); deconstruction is over; it can be brought to book and historicized. And if his theory possibly had, in its day, some originality to it as, precisely, *his* theory, woe betide the "disciples" who reproduce it: in doing so they become no more than nameless, meaningless pawns. It would accord with the momentum, though not the poised intelligence, of Guillory's critique to add to these commonplaces the most journalistic and fantastic of them all: that de Man invented his theory so as not to feel guilty about having written his youthful wartime journalism. Guillory rightly discerns a symptom at work in the phantasmatic equivalence between de Man and "theory," but his analysis exactly repeats the symptom's own grammar and terms. Recycling the personification of theory as "de Man," he alternately ignores or dismisses theory's critique of personification (personification, that is, as an inevitable but endlessly unstable trope), and necessarily repeats in negative form the fetishizing gesture of the transference. The result is that odd blend of originality and ordinariness that I have wondered about more than once in these pages. One might risk the somewhat fanciful diagnosis that, in wrestling with de Man, Guillory manages to internalize and incorporate anti–de Manian commonplaces so successfully that they become indistinguishable from his own remarkable accomplishment. I shall say more about what I find laudable about Guillory's reading, but first let me try to bring into sharper focus the outline of his resistance to theory—which, as noted, is not simply "his" resistance.

Peggy Kamuf was right, in the review I cited earlier, to diagnose as *Cultural Capital*'s sticking point the deconstructive insistence "on the technicity of the idea, on the iterability of the proper, on the divisibility of any mark of division, and therefore on the necessary contamination of any posed or supposed purity." Throughout his reading of de Man, Guillory works to separate the technical from the ideational and render the former an ornament of or supplement to the latter. We are told that the de Manian disciples do not really imitate the master's doctrine, which is a contentless content: "What is imitated rather is the form of the doctrine's iteration, in other words, its style" (201). Style separates from content, and it becomes on the one hand a sheer principle of mechanical reproducibility and on the other hand *l'homme même*—a mechanical reproduction of *this man*'s style. The "form of the doctrine's iteration" is thus at once expelled from meaning and subordinated to personality. When Guillory turns from the institutional propagation of theory via discipleship to the theory itself, he repeats a version of the same gesture: tropes become technical ornaments separate from, and subordinate to, the "themes" of rhetorical reading. Earlier I noted but did not comment on Guillory's claim that de Man conflates trope with the Saussurian signifier; let me say a word about that error now. Despite the proximity between the notions of trope and signifier (they are translatable: one can describe a trope as a signifier, and one can describe the relation between signifier and signified as a trope) the two concepts are not equivalent (the translation, that is, leaves a residue). Tropes, for de Man, always raise epistemological questions because they put into play the difference between literal and figurative meaning; thus, given that they perform semantic displacements, tropes involve the "signified" as much as they do the "signifier". Tropes are disruptive for de Man precisely because they twine together meaning (the "signified") and the principle of meaning's articulation (the "signifier") while disallowing a stable link between the two. Guillory identifies trope and signifier as part of his overall, tacit effort to segregate themes from their "technical" expression. The guiding thread is an affirmation of *presence*: of the professor to the seminar participant, of meaning to the mind, of objects to experience, of a theme to a text. And as we have seen, this logocentrism must endlessly condemn and expel what we may call the technicity of language: technicity, here, signaling not just "mechanical" iterability, but the irreducibility and irreducible unpredictability of *mediation*.[28] "There is no deconstruction," Derrida affirms, "which does not begin by again calling into question the dissociation between thought and technology. . . . This is why this deconstruction, at the very moment when it puts into question the hierarchical division between thought and technology, is neither technicist nor technological" (Derrida, *Memoires*, 108, 110).

It is with this caution in mind that we may now turn to the most original element of Guillory's argument: its powerful final reduction of de Man and de Manian theory to symptoms of institutional and social crisis and change. The technical plays an important role in this argument: having characterized de Man's tropological terminology as a sheerly technical excrescence on a pathos-driven theme, Guillory claims to have discovered a "valorization of the technical" in de Man: "just as the rhetorical terminology exists for the sake of the determinist thematic, that thematic in turn offers a means of recharacterizing the rhetorical terminology as technical or rigorous in *contemporary* terms" (Guillory 232). No longer a *technē rhētorikē*, this new, late twentieth-century art of rhetoric thematizes its technicity as "rigor." De Manian rigor is of course, for Guillory, a sham, an excuse for the pathos and the lurid figures it generates;[29] but the de Manian master-trope of rigor "facilitates an imaginary reduction of the social totality to the structure of trope," allowing "rhetorical reading to function as a political theory just by virtue of being *no more than* a theory of literature" (236). This "imaginary reduction of the social to an instance of the linguistic" in turn allows the disciples first to respond to the desire that criticism have political effect in a way that imposes "a *limit* to curricular revision, a limit intended to preserve theory as *literary* theory" (237) and second to imagine de Man as external to and subversive of the institution.

As to the first claim, which seeks to bring home the traditional left-wing antideconstructive argument that de Manian theory "defends" a high-literary canon, we may note that Guillory, who knows well that this theory offers (via its "technical" focus on rhetoric) "an extension of the category of the literary" that "removes any logical grounds for distinguishing between literature and any use of language whatsoever" (212), depends heavily upon his reduction-to-the-seminar and his restriction of the reception of de Manian theory to "disciples" who like their master read "a very select set of texts within the Romantic tradition" (216), in order to make his argument. Indeed, he goes on to note (with perhaps a touch of annoyance) "de Man's relative lack of interest in this consequence of his theorizing" (212). De Man, that is, writes on canonical texts but seems uninterested in affirming the virtues of the canon. Only by granting a canonical sense to references to "literature" in de Man's texts and ignoring statements that set out in a contrary direction can Guillory link de Man to a conservative canonical agenda. (The counterevidence is visible. As we saw in Chapter 1, de Man's programmatic essay "The Resistance to Theory" defines "literariness" very broadly, in opposition to aesthetic concepts of language and literature, and emphasizes the instability of the category of literature: "as a first casualty of [the discrepancy between truth and method], the notion of 'literature as such' as well as the clear distinction between history and interpretation can no longer be taken for granted" [*RT*, 4]. In the middle of this essay de Man tells us that literary theory "blurs the borderlines between literary and non-literary discourse" [11], and near its end he notes that the rhetorical dimension of language "can be revealed in any verbal event when it is read textually" [17].) It is, of course, true that de Man wrote almost exclusively about certain high-literary texts; it is almost certain that de Man, like Derrida or Blanchot, should be read as affirming the interest and power of the post-eighteenth-century discursive category of literature; it is furthermore highly probable that, in the context of his own training and tastes, and his own particular mandate as a pedagogue, de Man thought it his job to teach "literature." (Guillory—and we—will have more to say about de Man and professionalism in a moment.) It is also true, however, as Guillory rightly points out, that de Manian rhetorical reading in no way requires of its practitioners that they focus on Wordsworth or Hölderlin or Rousseau. This set of facts does not add up to an "aporia" or a "conceptual catachresis," as Guillory claims (215, 216); there is no logical impasse here—nor even a pragmatic or institutional one, as becomes obvious as soon as we broaden our horizon and look at the diverse kinds of critical projects that de Manian theory has in fact inspired over the last thirty-odd years (and was already inspiring by the time Guillory was writing this book in the early 1990s).[30] If critics have drawn on the idiom and procedures of rhetorical reading to address "texts" such as trauma theory or journalism or gender identity or the rhetoric of war, this is because in de Manian terms neither literariness nor the aesthetic are fundamentally "high-cultural" phenomena. They are aspects of language; and "language" is not, for de Man, a positive object among others, but is perhaps better thought of as the catachretic name for the possibility that understanding cannot catch up with—cannot understand—its own mediations.

I shall not comment much on Guillory's distortion of various remarks that de Manians have made about de Man being "outside" the institution; it is of course not the case that any competent deconstructive critic has ever imagined de Man to be simply or fundamentally external to the institutions of criticism and pedagogy. (The deconstructive position, as we saw Kamuf pointing out earlier, is that "the institution," despite having a fundamental power to exclude and include, is not a homogenous space that texts or textual practices can simply *inhabit*.) We may pass on to consider what Guillory considers the ideological freight of such imaginings. They serve, in his reading, a dream of autonomy, via an ideology of professionalism. Within a bureaucracy, professionalism is the ideology by means of which "the charisma of the master theorist appears to constitute a realm of *absolute* autonomy, and therefore, as we have noted, an 'other scene' of politics" (254, Guillory's emphasis). De Manian theory thus reasserts charismatic authority in the face of "technobureaucratic dominion" (256); but at the same time, in and through the valorization of the technical as "rigor," it transforms the work of reading into "an *unconscious mimesis* of the form of bureaucratic labor." "Rigor" supports a dream of autonomy even as it recapitulates, as positive qualities, the "boredom, monotony, predictability, and unpleasantness" of bureaucratic existence. "Just as the transference transferred in the pedagogic sphere imparts to 'rigor' the eros, the sexiness, of the master teacher, so in the bureaucratic sphere it signifies a *charisma of routinization*, the cathexis of routine" (257).

Now, on the one hand, as we have seen, every brick making up this massive conceptual edifice is a friable mixture of untruth, half-truth, hypothesis, or assertion. The seminar of the charismatic teacher, no doubt important enough in its way, is an imaginary reduction of the real technobureaucratic conditions for the propagation of theory. As for the theory being propagated, it is certainly not blind to the transference; it does not (despite its own self-resistance) rediscover the cognitive mastery of the subject as linguistic determinism; it is not securely theme-driven; it does not isolate trope from theme; it does not, except as deployed within very specific institutional contexts, "defend literature." Its practitioners no doubt imagine what they do to be irritating to the institution (infuriating, even, at times), but do not, if they are competent practitioners, labor under the illusion that either their discourse or that of anyone else, including the "master," occupies "a realm of *absolute* autonomy." Deconstruction has its suspicions about absolute autonomy. But on the other hand, Guillory's argument, marked at every turn by a negative transference and a determination to preserve the metaphysical hierarchies and conceptual distinctions that theory puts into question, makes visible the degree to which de Manian theory reflects on its own institutional conditions. We have noted how this theory builds into its allegory of itself a gloss on the transference and the moral ambiguities of pedagogy; we may now credit de Man's discourse with an allegory of its institutional unfolding. The discourse is not an "unconscious mimesis of the form of bureaucratic labor" (a claim that makes clear the degree to which the sociological critique ultimately relies upon a metaphysics of reflection); it is a registering and a reading of the technobureaucratic scene of theory's production. The empirical specificity of the historical event of theory—the fact that "pragmatically speaking . . . we know that there has been, over the last fifteen to twenty years, a strong interest in something called literary theory" (*RT*, 5)—may be aligned, as an empirical phenomenon, with the technobureaucratic development of the university within the wider regime of late capitalism and modern technics. Derrida, whose texts thematize such matters far more explicitly than de Man's, affirms as much: "it is not by chance that deconstruction has accompanied a critical transformation in the conditions of entry into the academic professions from the 1960s to the 1980s" (*Memoires* 16). "Pragmatically speaking," *rigor* signals the imperative to *produce readings*; and although this imperative outstrips any local performance of it, it *also* bears the traces of its context and addresses itself in the first instance to professionalized reader-producers within a scientific-bureaucratic organization. Rhetorical reading implicitly incorporates and reflects on its own institutional conditions of production, not in order to condemn its own institutionalization or celebrate its own professionalism, but because the imperative to read is infinite, and these conditions of production form part of the text to be read. The production of readings may then be characterized as a bureaucratic task that—whether or not the nominal topic is traditionally high-literary—in a very broad sense works performatively to "defend literature" (just as Guillory's book or mine or any other field-relevant academic publication does, by virtue of its participation in and contribution to criticism as an institution); but, arguably, no critical approach more consciously addresses itself to the complexities besetting its own performance than rhetorical reading. We return to a classic de Manian–deconstructive insight: the reading is not something we add to the text from the outside, but constituted the text from the beginning (the beginning, that is, of the reading). De Man's text, once we have read Guillory reading it, stands revealed not as a blind repetition of its own institutional conditions of production, but rather as an elaborate machine for registering those conditions. In the terms of *Blindness and Insight*: "The work can be used repeatedly to show when and how a critic diverged from it, but in the process of showing this, our understanding of the work is modified and the faulty vision shown to be productive" (*BI*, 109).

"Rigor" is indeed a charged figure in theory's production and propagation, but Guillory's analysis cannot stand in the form he offers it. There *is no* unambiguous "valorization of the technical" in de Man, as any careful inspection of "Aesthetic Formalization in Kleist" or the "Confessions" chapter of *Allegories of Reading*—to name only two particularly obvious texts—shows. Technical and aesthetic formalization in de Man is not just inhuman but also potentially damaging to humans (to Rousseau, entranced by the metal rolls [*AR*, 298]; to the mutilated man in Kleist's story who dances like a marionette [*RR*, 288–90]). Formalization obtains inhuman, machinelike powers of iterability in these de Manian readings, and formalization is all the more dangerous when it has been aestheticized and thereby rendered, fallaciously, a property of the "human" or a principle of political order. Rhetorical reading cannot help fetishizing "rigor," but is also a rigorous critique of rigor. Avital Ronell has argued that "Paul de Man's work is essentially engaged with and inflected by the question concerning technology";[31] what Guillory calls theory's ideology of rigor is a dimension of that engagement. Even as theory's invocation of rigor triggers the pathos and thrills of technical formalization, it enacts the imperative to read the uncertainties, the violent derivations and deviations of formalization.[32]

It is telling that, as his chapter approaches its end, Guillory's assaults on de Man grow conflicted, particularly in the orbit of some lines he cites from de Man's interview with Stephano Rossi:

So, personally, I don't have a bad conscience when I'm being told that, to the extent that it is didactic, my work is academic or even, as it is used as a supreme insult, just more New Criticism. I can live with that very easily, because I think that only what is, in a sense, classically didactic, can be really and effectively subversive. And I think the same applies there to Derrida. Which doesn't mean that there are not essential differences: Derrida feels compelled to say more about the institution of the university, but that is more understandable within the European context, where the university has such a predominating cultural function, whereas in the United States it has no cultural function at all, here it is not inscribed in the genuine cultural tensions of the nation. (*RT*, 117)

Guillory attacks immediately, in the hyperbolic mode we have encountered before: "No proposition could be more blind to its own meaning than the claim that the American university has no 'cultural function.' A claim of this sort would be hardly credible about any social institution" (241). But then comes—rather unexpectedly given the overall tone of this chapter— the next sentence: "Yet this is not to say that de Man's assertion has no basis whatsoever." The partial retraction is perhaps partly spurred by embarrassment over having pounced on a crumb (for obviously de Man, improvising in an interview, offers a loose phrase here, which he then follows with a tighter one); but as we read along it becomes apparent that part of Guillory's problem is that de Man is saying something close to what Guillory is saying, as Guillory eventually half-admits: "What de Man considered to be the cultural irrelevance of the university describes a real condition, perhaps, not of the university but of the literary curriculum" (264). In between these two moments in his essay Guillory has exempted de Man from the "outside the institution" fantasy that Guillory attributes to the disciples: "So far from inhabiting a space exterior to the institution, de Man proposes that fully implementing a deconstructive pedagogy would transform 'departments of English from being large organizations in the service of everything except their own subject matter into much smaller units, dedicated to the pro- fessional specialization that Professor [Walter Jackson] Bate deplores' [*RT*, 25–26]" (247). Guillory presses that citation toward a de Manian requirement that "the methodology of rhetorical reading be *identified* (how closely, we shall see) with the institution and its strictly institutional agenda"; but a few sentences later he nonetheless finds it necessary to distinguish de Man from the "aggressively 'professionalist' polemic" of a pragmatist such as Stanley Fish (247). Here, for a moment, de Man seems to float free, an inch or two above the clutches of polemic. De Man, we are told, "*identifies*," in italics, his theory with the institution— but he also doesn't quite. Guillory has come as close as he is able in this text to registering de Man's double or deconstructive reading of institutionality (and of the technically or rigorously or classically "didactic") as *both* determining and unstable, coercive yet open to certain possibilities.

Looking back over Guillory's long chapter, one has the sense of having watched a skilled archer, shooting over vast distances, clump arrows around but never quite in the bull's-eye—itself an extraordinary feat, and one perfectly capable of transforming our sense of the target by reframing it and allowing us to see it anew. If Guillory's persuasive critique of the "canon debate" should have led him to be leery of the temptations of personification (the trope that allows minority authors to become "representative" of experiences and constituencies, thereby effacing the institution through which this "representation" occurs), the fact that he repeats so fiercely the personifying gesture in his chapter on de Man suggests that no genuine account of canon formation—and, for that matter, no adequate history of literary theory—can be achieved in the absence of a fundamental rhetorical critique. As regards de Manian theory per se, most of Guillory's characterizations and propositions, as we have seen, offer at best secondary or derivative truths. The legendary transferential effects of de Man's seminar did indeed play an important if necessarily limited role in the diffusion of de Manian theory. One can hardly deny that de Man was a charismatic figure, and it would be nearly as hard to deny that the strange "rigor" of his method—which is inseparable from the strange violence of his readings—facilitated many of the transferential and ideological effects that Guillory describes. It is always tempting to imagine one's beloved teacher "outside" the institution, even if one knows better; and when the sociological context is one in which full-scale humanities instruction has largely retreated to elite enclaves and is being carried out—at best, in these enclaves—by a two-tier staff of bureaucratically integrated professionals and a casual workforce (this latter category including, of course, the master teacher's students so long as they are literally *students*), it becomes all the easier for the participants in this drama to reimagine the master's singularity as "absolute autonomy." But de Manian *theory* does not license these phenomena; it predicts and in a sense exploits and after a fashion repeats them, and this repetition is always also a critique. In his heart, perhaps, Guillory knows this, and perhaps we know he knows. That is why we are not, perhaps, completely taken by surprise when, on the final page of this chapter, Guillory offers us a half-smothered confession of impotence, telling us "how nearly impossible it is to imagine what lies beyond the rhetoricism of literary theory, and hence beyond the problematic of literariness" (265). That near-impossibility spurs a formulaic gesture toward some future moment, when "a much more thorough reflection on the historical category of literature" will allow us to "conceptualize a new disciplinary domain." The signifier "history," here, as so often in American academic criticism, points toward salvation from history and from the "disciplinary domains" within which we find ourselves.

This swerve from history by way of a redemptive historicism returns as a hyperbolic investment in the aesthetic at the end of *Cultural Capital*, as we have seen. As its final offering, Guillory's book proffers, as the prize of its wrestling match with de Man, the dream of an Aesthetic State in which the violence of social inequity is transformed into "pure 'symbolic distinction'" (339). On the purity of that distinction, and the enforceable difference between literal and figurative violence that its purity requires, the vision depends—desperately and impossibly; for such distinction can only be, always already, impure. Guillory is right to argue, against the historicists and neopragmatists, that aesthetic judgment cannot be evaded; just as little, however, can one evade the rhetorical critique that maps onto the singularity of aesthetic judgment the impossible imperative to judge without rule, suspended between literal and figural meaning, and pressured toward a confrontation with language's materiality—its resistance to human purpose or desire. Aesthetic humanism does not give up its dream easily. Indeed, that dream perhaps never gets quite erased, particularly if one is pursuing a career in the humanities in the American university, whether or not one sees oneself as practicing "theory." Thus, criticism continues to twist in the turns of aesthetic discourse while now and then registering its fascination and impatience with the critic who most obsessively and strangely followed out those turns. It is likely that this predicament will remain that of "literary criticism in the coming years."

6. Querying, Quarrying

Mark Tansey's Paintings of Theory's Grand Canyon

Any book that sets out to analyze the phenomenon of "theory" as "decon-struction in America," as I have here, never gets far from the question of the university's role in the cultural life of later twentieth-century America. Theory was produced although not exclusively consumed in the academy; this situation was enabled, I have suggested, by certain institutional and dis-cursive features characterizing the U.S. experiment in mass higher education and its cultural context. Over the last few decades, therefore, the nickname "theory" has had to refer both to a host of discursive transformations in professional academic practices that possess a substantial degree of profes-sional autonomy, *and* to a wider cultural and media event. The relationship between these entwined developments is complex. Theory exacerbated the already considerable distance between the professionalized humanities and nonacademic highbrow American literary culture; yet, even as it contributed to the further splintering of the public sphere, theory underwent surpris-ingly broad and energetic mass distribution, over the course of which it also tended to be narrowed down to a lurid core. Throughout this book I have stressed how inseparable the mediatization of theory has been from the scandal of "deconstruction," a scandal that culminated in the national broadcasting (and then, a quarter-century later, in 2014, the remarkable rebroadcasting) of the "de Man affair." And since I believe, and have done my best to demonstrate, that the texts and approaches we conventionally refer to as "deconstructive" have decisive analytic power, I have proposed that we understand the totemic role of de Man and Derrida—and, briefly, of that peculiar ensemble of "Yale Critics"—as the precipitate of a deep cul-tural anxiety about "language" in the broadest sense (mediation, figuration, deracination, iterability). The conflagration that resulted still gives off heat sporadically, decades later.

When one's focus is on journalistic "affairs," it is hard not to think of mediatization as a synonym for simplification. But that would be to simplify, and quite misleadingly. The association of mass mediatization with cultural degradation is a major postromantic trope; it correlates with a model of reception as echo and fall—an appealing plot when we are dealing with sound bites and hostile parodies, but not one that does justice to the complexity either of mediatization per se, or of the actual reception of theoretical texts beyond the academic context. Since its development in the middle to late nineteenth century, the postromantic institution we call the "art world" has been the place in Western societies where aesthetic notions, norms and practices are performed, shaken, destroyed, and reimagined; so it is hardly surprising that major authors and texts associated with theory in the academy have been taken up, sometimes quite powerfully, by artists in various media and by non- or para-academic writers in any number of genres.

I want to close this study with a close look at two paintings by Mark Tansey that examine very shrewdly and knowledgeably the phenomenon of "deconstruction in America." In a roughly two-year span around 1990, Tansey painted a number of canvases that in the present context we could call "theory paintings": high-concept, monochrome works that feature "landscapes" printed with blurred silkscreened lines of text, the identifiable portions of which reproduce either pages 146–47 of de Man's *Blindness and Insight* or pages 112–13 of Gayatri Spivak's translation of Derrida's *Of Grammatology*.[1] These paintings are well known, and several have served as cover art for theoretically inclined academic books.[2] *Under Erasure* (1990), which represents a waterfall partly "erasing" the *Of Grammatology* pages, circulated particularly widely as the cover art for the first edition of the *Norton Anthology of Theory and Criticism* (2001). (For the anthology's second edition in 2009, the editors substituted a fiery abstract by Cy Twombly—possibly, one has to suspect, in an effort to downplay the symptomatic and historical symbiosis between "theory" and "deconstruction.") The two paintings to be discussed here, *Derrida Queries de Man* and *Constructing the Grand Canyon*, both from 1990, make conceptual art out of the conceptual knot I have struggled to untie in this book. The first painting refigures Sidney Paget's famous illustration in *The Strand Magazine* for Arthur Conan Doyle's Sherlock Holmes story "The Final Problem" (1893), setting its totemic theory-figures in a landscape reminiscent of monumental romantic sublime painting, save for the fact that the cliffs and chasm feature only partly legible silkscreen reproductions of de Man's text. The second painting, also evocative of the tradition of sublime landscape painting, transforms the Grand Canyon into the textscape of "theory in America," with the Yale Critics framed and lit up at its vanishing point.

—|—

Let us begin with a first look, which of course will never be innocent. The two struggling or dancing figures are not so dwarfed by the chasm as to prevent an informed viewer from experiencing a shock of recognition (Figure 1). Hyperrealistically rendered, Paul de Man faces away from us, toward Jacques Derrida and the abyss. He appears to be leading: his weight is forward, and his right hand, now clasping Derrida's left hand, may soon be insinuating itself around his partner's waist. Derrida's body slants elegantly but precariously into the dance and toward the void; he seems to be standing on one foot. He will probably fall first—unless his yielding is a ruse. "He rushed at me and threw his long arms around me," Sherlock Holmes tells Watson in "The Adventure of the Empty House" (1903):

> We tottered together upon the brink of the fall. I have some knowledge, however, of baritsu, or the Japanese system of wrestling, which has more than once been very useful to me. I slipped through his grip, and he with a horrible scream kicked madly for a few seconds and clawed the air with his hands. But for all his efforts he could not get his balance, and over he went.[3]

The dance dissolved after all; the coupling was a feint, and only Holmes's double, the evil Professor Moriarty, fell. But Tansey's painting weaves a complex web of allusions. Watson had told a different tale ten years previously, when Arthur Conan Doyle was killing off Holmes in "The Final Problem" (1893), at the end of which Watson sees "two lines of footmarks" leading to the edge of the falls, and imagines detective and villain "reeling over, locked in each other's arms" (555). Sidney Paget's illustration for that story picks up on that phrase: he has Holmes grasping Moriarty rather than "slipp[ing] through his grip," and ready to be the first one to go over the edge (Figure 2). Tansey quotes extensively from Paget, but changes the arrangement of the bodies so that a violent struggle becomes an ambiguous dance, in which the near figure, de Man, acquires a shadowy version of Holmes's devastating grip, while the far figure, Derrida, slips off-balance like Moriarty. Will there be a winner, or will both lose? Or is such a question itself a slip-up?

Tempering the painting's neorealism is its monochromatic palette: an icy cyan. Monochrome suggests conceptual rather than representational space: a space able to support, as Tansey comments, "temporal disparities," and "impossible encounters and reconciliations."[4] The space-time of Derrida and de Man's impossible encounter is that of a difficult, ambivalently agonistic act of reading. The words "Blindness and Insight" leap out at us along the left edge of the chasm, extending the line of the dancer-wrestlers' bodies down

Figure 1. *Derrida Queries de Man* (1990) by Mark Tansey. Oil on canvas. 83¼ × 55″ (212.7 × 139.7 cm.). Collection of Mike and Penny Winton. Courtesy Gagosian Gallery. © Mark Tansey.

Figure 2. *The Death of Sherlock Holmes* (1893) by Sidney Paget. Image Select/Art Resource, NY.

the cliff. These words compose a hyper-recognizable phrase and title—the proper name of one of the theory-canon's most famous books, a book so famous that its title has taken on a life of its own as a shibboleth of "theory." This title is also an image. Tansey is reproducing here the running head at the top of even-numbered pages of *Blindness and Insight*. To theoretically oriented reader-viewers who have pored over their copies of this book over the years, these characters will be almost as recognizable by their typeface as by the words they compose or the meanings they trigger—almost as recognizable as the photorealistically rendered authorial figures above them. We "see" such signs the way we see faces, with such seeming immediacy that we forget, in the little pleasurable shock of the revelatory moment, that our seeing is always also an act of reading: a making-sense of iterable marks. The ironies multiply: we are enjoying here the act of perceiving mechanically reproduced signs that, in their original context, would have faded into the background to the point of being hard to see at all. When we pick up and reread *Blindness and Insight*, we will once again start going blind to these iconic, yet emptily and mechanically produced words—for who attends to a running head?[5] The edge of Tansey's cliff is a cut that blurs the difference between seeing and reading, perception and blindness, image and sign, singularity and iterability.

Elsewhere the texture of the cliffs is similarly textual, consisting of blurred lines of print silkscreened onto the canvas. Despite the smears, the *Blindness and Insight* typeface remains naggingly recognizable. And indeed, here and there an obsessive viewer can pick out words from page 146 of de Man's text. In the painting's upper left-hand quadrant, for instance, one can trace a vertical swath of legible words: "of th"/"past" /"[Man] wonders"/"to forget": these are fragments of the left margin of the middle of page 146, where de Man is introducing a block quotation with a paraphrase of Nietzsche ("The restlessness of human society, in contrast to the placid state of nature **of th**e animal herd, is diagnosed as man's inability to forget the **past**"), and then block quoting from Nietzsche's *On the Use and Abuse of History* ("**[Man] wonders** about himself, about his inability **to forget**. . . .").[6] On the right-hand cliff another fragment, "We saw," peeps out: these are the opening words of another of de Man's block quotes from Nietzsche on page 146 ("**We saw** that the animal. . . ."). The path leading up to the struggling figures seems to feature text from a different source (the typeface resembles that of *Blindness and Insight*, but the words legible on the path do not seem to come from any particular page in the book).[7] On the rest of the cliff faces, the lines of text are too smeared for me to be sure of their provenance, though they are probably from *Blindness and Insight*, possibly from the same page. Only in one place does a clearly different typeface announce itself—in the lower right corner, where the painting's own title, *Derrida Queries de Man*, overrides the blurry line of a silkscreened print line.[8]

We must beware the temptation to reduce this texture-text to a message—the temptation, that is, of imagining that if we consult *Blindness and Insight*, or, more specifically, "Literary History and Literary Modernity" (the chapter within which page 146 appears) we will access the hidden meaning of this painting. The painting has posted danger signals to slow us down and remind us that we will not be dealing with a key or code, or a stable allegorical structure in which a legend explains an image. As noted before, a different page (possibly from a different text) has left its traces on the text-path to the struggling or dancing figures. And there are plenty of other warning signs. On a formal or material level, most of the printed lines, as noted are too blurred to be readable, while the word fragments that I *can* read are shattered bits of reused and reframed words, for they are fragments not of de Man's words, but Nietzsche's, as *quoted* by de Man. On a representational or dramatic level, the reader-surrogate in the composition, "Derrida," is risking his life and not necessarily getting anywhere. On a symbolic level, the text to be read—*qui n'en est pas un*, whatever its nominal identity—is doubled, split across the two cliff faces, reiterating in sublime fashion the vexed doubleness of the Derrida–de Man reader-text pairing.

Yet just because a text is unreadable doesn't mean that we can stop trying to read it—or that we can interpret it arbitrarily. Any effective interpretation of Tansey's painting must take account of the fact that de Man's text signs the landscape (or at least much of the landscape); that "de Man," according to the embedded title, names the text to be queried; and that page 146 of *Blindness and Insight*, even though it fails to provide the path toward these dancer-fighters, has been made our entry-point into this daunting hermeneutic thicket. So we may take a short, cautious excursus through a few paragraphs of "Literary History and Literary Modernity."

As the fragmentary bits of it quoted earlier may have recalled, page 146 forms part of the first movement of the essay, where de Man is reading Nietzsche's meditations on "life" as a "dynamic concept of modernity . . . opposed to history": "'Life' is conceived not just in biological but in temporal terms as the ability to forget whatever precedes a present situation" (146). The ability to forget—to forget one's historical indebtedness and embeddedness—constitutes the ability to act historically.[9] Forgetting thus names "the radical impulse that stands behind any genuine modernity" (147). Readers determined to assimilate de Man's professional writing to the repression of his wartime journalism should pause before jumping too quickly to conclusions, however, for de Man has not yet arrived at his main point, which is that this forgetting, however necessary and constitutive, is also impossible. Nietzsche's text uncovers a deeper historicity that "implies the necessary experience of any present as a *passing* experience that makes the past irrevocable and unforgettable, because it is inseparable from any present or future" (148–49, de Man's italics). This unforgettable, authentic historicity is generated out of the rupturing act of modernity, which makes things happen; but modernity's blind impulse in no way constitutes an instance of self-presence, and instead reiterates the difference it disavows. Invention—the rupturing, history-making act—occurs, impossibly, in and through the archive. Tansey's painting itself echoes and illustrates this paradox: archive fever fuels its inventiveness. Gesture and meaning, act and interpretation, singularity and iterability, forgetting and remembering splice into each other. De Man's text signs that theme, as do so many other texts by other authors, all in their own singular fashion (in keeping with the drama before us, I have spliced some Derridean terminology into the last few sentences). And Tansey recollects, reproduces, and effaces de Man's text as part of a painterly act that has a certain proximity to the powerful kind of writing that de Man calls literary ("both an act and an interpretive process that follows after an act with which it cannot coincide," 152).

If a text by de Man, and by extension a dramatization of "de Man" as oeuvre, historical figure, phantasm and question orients this painting thematically, its figural composition draws most obviously, as noted earlier, on Sidney Paget's famous illustration for Conan Doyle's "The Final Problem." Why this illustration, and, more broadly, why Sherlock Holmes? I think Tansey's intuition is keen, and that he is summoning Holmes from the archive with the same deft touch that he displays in having Derrida "query" de Man rather than the other way around. Let us dwell with the asymmetry of the painting's title for a moment, and then think more about Holmes.

We just summarized portions of "Literary History and Literary Modernity," but in doing so we were reminded that Tansey could have reproduced other texts—texts by Derrida, most obviously—to capture broadly similar themes (e.g., the tension between knowing and doing, reading and seeing, structure and event, cognition and performance, to offer only a few of many pairings, each with its particular lines of force, that have played a role in the elaboration of deconstructive thought). For reasons having to do both with Tansey's general aesthetic project and with this specific painting, it is understandable that he might find particularly congenial de Man's privileged terms in "Literary History and Literary Modernity" (history, modernity; memory, forgetting), and I shall say a little more about that later; but it is important never to let go entirely of the point we stressed at the outset: smeared and broken and split as the (impossible) representational world of this painting is, *no* source text, not even the one we can read fragments of, can provide stable thematic content for it. In order to invent a viable reading of this painting, we must both remember and forget "Literary History and Literary Modernity."

Yet that paradox causes us to step back and ask the blanker, more abstract question: Why a text by de Man at all? Why *is* Derrida the one doing the querying? Of course, we have only the authority of the painting's title to go on here, and the painting makes its own title query-able. There is nothing in the disposition of these two struggling/dancing figures to establish that only one of them—or for that matter that either of them—is querying the other. Furthermore, the title, as part of the text-striated cliff-face, forms part of the painterly text to be read; it would behoove us not to trust that title blindly. Yet the fact that it forms part of the painting *also* means that we are not relieved of our question. The choice of title rhymes with the choice of a de Man text for the background. We may have every reason to feel we are teetering on an abyss, but we nonetheless have to persist with our query: Why is Derrida the querying reader; why is de Man the enveloping text? (Didn't de Man merely "domesticate" Derrida, according to a tenacious discourse-of-theory leitmotif of the 1970s and 1980s that we glanced at early on in this book? Wasn't it de Man who learned from Derrida by querying and quarrying him, rather than the other way around?)

On this point Tansey's painting, I think, knows perfectly well what it is doing. Derrida queries de Man (at least according to that suspiciously overly assertive title) on the edge of a de Manian abyss not just because by 1990 de Man had been dead for seven years, the "de Man affair" had occurred, and Derrida had published several of the intense, mournful struggles with de Man's texts that make up a salient part of his huge oeuvre during the last two decades of his life. Those empirical and biographical facts are certainly part of the story; but I think there is another, more thematic reason why Derrida is querying de Man so precariously in this phantasmatic landscape. He does so because Tansey's painting is addressing itself to "theory" as "deconstruction," "in America." In the discourse of "theory," as we know, de Man is the spectral embodiment of theory's charms and discontents. He is the theorist of the warped necessity and radical instability of personification—of, that is, the minimal sort of personification that he called prosopopoeia: the catachretic positional force through which signs are *taken* as signs, through which the possibility of signification is imposed so as to be presupposed. De Man *as figure* provides the face and the name of the possibility that faces and names might turn illegible. I shall return to this allegory of figure and landscape in Tansey's painting. But first let us spend some time appreciating the Sherlock Holmes intertext, which, by way of Paget's illustration, has provided the painting with its major figural reference points.

Sherlock Holmes, as Tansey's painting has the wit to remind us, plays a small, tangential, but interesting role in the prehistory of "theory" in the Anglo-American cultural archive. Holmes's interpretive activity is frequently troped as reading, and he is the keenest and closest of readers. Sometimes he interprets literal texts ("Have you read anything else in this message, Mr. Holmes?" [803, *Hound of the Baskervilles*]), though more typically his text is the world and its fungible signs ("If only I had been there! ... That gravel page upon which I might have read so much has been long ere this smudged by the rain and defaced by the clogs of curious peasants" [795, *Hound*]). Officially, to be sure, he is the opposite of the postmodern "theorist." He is the hero of hermeneutic closure: his mission is to discern a stable truth behind false appearances, and he inhabits a genre, the detective story, that orders the world into a tidy plot and thereby underwrites its protagonist's success. Close reading, performed by the master-interpreter within this sheltered narrative space, is supposed to lead to revelation, not ambiguity or blockage. Holmes's theorizing aspires to the counterintuitive yet rational movement of scientific thought (Holmes speaks of "the scientific use of the imagination" [804, *Hound*]), and thus aspires to greater referential power than any naïve empiricism could command. The flat-footed officials of Scotland Yard, whose reliance on unimaginative common sense causes them to "twist facts to suit theories, instead of theories to suit facts" (179, "A Scandal in Bohemia"), ritually and comically reconfirm the referential force of Holmes's scientific theorizing.

Still, the fact that the flat-footed officials call Holmes a *theorist*, in the peculiarly negative sense of the word that became available in the wake of the political polemics of the 1790s ("It's Mr. Sherlock Holmes the theorist" [120, "The Sign of Four"]), suggests lingering complications. We do not need to take up here in any direct way the question of the logical structure of Holmesian "observation" and "deduction," with its large admixture of intuition, imagination, and guesswork.[10] It suffices to note that the Holmes stories, which never fail to back up their hero's wildest interpretations, presuppose a universe "ruled by a sort of complicity between the author [and] his characters," as Umberto Eco has put it.[11] A theatrical and necromantic aura therefore clings to Holmes, and the stories register this ("theoretical") excess—this half-hidden textual violence—in various ways, perhaps most tellingly by granting Holmes the characteristics of a *fin-de-siècle* aesthete and decadent. The purple dressing gown, the Stradivarius, the cocaine addiction, the alternately bachelor-solitary or same-sex *ménage*, the love of theatrics and disguise, the not infrequent references to Continental literature; this Wildean world has at its dramatic center Holmes's willingness to link his "scientific use of the imagination" to high aestheticism.[12] He compares his art to Flaubert's in the closing words of the short story "The Red Headed League" (" '*L'homme c'est rien—l'oeuvre c'est tout,*' as Gustave Flaubert wrote to George Sand" [212]); Watson names the first adventure "a study in scarlet" because Holmes tells him to ("Why shouldn't we use a little art jargon" [28]). According to the racializing logic that often flickers into view in these texts, Holmes has come by his aestheticist and all-too-French leanings honestly; he tells Watson that he had "a grandmother, who was the sister of Vernet, the French artist. Art in the blood is liable to take the strangest forms" (502, "The Greek Interpreter"). We reencounter here, from a rather unexpected angle, the overlap between theoretical excess and "Frenchness" that has played such a long-standing role in Anglo-American chauvinism.

In principle, a Sherlock Holmes story is all about enlightenment, law enforcement, and effective policing—of causality and meaning, but also, quite concretely, of social and racial hierarchies and of the borders of empire and nation. The Holmes narratives patrol, unsettle, and reinforce hierarchies of race, class, and gender in ways familiar to students of late Victorian literature, and they feature a near-obsessive attention to the reflux of empire. Watson enters the narrative bearing wounds from the Anglo-Afghan War of 1878–80, and a large number of his subsequent adventures with Holmes feature threats stemming from far-flung reaches of the British Empire (particularly from India and Australia, as might be expected, though the lost colony in North America contributes a steady stream of murderous Mormons, gangsters from Chicago, and daughters of gold miners). Though Holmes makes a point of working only for the work's own sake, his clients tend to belong almost entirely to the upper to middle classes, and Watson frequently alludes to the great number of aristocratic and politically powerful clients whom Holmes has helped. The intimacy between Holmes and the governing apparatus of the nation grows more striking as the canon evolves, and in some of the late stories he becomes quite explicitly an agent of the British state.[13]

Yet the genre, like its main character, has a deviant side. In this urban-gothic, fog- and tobacco-smoke-blurred environment, signs and identities become at once hyperlegible and mobile. The world of Sherlock Holmes is saturated with signs far more fantastic than the scuffed trouser leg or smear of mud that we tend to associate with the stories. The face, a traditional gothic text, becomes a site of extravagant decoding. Holmes reads Watson's mind in several stories based on his facial expressions.[14] Faces convey guilt ("Look at their faces!" Holmes cries as part of his proof in "The Reigate Puzzle" [468]; in one quite weak late story, "The Adventure of the Sussex Vampire," an evildoer's facial expression constitutes essentially *all* of Holmes's proof). They record innate depravity ("an evil yellow face, a terrible animal face, all seamed and scored with vile passions" [849, *Hound*]). (Amazingly, this is the face of the wayward brother of a respectable, ordinary-looking character: in this particularly lurid example, a life of crime seems able to mark a face racially by turning it "yellow," presumably as part of the descent back to the "animal.") A sufficiently horrible facial expression can possess medusoid power (the victim in "The Crooked Man" dies with such a chilling facial expression that "more than one person fainted at the mere sight of him, so terrible was the effect" [479]). An agreeable pitch of comic absurdity is reached when Holmes deduces that a client is a piano teacher rather than a typist because "there is a spirituality about the face ... which the typewriter does not generate" (613, "The Adventure of the Solitary Cyclist").[15]

Such hyperlegible signs, inherited from melodrama and the gothic tradition, are in tension both with the thespian gift that allows Holmes repeatedly to don disguises that fool everyone, including Watson, and with the process of fission that produces a Moriarty out of a Holmes (or vice versa)—an ambiguity that also forms part of the texture of gothic narrative. The eagle-eyed protagonist splits and doubles: into a stolid foil (Watson), a superbrilliant double (Holmes's older brother Mycroft), and an evil double (Professor Moriarty).[16] The Holmes-Watson-Moriarty sequence mirrors a pattern laid down by Edgar Allan Poe in the Dupin stories; and the Poe stories themselves, as is well known, form an echo chamber of allusions and repetitions.[17] This vigorous splitting and redoubling—a fundamental gothic motif, as Eve Sedgwick and others have shown—bleeds into the even more uncontrollable processes of redoubling, replication, and identification that we have summed up at various points in this book as the movement of media or mediation.[18] Holmes's addiction to cocaine or even to tobacco pales in comparison to his addiction to news. Holmes reads newspapers obsessively, learns about cases from them, occasionally cracks cases by putting manipulative ads in them ("The Press, Watson, is a most valuable institution, if you only know how to use it" [688, "The Adventure of the Six Napoleons"]), and advances his reputation by having his exploits mentioned in them.[19] The famous Baker Street fog and smoke has newsprint in the spectrum of its particulates—sometimes almost literally, as when Watson, incapacitated by his war wound on a rainy day, surrounds himself "with a cloud of newspapers, until at last, saturated with the news of the day, I tossed them all aside and lay listless" (327, "The Adventure of the Noble Bachelor"). Watson's chronicling of Holmes's adventures, meanwhile, makes Holmes an ever more public figure, brings him more clients, and generates all sorts of unpredictable mediatic side-effects—not least the creation of fan organizations dedicated to pretending that Holmes and Watson are, or were, real.[20]

My point here is not to provide a full-scale reading, of course, either of the Holmes stories or of Sherlock Holmes as a cultural phenomenon.[21] My aim has been rather to suggest some reasons why an artist keen-eyed enough to discern the shape of the discourse of theory in 1990 might have turned his thoughts to Sherlock Holmes. This Edwardian detective long ago became a citizen of the global archive, available for all sorts of artistic repurposings. With his heart of steel, Holmes has many of the qualities that, as we saw in Chapter 1, the late twentieth-century discourse of theory will require of its personifications ("so many regard him as a machine rather than a man" [475, "The Crooked Man"]). His intelligence is a little too cold, a little too rational to be entirely human ("One of the most remarkable characteristics of Sherlock Holmes was his power of throwing his brain out of action and switching all his thoughts on to lighter things whenever he had convinced himself that he could no longer work to advantage" [1,093]).[22] Holmes is the theorist as hyperrational, hyperaesthetic superreader, quivering on the edge of "Frenchness," and bound up with the potentially uncanny workings of mass media. An artist like Tansey, interested in the phantasmatic reduction of theory to its two-headed avatar de Man/Derrida, and alert to the ways in which the discourse of theory becomes a "querying of de Man" at its moments of greatest intensity, can be counted on to read the archive with similar care. The Holmes intertext strengthens the hypothesis that this painting is querying "theory" in America.

—+—

The specific visual intertext, of course, is Sidney Paget's famous frontispiece illustrating Holmes's death in "The Final Problem"; and Tansey's choice of this image forms part of his deconstruction of Holmesian certitude.[23] This Paget drawing illustrates the conflict that Watson never sees. At the end of "The Final Problem," Watson and some unidentified "experts" who, in Holmesian fashion, have studied the signs, can only imagine this scene based on a textual landscape of footprints and marks and literal text.[24] (Holmes leaves physical marks on the finest text-receptive surface that the earth can provide—"The blackish soil is kept forever soft by the incessant drift of spray, and a bird would leave its tread on it" [554]—and he leaves a letter for Watson weighted down with his cigarette case on a rock. The landscape is already nearly as text-striated in Conan Doyle's story as it is in Tansey's painting.) Paget, offering a visual equivalent of the Holmesian "scientific use of the imagination," grants visibility to what was not seen—to an event that has had to be reconstructed through signs. Tansey, as noted earlier, redraws and resituates Paget's image so as to strip away the illusion of referential reliability. Tansey's scene can *only* be "seen"—hallucinated, imagined, read off from canvas, paint, and ink. (We may note in passing, though, that Paget's illustration is rich with strange detail. Coffin-shaped protuberances bulge out of the cliff face; Moriarty's arm thrusts skyward with mysterious rigidity and force; most strikingly there is that hat—the famous deerstalker that Paget is often credited with giving Holmes—falling ahead of the two combatants, looking rather like a breast, and floating just to the right of where their two groins are pressed together, offering itself to psychoanalytically inclined readers as something like an *objet petit a*: a fragment of alterity within the symbolic order.)[25] In the impossible space of Tansey's painting, Derrida is querying a dead de Man, at the edge of a text-cliff reached by a text-path that has been pulled out of scalable perspective as it drops toward us in the painting's lower left corner. (Paget's path also has a dizzying drop; Tansey accentuates it.) Uncertain to what extent we are seeing or reading, we recognize figures that are just that—*figures*, in and of a landscape that simultaneously encourages and destroys representational conventions. Within the representational convention, Derrida dances with and queries his dead other: querying him, he listens for a voice from beyond the grave—a little like Watson at the Reichenbach Falls, "listening to the half-human shout which came booming up with the spray out of the abyss" (552).[26] We might ourselves begin to hear echoing in this scene a famous, darkly sublime de Manian comment about reading-as-querying: "to read is to understand, to question, to know, to forget, to erase, to deface, to repeat—that is to say, the endless prosopopoeia by which the dead are made to have a face and a voice which tells the allegory of their demise and allows us to apostrophize them in our turn. No degree of knowledge can ever stop this madness, for it is the madness of words."[27] The dead voice of de Man continues its broadcast, thanks to its technical extension in print-media; and the message it sends—which is that "voice," always already mediatized, is originary only as trope—could be called the very motto of "theory." There is a sublime thrill to that message; and Tansey, building on Paget's illustration of Conan Doyle's prose, provides a visual equivalent in the idiom of sublime landscape painting. These dancers are so framed by falling, by the great sweep of the rift that scores six and a half feet of canvas, that they and their embrace seem just one more thing that the indifferent abyss will devour. Yet there they are nonetheless: fixed figures with whom we can identify; to whom we can grant faces, voices, vices; around whom minimal plot-elements can form.[28] This sublime economy of threat and consolation is further complicated by the painting's disruption of its representational codes, as well as by its nagging absurdity. Its monochrome field, its textual smears, and its comically fantastic scenario combine to urge us to consider how difficult it can be to decide whether we're being taught a lesson or told a joke, and whether we're seeing a mark, or reading a sign, or imagining a world.

In Conan Doyle's story, Holmes and Moriarty do not "query" each other. They rush into battle without a word, pushing the vexed question of reading back as far as it will go, straight into the mirrored face of the other ("I read an inexorable purpose in his grey eyes" [562]). Tansey delivers us from that clenched gothic agon, but only to enmesh us in a dance-struggle that, however often we remind ourselves of its irreality, or of its ambiguity (which is it: dance or struggle?), keeps us teetering around a circle of dancing, struggling, questioning. The question "what does the painting mean" spirals into the absurd yet unavoidable question, "what is Derrida asking de Man?" This question of the question receives two exemplary, if inevitably unsatisfactory, answers in the commentaries on this painting in the two books from the early 1990s that collect and survey Tansey's art. Rather ingeniously, Arthur C. Danto proposes that Tansey's two figures are "locked in eternal combat over the meaning de Man gave to the meaning that Derrida gave to Rousseau."[29] This is intelligent imagining: Danto has his eye on the intellectual, biographical, and textual history that joins and separates the oeuvres of Paul de Man and Jacques Derrida. The only drawback of this suggestion—apart of course from the mad gratuitousness that accompanies it or any other "answer" in this context—is that it does not really address itself to the question of the question as delivered to us by the statement of the title (why is only *Derrida* doing the querying, then?). Judi Freeman accounts for Derrida's role, though her prose takes an odd, symptomatic turn as she points us toward the most obvious, reductive, and inevitable interpretation of all. "The scene," she tells us,

> illustrate[s] the debate raging over the posthumous revelation in 1987 that de Man had ties to fascists in his native Belgium during World War II. . . . So why is Derrida now wrestling de Man? Because his defense, though impassioned, was often problematic, involving a selective marshalling of events and documents in support of de Man's integrity. No doubt he was "querying" the de Man he thought he knew as well as the one he did not know at all.[30]

"No doubt" is indeed the mantra here: the critic's apparent absence of doubt generates first a cascade of strenuously simplistic assertions, and then, in a more surprising development, carries her final sentence off into the historical past tense. A little like Sherlock Holmes fans getting caught up in their reimaginings of Baker Street, Freeman drifts briefly into the rhetorical equivalent of a referential fantasy—as though Derrida had once *really* stood there querying de Man in that Tansey painting. The more violently one demands answers in such contexts, the more vigorously one has to invest in personifications capable of providing them. But Freeman is right to at least this extent: the "de Man affair" forms part of the landscape of theory that is this painting's subject. Freeman's answer is scripted in advance, wired into the painting's aesthetic program—not as an "answer," of course, but as part of the question of the question. Tansey's foregrounding of a page of *Blindness and Insight* that cites Nietzsche on memory and forgetting may be adduced as, among other things, a discreet tracking device, oriented toward the media storm that marks the culminating point of the phantasmatics of theory in America.

Both de Man and Derrida question the question. Some of Derrida's most sustained writing in this difficult area occurs in *Of Spirit: Heidegger and the Question* (1987), a text that appeared in its original French edition just before the "Heidegger" and "de Man" "affairs" erupted in Europe and the United States.[31] Working his way toward a discussion of promising in relation to questioning, Derrida invokes de Man—once again; in the four years between de Man's death in 1983 and the publication of this text, Derrida has invoked, read, questioned de Man repeatedly. In *Of Spirit*, Derrida turns to de Man just as the running noose of his argument is tightening. He is about to affirm that the promise ontologically precedes the question, and at this point he recalls de Man's mock-Heideggerian pun in *Allegories of Reading*, "*Die Sprache verspricht (sich)*" ("language promises," but, with the addition of the reflexive pronoun, "language mis-speaks"). Here is de Man's complete sentence: "*Die Sprache verspricht (sich)*: to the extent that it is necessarily misleading, language just as necessarily conveys the promise of its own truth."[32] Derrida elaborates: "language or speech promises, promises itself, but also goes back on its word, becomes undone or unhinged, derails or becomes delirious, deteriorates. . . . Language always, *before any question*, and in the very question, comes down to [*revient à*] the promise."[33] Does Derrida's deployment of the de Man citation promise a dance or a struggle? As one might expect at this point, a question about Derrida on de Man on the question of the question is not going to generate a satisfying answer. But let us attempt a reading that respects the friendship between these two readers, and then leave them there, teetering on the cliff, to work things out.

The promise that lies (in all senses) before any question, Derrida tells us, performs what he goes on to call "a *yes* before all opposition of *yes* and *no*" (94): a dissymmetrical affirmation that cannot be brought into the cognitive order of yes/no, inside/outside, figurative/literal. Prior to the formation of any question, language is already there: promising itself, going back on itself, ex-posing itself. This thesis, I suggest—for Derrida, who has his own preferred idiom, certainly does not put it this way—overlaps with de Man's radicalization of the problem of figurative language. Derrida could have quoted from earlier in *Allegories of Reading* if he had been inclined to question de Man on the question more frontally, hands firmly around his friend's waist (searching, perhaps, for a "baritsu" hold). He would have turned in that case to the famous opening essay "Semiology and Rhetoric," where de Man submits the so-called rhetorical question to rhetorical intensification, to the point that the question becomes unsure of its own identity, without ceasing to have to question (itself). Once again the punch line is a pun—the most awful and baroque pun in de Man's oeuvre, and one that gathers Derrida into its serious joke:

> As long as we are talking about bowling shoes, the consequences are relatively trivial; Archie Bunker . . . muddles along in a world where literal and figurative meanings get in each other's way, though not without discomforts. But suppose that it is a *de*-bunker rather than a "Bunker," and a de-bunker of the arche (or origin), an archie Debunker such as Nietzsche or Jacques Derrida for instance, who asks the question "What is the Difference"—and we cannot even tell from his grammar whether he "really" wants to know "what" difference is or is just telling us that we shouldn't even try to find out. Confronted with the difference between grammar and rhetoric, grammar allows us to ask the question, but the sentence by means of which we ask it may deny the very possibility of asking. For what is the use of asking, I ask, when we cannot even authoritatively decide whether a question asks or doesn't ask? (*AR*, 9–10)

It can be tempting to grant idealizing humanist or negative-theological content to Derrida's affirmation of affirmation, and de Man's scene of skewed repetition ("what is the use of asking, I ask") can serve as a useful counterweight. (As can de Man's ironic tolerance of mayhem: as he writes in another context, it would be "naïve to ask over what one is fighting: one fights over whether or not there is a question.")[34] The Derridean "yes" that precedes the question is an exposure to futurity: futurity as the incalculable "*à venir*," as Derrida frequently puts it. De Man's tone is more darkly comic, and the language of temporality has been replaced by a rhetorical idiom; but his seriocomic staging of a compulsive inability to stop questioning enacts an instability that ontologically "precedes" the question. De Man calls that instability "reading." Reading, the inability (and necessity) to decide between literal and figural meaning, is the trap, the opportunity, the future that language gives. Is the question (really, literally) a question? We cannot be sure; we must decide; that vertiginous pressure is the "yes" of language as the opening of the (im)possibility of reading. De Man famously plots self-disarticulating reading-itineraries devoted to the renunciation of all satisfactions, including those of renunciation. When de Man offers bivouac points, they sound like bleak, exposed places ("No degree of knowledge can ever stop this madness, for it is the madness of words"). Yet perhaps—perhaps at least at certain points in the intimate and ambiguous Derrida–de Man encounter—that de Manian rhetorical mood may be characterized as affirmative, in its own grim, ironic way.

—+—

Constructing the Grand Canyon, another Tansey painting from 1990, offers a different environment (Figure 3). The monochromatic palette is cadmium red; it is daytime, time for work. Tansey's sly wit is more obviously in evidence. His preparatory studies for this painting include mock-questions to himself such as "How much does text weigh?" scrawled over rapid pen-and-ink sketches of figures pushing or pulling or hewing large blocks or fragments (Danto, 124). In the finished painting, minute human figures swarm through a textual Grand Canyon, "constructing" it. Presumably one constructs a canyon through a process of "deconstruction"—an activity that resembles Tansey's subtractive method of painting. He applies a coat of paint to a white gesso ground, and works the paint while it is wet. "Human figures can be painted in the first two hours," Tansey explains. "After three hours tacky paint can be blotted and smudged to create such naturalizing effects as atmospheric perspective and obscuring dusts. After five hours only scraping or abrasion is possible" (127). A Tansey painting is a race against time; like a fresco painter he composes his pictures in sections. According to Tansey the subtractive method, performed on a monochromatic field, emphasizes "interactions of time, memory, touch, and sight" as opposed to "the immediate opticality of color." Texture involves associations between appearance and memory: "If you see rock texture in a painting you read it as rock by associating the appearance with the memory of how rock feels." Furthermore,

Figure 3. Mark Tansey, *Constructing the Grand Canyon*. 1990. Oil on canvas. 88¼ × 127¾ × 2⅛″ framed. Collection Walker Art Center, Minneapolis. Gift of Penny and Mike Winton, 1990. © Mark Tansey.

there is also a built-in narrative element in that texture, in a sense, is the fossil-
ized record of action, both natural and cultural. Examples are geological strata,
a repeatedly marked text, an eroded surface, a piece of textile, a painting with
indexical marks. Texture is the trace of events. (Tansey, in Danto 128)

Constructing the Grand Canyon is thus among other things an allegory of the
activity of marking and inscribing that brought the painting into being. It is
an allegory of inscription as memory, and memory as inscription: an allegory
of the archive.

The archive swallows up its texts. Page 146 from *Blindness and Insight* may
have contributed to the construction of this Grand Canyon of Theory (one
of the rock climbers scaling the left wall is a miniature, near-exact replica
of the climbing figure who scales page 146 in another Tansey painting from
this period, *Close Reading*). But here, we can't be sure what is being climbed.
The text face on which the climber hangs seems to have changed, and the
print has become illegible (Figure 4). Tansey has used confetti-strips of text
this time, with different strips miming the texture of geological strata. Words,
occasionally groups of words, remain legible throughout the Canyon, but it
will take a reader more obsessed than I to recover even small portions of its

Figure 4. Mark Tansey, *Constructing the Grand Canyon*, detail.

textual archaeology. The Canyon is an archive in which texts shatter and blur, forgotten while being preserved. Like Borges's Library of Babel, this Canyon seems capable of containing everything, including other paintings by Mark Tansey. But (again like Borges's Library) its riches emerge as fragments. In the foreground a man pours rubbled, winnowed text, all A's, into a railcar (Figure 5).

Like *Derrida Queries de Man, Constructing the Grand Canyon* offers us a sublime scene—or at least it ought to: the Grand Canyon is an official locus the American natural sublime. It strikes us as paradoxical to speak of "constructing" the Grand Canyon; but Tansey's title and painterly praxis alert us to the constructedness not just of texts and paintings, but of psyches, lives, cultures, and not least, of course, national symbols and monuments, including "natural" ones. A historical study by Stephen J. Pyne, *How the Canyon Became Grand*, complements Tansey's painting nicely:

Figure 5. Mark Tansey, *Constructing the Grand Canyon*, detail.

The Grand Canyon was not so much revealed as created. More than once the Canyon was missed entirely or seen and dismissed. Then, with the suddenness of a summer storm, American society in the mid-nineteenth century mustered the capacity and the will to match its discovered opportunity and transformed land into place and place into symbol. The outcome was neither obvious nor inevitable. Popular instincts argued that river-dashed gorges were hazards, not adventures, and that immense chasms were geologic gaps, not gorgeous panoramas. A generation of intellectuals labored to instruct the public otherwise.[35]

As Pyne shows, an educated urban elite, nourished on romantic aesthetics and nineteenth-century nationalism, viewed and promoted the Canyon in ways that would never have occurred to the Native Americans, Spanish explorers, Mormon pioneers, and other settlers and mountain men who encountered the Canyon in earlier eras. "The creation of Canyon meaning was as arduous and dramatic as the excavation of its great gorges" (xiv). The pictorial arts played a role: Thomas Moran's seven by twelve foot *The Chasm of the Colorado* (1873), purchased by the U.S. Congress in 1874 to hang in the Capitol, is credited with having influenced Theodore Roosevelt's decision to name the Canyon a National Monument in 1908.[36] Tansey's painting (at 7 × 10.5 feet, nearly as large as Moran's) does not, however, directly quote *The Chasm of the Colorado* or any other famous rendition of the Grand Canyon. We have left the agonistic world of *Derrida Queries de Man* for a more diffusely archival universe. Rather than stage a parodic struggle-dance with a precursor, Tansey draws broadly here on the perspectival conventions of sublime landscape painting, as part of an even broader critique—and comically literalized "deconstruction"—of the textual and historico-aesthetic construction of sublime, national-symbolic space.

Derrida Queries de Man had left room in its textscape for waterfall-mist, a few straggling plants, and impressions of slick black rock; *Constructing the Grand Canyon* reduces its traces of "nature" to haze, light, and sky. The earth—the geologic archive—has become dehydrated strata, ribbons, blocks, and boulders of mechanically reproduced and reproducible text. We have entered the time of the Anthropocene: the era of geoengineering and climate change. And though the sublimity of the scene is not simply negated—the grand compositional conventions of this style of painting remain—everything goes slightly awry. A blend of wonder and absurdity—something like what Friedrich Schlegel called "sublime buffoonery"—infects the scene's grandeur. There is an overcrowded heterogeneity to the "construction" process. Some of the workers are dressed as Gold Rush miners, some as preppies; one or two, like the rock-climbing "close reader," are 1980s hardbodies.

In the middle foreground, to the left, variously clad figures sit in a circle like children and play with little hammers. The derricks and pulley mechanisms and most of the tools date from the pre–Civil War period, having migrated, like the tiny bison atop the left cliff, from popular illustrations of the Wild West. But on both left and right ridges, figures bend their bodies in postures known only to twentieth- and twenty-first-century labor, and blast away with jackhammers. Documenting its own (de)construction, this archive collects different styles and temporal strata of technology and work. The mix is absurd rather than dizzying. Not that comic absurdity in the least precludes critical insight. Limning those tiny toy buffalo on the ridge is a faint gleam of the political violence that "national-natural" spaces work to conceal. The buffalo relay the only trace left, in this archival space, of the native peoples whose literal displacement and figurative near-erasure was the precondition for the production of *nature* as a *national* monument. The buffalo relay that trace only in the faintest way, for of course they are themselves mass-produced clichés, plastic figurines to be arranged as part of a faux-mythic scene. Tansey's point—made all the more powerfully for remaining strictly within the kitsch-code of the Western-sublime landscape— is of course partly that archives are not innocent compendia. Archives are not "natural" or neutral; they remember certain things and forget others, sometimes strategically (and sometimes not: they also lose things accidentally, and preserve or repeat things without meaning to). Tansey's painting may be said to be remembering, here, in and through an act of ironic repetition, the massive power of forgetting commanded by natural-national-sublime landscape painting. But the mood is comic-ironic rather than tragic. The grand lineaments of the sublime have faded into an enormous, hot, monochrome space in which nature and culture, work and play, fray into each other to form an allegory of dubious gravity.

A Yale pennant, bright punch line at the heart of the joke, flutters near the visual center of the painting. It recalls the world of Stover at Yale, football culture, secret societies, and the other tokens and signs through which an elite institution preserves and nurtures its symbiosis with its clientele. Under the pennant are the famous figures, miniature but recognizable (Figure 6). Despite their central position in the landscape, they are comically out of place: they belong neither to the pennant's undergraduate college-culture, nor to the various worlds of the Canyon's athletes and laborers. De Man and Derrida, hailing from some markedly foreign clime, wear raincoats. They stand close to each other in easy intimacy, their friendship rather than their agon on display. In front of them, Geoffrey Hartman sprawls on the ground, and Harold Bloom, rather atypically dapper in tie and blazer, assumes a

Figure 6. Mark Tansey, *Constructing the Grand Canyon*, detail.

thinker's pose. I mentioned earlier that Tansey's painting eschews modeling itself (at least so far as I know) on any specific Grand Canyon painting; but now that we have gotten to the Yale School, we enter a painterly jest. The postures of all four critics quote Raphael's *School of Athens*, with de Man and Derrida cast as Plato and Aristotle (Figure 7). (Derrida here is also redupli-cating, in clothing and posture, the Derrida of an earlier Tansey painting, *Mont Sainte-Victoire* [1987]. We are looking not simply at a painted image of Derrida, but at a *repetition* of a painted image of Derrida.) Sitting rather precariously on—possibly scooching down off—a text-block near the left edge of the painting, Michel Foucault also wears the clothing of European authority (Figure 8).[37] But in this canyon, it seems, the Yale School reigns. The painting's light source forms a spotlight illuminating them. For we are in the country of myth: the myth of "Yale," of Theory in America.

Figure 7. *The School of Athens* (1510–12) by Raphael. Courtesy Scala/Art Resource, NY.

Figure 8. Mark Tansey, *Constructing the Grand Canyon*, detail.

Perspectivally speaking, we inhabit this space. Our access to *Derrida Queries de Man* had been shrugged off by the cliff shoulder and its dizzyingly vertical, out-of-perspective path. That Alpine scene belonged to its high, distant agonists. This Grand Canyon is no doubt equally impossible to live in, but its text-walls sweep outward, opening onto the imagined community of a nation. The phantasmagoria that it offers us as part of our world is an artist's version of a discursive landscape that we have been surveying throughout this book. It makes sense that these Yale critics seem out of place; even at that mythical moment when the theory-canyon was just opening for business, no one really believed that they had organized and financed it singlehandedly. We see what we always knew we would see when we peer around: many different-looking projects or nonprojects going on. If this is "theory," it is not a visibly coordinated enterprise. Yet the painting's dominant visual and conceptual pun—that a canyon's construction is its *de*construction—wittily repeats the rhetorical equation of theory with deconstruction that forms the matrix of the discourse of (the resistance to) theory. So does the metamorphosis of earth into mechanically reproduced text. In this painting, even more dramatically than in *Derrida Queries de Man* and the other "theory" paintings of 1990, Tansey comically literalizes and frames for inspection the crude misreading of "deconstruction" as "a textualism which would confuse text and discourse, page, book, and the world, society or history and the library."[38]

And so the figures of the famous critics shine out at us, key-stops of a fantastic roman à clef. As we know, the notion of a meaningful collective of "Yale Critics" is messy; Bloom and Hartman certainly seem lost in their own heads in this Canyon, and Hillis Miller has gone missing. But the center of the center was never in doubt. Precisely at the intersection of the painting's major perspectival lines of force stand de Man and Derrida, their heads haloed and framed by the sublime cascading U's of the receding text-canyon, their raincoats a visual rhyme. It is amazing that they are there, these foreign, trenchcoated figures, one of them beamed up from another Tansey painting and both of them playing the principals of *The School of Athens*; they certainly are not entirely real; yet without them neither Tansey's painting nor the discourse of theory it pictorializes and parodies would cohere.

We have been searching for language throughout this book to describe an illusion that also relays a kind of truth. It is unquestionably a desert-heat-crazed dream to equate theory with deconstruction, and to personify deconstruction as de Man and Derrida. The hallucinatory equation "theory-deconstruction-Derrida-de Man" has a symptomatic, but not in any way synecdochic or otherwise straightforwardly representative relation to the reality of professional practice in the academy. A proper intellectual historian of theory in America—a cousin of that beachcombing historian of structuralism whom we recalled Derrida imagining at the beginning of this book—might well decide, for instance, that, as far as actual discursive practices go, the most influential single figure over the past forty years across multiple fields, topics, and approaches in the humanities has been Michel Foucault. And the Canyon we are gazing at here does not necessarily disagree: we, too, might well decide that, traced down to the heterogeneous digging, measuring, and climbing activities being performed by these absurd little figures, the painting's visual pun of "construction through deconstruction" mutates into tropes of archaeological and archival recovery and production that practitioners of the variously Foucault-influenced styles of work of the last few decades might, in a humorous mood, be willing to claim as an ironic figure for their aspirations. But if, in this painting's shrewd visual commentary, Foucault sits on the sidelines, his face obscured, while the fetish-figures of theory, de Man and Derrida, with their "Yale" penumbra, occupy the Canyon's vanishing point (*je sais bien, mais quand même . . .*), it is because the writings of de Man and Derrida touched a nerve. In their different ways, both constructed reading practices that radically dismantled the illusions on which national-aesthetic ideologies rely. There would be many other ways of describing what their writings are about (particularly the extraordinarily inventive writings of Derrida, whose work crossed so many intellectual and institutional borders); but I have been focusing in this book on the Anglo-American phenomenon called "theory," and I have proposed that this phenomenon took shape in a context in which a radical critique of aesthetics (aesthetics in the broadest sense as the phenomenalization of signification, yet also in an institutional-discursive sense as a pedagogical ideology) was able to metastasize past what one might have imagined to be its natural scholarly boundaries.

One of theory's enabling conditions, I have suggested, was the structure and scale of the American research university system. The canyon-making, text-mining activity going on in Tansey's painting offers a figure for, among other things, academic work, particularly in the humanities—especially when interpretive work in the humanities is being quantified within university bureaucracies. (How much has been produced? Which, recoded as the visual joke of Tansey's painting, becomes: how much has been taken away?) In the American scholarly system, work has to be produced; and in literary and cultural fields, for the last half-century or so, this has above all meant that interpretations and arguments about interpretations have to be produced. If de Man had not inhabited such an institutional context, he could not have acceded—at least not in the same way—to the symbolic role that the discourse of theory accorded him, and that he so cagily filled. A fundamental but vexed role for academic work; a history of strident public discourse about the demise of the humanities; an ever more media-saturated and globalized yet also obsessively nationalistic culture: these were some of the broad features of the cultural ecosystem in which the discourse of theory evolved in the United States in the 1970s and 1980s. Tansey's painting not only tropes its own production, but also that of the professionalized criticism that constituted one of the conditions for "theory" to become a wider media phenomenon. And when we say that this painting tropes its own production, we mean not just that it figures the "subtractive" technique (that is, the drawing, scraping, and smudging processes mentioned earlier) through which it came physically into being, but also that it allegorizes its critical vision. To the degree that Tansey's painting deconstructs national-natural aestheticism by revealing the historicity, constructedness, and violence—in a word, the textuality—of a "national monument," this painting, like my interpretation of it here, announces itself as having been produced within the context of "theory." And when, within this context, we use the word *theory* to describe readings that demystify national aestheticism in this way, we pay homage willy-nilly to the difficult, routinely misrepresented, complexly influential writings of two thinkers whose work, at a crucial point in the discursive and institutional history of the American academy, thematized and performatively engaged the radical instability of signifying and techno-mediatic processes. That is why, as long as conditions obtain for the survival of the discourse of theory as we know it, Derrida and de Man will remain the mirage-like central figures in its landscape.

Acknowledgments ―|―

This book began many years ago, promptly ran off the rails, and more than a decade later got put back on track. My intention had always been to write about the peculiar academic-mediatic event of "theory" in the American academy, the attention accorded the so-called "Yale Critics" in the 1970s, and the quasi-allegorical way in which Jacques Derrida and Paul de Man—above all de Man—came to represent "theory" at its "highest" and, seemingly, its most threatening and alluring. But as I began to collect information about the reception of the Yale Critics, I became curious about the institutional history of literary instruction at Yale and got sidetracked. Visiting New Haven in 1999, I was fortunate to have the chance to interview Maynard Mack and Louis Martz, and, a year later, during a trip to Ithaca, A. Dwight Culler; they told me stories about the old school of text editing and historical scholarship at Yale, and about how Mack and others introduced Brooks and Warren's *Understanding Poetry* (1938) into their classes. During this same two-year period, which is to say around 1999–2000, Victor Brombert, Peter Brooks, Jacques Derrida, Shoshana Felman, Paul Fry, Thomas Greene, Geoffrey Hartman, Neil Hertz, Christopher Miller, J. Hillis Miller, and Ronald Paulson shared memories of and thoughts about the 1970s era with me. Once when I was passing through Baltimore, Richard Macksey welcomed me to his legendary library for an afternoon and regaled me with information about the epochal 1966 conference at Johns Hopkins. These fragments did not add up to a book—at least not one I am able to write—and those notes still sit in a box.

I mention this false start in order to thank the individuals who generously gave of their time. I also want to thank the staff of the Department of Manuscripts and Archives of Yale's Sterling Library, in particular Bill Massa, for their help, and the staff of the Department of Special Collections at the University of California at Irvine, in particular Eddie Yeghiayan and Bill Landis, for theirs. Kari Conness and Ellen Scheible helped me gather data during an early phase in my research. The project was supported over several summers by research grants from Claremont Graduate University and, later, from Brown University.

Fragments of these chapters have been given as talks on many occasions over a long period of time, and it is now impossible for me even to remember, let alone do justice to, most of the debts I have contracted along the way. A few stand out. I am particularly grateful to Barbara Herrnstein Smith for helping me reorient this project at a crucial point in its development. Jonathan Culler and Paul Fry read the manuscript with care and helped me improve it in many ways. There can be no better place than here, in the antechamber of a book about literary theory, to record my debt to these two scholars: long ago, Paul's undergraduate course on literary theory opened a new world of thought to me, and a couple of years later Jonathan's fall 1981 graduate seminar—a preview of his classic *On Deconstruction* (1982)—helped me begin mapping that world. A third former teacher is owed special thanks: J. Hillis Miller shared thoughts and answered questions on many occasions over many years, with the generosity for which he is legendary. His most recent act of kindness was to share with me his forthcoming text "Tales out of (the Yale) School," from which I quote in Chapter 1.

During the last four years I've had the privilege of being part of an extraordinary intellectual community that has come together at Brown University. Friends and colleagues who have commented on portions of the manuscript or discussed aspects of the topic with me include Ed Ahearn, Amanda Anderson, Susan Bernstein, Timothy Bewes, Stephen Foley, William Keach, Jacques Khalip, Kevin McLaughlin, Kristina Mendicino, Ourida Mostefai, Karen Newman, Saul Olyan, Gerhard Richter, Vanessa Ryan, Pierre Saint-Amand, Thomas Schestag, Zachary Sng, Suzanne Stewart-Steinberg, and Arnold Weinstein. Other friends whose conversation, writing, thought, and example have left their mark on my efforts to write about the "Yale Critics" over the years include Ian Balfour, Cathy Caruth, Cynthia Chase, David L. Clark, Evelyne Ender, Elizabeth Fay, William Flesch, Anne-Lise François, Michael Gamer, Kevis Goodman, Ortwin de Graef, Sara Guyer, Jerrold Hogle, Theresa Kelley, Kir Kuiken, Jeffrey Librett, Charles Mahoney, Elissa Marder, Brian McGrath, Martin McQuillan, Jan Mieszkowski, Kevin Newmark, Arkady Plotnitzsky, Forest Pyle, Laura Quinney, Tilottama Rajan, Arden Reed, Paul Saint-Amour, Charlie Shepherdson, Karen Swann, Rei Terada, Orrin N. C. Wang, Andrzej Warminksi, Samuel Weber, Deborah Elise White, Joshua Wilner, and Nancy Yousef.

I thank Mark Tansey for kindly permitting me to reproduce the paintings of his that I discuss in Chapter 6. Thanks also to the Gagosian Gallery for permission to reproduce their file of *Derrida Queries de Man*, and to the Walker Art Center for permission to reproduce *Constructing the Grand Canyon*. I am grateful to the Walker Art Center for allowing me to study this painting during a visit to Minneapolis some years ago.

Chapter 1 contains a paragraph extracted and repurposed from an afterword I wrote for *Art History versus Aesthetics*, ed. James Elkins (Routledge, 2005), plus a few fragments from an article, "Aesthetics, Theory, and the Profession of Literature: Derrida and Romanticism," *Studies in Romanticism* 46, no. 2 (2007). An early version of a portion of Chapter 2 appeared in *The Blackwell Companion to Romantic Poetry*, ed. Charles Mahoney (Blackwell, 2011), and a very early version of a portion of Chapter 4 appeared in *Historicizing Theory*, ed. Peter C. Herman (SUNY Press, 2003). Versions of a few paragraphs in Chapter 3 appeared in my introduction to a special issue of *The Wordsworth Circle* 37, no. 1 (2006). An earlier version of Chapter 5 appeared in a collection of essays that I edited, *Legacies of Paul de Man* (Fordham University Press, 2007). I thank the respective publishers for permission to republish these texts in revised form.

Helen Tartar talked with me about this book over more than a decade. She knew the story this book tells from the inside, and she should simply be receiving warm thanks here rather than also having to be remembered and mourned. The difference Helen made in the humanities over the last quarter-century is large enough to be called historical.

Tom Lay has taken up, caringly and skillfully, the impossible task of continuing Helen's work, and he has my thanks. I am grateful to Eric Newman and Gregory McNamee at Fordham for their help in preparing the manuscript for publication.

Heartfelt thanks to Molly for all those conversations that helped this book along its torturous way.

Notes

Introduction: The Strange Case of "Theory"

1. Jonathan Arac, Wlad Godzich, and Wallace Martin, eds., *The Yale Critics: Deconstruction in America* (Minneapolis: University of Minnesota Press, 1983), xi. Signs of discomfort proliferate. Since they miss "the coherence of a 'school,'" the editors will "focus on four 'critics'" after having subtracted Derrida: "Although Derrida is a regular visitor to Yale and lectures there, we do not devote an essay to him alone but allow his effect to be diffused throughout our discussion." Then, after mentioning Shoshana Felman, they explain why they are not including her: "Her work, however, we have judged part of another story. Written in French, it has helped make the 'Ecole de Yale' known in Paris, but it is only beginning to be known here, as translations of her major books appear" (xi–xii). By 1983, Felman had published influential papers in English and was known in particular for her great essay "Turning the Screw of Interpretation," *Yale French Studies* 55–56 (1977): 94–207, so Arac, Godzich, and Martin's reasoning is pretty lame. Barbara Johnson, herself another candidate for election as yet another "Yale Critic," offers a relevant analysis with respect to a different text in her essay "Gender Theory and the Yale School" (1984): "Would it have been possible for there to have been a female presence in the Yale School? Interestingly, in Jonathan Culler's bibliography to *On Deconstruction*, Shoshana Felman's book *La folie et la chose littéraire* is described as "a wide-ranging collection of essays by a member of the 'école de Yale.' Felman, in other words, *was* a member of the Yale School, but only in French. . . . For now, suffice it to say that there was no reason other than gender why Felman's work—certainly closer to de Man's and Derrida's than the work of Harold Bloom—should not have been seen as an integral part of the Yale School." Barbara Johnson, *A World of Difference* (Baltimore: Johns Hopkins University Press, 1987), 32–41, at 32–33. I think Johnson is unfair to Culler here (who, it seems to me, *does* consider Felman part of the Yale School; his shift to French seems little more than a bit of rhyming with the language of Felman's title); but Johnson has put her finger on a pattern that Arac, Godzich, and Martin's preface exemplifies.

2. Readers who want to read up on that history should begin with the following texts: Paul de Man, *Wartime Journalism, 1939–1943* (Lincoln: University of Nebraska Press, 1988) and *Responses: On Paul de Man's Wartime Journalism* (Lincoln: University of Nebraska Press, 1989). Both collections are edited by Werner Hamacher, Neil Hertz, and Thomas Keenan. I discuss the media uptake of the "de Man affair" in Chapter 1. Within the academy, the most important polemical exchange to know about is the one that took place in the pages of *Critical Inquiry* in response to Jacques Derrida's essay,

"Like the Sound of the Sea Deep Within a Shell: Paul de Man's War," trans. Peggy Kamuf, reprinted in *Responses* but originally published in *Critical Inquiry* 14, no. 3 (1988): 530–652. Six responses to Derrida's essay, several of them very angry, were published in *Critical Inquiry* 15, no. 4 (1989), as was Derrida's fierce reply, "Biodegradables: Seven Diary Fragments," trans. Peggy Kamuf (812–73).

3. There are, of course, numerous invaluable analyses of the institutional history of criticism, starting with Gerald Graff's classic *Professing Literature* (Chicago: University of Chicago Press, 1987), which emphasizes the ease with which the vertical and modular structure of the American university department accommodates (and quarantines) innovation.

4. About once every two years the American best-seller market supports another *cri de coeur* about the humanities at the university level; as I write, the book making the talk-show rounds is William Deresiewicz, *Excellent Sheep: The Miseducation of the American Elite and the Way to a Meaningful Life* (New York: Free Press, 2014). This genre of writing is hard to imagine outside the American context.

5. René Wellek, "Destroying Literary Studies," *The New Criterion* (December 1983).

6. Paul de Man, "The Resistance to Theory," in *The Resistance to Theory*, (Minneapolis: University of Minnesota Press, 1986), 12–13.

7. The French and perhaps more generally European tradition of the *maître-penseur* is the product of a quite different educational system, differently positioned within the public sphere. For an interesting study of the relationship between philosophy and the media in France during these years, see Tamara Chaplin, *Turning on the Mind: French Philosophers on Television* (Chicago: University of Chicago Press, 2007).

8. Jacques Derrida, "Some Statements and Truisms about Neologisms, Newisms, Postisms, Parasitisms, and Other Small Seismisms," in *The States of "Theory": History, Art, and Critical Discourse,* ed. David Carroll (New York: Columbia University Press, 1990), 71. Subsequent references are given parenthetically.

9. Culminating in Derrida's "Typewriter Ribbon: Limited Ink (2)," in *Without Alibi*, trans. Peggy Kamuf (Stanford: Stanford University Press, 2002). Andrzej Warminksi notes the dash of aggression that flavors Derrida's treatment of de Man in this late text. See "Machinal Effects: Derrida With and Without de Man," *MLN* 124, no. 5 (2009): 1072–90.

10. Paul de Man, *Aesthetic Ideology* (Minneapolis: University of Minnesota Press, 1996), 118.

11. Rodolphe Gasché, *The Wild Card of Reading: On Paul de Man* (Cambridge, Mass.: Harvard University Press, 1998), 1. Rapid genealogies that pair Derrida the philosopher with de Man the literary theorist easily devolve into simplistic hierarchies, as in the minor commonplace that has circulated in Anglo-American literary-theoretical argument since the mid-1970s, according to which de Man's literary deconstruction "domesticates" Derrida's more radical project. The most tough-minded version of this claim is to be found in Rodolphe Gasché's influential "Deconstruction as Criticism," *Glyph* 6 (1979): 177–215.

12. See Jacques Rancière, *The Politics of Aesthetics*, trans. Gabriel Rockhill (New York: Continuum, 2004): "I call the distribution [*partage*] of the sensible the system of self-evident facts of sense perception that simultaneously discloses the existence of

something in common and the delimitations that define the respective parts and positions within it" (12).

13. Romanticism had long been one of the strengths of Comparative Literature at Yale because of the influence of René Wellek, the inaugural chair of the department at its founding in 1946, and its institutionally dominant figure during the ensuing twenty years. The English Department, with its strong historicist, text-editing, eighteenth-century-studies and Christian–New Critical traditions, was another story; when Harold Bloom began graduate study there in 1951 he saw himself as having to do battle with the antiromantic legacy of the New Critics. (I provide a few details about this in Chapter 4.) By the 1970s, however, even the Yale English Department was arguably best known for its strength in romantic studies, thanks to Bloom and Hartman and the younger critics they influenced (e.g., Thomas Weiskel, Paul Fry, Leslie Brisman).

14. I have discussed the mutual interference among theory, aesthetics, and romanticism in *The Politics of Aesthetics: Nationalism, Gender, Romanticism* (Stanford: Stanford University Press, 2003).

15. See Rancière, *The Politics of Aesthetics*, 22, passim. "The aesthetic regime of the arts is the regime that strictly identifies art in the singular and frees it from any specific rule, from any hierarchy of the arts, subject matter, and genres" (23).

16. Harold Bloom, *The Visionary Company: A Reading of English Romantic Poetry* (New York: Doubleday, 1961). Different sorts of interpretations of romanticism as "escapist" were offered by the New Humanists at the beginning of the twentieth century and by the "New Historicists" at the end of it.

17. See Chapter 1 for a brief discussion of *Deconstruction and Criticism* (1979), and see Chapter 2 for an account of J. Hillis Miller's contributions to the field of romanticism during this period.

18. Geoffrey Hartman, "Preface" to *Deconstruction and Criticism*, by Harold Bloom, Paul de Man, Jacques Derrida, Geoffrey H. Hartman, and J. Hillis Miller (New York: Seabury Press, 1979), ix.

19. This book grants more attention to Bloom and Hartman than to Miller for precisely this reason. As I am about to summarize, a resistance to ("de Manian") theory attains complex figuration in Hartman's writing on the romantic imagination, and in Bloom's various self-stagings as well as in his theoretical writings from the 1970s. Miller's closeness to de Man and Derrida certainly does not mean one cannot try to discover patterns of resistance in his texts to the very deconstructive insights for which they argue (I attempt just such a reading in Chapter 2, and of course de Man's and Derrida's texts can be read similarly). But Miller is working in conscious proximity to de Man and Derrida; and though it would be possible and valuable to tease out the singularity of Miller's approach, I have preferred here to train attention on the more dramatic internal differences composing the "Yale Critics." My focus on romanticism has also kept me from giving as much space to Miller's work as it deserves. So much of Miller's extensive oeuvre appeared after the 1970s, furthermore, that a differently oriented book would be required to address it.

20. Paul de Man, "The Intentional Structure of the Romantic Image," in Harold Bloom, ed., *Romanticism and Consciousness: Essays in Criticism* (New York: Norton, 1970), 65–77, at 76–77.

21. John Guillory, *Cultural Capital: The Problem of Literary Canon Formation* (Chicago: University of Chicago Press, 1993), xii.

22. As responsible voices have emphasized, it is a cultural myth that the humanities major is in rapid decline. Humanities majors dropped off in the 1970s and early 1980s (as did social science majors, even more sharply), but since then the numbers of humanities majors have known no sharp changes, holding at 8–9 percent of total degrees granted in the United States. (The big shift in the 1970s–1980s was toward degrees in fields such as business and health services, largely driven by the marketing of college to new populations and the expansion of the credentialing system into new areas.) As Michael Bérubé comments: "The real story should be this: amazingly, remarkably, counterintuitively and bizarrely, humanities majors in the United States, as a percentage of all bachelor's degrees, have held steady since about 1990—since the onset of the culture wars, in fact." Michael Bérubé, "Breaking News: Humanities in Decline! Film at 11" (November 16, 2010), *Out of the Crooked Timber* website (accessed May 4, 2014). See also Bérubé's more recent "The Humanities, Declining? Not According to the Numbers," *The Chronicle Review* (July 1, 2013) (accessed May 4, 2014). The best summary of the numbers is Ben Schmidt, "A Crisis in the Humanities?" (June 10, 2013), guest-blogging for David Silbey, *Chronicle Blog Network* (accessed May 4, 2014). I thank Vanessa Ryan for pointing me to these and many other sites.

23. The changes effected in the consumption and distribution of literature under the impact of new media forms (many of which, of course, postdate Guillory's book) would also need careful weighing here. For a trenchant analysis of the contemporary neoliberal assault on cultural and political institutions, see Wendy Brown, *Undoing the Demos: Neoliberalism's Stealth Revolution* (Cambridge, Mass.: MIT Press, 2015).

24. Guillory's work since the publication of *Cultural Capital* has explored various archaeological layers of the American educational and research system; see e.g., "The System of Graduate Education," *PMLA* 115, no. 5 (2000): 1154–63, which addresses, among other topics, the modern university's double function of credentialing and research (1156).

25. I borrow the term "nickname" as a way of describing the curious status of this idiomatic use of the word *theory* from Jonathan Culler. See, among other texts, *On Deconstruction: Theory and Criticism After Structuralism* (Ithaca, N.Y.: Cornell University Press, 1982), 8. Culler comments that "the writings to which this term alludes . . . are a puzzling mixture."

26. Jonathan Culler, *The Literary in Theory* (Stanford: Stanford University Press, 2007), 3.

27. I borrow the term "allergen" from J. Hillis Miller; see "Paul de Man as Allergen," *Others* (Princeton: Princeton University Press, 2001), 219–58.

28. Evelyn Barish, *The Double Life of Paul de Man* (New York: Norton, 2014), xvii, passim.

29. Claire Colebrook offers a representative anecdote: "I began writing on de Man while living in Manhattan. I was surrounded by educated, well-read, thoughtful, highly literate but not necessarily academic types. When I mentioned that I was writing on de Man they all either knew de Man almost solely via the 'de Man affair' or had de Man introduced to them there and then (by me) through an account of the

de Man affair." Claire Colebrook, "Introduction," *Theory and the Disappearing Future: On de Man, on Benjamin*, by Tom Cohen, Claire Colebrook, and J. Hillis Miller (New York: Routledge, 2012), 3.

30. David Lehman, *Signs of the Times: Deconstruction and the Fall of Paul de Man* (New York: Poseidon Press, 1991 [1992, with a new afterword]). For a witty and incisive review, see Ortwin de Graef, "A Bad Liver," *The Minnesota Review* 39 (1992–93): 157–65.

31. Jonathan Freedman, "Deconstructing de Man in the Digital Age," *Los Angeles Review of Books*, April 22, 2014.

32. I share, at least to some extent, the fascination with de Man as a biographical subject; it is a real pity that this very complicated man has yet to find a biographer or novelist talented enough to put aside the vitiating allegorical association of de Man with "theory" and imagine this life from the inside with the necessary subtlety and insight. To my knowledge, de Man's life has inspired at least four novels to date; of these the earliest, in my opinion, is the only one worth reading (and it may be no accident that this one good *roman à clef* centered on a "de Man" figure predates the "theory" era): Henri Thomas, *Le parjure* (*The Perjurer*) (Paris: Gallimard, 1964). According to Derrida, de Man recommended this novel to him: see Derrida, "Le Parjure, Perhaps," in *Without Alibi*, trans. Peggy Kamuf (Stanford: Stanford University Press, 2002), 161–201 (esp. 170ff). Sensational aspects of de Man's life (reduced for the most part to the coercive, bare-bones formula: "master-theorist covers up fascist past") are fictionalized in Gilbert Adair's *The Death of the Author* (1992), John Banville's *Shroud* (2002), and Bernhard Schlink's *Die Heimkehr* (2006; *Homecoming*, trans. Michael Henry Heim, 2008). (I thank Timothy Bewes for calling the Adair novel to my attention.) For an intelligent review of Banville's and Schlink's novels that ponders the motives behind their hysteria-laced approach to their subject matter ("why do these novels go in for the final shocking revelation as if the best response to the de Man affair is to be sent reeling?"), see Jacqueline Rose, "The Iron Rule," *London Review of Books* 30, no. 15 (2008): 21–24.

33. The image is signed "David Plunkert for the *Chronicle*." Romano's article and Plunkert's illustration appeared in the March 3, 2014, issue of *The Chronicle Review*. They may be accessed online; see http://chronicle.com/article/Paul-de-Man-Deconstructed/144991.

34. Paul de Man, *The Rhetoric of Romanticism* (New York: Columbia University Press, 1984), 122.

35. For instance, accounts that portray deconstruction as "a textualism which would confuse text and discourse, page, book, and the world, society or history and the library" ("Some Statements and Truisms," 89). The paintings by Mark Tansey that I discuss in my final chapter could be said to be parodying consciously the kind of involuntary parody of deconstruction that Derrida is discussing.

36. Jacques Derrida, *Of Grammatology*, trans. Gayatri Spivak (Baltimore: Johns Hopkins University Press, 1976), 6, Derrida's italics, translation slightly modified. See also the famous opening of "Force and Signification" (1963), which I cite and discuss at the beginning of my next chapter: "the fact that universal thought . . . should be receiving a formidable impulse from an anxiety about language—which can only be an anxiety of

language, within language itself—is a strangely concerted development." Jacques Derrida, *Writing and Difference* (Chicago: University of Chicago Press, 1978), 3.

1. Theory, Deconstruction, and the Yale Critics

1. Jacques Derrida, *Writing and Difference*, trans. Alan Bass (Chicago: University of Chicago Press, 1978), 3.

2. François Cusset, *French Theory: How Foucault, Derrida, Deleuze & Co. Transformed the Intellectual Life of the United States*, trans. Jeff Fort (Minneapolis: University of Minnesota Press, 2008), 105. The subtitle may post a warning, but even so, the superficiality and inaccuracy of this book outstrip expectation. At its best it offers a helpful narrative overview of famous colloquia, names, texts, arguments, and so forth, but its understanding of French philosophy is erratic and its grasp of American culture and institutional practices shaky. Cusset's tone veers between enthusiasm and condescension, and his pose is mock-anthropological (he is explaining America to French readers, and filtering his subject through the usual clichés). There are a great number of minor but distracting factual errors (e.g., Jonathan Culler described as an "English" critic) and glitches produced by hasty note-taking (e.g., Cusset telling us that, in their contributions to *Deconstruction and Criticism*, "de Man and Bloom diverge in their readings of Shelley" [114]: Bloom's essay, which is mainly on Ashbery, does not even mention Shelley once). It is too bad, because a broad survey of the history of "French theory" in America, done carefully, would make a valuable addition to the archive.

3. I allude here to the title of the revised edition of the proceedings of the 1966 conference: see Richard Macksey and Eugenio Donato, eds., *The Structuralist Controversy: The Languages of Criticism and the Sciences of Man* (Baltimore: Johns Hopkins University Press, 1972). Subtitle and title are reversed in the first edition of 1970. "The Languages of Criticism and the Sciences of Man" was the title of the famous conference itself. Jacques Derrida's equally famous paper, "Structure, Sign and Play in the Discourse of the Human Sciences," is available both in that collection and in *Writing and Difference*, 278–94.

4. Thus Mark Currie, in *The Invention of Deconstruction* (London: Palgrave Macmillan, 2013), posts ironic reservations but sticks to the script: "The moment of invention, supposedly, was 21 October 1966, when Jacques Derrida presented 'Structure, Sign and Play' at a conference about structuralism in the social sciences at Johns Hopkins University, but the idea of this as an inaugural event is something of an absurdity" (3). Currie's book offers a valuable history of deconstruction in the United States. My account differs considerably from Currie's: his historical narrative functions mainly as a frame to compare and contrast the theoretical positions of de Man and Derrida, to the advantage of the latter, whereas I am interested in "theory" in the ways outlined in my Introduction and in the present chapter, and shall therefore be focusing mainly on de Man.

5. As discussed in the Introduction, Derrida emphasized this citational aspect in his one extended comment on "theory" in the idiomatic sense we are exploring here. See Jacques Derrida, "Some Statements and Truisms about Neologisms, Newisms, Postisms, Parasitisms, and Other Small Seismisms," in *The States of "Theory": History, Art,*

and Critical Discourse, ed. David Carroll (New York: Columbia University Press, 1990), 63–94.

6. David Lehman, *Signs of the Times: Deconstruction and the Fall of Paul de Man* (New York: Poseidon, 1991), 266–68.

7. Paul de Man, "The Resistance to Theory," in *The Resistance to Theory* (Minneapolis: University of Minnesota Press, 1986), 3–20, at 17, 19. Subsequent references to this text will be given by page number and acronym *RT.*

8. Derrida's reflections on deconstruction and "America" were more careful and infrequent than is sometimes assumed. He did, famously, and possibly to his regret, flirt with (before rejecting, a few sentences later) the phrase "America is deconstruction" in *Memoires: For Paul de Man* (1986), and in a talk titled "The Time is Out of Joint" in 1993, he gingerly engaged the title of the conference at which he was speaking, "Deconstruction is/in America" (the proceedings of which were later published as a book under that title). In later years he was careful to contextualize these remarks in interviews. For a convenient assembly of Derrida's reflections on this theme, see the chapter titled "Deconstruction is America?" in Catherine Malabou and Jacques Derrida, *Counterpath: Traveling with Jacques Derrida,* trans. David Wills (Stanford: Stanford University Press, 2004), 219–29. For a fine discussion of these texts in the context of Derrida's complex ties to and reflections on the United States, see Michael Naas, "Derrida's America," in *Derrida's Legacies: Literature and Philosophy,* ed. Simon Glendinning and Robert Eaglestone (New York: Routledge, 2008), 118–37; see also Peggy Kamuf, "The Affect of America," ibid., 138–50.

9. J. Hillis Miller, "The Year's Books: On Literary Criticism," *New Republic* 173, no. 22 (November 29, 1975), 30–33, at 33.

10. Geoffrey H. Hartman, *A Scholar's Tale: Intellectual Journey of a Displaced Child of Europe* (New York: Fordham University Press, 2007), 41–42.

11. Email to author, August 13, 2013. Hartman also comments that he thinks Bloom first met de Man many years before he himself did, since Bloom "was invited to visit (with the idea of joining) the Harvard Junior Fellows Program shortly after we met at Yale in our basement offices" (in 1955, when Hartman and Bloom were hired as instructors in English). De Man was in Paris in 1955, however—which is the year Derrida spent at Harvard; he and de Man missed meeting each other that year, and it seems likely that de Man and Bloom did too. Nor did Miller and de Man encounter each other at Harvard: Miller took his Ph.D. in 1952, the year de Man began his studies.

12. Personal communication. For decades, Miller and Derrida preserved the ritual of having lunch together every Tuesday whenever Derrida was visiting (first at Hopkins, then at Yale, then at Irvine). As for Miller's meeting with de Man in 1964: as chance would have it, the colloquium was at Yale. Miller has an anecdote to offer: "I first met de Man at that conference. He delivered there the admirable paper on Lukács that subsequently appeared in *Blindness and Insight* (1971). In our first private conversation, walking down New Haven's Wall Street at lunch time during the conference, I told de Man I was deeply interested in 'later Heidegger.' 'Oh no,' said de Man, with great urgency, 'later Heidegger is very dangerous. If you must read Heidegger, read *Sein und Zeit.*'" J. Hillis Miller, "Tales Out of (the Yale) School," in *Theoretical Schools and*

Circles in the Twentieth-Century Humanities, ed. Marina Grishakova and Silvi Salupere (New York: Routledge, 2015).

13. Derrida's ties to Yale preceded de Man's arrival. Jacques Ehrmann, a professor of French at Yale who had edited an important special issue of *Yale French Studies* on "Structuralism" in 1966, invited Derrida to lecture at Yale when Derrida was teaching at Hopkins, in 1968 and again in 1971. But for his untimely death in 1972, Ehrmann would probably have played a substantial role in the story of "theory" at Yale in the 1970s.

14. Jonathan Culler, "Criticisms and Institutions: The American University," in *Post-Structuralism and the Question of History*, ed. Derek Attridge, Geoff Bennington, and Robert Young (Cambridge: Cambridge University Press, 1987), 82–98, at 85. Thus we speak casually of "the hegemony of the New Criticism in the forties and fifties," for instance; but in fact most of the criticism written during that period, as Culler notes, moves eclectically between new critical practices and "an interest in authors and in literary history" (86).

15. Currie makes the sensible suggestion that historians of this period need to keep in mind translation lag. Prior to David Allison's translation of *Speech and Phenomena* (1973) and Gayatri Spivak's epochal translation of *Of Grammatology* (1976), non-French-reading American academics knew Derrida only through a handful of essays in translation: "Structure, Sign and Play" (in the proceedings of the Hopkins conference); "The Ends of Man" (in *Philosophy and Phenomenological Research* in 1969); "Positions" (an interview published in two parts in *Diacritics* in 1972–73); "Freud and the Scene of Writing" (in an important issue of *Yale French Studies* in 1973 that also featured Lacan's "Seminar on the Purloined Letter"); and "White Mythology" (in *New Literary History* in 1974). See Currie, *The Invention of Deconstruction*, 35–36 (he misses the *Yale French Studies* essay). Currie's overall argument is that Derrida's reception in the United States pressed him into a peculiarly American argument between historical and formalist or textualist approaches to literature, and that until about 1975 Derrida's was often invoked as a historicizing thought (in contrast to structuralism).

16. See Richard Klein, "The Blindness of Hyperboles: The Ellipses of Insight," *Diacritics* 3, no. 2 (Summer 1973): 33–44.

17. References to Bloom are everywhere in the archive during these years. For one telling instance, see the "Interview" with Edward Said in *Diacritics* 6, no. 3 (Autumn 1976): 30–47; the interviewer leads with the remark that Said "recently expressed considerable sympathy for the deeply philosophical criticism of Harold Bloom" (30). We may note in passing that in this interview Said uses the phrase "Yale critics" (31); it had become a standard metonym by this point.

18. J. Hillis Miller, "Stevens' Rock and Criticism as Cure, II," *The Georgia Review* 30, no. 2 (Summer 1976): 330–48, at 336. Under the editorship of John T. Irwin, *The Georgia Review* was transformed from regionalist publication to avant-garde forum for literary theory, and particularly for Yale-based critics: from the fall of 1974 to the fall of 1977, nearly every issue featured articles by at least one of the following: Bloom, Hartman, de Man, Miller, Derrida, Leslie Brisman, Peter Brooks, Thomas Weiskel. Miller's article, quoted here, attracted wide notice. It goes on to distinguish between "uncanny" and "canny" critics: "Jacques Derrida teaches a seminar early each fall at Yale and so

may be included among the Yale group. These critics may be taken by a convenient synecdoche as 'examples' of criticism as the uncanny, but there are of course others, for example Derrida's associates in France, Sarah Kofman, Philippe Lacoue-Labarthe, Jean-Luc Nancy, Bernaurd Pautrat (essays by whom are gathered in their new book, *Mimesis*). The American critic Edward Said admirably explores an uncanny topic in *Beginnings*" (ibid.). Much of the rest of the essay describes what Miller sees as the uncanniness of the writing of Bloom, Derrida, de Man, and Hartman. Uncanniness means here a resistance to "rational or logical formulation" (343); Miller contrasts the work of the uncanny critics with that of the "canny" practitioners of semiotics or the human sciences such as Jonathan Culler or A. G. Greimas, "who are lulled by the promise of a rational ordering of literary study on the basis of solid advances in scientific knowledge about language" (335).

19. William Pritchard, "The Hermeneutical Mafia, or, After Strange Gods at Yale," *The Hudson Review* 28, no. 4 (1975): 601–610, at 601 n. 2. Pritchard's earlier reference is to Richard Poirer, "A Star Trek in the Theory of Poetics," review of Hartman's *The Fate of Reading*, *New York Times Book Review* (April 20, 1975), 21–26. Neil Hertz reminds me that Pritchard, who taught at Amherst, knew de Man from Harvard, so a personal relationship may be helping his judgment of de Man's work here.

20. Hilton Kramer, "The Triumph of Misreading," *New York Times*, August 21, 1977, 3, 28. I thank William Flesch and Laura Quinney for drawing my attention to this article. As regards my speculation in the previous sentence—that this might be the first all-out attack on an academic literary critic in the postwar era in a mass-circulation publication—I admit to having done no systematic homework to back it up. I am at least certain that Bloom was the first of the "Yale Critics" to be so treated. Kramer's polemic is remarkable for appearing in the main newspaper (Kramer was at this point the chief art critic of the *Times*), not in the *New York Times Book Review*.

21. Gerald Graff, "Fear and Trembling at Yale," *The American Scholar*, 46, no. 4 (Autumn 1977): 467–78, at 470. In fairness to these critics, it may be admitted that some of Hartman's writing in *The Fate of Reading* is mannered to the point of sounding, at least to the present reader, off-key; yet this book also contains powerful essays such as "Poem and Ideology" or "Evening Star and Evening Land" in which Hartman's prose earns pretty much all of its turns, reflecting with extraordinary subtlety on particular poems and contexts. Pritchard's and Graff's reaction to this book needs to be understood as a symptom of a deeper disquiet.

22. Harold Bloom, *The Flight to Lucifer: A Gnostic Fantasy* (New York: Farrar, Straus and Giroux, 1979); Geoffrey H. Hartman, *Akiba's Children* (Emory, Va.: Iron Mountain Press, 1978).

23. Geoffrey H. Hartman, "How Creative Should Literary Criticism Be?" *New York Times*, Sunday Book Review, April 5, 1981.

24. These critics were not infrequently referred to as "Yale critics" or "Yale formalists" in the 1950s and 1960s. Later in this book, I briefly discuss the differences between the English and Comparative Literature Departments at Yale in the context of Bloom's and Hartman's different experiences as graduate students in the early 1950s. Part of the lore of the Yale English Department concerns the introduction, by eager junior faculty (Maynard Mack, Louis Martz, John Pope, Richard Sewell, Eugene Waith,

William Wimsatt), of Cleanth Brooks and Austin Warren's hugely influential textbook *Understanding Poetry* (1938) into undergraduate classes at Yale in 1939. There was initial resistance from senior faculty, but in the end the new methods prevailed relatively easily. Cleanth Brooks joined the Yale faculty a decade later, in 1947. (Wellek was hired as Professor of Slavic and Comparative Literature at Yale in 1946, and subsequently founded the Comparative Literature Department.)

25. Of course, "conservative" means different things in different contexts, but the generalization seems fair. During the colonial era, Yale stood for Calvinist orthodoxy; in the nineteenth century, Yale was particularly famous and influential as a champion of the classical curriculum, which had come under fire in the early decades of the century but was resoundingly affirmed in the "Yale Report" of 1828. (This report influenced colleges throughout the United States, and was sufficiently famous that it received approving mention more than a century later in the 1951 *Time* Magazine article on Directed Studies, from which I shall be quoting a little later.) Until the admissions reforms of the mid-1960s, the opening of the undergraduate college to women in 1969, and (above all) the Black Panther trial and student demonstrations in 1970, Yale maintained a reputation as a stolid place. (It did not come up to William F. Buckley's standards, of course, who faulted the university's economics and political science departments for their liberalism in his bestselling *God and Man at Yale* in 1951—though he had a positive assessment of the English Department; see my note on this in Chapter 4.) Yale was especially famous as a target of CIA recruitment during the Cold War era, and as the alma mater of choice for the OSS during World War II. See Robin Winks, *Cloak and Gown: Scholars in the Secret War, 1939–1961* (New Haven: Yale University Press, 1996 [1987]).

26. It is perhaps worth emphasizing that Miller was the only one of the four Yale Critics to be squarely in English. Hartman was in Comparative Literature and English; Bloom was able to remove himself from all responsibilities in English and become a "department of one," as he liked to put it, in 1974; de Man, of course, was in French and Comparative Literature, and Derrida's guest appointment ran through those departments.

27. De Man seems to have been the main figure behind the creation of the undergraduate course "Lit Z" at Yale in the mid-1970s, which sought to provide an updated version of Reuben Brower's HUM 6 course at Harvard that so impressed de Man when he served as a teaching assistant for it, as he recounts in "The Return to Philology" (*The Resistance to Theory*, 21–26). For a description of Lit Z and a reprint of the internal memo (unsigned, but almost certainly by de Man) that proposed its creation, see the appendices to *Legacies of Paul de Man*, ed. Marc Redfield (New York: Fordham University Press, 2007), 179–90. As I comment in my explanatory headnote to that memo, Lit Z not only offered de Man a way to reach undergraduates, it also provided de Man's graduate students with a platform to develop work. The course was a team-taught lecture course (in the first years, de Man and Hartman team-taught it) that employed TAs for sections (de Man and Hartman also taught sections); the TAs each gave one guest lecture over the course of the semester. Many of the first rhetorical readings by students of de Man took shape as lectures for Lit Z. (TAs who eventually published article versions of their lectures included Timothy Bahti, Claudia Brodsky, Cathy

Caruth, Tom Cohen, Deborah Esch, David Ferris, Barbara Johnson, Tom Keenan, Kevin Newmark, and Andrzej Warminski.) De Man's interest in pedagogy remains an understudied field, though for a wide-ranging study of de Man's critique of aesthetics in relation to pedagogy, see Cynthia Chase, "Trappings of an Education: Toward that which we do not yet have," in *Responses*, 44–79; and for an examination of de Man's complexly ironic relation to his graduate students, see Sara Guyer, "At the Far End of This Ongoing Enterprise," in *Legacies of Paul de Man*, 77–92.

28. The French Department had a number of faculty and students interested in psychoanalysis, and Shoshana Felman was becoming one of the most prominent literary interpreters of Lacan in the United States. As I shall have occasion to recall a little later in this chapter, Fredric Jameson was also a member of the Yale French Department during the height of the "Yale Critics" era (he had been hired in 1975), so the avant-garde theoretical options were quite diverse at Yale during this period, overshadowed though they were—for reasons this book is pursuing—by "deconstruction" and rhetorical reading.

29. Andrzej Warminski, "Interview: 'Deconstruction at Yale,'" interview with Stuart Barnett, in Warminski, *Material Inscriptions: Rhetorical Readings in Practice and Theory* (Edinburgh: University of Edinburgh Press, 2013), 228.

30. Hannah Arendt, "Martin Heidegger at Eighty," trans. Albert Hofstadter, *New York Review of Books*, October 21, 1971. Arendt is describing the rumor of Heidegger's teaching prior to his publication of *Being and Time* in 1927: "There was hardly more than a name, but the name traveled all over Germany like the rumor of a hidden king."

31. Harold Bloom, Paul de Man, Jacques Derrida, Geoffrey H. Hartman, and J. Hillis Miller, *Deconstruction and Criticism* (New York: Seabury Press, 1979). According to Miller, Bloom was the animating spirit behind the volume: "Harold Bloom picked up on my brief article. He then concocted, with his remarkable gift for publicity, the idea of a collective volume gathering essays by each of the five of us and to be published by Seabury Press, where he had an 'in.'" That claim is supported by remarks in a letter de Man wrote to Derrida on 14 May 1977 (these letters are being edited for publication by Patricia de Man, Martin McQuillan, Kevin Newmark, and Marc Redfield). The original idea was that the contributors were all to write on Percy Shelley's *The Triumph of Life*. Only de Man and Miller really did so, though Derrida offered a few reflections on the poem in an essay that was really about Maurice Blanchot's novel *L'arrêt de mort*. Bloom, as noted earlier, ignored the assignment entirely and wrote mainly on Ashbery; Hartman wrote on Wordsworth.

32. Geoffrey H. Hartman, "Literary Criticism and its Discontents," *Critical Inquiry* 3, no. 2 (Winter 1976): 203–20, at 212. Hartman responds in this essay to "complaints"—such as Pritchard's, though Hartman names no names—"against the post–New Critical critics: their demanding style" (207) and to the "charges that a new elitism is creeping into literary studies. . . . Instead of subordinating himself to the literary work, [the critic] puffs his own activity until criticism becomes a rival of literature" (209). Hartman's defense produced a response from Wallace Martin, "Literary Critics and their Discontents: A Reply to Geoffrey Hartman," *Critical Inquiry* 4, no. 2 (Winter 1977): 397–406. This was one of several high-profile polemical exchanges about deconstruction and the "group at Yale" during the mid-1970s: two that involved Miller are

mentioned later in this chapter. By far the most memorable polemical exchange having to do with deconstruction during this period, however, had nothing to do with Yale; that was the debate between Derrida and John Searle in the pages of *Glyph* in 1977 (see note 36).

33. S. L. Goldberg, "The Deconstruction Gang," *London Review of Books*, 22 May–4 June 1980, 14–16.

34. Denis Donoghue, "Deconstructing Deconstruction," *New York Review of Books*, June 12, 1980.

35. Jonathan Arac, Wlad Godzich, and Wallace Martin, eds., *The Yale Critics: Deconstruction in America* (Minneapolis: University of Minnesota Press, 1983). The editors waffle on whom to include and treat Derrida as a marginal case; see my note to the Introduction of the present book on their ambivalent exclusion of other critics such as Shoshana Felman.

36. Earlier I flagged parenthetically the strange hypertrophy of the term *deconstruction*; we may add here, as an ironic coda, Warminski's recollection that he and de Man's other students "never conceived of what we were doing as 'deconstruction'" (219–20). "It may seem a little funny in retrospect, but I have to say that, from our point of view at Yale, 'deconstruction' was rather what was taking place at Johns Hopkins and *not* at Yale—especially with the founding of *Glyph* and the manifesto-like impact of the work produced by the *Glyph* circle at Hopkins" (221). The semiannual journal *Glyph* was founded at Hopkins in 1977 by Samuel Weber; its first issue included de Man's "The Purloined Ribbon" (an essay that became the "Confessions" chapter of de Man's *Allegories of Reading*, and that I discuss glancingly in Chapter 2), a translation of Derrida's "Signature Event Context," and a hostile reply to Derrida by John Searle; its second issue included Derrida's hostile reply to Searle, "Limited Inc a b c," which Derrida also gave in 1977 as his first public lecture in English at Yale. This grand opening salvo may indeed have given *Glyph* a manifesto-like aura, but its content was not programmatically Derridean and its editors had little institutional purchase at Johns Hopkins. Though I have no reason to doubt Warminski's memory of the prevailing attitude among de Man's students at Yale, it seems clear to me that during the late 1970s, Yale considerably outweighed Johns Hopkins as a symbolic (and phantasmatic) locus of "deconstruction in America."

37. Jacques Derrida, *Parages* (Paris: Galilée, 1986), 118. On the original idea that Bloom, Derrida, de Man, Hartman, and Miller would all write on *The Triumph of Life*, see note 31. On Derrida's lack of investment in the notion of "romanticism," see note 62. But for a careful and acute reading of Derrida that discovers in "Living On" an important resource for thinking about romanticism, see Sara Guyer, "The Rhetoric of Survival and the Possibility of Romanticism," *Studies in Romanticism* 46, no. 2 (2007): 247–63. This special issue of *Studies in Romanticism*, titled *Romanticism and the Legacies of Jacques Derrida*, ed. David L. Clark, collects valuable studies exploring the difference Derrida's thought has made for this field.

38. J. Hillis Miller, "Georges Poulet's 'Criticism of Identification,'" in *The Quest for Imagination: Essays in Twentieth-Century Aesthetic Criticism*, ed. O. B. Hardison Jr. (Cleveland: Case Western Reserve University, 1971), 191–224. "All the apparent assumptions of Poulet's criticism are interrogated by Derrida and found wanting (though

without reference to Poulet)" (216). Miller's essay stages a dramatic turn by announcing in its sixth section that its first previous sections were "written in 1963" (205); the final sections of the essay represent the turn to Derrida. The twist of that turn is that Miller claims to be critiquing Poulet's "*apparent* assumptions"; "The more deeply and carefully one reads Poulet's criticism, however, the more clearly it emerges that it challenges its own assumptions" (216).

39. In addition to the back-and-forth with Abrams, which occurred across several journals and several years, Miller conducted a public argument with another critic interested in Derrida, but, in Miller's view, still too indebted to Heidegger, Joseph Riddell: see Miller's review of Riddell's book *The Inverted Bell*, "Deconstructing the Deconstructors," *Diacritics* 5, no. 2 (1975): 24–31, and Riddell's response, "A Miller's Tale," *Diacritics* 5, no. 3 (1975): 56–65.

40. Vincent B. Leitch, "The Lateral Dance: The Deconstructive Criticism of J. Hillis Miller," *Critical Inquiry* 6, no. 4 (Summer 1980): 593–607, at 603. The weirdly overheated description continues: "Miller, the relentless rift-maker, refuses any apparent repair and rampages onward, dancing, spell-casting, destroying all. As though he were a wizard, he appears in the guise of a bull-deconstructor loose in the china shop of Western tradition" (ibid.). In addition to testifying to Miller's influence, Leitch's article offers a usefully detailed account of Miller's publications during this decade.

41. To represent this moment in de Man's writing as a turn or *Kehre* is to press his oeuvre into the distorting pattern of a conversion narrative; close readings of his earlier work have revealed the inadequacy of dividing it into a "before" and "after." Readers who read French can profit from Cynthia Chase's particularly informed and nuanced account of some of de Man's early work in "Hölderlin lectuer: De Man avant Derrida," *Le tour critique* 3 (2014): 16–28. That said, it is clear enough that a new idiom and focus enters de Man's work in the transitional period 1969–71.

42. Paul de Man, "Foreword to Revised, Second Edition," *Blindness and Insight: Essays in the Rhetoric of Contemporary Criticism* (Minneapolis: University of Minnesota, 1983 [1971]), xii. Subsequent references to this volume will be given by page number and acronym *BI*.

43. De Man's argument with Derrida is a work in progress during these years; he at once modifies and reaffirms his position in a slightly later essay, "Theory of Metaphor in Rousseau's *Second Discourse*" (1973; this essay became the important Chapter 7 of *Allegories of Reading*; I discuss it briefly in Chapter 5). Clearly quite important for de Man during this transitional period was Derrida's great essay, "White Mythology: Metaphor in the Text of Philosophy" (1971). Warminski goes so far as to credit "White Mythology" as being "much evident in de Man's turn to rhetoric—and perhaps in his rethinking and revising of his initially suspicious reading of *De la grammatologie*" (226). Essays on Nietzsche by Philippe Lacoue-Labarthe and Sarah Kofman that appeared in the same issue of *Poétique* as Derrida's "La mythologie blanche" are used as leverage in de Man's essay on Nietzsche, "Genesis and Genealogy" (now Chapter 4 of *Allegories of Reading*): that issue, *Poétique* 5 (1971), clearly played an important role in de Man's early elaboration of rhetorical reading.

44. Miller, "Stevens' Rock and Criticism as Cure, II," 333. Miller goes on to grant authority to de Man and Derrida: "If Paul de Man is the master, no master, of the

aporia, then Jacques Derrida is, as Geoffrey Hartman calls him, a 'boa-deconstructor'"
(341).

45. These are only a few indications among many. Here are a couple more. In early
1977 there appeared the extraordinary issue of *Yale French Studies* 55–56, "Literature and
Psychoanalysis. The Question of Reading: Otherwise," edited by Shoshana Felman,
featuring Felman's "Turning the Screw of Interpretation" (94–207) and Barbara Johnson's "The Frame of Reference: Poe, Lacan, Derrida" (457–505). (Johnson republished
her essay as part of *The Critical Difference*.) Both of these classic essays perform, in their
different ways, the "Yale" (de Manian) move of reading the literary text as predicting
the error of its interpreters. It would be misleading to identify Felman as a straight-line
de Manian critic, given her interest in Lacan and her original style and emphases, but
de Man's influence is palpable in this and other texts that Felman published (in French
as well as English) from the mid-1970s onward. Felman was de Man's junior colleague
(she was hired at Yale in 1969 and became the first woman to receive tenure in the
Yale French Department); Johnson was de Man's student (she began graduate study
in 1969—which, incidentally, is the year the first freshman class to include women arrived at Yale College). Essays written by de Man's students in the idiom of de Manian
rhetorical reading were appearing in the most prestigious journals in the late 1970s:
e.g., Cynthia Chase, "The Decomposition of the Elephants: Double-Reading Daniel
Deronda," *PMLA* 93, no. 2 (1978): 215–27.

46. According to the editor of *PMLA*, out of a pool of thirty-five essays considered for publication by the board at its meeting in June 1979, the highest citation
count went to Jacques Derrida (cited in ten essays) and Roland Barthes (seven); after
that came "the Connecticut theorists whose influence is obviously powerful right
now . . . J. Hillis Miller (quoted in six essays), Paul de Man (five), Harold Bloom (four),
and Geoffrey Hartman (four)." Joel Connaroe, "Editor's Column," *PMLA* 95, no. 1
(1980): 3; I was alerted to this factoid by Arac, Godzich, and Martin in their preface to
The Yale Critics, xii.

47. Hartman remained an authoritative figure in the burgeoning field of "theory";
he took over from Murray Krieger as director of the School of Criticism and Theory
and led it from 1981 to 1987 (Krieger had founded it in 1976, at the brand new University of California at Irvine). Yet Hartman had a complexly ambivalent relationship to
"theory," as suggested by the two quite different books he published at the beginning of
the new decade: on the one hand, a wide-ranging collection that seeks to revisit traditionally Arnoldian questions about criticism and society, *Criticism in the Wilderness: The
Study of Literature Today* (New Haven: Yale University Press, 1980); on the other, a more
theoretically ambitious meditation on Derrida, language, and style, *Saving the Text:
Literature, Derrida, Philosophy* (Baltimore: Johns Hopkins University Press, 1981), a text
that in its strongest moments returns forcefully to Hartman's deep and long-standing
preoccupation with the power—the aesthetic but also the wounding power—of words.
Words imply a trust or recognition that can always be broken, and thus "language
itself . . . exposes us to continual psychic hurt" (139). I explore the theme of "wounds
and words" by way of earlier texts of Hartman's in Chapter 3.

48. I do not have any statistics to offer to back up my claim about the singular
mediatization of deconstruction within the academy, but my sense is that most in-

formed observers would agree with Vincent B. Leitch in *American Literary Criticism from the Thirties to the Eighties* (New York: Columbia University Press, 1988): "By the mid-eighties there were evidently more books, articles, reviews, and conference papers dedicated to explaining, assessing, applying, and/or criticizing deconstructive criticism than any school or movement had received in the period covered by this history of American literary criticism" (302). Leitch's chapter on poststructuralism offers a helpful history of deconstruction in America that, precisely because it aspires to be clear and compact, obeys all the genre rules I have been pointing to (the origin at the Hopkins conference; the role of the Yale School; etc.): see 267–306.

49. Mitchell Stephens, "Deconstruction and the Get-Real Press," *Columbia Journalism Review*, September–October 1991, n.p. According to Stephens, the *Times* learned of the story "not because of its crack staff of reporters, but because a *Times* news clerk had spotted a two-sentence mention of 'Paul de Man's early fascist writings' on page 150 of *The Village Voice*." Denunciations of de Man and deconstruction appeared in most of the major American venues (among others, *Newsweek*, *The Nation*, and the *VLS*), and in a few overseas newspapers (e.g., the *Frankfurter Allgemeine Zeitung*).

50. Thus, for instance, Stephens does not mention Hartman's piece in *The New York Times* mentioned above, or Hillis Miller's 1975 *New Republic* piece, or Hilton Kramer's 1977 attack on Bloom in *the New York Times*, or (a piece we have not looked at) Peter Shaw's "Degenerate Criticism: The Dismal State of English Studies," *Harper's*, October 1979, 93–99. There would be many other articles of a similar sort; my own list is contingent and incomplete. A full report on the early representation of literary theory in the wider print media would be useful to have.

51. Kenneth L. Woodward et al., "A New Look at Lit Crit," *Newsweek*, June 22, 1981, 80, 82–83, at 80. The Cold War slur "Gang of Four" rhymes with other polemical activations of the lexicon of organized crime ("hermeneutical Mafia," "Deconstruction Gang").

52. Robert Alter, "Deconstruction in America," *New Republic*, April 25, 1983, 27–32, here 32. Alter is reviewing Arac, Godzich, and Martin's collection *The Yale Critics* along with Jonathan Culler's *On Deconstruction* and several other books.

53. Colin McCabe, "The Tyranny of the Yale Critics," *New York Times Magazine*, February 9, 1986.

54. David Lehman, "Yale's Insomniac Genius," *Newsweek*, August 18, 1986, 56. I discuss this piece and others like it in Chapter 4.

55. See Francis Oakley, "Ignorant Armies and Nighttime Clashes: Changes in the Humanities Classroom, 1970–1995," in *What's Happened to the Humanities?*, ed. Alvin Kernan (Princeton: Princeton University Press, 1997), 63–83. When he wrote this piece in 1994, Oakley had just stepped down from the presidency of Williams College. Of the 3,595 institutions that have Carnegie recognition, he notes, "specialized institutions, community colleges, and junior colleges make up no less than 61 percent of the total, while the 250 or so institutions categorized in the top ranks of research universities and liberal arts colleges together add up to no more than 9 percent. And yet my own reading suggests to me that the bulk of the critical commentary on the current state of teaching in the humanities—frequently characterized by sweeping and sensationalist claims and a species of disheveled anecdotalism—has been based on what is supposed

to be going on at probably no more than a dozen of the nation's leading research universities and liberal arts colleges" (65).

56. See especially *The Politics of Aesthetics: Nationalism, Gender, Romanticism* (Stanford: Stanford University Press, 2003), 1–42.

57. David Lloyd and Paul Thomas, *Culture and the State* (New York: Routledge, 1998), 2. "As culture comes to represent the fundamental common identity of human beings," the authors argue, "so the state is conceived, ideally, as the disinterested ethical representative of this same common humanity" (146). Arguing for the historical and institutional force of this idea of culture, Lloyd and Thomas align themselves with Gramsci and to some extent against Foucault by insisting on "the ultimate unity of the state formation as an instrument of class rule" (21). (It may be added that Lloyd and Thomas are in a sense doing no more than take Matthew Arnold at his word and follow out the consequences: see note 73). I have discussed the overlap between aesthetic discourse and Foucault's notion of biopower and governmentality in "Aesthetics, Biopower, Modernity: From Schiller's *Über die ästhetische Erziehung des Menschen* to Goethe's *Unterhaltungen deutscher Ausgewanderten*," in *Romantic Circles Praxis Series*, special issue on "Romanticism and Biopolitics," ed. Matthias Rudolf and Alistair Hunt (December 2012).

58. Pierre Bourdieu, *Distinction: A Social Critique of the Judgment of Taste*, trans. Richard Nice (Cambridge, Mass.: Harvard University Press, 1984).

59. Forest Pyle, *Art's Undoing: In the Wake of a Radical Aestheticism* (New York: Fordham University Press, 2014), 6.

60. The sense that "romanticism" demands a theoretical account of itself goes back to the early days of professional literary study. Here is a lecturer speaking in 1915: "Between these two dates [1783 and 1832] a great company of English writers produced a literature of immense bulk, and of almost endless diversity of character. Yet, one dominant strain in that literature has commonly been allowed to give a name to the whole period, and it is often called the Age of the Romantic Revival. We do not name any other notable period of our literature in this fashion. *The name itself contains a theory*, and so marks the rise of a new philosophical and aesthetic criticism." Sir Walter Raleigh, *Romance: Two Lectures* (Princeton: Princeton University Press, 1916), cited in George Whalley, "England/Romantic—Romanticism," in Hans Eichner, ed., *"Romantic" and Its Cognates: The European History of a Word* (Toronto: University of Toronto Press, 1972), 157–262, at 255, my emphasis. Perhaps a further word on institutional history will be helpful. The older typologizing opposition romantic-classic, popularized by Mme. de Staël and A. W. Schlegel, survived through the first two decades or so of twentieth-century academic and proto-academic writing; but already in the earliest scholarly studies such as William Lyon Phelps's *The Beginnings of the English Romantic Movement* (1893) or Henry A. Beers's *History of English Romanticism in the Eighteenth Century* (1899), the typological sense has become subordinate to historical periodization (that is, these authors no longer have any inclination to speak in Schlegelesque fashion of Dante's or Shakespeare's writing as "romantic"). (Both Phelps and Beers, as it happens, were professors at Yale.) The period term "romanticism," therefore, emerges with the professionalization of literary study; see John Rieder, "The Institutional Overdetermination of the Concept of Romanticism," *The Yale Journal of Criticism* 10, no. 1 (1997):

145–63. For further discussion of the conceptual intersections of romanticism, aesthetics, and theory, see my *Politics of Aesthetics*.

61. David L. Clark, "Lost and Found in Translation: Romanticism and the Legacies of Jacques Derrida," *Studies in Romanticism* 46, no. 2 (2007): 167–68.

62. My allusion here is of course to Jerome McGann's exemplary *The Romantic Ideology: A Critical Investigation* (Chicago: University of Chicago Press, 1983). The association of romanticism with excessive aestheticism and idealism is by no means simply an American habit; it is also a cliché in the major European traditions, and appears as such in work by, e.g., René Girard, Alain Badiou, and so on (Jacques Rancière is something of an exception; precisely because he is interested in redeeming and granting power to the concept of the aesthetic, he privileges the notion of romanticism: see my note on this in the Introduction.) Even Derrida, despite his close personal ties to the "Yale Critics" and many other American romanticists over many years, falls into this pattern. A trawl through his texts elicits little more than the rare throwaway usage of the word *romantic*, as when, during a late interview focused on books and electronic media, he warns an interlocutor to "be wary of a progressivist—and sometimes 'romantic'—optimism, ready to endow the new distance technologies of communication with the myth of the infinite book without material support." *Paper Machine*, trans. Rachel Bowlby (Stanford: Stanford University Press, 2005), 17. "Romantic" is here, of course, being given its standard sense of excessive idealism. Derrida was well aware of what his American romanticist friends were up to, as another rare appearance of the word *romanticism* in his oeuvre—the noun, this time, capitalized—makes clear. "One cannot understand [de Man's] privileging of allegory—I was long puzzled by it for this very reason—if one is not familiar with the internal debates of Anglo-American criticism concerning Romanticism." *Memoires for Paul de Man*, rev. ed., trans. Cecile Lindsay, Jonathan Culler, Eduardo Cadava, and Peggy Kamuf (New York: Columbia University Press, 1989), 77. So far as one can tell, Derrida never actually became familiar with those "internal debates"; they were alien to his training and presumably never greatly interested him.

63. Pyle, *Art's Undoing*, 21, 5. Pyle defines radical aestheticism as part of the "legacy of Romanticism" (1), and examines texts by Shelley, Keats, Dickinson, Hopkins, Rossetti, and Wilde. Radically aesthetic textual events "reflect on art" (3) while performing "the undoing of any claim to an aesthetic autonomy or self-reflexive totality" (4). Pyle distinguishes between his notion of radical aestheticism and de Man's notion of materiality (13), though he often seems very close to the latter, e.g. in his reading of Shelley's "shape all light" in *The Triumph of Life* as an event that "undoes the possibility of historical reckoning" or any other redemptive motion. I am not at all sure that the excessive phenomenality ("to the point of white-out" [64]) to which Pyle directs our attention can be cleanly distinguished from what de Man calls materiality (a materiality that, we recall, manifests itself as sheer seeing in de Man's famous reading of Kant—an impossible act in Kantian philosophy, for which there is no such thing as unmediated perception: see "Phenomenality and Materiality in Kant," 80–81, passim).

64. Already in the catalogue of contending voices with which A. O. Lovejoy begins his famous essay, "On the Discrimination of Romanticisms" (1924), the contagiousness of romanticism shadows and spurs the need to pursue discriminations; for romanticism

is apparently everywhere, above all in the texts of the critics who abjure it: "It is to be observed, for example, that Messrs. Lasserre, Seillière, Babbitt and More (to mention no others) are engaged in arguing that something called Romanticism is the chief cause of the spiritual evils from which the nineteenth century and our own have suffered; but that they represent at least three different opinions as to what these evils are and how they are to be remedied. . . . [M. Seillière] therefore intimates that the school of opinion which M. Lasserre ably represents is itself a variety of Romanticism. But it is equally certain that M. Seillière's own philosophy is one of the varieties of Romanticism defined by Mr. Babbitt and Mr. More; while Mr. Babbitt, in turn, has been declared by more than one critic of his last brilliant book, and would necessarily be held by M. Seillière, to set forth therein an essentially Romantic philosophy." A. O. Lovejoy, "On the Discrimination of Romanticisms," in *Essays in the History of Ideas* (Baltimore: Johns Hopkins University Press, 1948), 228–54, at 233.

65. T. S. Eliot, "The Metaphysical Poets" (1921) in *Selected Essays* (New York: Harcourt, Brace, 1950), 241–50, at 247.

66. Louis Menand, *Discovering Modernism: T. S. Eliot and His Context*, 2nd ed. (New York: Oxford University Press, 2007 [1987]), 177.

67. Geoffrey Hartman, "Romanticism in France," in David Thorburn and Geoffrey Hartman, eds., *Romanticism: Vistas, Instances, Continuities* (Ithaca, N.Y.: Cornell University Press, 1973), 38–61, at 38.

68. Laurence R. Veysey, *The Emergence of the American University* (Chicago: University of Chicago Press, 1965).

69. Wilhelm von Humboldt, "On the Spirit and the Organizational Framework of Intellectual Institutions in Berlin," trans. Edward Shils, *Minerva* 8 (1970): 242–50, at 243.

70. Gerald Graff, *Professing Literature* (Chicago: University of Chicago Press, 1987). The opposition between philology and bellelettrism is also explored and analyzed in John Guillory, "Literary Study and the Modern System of the Disciplines," in *Disciplinarity at the Fin de Siècle*, ed. Amanda Anderson and Joseph Valente (Princeton: Princeton University Press, 2002), 19–43. In the case of English, a remedial mission has also weighed on the field; this has often resulted in the development of separate composition and writing programs. In the foreign languages, language instruction overlaps to some extent with the acculturative mission, but on its lower levels is often relegated to non-tenure-line teaching staff, like remedial writing instruction in English departments.

71. *The Teaching of the Arts and Humanities at Harvard College: Mapping the Future* (web). This report, released in June 2013, reinvests in the high aesthetic idiom: "We might reflect that we have tended to emphasize specialist knowledge (*Wissenschaft*) over the formation of truly educated citizens (*Bildung*), a division built deep into the shape of our disciplines over the century and most of the modern disciplines. We have, that is, possibly become too specialized, allowing the research culture of our faculty and graduate constituencies to dominate the general needs of the undergraduate" (30). An equivalent affirmation may be found in the *Report on Yale College Education* (April 2003), 10, available on the Yale web site.

72. Geoffrey Galt Harpham, *The Humanities and the Dream of America* (Chicago: University of Chicago Press, 2011), 147.

73. Here is the equivalent passage in Arnold: "But by our *best self* we are united, impersonal, at harmony. We are in no peril from giving authority to this, because it is the truest friend we all of us can have; and when anarchy is a danger to us, to this authority we may turn with sure trust. Well, and this is the very self which culture, or the study of perfection, seeks to develop in us; at the expense of our old untransformed self, taking pleasure only in doing what it likes or is used to do, and exposing us to the risk of clashing with every one else who is doing the same! So that our poor culture, which is flouted as so unpractical, leads us to the very ideas capable of meeting the great want of our present embarrassed times! We want an authority, and we find nothing but jealous classes, checks, and a dead-lock; culture suggests the idea of *the State*. We find no basis for a firm State-power in our ordinary selves; culture suggests one to us in our *best self.*" Matthew Arnold, *Culture and Anarchy*, in *Culture and Anarchy and Other Writings*, ed. Stefan Collini (Cambridge: Cambridge University Press, 1993), 99.

74. Harpham, *The Humanities and the Dream of America*, 165, citing from page 1 of the ACLA report. (The line sounds right out of *Dr. Strangelove*—we cannot afford a humanities gap.) Older readers will recall that, in the context of the "theory" and "canon" "wars," NEH chairs William Bennett (1981–85) and Lynne V. Cheney (1986–93) proposed closing the NEH down because scholars were not working for nation and humanity.

75. The NEA and the NEH were created through the National Foundation on the Arts and Humanities Act. Signing the act into law on September 29, 1965, President Lyndon B. Johnson commented: "Art is a nation's most precious heritage, for it is in our works of art that we reveal to ourselves, and to others, the inner vision which guides us as a nation." Cited in Michael Brenson, *Visionaries and Outcasts: The NEA, Congress, and the Place of the Visual Artist in America* (New York: New Press, 2001), 1–2.

76. Yale is still probably associated in the public mind with a humanities education, since such associations are tenacious (thus Oxford still calls up—and markets—fantasies of *Brideshead Revisited* despite having essentially become a state university focused on science and technology after the Second World War). Yale changed considerably between the 1970s and the present, however. Like other well-off American universities, it grew much richer after the passage of the Bayh-Dole Act of 1980, which allows universities to patent the results of publicly funded research. Yale also benefitted from the economic boom at the end of the twentieth century; its endowment passed the billion-dollar mark in 1983, had doubled by 1987, doubled again by 1995, and was $10.7 billion by 2001. The university invested heavily in the sciences and is now very strong in many fields, particularly biotech. The profits from one exceptionally lucrative product, the Yale-discovered AIDS drug Zerit, helped pay for Yale's Anlyan Center for Medical Research and Education, which opened in 2003.

77. *Time*, 11 June 1951, 74, 82. We may note in passing that *Time* was founded in 1923 by two Yale graduates (and members of Skull and Bones), Henry Luce and Britton Hadden. Another Yale alumnus and Bonesman, W. Averell Harriman, founded a magazine called *Today* in 1932 that merged with a floundering *News-Week* to become *Newsweek* in 1937. Yale has tended to be well represented in the pages of these iconic newsmagazines.

78. Immanuel Kant, *The Conflict of the Faculties / Der Streit der Fakultäten*, trans. Mary J. Gregor (New York: Abaris Books, 1979), 25, 27, 45.

79. Brooks Mathers Kelley, *Yale: A History* (New Haven: Yale University Press, 1974), quoting the faculty report that founded Directed Studies, 409. Unlike the general education programs at Columbia, Chicago, and Harvard, Directed Studies was originally a four-year program, though it soon shrank into a two-year one, with the second year optional; it had persistent funding difficulties, and at one point had to be rescued by a grant from the millionaire Paul Mellon; but it survived, and at present writing still survives (it is now a one-year program consisting of three year-long seminars in philosophy, literature, and political philosophy).

80. John Stuart Mill, "Inaugural Address at St. Andrews," in F. A. Cavenagh, ed., *James and John Stuart Mill on Education* (Westport, Conn.: Greenwood Press, 1979), 134.

81. Daniel Bell, *The Reforming of General Education: The Columbia College Experiment in its National Setting* (New York: Columbia University Press, 1966).

82. Arnold's famous phrase is from "The Function of Criticism at the Present Time" (1864); see *Culture and Anarchy and Other Writings*, 26–51. I provide a reading of "The Function of Criticism" in my *Politics of Aesthetics*, 74–92.

83. Theodor Adorno, *Aesthetic Theory*, trans. C. Lenhardt (New York: Routledge, 1984), 179. Actually, the translator wrote more of that sentence than Adorno did. Adorno's own sentence reads: "*An der Wut darüber hat teil, daß solche Werke die Verständlichkeit auch der traditionellen erschüttern*"; literally translated, "The anger about them [i.e., hermetic works, mentioned in Adorno's previous sentence] has partly to do with the fact that such works also shake the comprehensibility of traditional artworks." *Ästhetische Theorie, Gesammelte Schriften* (Frankfurt: Suhrkamp, 1970), 7:186.

84. In classical Greek, *theōria* originally meant the beholding of a spectacle, and the sending of ambassadors or witnesses (*theōroi*) to oracles or games. For a study of the context behind Plato's and Aristotle's various appropriations of this word, see Andrea Wilson Nightingale, *Spectacles of Truth in Classical Greek Philosophy: Theoria in Its Cultural Context* (Cambridge: Cambridge University Press, 2004).

85. Edmund Burke, "Thoughts on French Affairs" (1791), in *Further Reflections on the Revolution in France*, ed. Daniel E. Ritchie (Indianapolis: Liberty Fund, 1993), 208; *Reflections on the Revolution in France* (1790), ed. Conor Cruise O'Brien (Harmondsworth: Penguin, 1986), 128. Elsewhere we read that "the pretended rights [i.e., the "Rights of Man"] of these theorists are all extremes; and in proportion as they are metaphysically true, they are morally and politically false. . . . By these theorists the right of the people is almost always sophistically confounded with their power" (153). These theorists are "so heated with their theories" that they are willing to ruin themselves and the state for the sake of a theory (148). More frequently, Burke rings changes on the word *speculation*, both in the intellectual and the monetary sense: he speaks of "the dissoluteness of an extravagant speculation" (154), "these ranting speculations" or "speculative designs" (155); etc. At one point, amusingly to a twentieth- or twenty-first-century reader, these speculators are called "professors" (because they profess mad speculations, 155). All of this is opposed to "a sort of native plainness and directness of understanding" (186) with which Englishmen are generally blessed.

86. In his important study, *Romanticism, Nationalism, and the Revolt Against Theory* (Chicago: University of Chicago Press, 1993), David Simpson cites "Arthur Young . . . in 1793 getting his licks in at what he calls, in a prophetic phrase, 'French theory'" (9).

Simpson sketches a compelling genealogy for late-twentieth-century antitheoretical writing in counterrevolutionary polemic in the 1790s, and studies the development of the nationalist motifs on which that polemic drew (and on which antitheoretical polemic continues to draw): British common sense and "French" excess.

87. Jacques Derrida, "The Principle of Reason: The University in the Eyes of its Pupils," *Diacritics* 13, no. 3 (1983): 2–20, at 8, 9. The lecture was first given at Cornell University, and the "abyss" is also a play on the famous gorges scoring the Cornell campus.

88. Once again, see my brief discussion in the Introduction to this book of the one essay in which Derrida discusses at length the idiomatic North American use of "theory," "Some Statements and Truisms."

89. See Graff, *Professing Literature*, and Culler, "Criticism and Institutions." Culler offers a useful point-by-point contrast between the British and American systems (as of the late 1980s, when Culler was writing). In the highly professionalized American system, professors have to produce more for tenure than in Britain; graduate students undergo extensive formalized training; the Cold War boom has resulted in structures supporting research, including grants; departments compete for resources; universities compete for outstanding faculty; increased gender diversity in particular has spurred "a new area of critical debate" (91).

90. Jonathan Culler, *Literary Theory: A Very Short Introduction* (New York: Oxford University Press, 1997), 2.

91. For a somewhat different account, see David R. Shumway, "The Star System in Literary Studies," *PMLA* 112, no. 1 (1997): 85–100. Shumway dates the rise of the academic "star system" to "the rise of theory in the 1970s" (86) and claims that "Colin Campbell's 'The Tyranny of the Yale Critics,' which appeared in *The New York Times Magazine* in 1986, was perhaps the first major exposure of academic stars in the national media" (90–91). Shumway is particularly interested in the photographs that accompanied Campbell's piece, and points to the difference between the "starlike" portrait of Derrida and the rumpled-professor-shots of Bloom, Hartman, and Miller; he also briefly discusses Mark Tansey's painting *Derrida Queries de Man* (which I discuss at length in Chapter 6) as a registering and a reperformance of the literary theorist as "star." With all this I am in agreement; I would also agree with a couple of other points Shumway makes—that the lecture circuit has made performance an aspect of academic celebrity; that the fad for autobiographical writing can be connected to a post-1970s form of academic celebrity. But the photos and, I think, even the lecture performances play a secondary role in the academic functioning of "stardom" (if that really is the right word for academic celebrity). As Shumway goes on to stress in the sentence I am about to quote, the proper name functions as the primary marker of authority in theoretical discourse.

92. Amanda Anderson, *The Way We Argue Now* (Princeton: Princeton University Press, 2006), 15. My analysis differs from that offered by Anderson, who is interested in "agent-centered ideas of character" (9).

93. The charge of corrupting the young in the name of false abstractions has an ancient pedigree: Socrates is he who "speculates about things on high, searches out all things under the earth, and makes the weaker argument appear stronger" (as Socrates

himself relays the charges against him in *Apology* 18b, playing on the role of sophist and natural philosopher as Aristophanes had rendered him in *The Clouds*).

94. The "Yale School" was a "male school," as Barbara Johnson pointed out in a famous article, "Gender Theory and the Yale School" (1984), in *A World of Difference* (Baltimore: Johns Hopkins University Press, 1987), 32–41. But the question arises: what happens when a woman undergoes mediatization as a theorist, as happened in the case of Judith Butler and to some extent Eve Sedgwick in the 1990s? My sense is that the governing clichés of antitheoretical discourse persist, though one can expect them to be refracted through antifeminist prisms. Like her male counterpart, the theorist-as-woman will be accused of obscurity, of running on charisma, and of leeching the warmth and humanity out of life. Though I have to leave the exploration of this question—and a related one: how race, along with sexual orientation and sexual difference, might inflect the stereotypes of the "theorist"—to another occasion or another critic, see, for examples of the kind of hostile writing that Butler and Sedgwick have inspired, Martha Nussbaum's attack on Butler, "The Professor of Parody," *New Republic* (February 22, 1999). Nussbaum writes: "Some precincts of the continental philosophical tradition, though surely not all of them, have an unfortunate tendency to regard the philosopher as a star who fascinates, and frequently by obscurity, rather than as an arguer among equals. . . . The thinker is heeded only for his or her turgid charisma." Sedgwick is the main target of one of the most troubled and troubling essays in the anti-theoretical collection *Theory's Empire: An Anthology of Dissent*, ed. Daphne Patai and Will H. Corral (New York: Columbia University Press, 2005), an attack on queer studies by Lee Siegel, "Queer Theory, Literature, and the Sexualization of Everything: The Gay Science," 424–41. Clearly quite a number of anxieties and transferential investments are driving Siegel (who at one point even pauses to ask, "Why am I being so hard, so mean?" [438]). Sedgwick's and Butler's portrayals in the academic and wider media are by no means the same, but I mention these critics because it seems to me that in their cases—and perhaps only in theirs—the "theorist" code was activated as an intrinsic part of the media attention they received in the United States in the 1990s. I should stress the importance of *mediatization* in this analysis. Most theorists, of whatever gender or announced or presumed sexual orientation, however famous they are in the academy, have not triggered that extra bit of media uptake—Barbara Johnson, for instance, did not; arguably even Gayatri Spivak has not; one imagines that Avital Ronell could, but her mediatization seems thus far restricted to alternative and international channels, and has not (yet) precipitated a theory-scandal per se in non- or para-academic American media. Indeed, the case can be made that only Judith Butler has undergone mediatization in the United States in a way reminiscent of the media uptake of Derrida and de Man.

95. Rei Terada, *Feeling in Theory: Emotion after the "Death of the Subject"* (Cambridge, Mass.: Harvard University Press, 2001), 16. Terada appends a footnote documenting the prevalence of the notion that deconstruction is "pathologically austere": see 162 n. 1. Her work rebuts this commonplace by way of careful readings of Derrida and de Man.

96. See, for instance, feature articles written by Mitchell Stephens for *the New York Times Magazine*, January 23, 1994, and *the Los Angeles Times Magazine*, Sunday July 21,

1991; see also the interesting interview Derrida accorded Kristine McKenna, "The Three Ages of Jacques Derrida," *LA Weekly*, November 6, 2002. Various interviews with Derrida published in French and German newspapers over the decades are collected in Jacques Derrida, *Points. . . : Interviews, 1974–1994*, ed. Elisabeth Weber, trans. Peggy Kamuf et al. (Stanford: Stanford University Press, 1995); and Jacques Derrida, *Paper Machine*, trans. Rachel Bowlby (Stanford: Stanford University Press, 2005). The ways in which and institutional reasons for which Derrida broke through the "theory" stereotype are numerous. Within the American academy, for instance, he had become over the decades such a figure of interest for religion departments (and even a few philosophy departments) that halfway competent observers could no longer simply associate him with literary study. The art house popularity of Kirby Dick and Amy Zierling Kofman's documentary film *Derrida* also suggests that Derrida's non- or para-academic reception in America was gaining complexity by the end of the twentieth century.

97. Jonathan Kandell, "Jacques Derrida, Abstruse Theorist, Dies in Paris at 74," *New York Times*, October 10, 2004. The *Times* had clearly charted its course well in advance, assigning the obituary to a freelance reporter whose sole qualification was that he had shown he could write stinging obituaries (e.g., of the billionaire Laurence Tisch). Some responses, letters to the editor, and other related material may be found at the memorial page for Derrida on the UC Irvine web site. The *Times* obituary was picked up by many American papers, but elsewhere in the English-speaking world leading newspapers often carried far more positive obituaries: see, e.g., Martin Bright, "'World's Greatest Philosopher' Dies," *The Observer*, October 10, 2004.

98. Frank Lentricchia, *After the New Criticism* (Chicago: University of Chicago Press, 1980), 283–84. Admirer of de Man's work though I am, Lentricchia's account of de Man predicting the work of Bloom, Hartman and Miller strikes me as saying more about Lentricchia's fantasized image of de Man than about the history of literary criticism.

99. This small cento of quotations is drawn from *Yale French Studies* 69 (1985), "The Lesson of Paul de Man," ed. Peter Brooks, Shoshana Felman, and J. Hillis Miller, which opens with tributes offered at the memorial service for Paul de Man on January 18, 1984. Here are some more extracts. J. Hillis Miller: "Paul de Man would have smiled ironically. . . . He would have smiled ironically again. . . ." (3); A. Bartlett Giamatti: "I think of Paul de Man always in terms of lucidity, as a radiant presence. . . . I shall always see his shy and candid smile" (6); Geoffrey Hartman: "Who will forget his smile, which remained with him almost to the end? . . . [Once after a talk by de Man, a] challenger from the audience pointed triumphantly to Paul's own presence—why are you here, in person, if you believe as you do—and Paul's smile became a glint of steel, as he replied: the text matters, what you write matters, everything else is vanity" (7); E. S. Burt: "On those of us who took his courses, who read him avidly, who sat for hours in his office, the fascination was particularly strong. It was first attached to the man—to his gait, to the shrug of the shoulders, the set of the head, the quizzical smile" (11); Jacques Derrida: "As you know, Paul was irony itself . . ." (French 14; English 324); Yves Bonnefoy: "This head with the slanted forehead, leaning over a sudden big smile, above which would filter the very blue gaze" (French 17; English, translation modified, 327).

100. John Guillory, *Cultural Capital: The Problem of Literary Canon Formation* (Chi-

cago: University of Chicago Press, 1993), 178. Other informed observers were making similar claims during these years, e.g.: "It seems to me, more than any other figure, 'de Man' has become a synecdochal figure for theory and its stakes these past fifteen years." Jeffrey Williams, "The Shadow of de Man," *South Central Review* 11, no. 1 (Spring 1994): 44–55, at 44.

101. As J. Hillis Miller comments, "The use of some proper name or pronoun, or at least the barely visible traces of some already effaced prosopopoeia, seems to be another of those irresistible necessities of language." J. Hillis Miller, "'Reading' Part of a Paragraph in *Allegories of Reading*," in *Reading de Man Reading*, ed. Lindsay Waters and Wlad Godzich (Minneapolis: University of Minnesota Press, 1989), 155–70, at 166.

102. Barbara Johnson, *The Wake of Deconstruction* (Oxford: Blackwell, 1994), 72. Anyone seeking to trace the workings of personification owes an enormous debt to Johnson's rigorous and innovative rhetorical analyses over many books and essays.

103. Paul de Man, *The Rhetoric of Romanticism* (New York: Columbia University Press, 1984), 75–76. Subsequent references to this collection will be given as *RR* and page number.

104. I am unfairly compounding a rich array of theoretical and thematic lines of inquiry: animal studies, ecological criticism, so-called speculative materialisms, etc., all of which, of course, address fundamental questions while inspiring work of wildly varying quality and reach. A particularly noticeable evasion of the problem of language, I think, is evident in contemporary vitalist and materialist speculation. Elsewhere I have examined an apocalyptic scenario that one well-received writer in this tradition, Ray Brassier, constructs at the end of *Nihil Unbound: Enlightenment and Extinction* (New York: Palgrave, 2007); see my "Wordsworth's Dream of Extinction," *Qui Parle* 21, no. 2 (Summer 2013): 61–68. Brassier celebrates in remarkably idealizing terms the power of human thought to think extinction: "the will to know is driven by the traumatic reality of extinction, and strives to become equal to the trauma of the in-itself whose trace it bears. In becoming equal to it, philosophy achieves a binding of extinction, through which the will to know is finally rendered commensurate with the in-itself" (239). In this darkly Hegelian plot, knowledge catches up with its object when we recognize that we are "already dead"—when, that is, we acknowledge that we are consigned to extinction, like the sun (in 4.5 billion years) and the universe itself ("the ultimate horizon, when, roughly one trillion trillion trillion [10 to the 1728] years from now, the accelerating expansion of the universe will have disintegrated the fabric of matter itself, terminating the possibility of embodiment" [228]). De Manian rhetorical reading generates its own grim sublimity, as noted earlier; but in doing so it short-circuits this sort of covert idealism. We clever animals, as Nietzsche would say, do not just have to die; worse, we never even attain the satisfaction of knowing that we are "already dead," insofar as we are caught in a linguistic machine that prevents understanding from being "commensurate with the in-itself."

105. The verb itself is remarkably consistent: the critic *calls* (or, even more often, is described by another critic as *calling*) for an approach that would do X without sacrificing or marginalizing Y. This rhetorical tic is particularly visible in politically engaged Anglophone literary and cultural criticism; the rhetorical attitude is mildly messianic or millennial, and the verb *call* underscores the critic's inability actually to provide what

she or he is calling for. We shall encounter an example (one among thousands in the contemporary archive) near the beginning of Chapter 2, where we shall look at sentences by Virginia Jackson and Yopie Prins that, if summarized according to the code to which I am pointing here, would be described as *calling* for an "unraveling" of the generic notion of the lyric.

106. As we shall see in Chapter 5, De Man's late work conceives of this interruption of the aesthetic as the pressure of a certain materiality at work in phenomenalization: "The bottom line, in Kant as well as in Hegel, is the prosaic materiality of the letter and no degree of obfuscation or ideology can transform this materiality into the phenomenal cognition of aesthetic judgment." "Phenomenality and Materiality in Kant," in *Aesthetic Ideology* (Minneapolis: University of Minnesota Press, 1996), 90. Insofar as a close reading of a textual rendering of aesthetic judgment takes de Man to that "bottom line," his critical project aligns to a certain extent with the tradition that, from Kant to Adorno and Heidegger and through to the present, finds in art and aesthetic judgment resources for critical thought. An affirmation of the critical power of the artwork—some version of an "internal distance," in Louis Althusser's formulation—usually characterizes sophisticated Marxist criticism. For a comparison of de Man with Althusser, see Michael Sprinker, "Art and Ideology: Althusser and de Man," in *Material Events: Paul de Man and the Afterlife of Theory*, ed. Tom Cohen et al. (Minneapolis: University of Minnesota Press, 2001), 32–48.

107. De Man puts the cross-linguistic pun on *Fall* to work in "Aesthetic Formalization in Kleist," particularly when the essay is stressing "the trap of an aesthetic education which inevitably confuses dismemberment of language by the power of the letter with the gracefulness of a dance." For a study of the pedagogical complexity of rhetorical reading, see Brian McGrath, *The Poetics of Unremembered Acts: Reading, Lyric, Pedagogy* (Evanston, Ill.: Northwestern University Press, 2013).

108. Cathy Caruth, "The Falling Body and the Impact of Reference (de Man, Kant, Kleist)," in her *Unclaimed Experience: Trauma, Narrative, and History* (Baltimore: Johns Hopkins University Press, 1996), 74. Caruth suggests that this figure helps us understand how reference functions in de Manian theory: "In de Man's text, as in Kant's, the impact of reference is felt in falling: in the resistance of the example of falling to a phenomenal or perceptual analogy that would turn it into the mere figure of an abstract principle" (89). Her conclusion is "that reference emerges not in its accessibility to perception but in the resistance of language to perceptual analogies. . . . What theory does, de Man tells us repeatedly, is fall; and in falling, it refers" (90).

109. See Kevin McLaughlin, *Poetic Force: Poetry after Kant* (Stanford: Stanford University Press, 2014), for a rigorous examination of the "unforce" of "poetic force."

2. Theory and Romantic Lyric: The Case of "A slumber did my spirit seal"

1. Jonathan Culler, "Lyric, History and Genre," *New Literary History* 40, no. 4 (2009): 879–99, at 884. The adverb "finally" registers Culler's ongoing debate with critics who take a more nominalist position on lyric as a genre, about which more later. The minor role accorded the generic notion of the lyric prior to the romantic era is documented with his usual wit and acuity by Gérard Genette in *The Architext: An Introduction*, trans. Jane E. Lewin (Berkeley: University of California Press, 1992 [1979]).

2. Jonathan Culler, "Changes in the Study of the Lyric," in *Lyric Poetry: Beyond New Criticism*, ed. Chaviva Hosek and Patricia Parker (Ithaca, N.Y.: Cornell University Press, 1985), 41.

3. "The two readings have to engage each other in direct confrontation, for the one reading is precisely the error denounced by the other and has to be undone by it." Paul de Man, *Allegories of Reading* (New Haven: Yale University Press, 1979), 11.

4. Paul de Man, *The Rhetoric of Romanticism* (New York: Columbia University Press, 1984), 261.

5. Paul de Man, "Lyrical Voice in Contemporary Theory: Riffaterre and Jauss," in Hosek and Parker, *Lyric Poetry*, 55.

6. Virginia Jackson, *Dickinson's Misery: A Theory of Lyric Reading* (Princeton: Princeton University Press, 2005), 99.

7. In referring to new historicist romantic studies, I have in mind Jerome Mc-Gann's notion of a "romantic ideology." See McGann, *The Romantic Ideology: A Critical Investigation* (Chicago: University of Chicago Press, 1985). There are significant differences between McGann and Jackson: McGann ascribes "romantic ideology" to the romantics and represents twentieth-century criticism as entrapped by romanticism's self-representations, whereas Jackson forcefully distinguishes pre-nineteenth-century writing practices (above all Dickinson's, of course) from a process of "lyric reading" that is really a twentieth-century practice, though one with nineteenth-century roots. Yet McGann will also suggest that twentieth-century romantic studies projects its idealizations backward; and both McGann and Jackson are committed to a model of text-production in which an original rich, human communicative relationship gets vaporized into the abstractions of romantic (or lyric) ideology.

8. *The Lyric Theory Reader: A Critical Anthology*, ed. Virginia Jackson and Yopie Prins (Baltimore: Johns Hopkins University Press, 2014), 7.

9. They slacken the pressure for a moment in commenting on Craig Dworkin's "conceptual poem" on lyric and music: "We could call that poem a lyric, or you could call it whatever you like" (459).

10. Rei Terada, "After the Critique of Lyric," *PMLA* 123, no. 1 (2008): 195–200, at 196. Terada is introducing a cluster of papers originally given at the 2006 convention.

11. Culler, who has emphasized the importance of poetics throughout his career, offers an important counterperspective to the positions taken by Jackson and Prins or Terada. In Culler's view, genres are historical but not simply empirical; they are not just what people in a particular period thought, but rather involve norms, "fundamental structures that may be at work even when not manifest" ("Lyric, History, and Genre," 883). In this view, it is part of the job of literary theory and criticism to keep trying to build a good definition of lyric. Culler's considered reflections are forthcoming in his *Theory of Lyric* (Cambridge, Mass.: Harvard University Press, 2015). See also Timothy Bahti's *Ends of the Lyric: Direction and Consequence in Western Poetry* (Baltimore: Johns Hopkins University Press, 1996), which argues that lyric as a genre is marked by "tropes of inversion" (254).

12. Although de Man, as I am arguing throughout this book, is the symbolic "proper name" of the rhetorical deconstruction of voice, Culler deserves to be credited with a path-breaking publication on the rhetorical character of lyric voice: "Apostro-

phe," originally published in *Diacritics* in 1977 and subsequently collected in *The Pursuit of Signs: Semiotics, Literature, Deconstruction* (Ithaca, N.Y.: Cornell University Press, 1981). Of course, the shadow of Derrida's massive rewriting of the speech/writing distinction looms over any theoretically informed engagement with the question of "voice."

13. Barbara Johnson, "Anthropomorphism in Lyric and Law," in *Persons and Things* (Cambridge, Mass.: Harvard University Press, 2008), 188–207, at 189. Jackson and Prins include this essay in their anthology and direct at it (and at de Man, of course) their sentence about poststructuralism's making lyric into a "modern icon."

14. The first edition of *The Norton Anthology of Theory and Criticism*, ed. Vincent Leitch et al. (New York: Norton, 2001) includes, in addition to the two essays I am about to mention, a handful of texts that address poetry: de Man, "Semiology and Rhetoric," (1514–26); an extract from Bloom's *Anxiety of Influence* (1797–1805); Stanley Fish, "Interpreting the Variorum" (2071–88); and excerpts from two texts by Roman Jakobson: "Linguistics and Poetics" (1258–65) and "Two Aspects of Language and Two Types of Aphasic Disturbances" (1265–69). Of course, the *Norton* could have tweaked its selection a bit, but even if this or that editorial decision had gone another way, the anthology would inevitably document the marginal role that lyric poems have played as objects of analysis in the most-taught texts of the "theory canon" in the United States.

15. The archive of secondary work on these de Man essays is considerable; if one is starting out, one could hardly do better than begin with Barbara Johnson's "Anthropomorphism in Lyric and Law" (see note 13), which offers an exceptionally lucid account of de Man's "Anthropomorphism and Trope." De Man's essay "The Purloined Ribbon," which analyzes Rousseau's story of his theft of a ribbon early in his *Confessions*, became the closing chapter of *Allegories of Reading* under the title of "Excuses."

16. Quoted from William Wordsworth, *Selected Poetry*, ed. Stephen Gill (New York: Oxford University Press, 2008).

17. In its first publication in the 1800 edition of *Lyrical Ballads*, "seemed" was "seem'd," "Rolled" was "Roll'd," and punctuation was light (a comma after "seal"; a colon after "fears"; no punctuation after "feel"; a period after "years"; then no end-stopping punctuation at all in the second stanza—even after "sees"—until the final line, which received an exclamation point, but contained no internal commas: "With rocks and stones and trees!"). Wordsworth revised the punctuation for the 1802 edition.

18. The other "Lucy" poems are "Strange fits of passion have I known," "She dwelt among the untrodden ways," "I traveled among unknown men," and "Three years she grew in sun and shower." Critics have often added other poems, e.g., "Lucy Gray," to the group. For a scholarly overview see Herbert Hartman, "Wordsworth's 'Lucy' Poems: Notes and Marginalia," *PMLA* 49 (1934): 134–42. In the 1800 and subsequent editions of *Lyrical Ballads*, Wordsworth grouped "A slumber" with "Strange fits" and "She dwelt," but in his 1815 *Poems* he placed "A slumber" and "Three years she grew" under "Poems of the Imagination," but "Strange fits," "She dwelt," and "I traveled" (first published in 1807) under "Poems Founded on the Affections." As Brian Caraher cautiously remarks in *Wordsworth's "Slumber" and the Problematics of Reading* (University Park: Pennsylvania State University Press, 1991): "Wordsworth did not actively discourage an association of 'A slumber' with at least some of the poems in the 'Lucy' group" (41). The real-life candidates for "Lucy" are usually Dorothy Wordsworth (who plays

a charged and complex role in several of her brother's poems) and Margaret Hutchinson (who died young in 1796; she was the sister of Wordsworth's future wife, Mary). "Lucy," however, was also a stock elegiac name in the eighteenth century. For a summary of the biographical background, see Mary Moorman, *William Wordsworth: A Biography: The Early Years, 1770–1803* (Oxford: Clarendon Press, 1957), 423–25.

19. It is possible to mount an informed and coherent interpretation of the poem according to which the "she" refers throughout to the narrator's "spirit": see Hugh Sykes Davies, "Another New Poem by Wordsworth," *Essays in Criticism* 15 (1965): 135–61. Davies also argues that Wordsworth did not in fact consider "A slumber" part of the "Lucy" sequence. Most scholars, however, including all the critics I am about to mention who offer interpretations of the poem (Bateson, Brooks, Hirsch, de Man, Miller, Abrams—leaving aside Knapp and Michaels, who do not offer an interpretation), have taken the "she" to refer to a female personage separate from the narrator, and associable with the young girl of the "Lucy" group. Caraher adds a twist: he claims that the poem encourages us to refer the "she" back to "spirit" in its first stanza, but then, in its second stanza, forces us to discard that assumption so as to refer the "she" to a female personage separate from the narrator. (That is, the poem shakes us out of our pronominal slumber into intersubjectivity, as we repeat as readers the drama of the "I" in the poem.)

20. Hirsch was an assistant professor at Yale in 1960; his first book, *Wordsworth and Schelling*, a revision of his Yale dissertation of 1957, also appeared in 1960. "Objective Interpretation" was first published in *PMLA* 75, no. 4 (1960): 463–79. As a gesture of acknowledgment toward the institutionalization of theory, which is part of what we are studying in this book, I shall quote from Hirsch's and Knapp and Michaels's essays as republished in the *Norton Anthology of Theory and Criticism* (1684–1708 for Hirsch, 2460–74 for Knapp and Michaels). Hirsch's essay is also available in his *Validity in Interpretation* (New Haven: Yale University Press, 1967).

21. The texts Hirsch discusses are: F. W. Bateson, *English Poetry: A Critical Introduction* (New York: Barnes and Noble, 1950); and Cleanth Brooks, "Irony as a Principle of Structure," in Morton D. Zabel, ed., *Literary Opinion in America*, 2nd ed. (New York: Harper & Row, 1951), 729–41. (Of the two, Brooks's essay is in fact the earlier text; it was originally published in 1949.)

22. Both Brooks and Bateson are charged with being at once insufficiently formal and insufficiently historical in Geoffrey Hartman's classic essay "Beyond Formalism" (1966); both, according to Hartman, offer "essentially unhistorical descriptions of Wordsworth's style." See *Beyond Formalism: Literary Essays 1958–1970* (New Haven: Yale University Press, 1970), 43–51, at 45. Hartman's history of style, however, does not solve the problem of mutually exclusive interpretations that preoccupies Hirsch.

23. Brooks's interpretation, which does indeed strike the present reader as rather more plausible than Bateson's, is worth quoting at slightly greater length (these sentences are in fact cited by Hirsch, 1697–98): "Part of the effect, of course, resides in the fact that a dead lifelessness is suggested more sharply by an object's being whirled about by something else than by an image of the object in repose. But there are other matters which are at work here: the sense of the girl falling back into the clutter of things, companioned by things chained like a tree to one spot or by things completely inanimate like rocks and stones. . . . [She] is caught up helplessly into the empty whirl of the

earth which measures and makes time. She is touched by and held by earthly time in its most powerful and horrible image" (Brooks, 736).

24. Bateson's position, though unsatisfactory to some, is by no means a dead issue. It has been updated by Marjorie Levinson in "A Motion and a Spirit: Romancing Spinoza," *Studies in Romanticism* 46 (2007): 367–95. Levinson argues the case for "hearing the Spinozistic echo" in certain words and turns of Wordsworth's poetry, and proposes that "A slumber" "signpost[s] Spinoza, who ... distinguishes things from each other, from their background, and from what we think of as more-than-things (e.g., humans, animals, and less complex organisms) only on the basis of proportions of motion-and-rest" (389). When Levinson gets to the crux of her interpretation, her presentation of the poem's "consolation" sounds very like Bateson's claim that Lucy is actually more alive when dead (Levinson's version runs: "indeed, now for the first time, the narrator sees her and therefore himself as part of the whole, part of the larger, more active and complex body in which Lucy participates" [391]; compare Bateson: "the grander dead-Lucy ... has become involved in the sublimer processes of nature" [59]).

25. I certainly have no stake in arguing for any specifiable tipping-point, but am thinking here of the fact that 1979 is the year that the so-called Yale Critics' *Deconstruction and Criticism* and de Man's *Allegories of Reading* appeared. So did a special issue of *Studies in Romanticism* 18, no. 4 (1979), with an introduction by de Man and essays by several of his graduate students, as did an issue of *Diacritics* 9, no. 4 (Winter 1979), featuring a text by Heinrich von Kleist, a de Manian reading of it by Carol Jacobs, and de Manian responses to Jacobs's reading by Cynthia Chase and Andrzej Warminskski. "Theory at Yale" arguably entered the height of its visibility in 1979.

26. Both Miller's essay and Abrams's will be cited from Morris Eaves and Michael Fischer, eds., *Romanticism and Contemporary Criticism* (Ithaca, N.Y.: Cornell University Press, 1986): see Miller, "On Edge: The Crossways of Contemporary Criticism" (96–111), and Abrams, "Construing and Deconstructing" (127–58). In the Eaves and Fischer collection, Miller's essay is followed by a "Postscript 1984" that responds to M. H. Abrams's "Construing and Deconstructing," plus a transcript of questions and answers relevant to the exchange (118–26); Abrams's essay is also followed by questions and answers (158–82).

27. During most of his years of teaching at Johns Hopkins (1953–1972), Miller had left romantic poetry to his senior colleague Earl Wasserman; but his turn from phenomenology to deconstruction around 1970 took first published form not only as the long essay on Georges Poulet to which I made brief reference in Chapter 1, but also as "The Still Heart: Poetic Form in Wordsworth," both of which appeared in 1971. In fact, Miller's "job talk" for Yale that year was also on Wordsworth—he gave a version of an essay that he then published shortly afterward on the "Dream of the Arab" episode in Book 5 of *The Prelude* (personal communication). It should be noted, too, that although Miller was particularly famous as a Dickensian and critic of narrative when he moved to Yale, he had always published actively on poetry. His earliest publication in a major journal was on Hopkins (in *ELH* in 1955); his third book was on twentieth-century poetry (*Poets of Reality* [1965]), with chapters on Yeats, Eliot, Thomas, Stevens, and William Carlos Williams.

28. M. H. Abrams, *Natural Supernaturalism: Tradition and Revolution in Romantic Lit-

erature (New York: Norton, 1971); J. Hillis Miller, "Tradition and Difference," *Diacritics* 2, no. 4 (1972): 6–13; M. H. Abrams, "The Deconstructive Angel," *Critical Inquiry* 3, no. 3 (1977): 425–38. For a brief discussion of Miller's shift, around 1970–71, from a phenomenological to a deconstructive approach, see Chapter 1.

29. For the original publication, see J. Hillis Miller, "On Edge: The Crossways of Contemporary Criticism," *Bulletin of the American Academy of Arts and Sciences* 32, no. 4 (1979): 13–32. As noted, I shall quote from the Eaves and Fischer reprint. As we saw in Chapter 1, Miller published several essays during the 1970s that fall under the category mentioned here: the two high-profile polemical book reviews, of Abrams in 1972, and of Joseph N. Riddel's *The Inverted Bell* (1974) in 1975; the two-part essay "Stevens' Rock and Criticism as Cure" and "Stevens' Rock and Criticism as Cure II," *Georgia Review* 30 (Spring 1976).

30. Miller defines "metaphysical" sketchily as "the system of assumptions coming down from Plato and Aristotle which has unified our culture. This system includes the notions of beginning, continuity, and end, of causality, of dialectical process, of organic unity, and of ground, in short of logos in all its many senses" (100–101).

31. Although Miller will go on to complicate this set-up reading, I do not think his text ever reads the death of the "she" as a rupturing *event* in the poem. That is one of the main points of de Man's interpretation, as I understand it, in "The Rhetoric of Temporality" (1969), reprinted in de Man, *Blindness and Insight: Essays in the Rhetoric of Contemporary Criticism*, 2nd rev. ed. (Minneapolis: University of Minnesota Press, 1983), 187–228. De Man's reading is seemingly in harmony with Brooks's (and with Miller's first move here) insofar as for de Man the poem narrates a movement from delusion to bleak wisdom: "The stance of the speaker, who exists in the 'now,' is that of a subject whose insight is no longer in doubt and who is no longer vulnerable to irony. It could be called, if one so wished, a stance of wisdom. There is no real disjunction of the subject; the poem is written from the point of view of a unified self that fully recognizes a past condition as one of error and stands in a present that, however painful, sees things as they actually are" (224). De Man goes on to stress, however, the fictionality and non-presence of this "now," in a sentence that is itself slightly fragmentary: "The 'now' of the poem is not an actual now, which is that of the moment of death, lies hidden in the blank space between the two stanzas" (225).

32. All of Miller's major essays in the 1970s build their interpretations out toward fundamental claims about reading and textuality, but my own sense is that the outward movement is usually more tightly wound around the chosen text. In Miller's reading of Stevens's "The Rock," for instance, "the interpreter is led further and further into a labyrinth of branching connections going back through Whitman and Emerson to Milton, to the Bible, to Aristotle, and behind him into the forking pathways of our Indo-European family of languages" ("Stevens' Rock and Criticism as Cure," 31), but not toward any equivalent of the "obscure sexual drama" that particularly exercises Abrams.

33. Walter Benn Michaels, "Against Formalism: Chickens and Rocks," in *Interpreting Law and Literature: A Hermeneutic Reader*, ed. Sanford Levinson and Steven Mailloux (Evanston, Ill.: Northwestern University Press, 1988), 215–25, at 222. Michaels is referencing the Brooks-Bateson debate as presented by Hirsch: to a pantheist, presumably, a rock would be in some sense "alive." He is pursuing a thread that, with Steven Knapp,

he brushed against in the position paper "Against Theory" that I discuss later in this essay.

34. See Nancy J. Vickers, "Diana Described: Scattered Woman and Scattered Rhyme," *Critical Inquiry* 8, no. 2 (1981): 265–79. Jackson and Prins, who include it in their reader, brought my attention to this essay. Vickers notes that the Petrarchan speaker and the female addressee mirror each other's scattering through the *Rime sparse*: Laura is of course constantly fragmented into cherished body parts, but the "I" also suffers this fate. Vickers focuses on the fetishistic economy of gaze, identification, and dispersal in the Actaeon stanza of Petrarch's twenty-third *canzone*: "Woman's body, albeit divine, is displayed to Actaeon, and his body, as a consequence, is literally taken apart" (273).

35. John Baker Jr., "Grammar and Rhetoric in Wordsworth's 'A Slumber did my spirit seal': Heidegger, de Man, Deconstruction," *Studies in Romanticism* 36 (1997): 103–123, at 122.

36. The original text may be found in *Critical Inquiry* 8, no. 4 (1982): 723–42. Later I shall be considering important critiques of this essay by Peggy Kamuf and Orrin Wang; but I should note that "Against Theory" inspired a vigorous debate that will *not* be summarized here among intentionalist and pragmatist critics in the pages of *Critical Inquiry*. These responses to "Against Theory" (by, among others, E. D. Hirsch, Stanley Fish, and Richard Rorty), plus a rejoinder from Knapp and Michaels, are collected in W. J. T. Mitchell, ed., *Against Theory: Literary Studies and the New Pragmatism* (Chicago: University of Chicago Press, 1985). Though that collection certainly repays study, it is being left aside in the present context because its contributors, most of whom agree with some portion or other of Knapp and Michaels's argument, do not address the challenge of deconstruction.

37. Peggy Kamuf, "Floating Authorship," *Diacritics* 16, no. 4 (1986): 3–13. Kamuf adduces and puts pressure on an affirmation Knapp and Michaels make in "A Reply to Our Critics" (originally published in 1983, republished in Mitchell, 95–105): "What can the word 'author' mean if not the composer of the text?" ("A Reply," 101; discussed in Kamuf, "Floating Authorship," 7).

38. The wave poem activates various associations and pretexts, many of them surely intended by Knapp and Michaels. They probably had the Derrida passage from "Force and Signification" in mind, and probably also this well-known passage in Kant's *Critique of Judgment*: "Suppose that someone coming to a seemingly uninhabited country perceived a geometric figure, say a regular hexagon, traced in the sand . . . following reason, he would not judge that such a figure is made possible by the sand, the adjoining sea, the wind, or even animals that leave footprints familiar to him, or by any other nonrational cause." Immanuel Kant, *Critique of Judgment*, trans. Werner S. Pluhar (Indianapolis: Hackett, 1987), 248. Knapp and Michaels might also have recalled (why not?) an interesting moment in the sixth chapter of Freud's *Interpretation of Dreams*: "and if the whole picture is intended to represent a landscape, letters of the alphabet are out of place in it since such objects do not occur in nature." (I am citing from the extract published in the *Norton Anthology of Theory and Criticism*, 919–28, at 924.) Orrin Wang suggests further echoes in his extensive critique of Knapp and Michaels: "Defoe's Crusoe coming upon a footprint on the beach, Kant likewise coming upon a hexagon,

Wordsworth's Dream of the Arab, and Shelley's Rousseau's 'brain be[coming] as sand' [in Shelley's *Triumph of Life*, l. 405]; and, more close to the wave poem's inception, Foucault's concluding image in *The Order of Things* of a future where 'man would be erased, like a face drawn in sand at the edge of the sea'." Orrin Wang, *Romantic Sobriety: Sensation, Revolution, Commodification, History* (Baltimore: Johns Hopkins University Press, 2011), 87. The last reference is to Michel Foucault, *The Order of Things: An Archeology of the Human Sciences* (New York: Vintage, 1973), 387. Wang thanks David L. Clark "for the Foucault reference" (308 n. 4), and I relay the echo.

39. See Jackson, *Dickinson's Misery*, 110–14. Jackson accuses Knapp and Michaels of falling into the specifically lyric trap of idealizing genre out of existence, because their parable presents intentions as separate from generic conventions and constraints. She suggests that if the parable had featured the opening sentence of *Middlemarch*, the intent of the author would be less immediately prominent as a problem: "wondering how these words appeared in this place and wondering what the words say would remain two distinct questions" (113).

40. Jacques Derrida, "Signature Event Context" trans. Samuel Weber, in Jacques Derrida, *Limited Inc* (Evanston, Ill.: Northwestern University Press, 1988), 8. This volume also collects Derrida's reply to John Searle, "Limited Inc, a b c . . ."; both originally appeared in *Glyph* in 1977.

41. P. D. Juhl, *Interpretation: An Essay in the Philosophy of Literary Criticism* (Princeton: Princeton University Press, 1980), 12.

42. To this sentence Juhl attaches a footnote: "A reader who finds these examples too improbable is invited to substitute his own. The only requirement is that the text have been produced by chance. Computer poetry is a more realistic example. The reason I have decided to use the example of a text produced by a monkey (or by water erosion) is that it is less easily associated with a person's intentions" (72 n. 9). Responding to Juhl's invitation, Knapp and Michaels seem to have felt obliged to "substitute" not a less but a *more* improbable example. As I hope to show in the pages that follow, that is because Wordsworth's poem spurs critics to repeat and disavow figures of personification.

43. Wang's critique of "Against Theory" forms part of a two-chapter sequence in *Romantic Sobriety* that goes on to engage at length Walter Benn Michaels's *The Shape of the Signifier: 1967 to the End of History* (Princeton: Princeton University Press, 2004). Wang explores the way these texts seek to align sensory experience with the non-linguistic (the way that they seek to maintain that a "mark" can be *seen* as looking like but not being a letter). This critique forms part of Wang's analysis of the way in which tropes of sensation and sobriety define the reception of romanticism and inflect contemporary critical thought. An ambitious account of the intersections among romanticism, deconstruction, and Marxism, in the context of our ongoing romantic predicament, composes the broader argument of this important study.

44. This is not to say that repetitions do not make a difference. Knapp and Michaels's imaginative troping of Wordsworth's poem as a wave poem, for instance, opens to view the text's own staging of the possibility that it is being written by waves of vowels. For the movement from the first to the second stanza is not only from past to present tense, from first-person to impersonal narrative, and, more dubiously, from life

to death and from innocence to experience, but also a turn from *i*'s and *e*'s to the long and short *o*'s made emphatic by the promoted negatives making up spondees: Nó mó-tion has she nów, nó fórce (a pattern repeated in the slighter promotion of the negating *o*-word in nór sées, and strongly repeated in rólled róund; the *o*-emphasis is sustained at the end of the line with cóurse, and closed off as the poem closes with the long and short *o*'s of the near-stutter rócks and stónes). Perhaps the generative principle of the poem consists in the achievement of a line of *o*'s—an achievement indistinguish-able from poetic craft, yet, as a generative principle, utterly alien to the intersubjective drama, since the poem's narrative would then be driven not by any representational logic but by the particular vowels that happen to be found in particular words.

3. What Remains: Geoffrey Hartman and the Shock of Imagination

1. The history of the reception of romanticism during the first decades of the professional era is complex, but as has often been noted, many of the prominent in-tellectual movements and literary figures of the day (T. E. Hulme, Irving Babbitt and the New Humanism; T. S. Eliot and his New Critical admirers through to the young Cleanth Brooks) frequently defined themselves in opposition to something they called "romanticism." Polemical engagements with romanticism did not disappear in the 1960s by any means—one need think only of Jerome McGann's *The Romantic Ide-ology* (1983) and its considerable progeny. For reasons that I have discussed elsewhere—briefly in Chapter 1, and much more extensively in *The Politics of Aesthetics: Nationalism, Gender, Romanticism* (Stanford: Stanford University Press, 2003)—romanticism remains a scholarly field scored by periodic waves of defensiveness and embarrassment. Here my point is simply that a certain professional normalization had set in by the 1960s.

2. Hartman, who began graduate study in comparative literature at Yale in 1949, had been relatively unaware of and sheltered from the antiromantic, Christian, and genteelly anti-Semitic mindset that Bloom encountered in the English Department when he began his studies there in 1951. In the Department of Comparative Literature, Hartman had a distinguished romanticist, René Wellek, and a very great literary scholar who was Jewish, Erich Auerbach, as teachers and role models.

3. As in, e.g., René Wellek's famous formula for the "system of norms" that, in his view, defines romanticism: "imagination for the view of poetry, nature for the view of the world, and symbol and myth for poetic style." See Wellek, "The Concept of Ro-manticism in Literary History," in *Concepts of Criticism* (New Haven: Yale University Press, 1963), 128–98, at 161.

4. Geoffrey Hartman, *Wordsworth's Poetry, 1787–1814* (New Haven: Yale University Press, 1977 [1964]), 33. Subsequent references are given parenthetically by page number and acronym *WP*.

5. Hartman told me in 2013 that he met de Man "at an MLA meeting around 1960," at which de Man told him "that he had read *The Unmediated Vision* and was struck by a coincidence of interest"; they did not become friends, however, until 1965, when de Man invited Hartman to join him in founding a comparative literature pro-gram at Cornell. See Chapter 1 for a brief summary of Hartman's career as well as Bloom's, de Man's, and Miller's.

6. Bloom would also have been alerted to de Man's essay by the notice accorded it in René Wellek's survey of the field, "Romanticism Re-considered" (1963), in *Concepts of Criticism* (New Haven: Yale University Press, 1963), 199–222 (see 219–20). Evelyn Barish reports in her lurid biography *The Double Life of Paul de Man* (New York: Norton, 2014) that "Structure intentionnelle" got de Man his job at Cornell in 1960. M. H. Abrams told Barish that he discovered de Man's essay on his own, but "Hartman reported that he was the one who had called Abrams' attention to it" (421). De Man's essay had a remarkable impact among cognoscenti in the United States in the 1960s despite its being available only in French.

7. Paul de Man, "A New Vitalism," *Critical Writings 1953–1978*, ed. Lindsay Waters (Minneapolis: University of Minnesota Press, 1989), 90–96, at 94. A few subsequent references to this review are given parenthetically by page number.

8. Geoffrey H. Hartman, *The Unmediated Vision: An Interpretation of Wordsworth, Hopkins, Rilke, and Valéry* (New Haven: Yale University Press, 1954), 132. Subsequent references are given parenthetically by page number and the acronym *UV*. Bloom's footnote in *The Visionary Company: A Reading of English Romantic Poetry* (New York: Doubleday, 1961) ascribes the quotation to Hartman's "forthcoming book on Wordsworth" (455): a token of the rich exchange of ideas and manuscripts between Bloom and Hartman during these early years, though also a token of Bloom's casual documenting of his tenacious mental archive.

9. De Man's critique of Bloom stresses what he sees as Bloom's uncritical patterning of Wordsworth's imaginative relationship to nature on what Bloom himself calls the "sexual analogy" (*Visionary Company* 123, cited by de Man, 94). De Man writes: "The passages on a masculine Wordsworth trying to conquer a feminine nature (coupled with suggestions that his virility was not quite up to the task) are not to the point. Far from being Blake's pure energy, Wordsworth's imagination is an extended mode of seeing, originating in the act of visual perception and not in sexuality" (94). (De Man assimilates "sexuality" here to the natural cycle of generation proper to Blake's Beulah.)

10. Paul de Man, "The Intentional Structure of the Romantic Image," in Harold Bloom, ed., *Romanticism and Consciousness: Essays in Criticism* (New York: Norton, 1970), 65–77, at 76–77. For the original French text, see "Structure intentionnelle de l'image romantique," *Revue internationale de philosophie* 51(1960): 68–84. De Man is, among other things, writing slantwise against Sartre in this essay: see Jean-Paul Sartre, "Structure intentionnelle de l'image," *Revue de Métaphysique et de Morale* 45, no. 4 (1938): 543–609. Tillottama Rajan notes the references to Sartre and comments briefly on differences between de Man's French and English versions of his essay (as do I, later) in *Deconstruction and the Remainders of Phenomenology: Sartre, Derrida, Foucault, Baudrillard* (Stanford: Stanford University Press, 2002). For a reading of de Man's essay in the context of his early work, see Ortwin de Graef, *Serenity in Crisis: A Preface to Paul de Man, 1939–1960* (Lincoln: University of Nebraska Press, 1993), 163–73.

11. In the original French version from 1960, de Man makes a qualified exception for Hölderlin: "Les oeuvres du premier romantisme, à la seule et possible exception de certains poèmes de Hölderlin précédant de peu sa folie, ne nous en fournissent guère d'exemples" (83).

12. I have in mind here de Man's famous concluding sentence to this essay, which,

it should be noted, is slightly darker in the English version of 1970 than in the French one of 1960. The essay in *Romanticism and Consciousness*, on which generations of American romanticists cut their teeth from 1970 onward, has as its last sentence: "We are only beginning to understand how this oscillation in the status of the image is linked to the crisis that leaves the poetry of today under a steady threat of extinction, although, on the other hand, it remains the depositary of hopes that no other activity of the mind seems able to offer" (77). In the original French, however, the threat [*menace*] is left general, and the "hopes" have a markedly religious tinge ("la crise qui semble laisser le langage poétique contemporain sous le signe constant de la menace, tout en le laissant dépositaire d'espérances de résurrection que nulle autre activité de l'esprit ne semble en mesure d'offrir," 84). To complicate matters, de Man seems to have tweaked this closing sentence again when he republished it in *The Rhetoric of Romanticism* (New York: Columbia University Press, 1984), changing the English word depositary ("a person to whom something is lodged in trust," according to Merriam-Webster)—which accurately renders the French word he had used in 1960, *dépositaire*—to depository ("a place where things are stored") (17). Using this last version as his text, Forest Pyle comments, in a powerful reading of de Man's essay and of the entire problematic of the romantic image, that "*depository* is a curious word to describe this function of poetry: as a depository, poetry would be the place where hopes are kept, but out of circulation," and notes that the promise of poetry is being made to oscillate "with its tendency to oblivion." See Pyle, "The Romantic Image of the Intentional Structure," in *Releasing the Image: From Literature to New Media*, ed. Jacques Khalip and Robert Mitchell (Stanford: Stanford University Press, 2011), 181–203, at 202–203. I will shortly be examining ways in which Hartman, in his turn, has extinction (ambivalently) shadowing imagination.

13. Jean Paulhan, *Les fleurs de Tarbes, ou, La terreur dans les letters* (Paris: Gallimard, 1941). De Man's argument about literature's fractured dependence on literary history and desire for modernity, and Bloom's writings on the anxiety of influence may also be understood as (quite different) variations on this theme. I discuss Bloom's theory in Chapter 4, and refer to de Man's essay "Literary History and Literary Modernity" in Chapter 6.

14. Geoffrey H. Hartman, *Beyond Formalism: Literary Essays, 1958–1970* (New Haven: Yale University Press, 1970), ix. Subsequent references to this collection are given by page number and the acronym *BF*, with the titles and dates of the individual essays provided parenthetically on first reference.

15. I should stress that I am tracking only one particular line of development of Hartman's thought. In the decade separating these two books Hartman matured as a scholar and critic in many ways, as he summarizes in his autobiography *A Scholar's Tale: Intellectual Journey of a Displaced Child of Europe* (New York: Fordham University Press, 2007): "I now [that is, in the years following *The Unmediated Vision*] began to see what subtlety of thought, sensory dialectics, verbal choices, intertextual echoes, and complex social concerns were embedded in my strong impression of Wordsworth's originality. . . . The 'unmediated' turned out to be a construct, or the historical outcome of an extraordinary individual achievement that included a fortunate forgetting or ignorance of historical precursors" (22).

16. This closing flourish is one of several indications that Hartman may be writing consciously with and against de Man's "Structure intentionnelle"; compare de Man's closing sentences as cited in note 12. We have here a rare case of Hartman sounding grimmer than de Man.

17. "The morbidity of his intellect"; "the ravage of self-consciousness and the 'strong disease' of self-analysis"; "these maladies"; "the dangerous passageways of maturation"; "a passion that 'murders to dissect'"; "the corrosive power of analysis and the fixated self-consciousness" (BF, 298, 299).

18. To be sure, the theme of gentling is already announced in Hartman's first published scholarly article, "Milton's Counterplot" (1958, BF, 113–23), his remarkable pastoralizing, one could even say "Wordsworthian" reading of Paradise Lost. But not until Wordsworth's Poetry is this theme fully developed as a dialectic internal to the imagination.

19. For a comprehensive review of Hartman's oeuvre particularly attuned to themes of romanticism, trauma, and community, see Pieter Vermeulen, Geoffrey Hartman: Romanticism after the Holocaust (New York: Continuum, 2010). Continuities and differences between the two most prominent loci of Hartman's intellectual career, his work on Wordsworth and his work on Holocaust testimony, are explored in Cathy Caruth, "An Interview with Geoffrey Hartman," in Helen Regueiro Elam and Francis Ferguson, eds., The Wordsworthian Enlightenment: Romantic Poetry and the Ecology of Reading (Essays in Honor of Geoffrey Hartman) (Baltimore: Johns Hopkins University Press, 2005), 296–317. (Citations from this interview will be given by page number and identifier "Caruth.") The discussion engages questions of trauma and circles repeatedly back to the Boy of Winander episode in The Prelude. Hartman offers at one point a humorous summary of his thinking: "Look, everything works against trauma in Wordsworth, yet the basis of trauma is there. 'A gentle shock of mild surprise.' Now really!" (Caruth 304).

20. Cited from The Prelude: 1799, 1805, 1850, ed. Jonathan Wordsworth, M. H. Abrams, and Stephen Gill (New York: Norton, 1979).

21. Hartman's student, Thomas Weiskel, developed Hartman's reading of Wordsworth in this direction in his The Romantic Sublime: Studies in the Structure and Psychology of Transcendence (Baltimore: Johns Hopkins University Press, 1976). My line of inquiry here runs slightly differently, closer to Freud's much-discussed speculations in Beyond the Pleasure Principle on consciousness as a defense against shock.

22. For a sustained discussion of "nature" in Wordsworth and a rigorous effort to recover this term for an understanding of the power of his poetry, see Paul H. Fry, Wordsworth and the Poetry of What We Are (New Haven: Yale University Press, 2008): "nature is our own nonhuman existence, forgotten once named" (67).

23. Geoffrey H. Hartman, "Wordsworth Revisited," in The Unremarkable Wordsworth (Minneapolis: University of Minnesota Press, 1987), 3–17, at 3.

24. The pedagogical narrative has many subtle variants, e.g.: "Nature's only guidance is to intimate an imperishable consciousness which outlives even nature" (WP, 217, Hartman's emphasis); "Wordsworth's childhood experiences work in two conflicting ways, they 1) prophesy the independence from nature of his imaginative powers, and 2) impress nature ineradicably on them" (WP, 218, Hartman's emphasis).

25. A "fear of the death of nature" is fundamental to Wordsworth's sense of self, in Hartman's reading, which in many respects anticipates ecological interpretations of a later era (*WP*, 338). As he approaches Wordsworth's turn from surmise, however, Hartman turns more than once, with surprising energy, toward Blake—possibly in response to a decade's worth of conversations with Harold Bloom: "At Yale, in 1955, I met Harold Bloom, like myself on first appointment, and our conversation (which has lasted) made me attend more closely to the example of William Blake and his deceptive use of traditional apocalyptic imagery. A ghostly dialogue started in my head between Blake and Wordsworth. Allegorists might even say between Bloom and myself" (*A Scholar's Tale*, 41–42). At one point in *Wordsworth's Poetry*, Hartman in fact stages a fanciful dialogue between Wordsworth and Blake, at the end of which Wordsworth has to decide to either come up with placating last words or else stalk off, "an affrighted shade" (*WP*, 233). Somewhat later, Hartman remarks in an uncharacteristically Blakean idiom that Chaucer and Shakespeare "know nature is a constipated or frozen form of imagination and refuse to worship its randomness" (*WP*, 298).

26. Of such border figures, Hartman writes: "What sustains them? Their acceptance of the injuries of time evokes the idea of a soul that is invulnerable, because it dwells in Abraham's bosom or nature's. One of these is life, the other death, but in such border figures life and death, like natural and supernatural faith, are no longer separable" (*WP*, 225).

27. I believe this claim to be congruent with Forest Pyle's stress on the romantic imagination's constantly being "assigned the responsibility of making a linkage, an articulation," not least with the "language of 'community'": see Pyle, *The Ideology of Imagination: Subject and Society in the Discourse of Romanticism* (Stanford: Stanford University Press, 1995), 2. "This means that the imagination, as it undertakes an articulation or tries to speak the language of community, necessarily points to the prior existence of a rift, a fissure, a disjunction that must be crossed or healed" (Pyle 2–3). For a recent study that also stresses the communal and political dimension of the romantic imagination, mapping these tensions onto the problem of political sovereignty, see Kir Kuiken, *Imagined Sovereignties: Toward a New Political Romanticism* (New York: Fordham University Press, 2014).

28. I shall be discussing Hartman's engagement with the Philomela myth in the next section of this chapter. The Perseus myth provides the motif for the final chapter of Hartman's *Unmediated Vision*, "The New Perseus," 156–73. The "new" Perseus "disdains or has lost Athene's mirror, and goes against the monster with naked eye"—that is, without the technico-rhetorical supplementation or mediation that keeps the mythological Perseus safe from the Medusa's petrifying power (*UV*, 156). Hartman never mentions whether the modern poet has also discarded the sword with which Perseus beheads his victim.

29. Geoffrey H. Hartman, "The Philomela Project," in *Minor Prophecies: The Literary Essay in the Culture Wars* (Cambridge, Mass.: Harvard University Press, 1991), 164–75, at 169.

30. In his interview with Cathy Caruth, Hartman emphasizes the point: "I try to describe that structure as, basically, overspecified ends ("voice" and "shuttle") and something in the middle that is muted or left out. And I suggest that all figurative lan-

guage has these overspecified ends, as if the middle were cut out. It is the cutting out that's important" (Caruth 307).

31. Hertz's most systematic exposition of the "end of the line" structure is in the "Afterword" to *The End of the Line: Essays on Psychoanalysis and the Sublime* (New York: Columbia University Press, 1985); see also the important essay, "The Notion of Blockage in the Literature of the Sublime" (1979), collected in The *End of the Line*.

32. The association of poetic song with the sound shuttles make on the loom seems to have been a feasible one in Greek literary culture. The LSJ entry for *kerkis*, shuttle, offers among its illustrative quotations, in addition to Sophocles's *kerkidos phōnē* ("voice of the shuttle") another Sophoclean fragment, *kerkidos humnois* ("with the songs of the shuttle"), and a Euripidean fragment, *kerkidos aoidou* (either "the bard's shuttle" or "of the shuttle that is a bard"). Weaving, besides being the only form of work proper to aristocratic Greek women and goddesses, is of course one of Western culture's great tropes for narrative, from Homer on (when we first meet Helen she is weaving the story of the *Iliad* itself: see *Iliad*, III, 125–29). I thank Molly Ierulli for her help with this matter.

33. The violence, mutilation, and muting is of course gendered in the Philomela story, and feminist critics have suggested that the generality of Hartman's conclusions elides the way in which, as Barbara Johnson puts it, "once again, an 'aesthetics of silence' turns out to involve a male appropriation of female muteness as aesthetic trophy accompanied by an elision of sexual violence." *The Feminist Difference: Literature, Psychoanalysis, Race and Gender* (Cambridge, Mass.: Harvard University Press, 1998), 136. Johnson is referencing Patricia Joplin, "The Voice of the Shuttle Is Ours," *Stanford Literature Review* 1, no. 1 (1984).

34. In his interview with Caruth, Hartman stresses the dark heart of his essay: "I began this line of thinking in 'The Voice of the Shuttle,' where muteness and trauma are at the center, Philomela's tongue having been cut out" (Caruth, 307).

35. On the Greek tradition of associating the swallow's twitter with the meaningless noises of barbarians, see D'Arcy W. Thompson, *A Glossary of Greek Birds* (Oxford: Clarendon Press, 1966 [1895]), 320. As Thompson summarizes, "Philomela and Procne are frequently confused. . . . In Greek authors Philomela is the name of the Swallow, and Procne of the Nightingale" (22). Procne, the mother of Itys, naturally assumes the form of nightingale in Greek mythic thought, since as early as the Odyssey the nightingale is associated with mourning mothers. On the nightingale, *aēdōn*, see Thompson, 16–22; Thompson notes that the swallow is also linked with melancholy, especially when paired with the nightingale in the Philomela story (321). For a rich study of mourning mothers in fifth-century Athenian literature and culture, see Nicole Loraux, *Les mères en deuil* (Paris: Seuil, 1990); on the nightingale as mourning mother, see in particular her chapter "Le deuil du rossignol," 87–100. The Latin and medieval tradition tended to reverse the attributions and make Philomela the nightingale. Ovid, in his famous rendition, rather cagily does not tell us which sister becomes which bird—though with typical insight he suggests that Philomela's loss of speech is catching: Procne, reading the speaking tapestry—it has become a poem or song: *carmen*—keeps silent, her mouth closed by anguish: *carmen miserabile legit / et (mirum potuisse) silet. Dolor ora repressit . . .* (*Metamorphoses* VI:582–83). Once again I owe this swatch of philological lore to Molly Ierulli.

36. The essays making up *Beyond Formalism* vibrate again and again to this frequency: e.g., the closing movement of "Adam on the Grass with Balsamum": "'In the beginning was the Word, and the Word was contaminated'—the artist's freedom and the critic's mission arise, perhaps from the same trauma" (*BF*, 150).

37. Geoffrey H. Hartman, *Scars of the Spirit: The Struggle Against Inauthenticity* (New York: Palgrave Macmillan, 2004), 68.

38. A world characterized as an assault on the senses, particularly on the eye. In the background here are both Walter Benjamin's writings on the shock experience, and Hartman's own career-long meditation on Wordsworth's attempts to counter the "tyranny of the eye." It may be noted in passing, however, that the dialectic of the senses in Hartman is always a supple one: the eye-ear relationship is reversible. In *Saving the Text*, for instance, the ear constitutes exposure to real or potential trauma, whereas the eye takes on the role of Apollonian shield: "I have sometimes thought that design perception and interpretive brooding were separate gifts, and that we have genuine criticism only when interpretation reinforces perception or does not erode it." *Saving the Text: Literature / Derrida / Philosophy* (Baltimore: Johns Hopkins University Press, 1981), 150. The eye promises form; the ear is vulnerable to "sounds that cannot be refused entry, but penetrate and evoke something too powerful for any defense" (*Saving the Text*, 123).

39. Citations from this and later drafts of *The Ruined Cottage* are from William Wordsworth, *"The Ruined Cottage" and "The Pedlar"* (Ithaca, N.Y.: Cornell University Press, 1979), ed. James Butler; "Incipient Madness" is at 468–69, and *The Ruined Cottage* is at 42–75.

40. In the B manuscript the lines read slightly differently: "four clay walls / That stared upon each other" (lines 30–31; Wordsworth 44).

41. For a reading of the figure of Margaret attentive to the intersecting pressures of gender and genre in *The Ruined Cottage*, see Karen Swann, "Suffering and Sensation in the Ruined Cottage," *PMLA* 106, no. 1 (1991): 83–95. For an emphatic reading of the poem as a text about dwelling in disaster, see Jacques Khalip, "The Ruin of Things," *Romantic Praxis*, Special Issue, "Romantic Frictions," ed. Theresa M. Kelley (September 2011), accessed August 20, 2013.

4. Literature, Incorporated: Harold Bloom, Theory, and the Canon

1. Harold Bloom, interviewed by Antonio Weiss, "Harold Bloom, The Art of Criticism, No. 1," *The Paris Review* 118 (Spring 1991).

2. The department's grand old man, Chauncey Brewster Tinker (the eighteenth-century specialist who directed the dissertations of practically the entire next generation of Yale English professors: Frederick Pottle, Maynard Mack, Frederick W. Hilles, Louis Martz, William K. Wimsatt, and A. Dwight Culler, among others), had blocked Lionel Trilling's nomination to a professorship on racial-religious grounds. Not until Tinker's retirement in 1945 did the departmental door begin to open, slowly and reluctantly, to Jewish scholars. According to Dan A. Oren, "the first known Jew to hold a teaching position in English at Yale" was Charles Feidelson, who was appointed to an instructorship in 1947 and tenured a decade later: see Oren, *Joining the Club: A History of Jews at Yale* (New Haven: Yale University Press, 1985), 260.

3. Buckley describes Maynard Mack in *God and Man at Yale* (Chicago: Regnery, 1951) as "a straightforward Christian whose attitudes become apparent in his lectures on Shakespeare" (12). Cleanth Brooks, William K. Wimsatt, and Louis Martz were all devout Christians. Bloom studied with the historicist critic Frederick Pottle (also a devout Christian) and avoided the New Critics except for Wimsatt, from whom he took a course and with whom he subsequently became friends. Bloom also became friends with Robert Penn Warren, who, we may note in passing, was the one contributor to the Southern Agrarian manifesto *I'll Take My Stand* (1930) to renounce his earlier political positions and join the civil rights movement in the 1960s.

4. Geoffrey Hartman, *A Scholar's Tale: Intellectual Journey of a Displaced Child of Europe* (New York: Fordham University Press, 2007), 31. As noted in the previous chapter, Hartman, who did his graduate work in the much more cosmopolitan Comparative Literature Department, had an easier itinerary through early-1950s Yale than Bloom did in English.

5. According to David Miekes in a recent article on and conversation with Bloom, Bloom was "tenured in a reportedly very close vote." Miekes elicits the following from Bloom in conversation: "You know, a young fellow, still a rough yiddishe boy from the Bronx, and a proletarian too, arriving at the Yale English Department in the autumn of 1951, was not exactly what they wanted, and I certainly didn't want them. . . . Pottle forced my appointment as a faculty instructor on his colleagues who didn't want me, and they tried to get rid of me constantly, for the next seven years." David Miekes, "Harold Bloom Is God," *Tablet: A New Read on Jewish Life* (January 2, 2013).

6. The quote is from John Hersey, and the passage is worth quoting at length since it affords a glimpse of Bloom (unnamed but recognizable) at the time of the disturbances at Yale during the Black Panther trial in the spring of 1970 (Hersey was a master of one of Yale's undergraduate residential colleges): "Shortly after Mayday I sat in a meeting of a faculty committee [Yale University president Kingman] Brewster had set up to give advice on admissions policy, and I heard a professor in the English department, a brilliant critic, a man of massive intellect who can, I am told, recite from memory the entire body of English romantic verse of the nineteenth century, ask in a trembling voice if the admissions people couldn't let in what he called a 'buffer quota,' a large number of obviously solid and talented students who would serve as insurance against the destructive radical rebelliousness of the underprivileged high-risk students everyone seemed to think the university was obliged by social necessity to admit in these times." John Hersey, *Letter to the Alumni* (New York: Knopf, 1970), 123–24. Bloom's hostility toward the student movements at Yale, and, a year previously, at Cornell, where he had been a fellow of the Society of the Humanities, reads in retrospect as an identification with a threatened institution that would be retrofitted into an identification with a threatened "canon" a few years later. This was arguably the only way in which Bloom can be said to have played the role of assimilated Jew in these Ivy League institutions. Otherwise, according to copious report, Bloom flaunted his working-class and Jewish origins, eschewed the coat-and-tie code of 1950s and 1960s Yale, wrote a dissertation on a topic antithetical to the Yale norm, and generally, to the extent that it was possible to do so, seems to have forced Yale to accommodate him rather than the other way

around: an extraordinary achievement by any measure, as the previous notes have sought to indicate.

7. Harold Bloom as cited in John Taylor, "Bloom's Day: Hanging Out with the Reigning Genius of Literary Criticism," *New York* (November 5, 1990), 52–58, at 55.

8. John Guillory, *Cultural Capital: The Problem of Literary Canon Formation* (Chicago: University of Chicago Press, 1993), viii, x.

9. The Chelsea House project began as an updated version of the New Critical–era Twentieth Century Views, edited volumes of essays focused on a particular writer; it ran into trouble in the late 1980s and had to scale back, but continued to produce books and at present writing is still generating product lines under what is now literally the brand name "Bloom." The web page of Infobase Publishing (which houses Chelsea House) has an entire category called "Bloom's" on its selection bar, where one can browse an array of multi-volume sets and series marketed as for "grade 9 and up," with each volume featuring an introduction by Bloom. If one is planning a trip to St. Petersburg, for instance, one can purchase the relevant volume from the series "Bloom's Literary Places." See the Sets & Series section of www.infobasepublishing.com (accessed August 16, 2012).

10. David Lehman, "Yale's Insomniac Genius," *Newsweek*, August 18, 1986, 56. The photo is by Bernard Gotfryd. Bloom had appeared very briefly in the *Newsweek* article from a few years earlier that we mentioned in Chapter 1, "A New Look at Lit Crit," by Kenneth L. Woodward et al. (June 11, 1981), but the difference is striking: Woodward's article, focused on Derrida and the "Gang of Four" at Yale, barely mentions Bloom.

11. Paul Gray, "Hurrah for Dead White Males!" *Time*, October 10, 1994, 62–63; photo by Ted Thai. Indeed, the twin bed suggests this body's further extension and exposure along the bookshelves' horizontal plane. (I wish to thank Paul Saint-Amour for drawing my attention to this article, to Taylor's, and to Begley's mentioned later.)

12. Adam Begley, "Colossus among Critics: Harold Bloom," *New York Times Magazine,* September 25, 1994; photos by Ken Shung and Luc Novovitch.

13. Some of this appears even in Colin Campbell's "The Tyranny of the Yale Critics," *New York Times Magazine*, February 9, 1986: Bloom, though not the sole focus of the article, is the "Yale Critic" whose body Campbell most vigorously associates with both physicality and writing: "He is large, shaggy-haired and courteous. His belly sags. His pants look as wide as two old shopping bags," etc. "Chuckling, he swims toward a sort of Danish Lazy Boy and stretches out, nearly supine. Instantly, he is thinking aloud, his large dark eyes gazing at the ceiling, his brow a wall of hieroglyphic runes."

14. Larissa MacFarquhar, "The Prophet of Decline: Harold Bloom's Influential Anxieties," *The New Yorker*, September 30, 2002, 88. Photo by Richard Avedon. Throughout this article a truly obsessive degree of attention is granted Bloom's body, and the body's size is rendered an explicit figure of its inhabitant's spiritual gigantism: "Bloom suffers the insomnia of giants" (97).

15. Bloom describes himself as "Falstaffian" on a great many occasions; this particular quote is from *Omens of Millennium: The Gnosis of Angels, Dreams, and Resurrection* (New York: Riverhead Books, 1996), 133. Bloom's much-publicized fascination with Falstaff, which culminated in reading the part of Falstaff in public performances in Boston and New York in the fall and spring of 2000–2001 (the New York performance

was at the Kaye Playhouse on March 12), may be taken as a version of this fantasy, which hesitates, coyly, between play-acting and seriousness. Bloom is not really Falstaff; he is just pretending—but not quite as an actor pretends: we are to take his identification with this literary character as a partial expression of his omnivorous incorporation of the literary.

16. One way to get a quick sense of the historical shape of the canon debate is to note that, in his time, Samuel Johnson rarely if ever elicited fantasies of literary incorporation comparable to those inspired by Bloom, though the conventions of Augustan satire certainly encouraged associations between, for instance, a critic's physical size and the voraciousness of his reading. Eighteenth-century British culture had no real equivalent for our anxious fantasy of the "canon." There is, of course, considerable literature on Johnson's appearance and habits (he may have suffered from Tourette's syndrome), often in some supporting relation to his literary performances: e.g., Macaulay: "[Johnson] uttered his short, weighty, and pointed sentences with a power of voice, and a justness and energy of emphasis, of which the effect was rather increased than diminished by the rollings of his huge form, and by the asthmatic gaspings and puffings in which the peals of his eloquence generally ended." Lord Macaulay, *Essays and Lays of Ancient Rome* (London: Cassell and Co., 1909), 435. But one finds—I, at least, have found—surprisingly few analogies between Johnson's body and the extent of his learning (and I thank Robert Folkenflik and Helen Deutsch for offering their expert testimony in support of my hunch). Like Bloom, however, Johnson excited comment on his ability to remember what he read, and the speed with which he could read. The figure of the scanner or tape recorder that one encounters repeatedly in discourse about Bloom—and which I shall be discussing in greater detail—may be taken as the postmodern twist on what Boswell tends to present as the *non*physical character of Johnson's reading style. Remarkably for his time, Johnson had no need to sound out words and could thus read faster than he could speak: "The adulatory biographer was eager to make Johnson an 'eye-reader' . . . by describing his reading as nonphysical . . . he implied that it was interior and intellectual in the highest degree." Robert DeMaria Jr., *Samuel Johnson and the Life of Reading* (Baltimore: Johns Hopkins University Press, 1997), 23.

17. Jacques Lacan, *The Seminar of Jacques Lacan, II: The Ego in Freud's Theory and in the Technique of Psychoanalysis, 1954–55*, trans. Sylvana Tomaselli (New York: Norton, 1988), 166. For a fuller examination of the conflicted figure of the body in aesthetic discourse, see my *The Politics of Aesthetics: Nationalism, Gender, Romanticism* (Stanford: Stanford University Press, 2003), 74–92.

18. Bloom has always insisted that the appendix with the three-thousand title list was demanded of him by his publisher; I am certain this is true, but there is a way in which Bloom's writing lends itself, and has always lent itself, to list-making. The list is a version of Bloom's modular, proper-name-oriented style, about which I shall say a little more later.

19. G. W. F. Hegel, *Enzyklopädie der philosophischen Wissenschaften, III*, in *Werke*, ed. Eva Moldenhauer and Karl Markus Michel (Frankfurt am Main: Suhrkamp, 1986), X, 281 (Par. 463).

20. Taylor, "Bloom's Day," 55. Or again, asked about his memory by Antonio Weiss: "It was immediate and it was always triggered by text, and indeed always had an aes-

thetic element. I learned early that a test for a poem for me was whether it seemed so inevitable that I could remember it perfectly from the start" (Weiss).

21. The genius is never far from the monster in popular iconography. The classical art of memory, with its emphasis on spatial relationships and lurid (and thus memorable) figures, plays a weirdly prominent role in Thomas Harris' bestseller *Hannibal* (New York: Delacorte Press, 1999), in which much is made of the eponymous cannibal-hero's mnemotechnic. Though one could hardly imagine two literary characters more different in most respects than Harold Bloom and Hannibal the Cannibal, Harris's gothic thriller nonetheless suggests that the fantasies that go into the making of "Bloom" as the canon incorporate also circulate more widely. Hannibal Lecter (the pun on reading is intentional, of course) is a Renaissance man of superhuman—that is, monstrous—proportion: like Bloom, he has internalized the high points of Western culture, and his memory is the ur-technic that makes this masterful, aesthetic internalization possible. Harris is explicitly indebted to Frances Yates's classic *The Art of Memory* (Chicago: University of Chicago Press, 1966), a book Bloom will reference implicitly in the passage from *The Western Canon* mentioned in note 38.

22. See also Martin Kihn's account in his scandal-mongering "Bloom in Love," *GQ*, November 1990: "Forty years ago when he was drunk and in college at Cornell, he would recite Hart Crane's *The Bridge* backward, like some satanic tape recorder: 'Return lark's the of precincts agile the . . .'" (151). Charles McGrath, a former Yale graduate student turned cultural journalist, updates the tape recorder trope for the digital age in his *New Yorker* review of *The Western Canon*, imagining a Bloom "beleaguered by his own influences and unable to turn off that flood of remembered text scrolling endlessly through his brain," thereby losing the preeminence of *voice* that Bloom always insists on ("Loose Canon," *The New Yorker*, September 26, 1994, 105).

23. "It turns out the legend that Harold Bloom can read 1,000 pages an hour is simply not true," John Taylor assures us, Bloom having pointed out that "no human being" could accomplish such a feat ("You can't turn pages that quickly"). According to this account, Bloom can read "a 400-page book in just about an hour," and retain from it what he wants.

24. Paul de Man, "Review of Harold Bloom's *Anxiety of Influence*," in *Blindness and Insight: Essays in the Rhetoric of Contemporary Criticism*, 2nd ed. (Minneapolis: University of Minnesota Press, 1983), 267–76. The quotations in this paragraph are at 269–71. The review was originally published in *Comparative Literature* 26, no. 3 (1974).

25. In case these revisionary ratios in *The Anxiety of Influence* are (or have grown) unfamiliar to the reader: they are strategies that a belated poet adopts in defending against and wrestling with a precursor; their names come from a variety of hermetic traditions. *Clinamen*, the term that Lucretius uses to describe the swerving of atoms, represents the ephebe's general swerve from the precursor; *tessera*, signifying the broken pieces of pottery that, put together, allowed participants in Pythagorean ritual to recognize each other, represents the defensive gesture of "completing" the precursor; *kenosis*, Paul's term for the becoming-human of Christ, is the defense of diminishment (of the self and of the precursor); *daemonization*, a word that draws on various esoteric sources, is the defense of repression translated into self-expansion in the register of the sublime; *askesis*, a term from medieval spiritual discipline, is the defense of partial self-sacrifice

(as opposed to the more general diminishment of *kenosis*); and *apophrades*, the days of commemorating the dead in ancient Athens, is the defense of reversal or return, where the latecomer seeks rhetorically to be "earlier" than the precursor—to make the precursor into the latecomer's latecomer. I have drawn on, modified and abbreviated here the excellent summary provided by Agata Bielik-Robson in *The Saving Lie: Harold Bloom and Deconstruction* (Evanston, Ill.: Northwestern University Press, 2011), 12.

26. Harold Bloom, *A Map of Misreading, With A New Preface* (New York: Oxford University Press, 2003 [1975]): "My late friend, Paul de Man, to whom this book continues to be dedicated, cheerfully provoked it by a brilliant polemical review of *The Anxiety of Influence*. His challenge returned me to rhetoric, and to the ancient identification of figurative language with cosmology and psychology" (xiii). In addition to incorporating de Man's suggested tropes, Bloom also drew on Anna Freud's taxonomy of psychic defenses. Thus, as Bielik-Robson helpfully summarizes, "*clinamen* is irony and reaction formation; *tessera* is synecdoche and reversal; *kenosis* is metonymy and undoing; *daemonization* is hyperbole and repression; *askesis* is metaphor and sublimation; and *apophrades* is metalepsis and introjection. . . . And in *A Map of Misreading* . . . there will also appear concepts derived from Isaac Luria, Bloom's favorite kabbalist: contraction and restitution, or, in his rendering: limitation and representation, attributed alternately to all six stages" (13).

27. Harold Bloom, *Wallace Stevens: The Poems of Our Climate* (Ithaca, N.Y.: Cornell University Press, 1977), 386, 393.

28. Helpful summaries and analyses of Bloom's theoretical writing may be had in Graham Allen, *Harold Bloom: A Poetics of Conflict* (Hertfordshire: Harvester, 1994), Peter de Bolla, *Harold Bloom: Toward Historical Rhetorics* (London: Routledge, 1988), and David Fite, *Harold Bloom: The Rhetoric of Romantic Vision* (Amherst: University of Massachusetts Press, 1985). Allen provides a good general overview; Fite focuses particularly on Bloom's writing on romanticism and the romantic imagination; de Bolla offers the most extensive account of Bloom's theoretical speculations. Articles on Bloom were quite numerous during the "Yale Critics" era, and in this context I should mention Ann Wordsworth's "An Art That Will Not Abandon the Self to Language: Bloom, Tennyson, and the Blind World of the Wish," in *Untying the Text: A Post-Structuralist Reader*, ed. Robert Young (London: Routledge, 1981), 207–222, which focuses particularly on Bloom's struggle with de Man. Critical writing about Bloom has been sparse since the mid-1980s, but studies continue to appear. Along with Agata Bielik-Robson's important monograph *The Saving Lie,* cited earlier, three essay collections have been published in recent years: *Harold Bloom's Shakespeare,* ed. Christy Desmet and Robert J. Sawyer (New York: Palgrave, 2002), the ambitious *Salt Companion to Harold Bloom,* ed. Roy Sellars and Graham Allen (London: Salt Publishing, 2007), and *Reading, Writing, and the Influence of Harold Bloom,* ed. Alan Rawes and Jonathon Shears (Manchester: Manchester University Press, 2010). Roy Sellars has alerted me to Alistair Hayes's *The Anatomy of Bloom: Harold Bloom and the Study of Influence and Anxiety* (New York: Bloomsbury, 2014). Perhaps a small renaissance in Bloom studies is in the offing.

29. Bielik-Robson, *The Saving Lie,* 85; the point is also made forcefully by de Bolla. I do not think, however, that such defenses of Bloom address the main issue that deconstructively oriented critics of Bloom, at least, are raising when they question

Bloom's invocations of the Oedipal plot. Jonathan Culler, for instance, argues—rightly, as I see it—that "Bloom transforms intertextuality from an endless series of anonymous codes and citations to an oedipal confrontation, one of whose effects is to preserve the integrity of his poets as agents of the poetic process." See Culler, "Presupposition and Intertexuality," in *The Pursuit of Signs: Semiotics, Literature, Deconstruction* (Ithaca, N.Y.: Cornell University Press, 1981), 111. Culler's point is that Oedipal emplotment, even when shorn of literalizing content, provides a *structure* that shores up a subject's sense of agency. On this point, see Neil Hertz's classic discussion of "The Notion of Blockage in the Literature of the Sublime," in *Psychoanalysis and the Question of the Text*, ed. Geoffrey Hartman (Baltimore: Johns Hopkins University Press, 1978), an essay that may be taken as, among other things, an indirect critique of Bloom. See also Culler's sharp review of *A Map of Misreading*, "Reading and Misreading," *Yale Review* 65 (1975): 88–95.

30. Harold Bloom, *The Anxiety of Influence: A Theory of Poetry* (New York: Oxford University Press, 1997 [1973]), 71.

31. The point was made in passing by de Man (268); Fry makes it carefully and sympathetically in "How to Live with the Infinite Regress of Strong Misreading," in *Reading, Writing, and the Influence of Harold Bloom*, 217–39.

32. This is a claim with far-reaching consequences. Arthur Bradley, in "The Impossibility of Reading: Bloom and the 'Yale School' of Criticism," in *Reading, Writing, and the Influence of Harold Bloom*, 259–82, presses this aspect of Bloom's thought in order to suggest that for Bloom, "'reading' is impossible because any interpretation of [a] poem can only be the interpretation of the poem's own interpretation of other, earlier poems" (264). (Fry also notes the infinite regress implied by Bloom's model of literary history as influence: poetic swerving continues "back to the J-text and its precursor" [232].) Bradley persuasively suggests that Bloom, de Man and Derrida all in different ways stress the "impossibility of reading" and "the singular act or event of a reading" over and above any theory (260). I agree; my interpretation here seeks to keep Bloom's proximity to de Man and Derrida in mind while also examining his complex and ambivalent (and at times violent) resistance to their thought.

33. Bloom's sporadic and certainly rather unsatisfactory attempts to define the "poet-in-the-poet" carry through to *The Anatomy of Influence: Literature as a Way of Life* (New Haven: Yale University Press, 2011), 11.

34. Harold Bloom, *The Breaking of the Vessels* (Chicago: University of Chicago Press, 1982), 4. There are many similar formulations, e.g., "the will to utter within a tradition of uttering" (*Wallace Stevens*, 393).

35. Elizabeth Bruss, *Beautiful Theories: The Spectacle of Discourse in Contemporary Criticism* (Baltimore: Johns Hopkins University Press, 1982), 345. Bruss's book ought to be better known: published while the first wave of "theory" was still breaking in the American university, it remains an important study.

36. E.g., in this rather tortured sentence that works to situate the will outside of language, and establish time as the ultimate referent: "The trope is a cut or gap made into the anteriority of language, itself an anteriority in which 'language' acts as a figurative substitute for time" (*Wallace Stevens* 393). Bloom frequently insists that poems are not simply linguistic (in a moment I will be quoting a passage from *The Breaking of the Vessels* that makes that claim in passing). The "will" is a productive source of anxiety in

Bloom, for it names anxiety itself: "what does the anxiety of influence concern but the energy, the force, the will? Are they one's own, or emanations from the other, from the precursor?" (*Anxiety* 52).

Bloom's writing sometimes indulges in gendered fantasies that figuratively anchor extralinguistic reality in the body of the mother, positing in *A Map of Misreading*, for instance, a maternal and material "ocean of incarnation" from which "poets whose sexual natures manifest unusual complexity . . . never get far" (13). Literalizing appeals of this sort to normative sexuality are relatively rare in Bloom's oeuvre, but they follow from that oeuvre's tendency to invoke the "metaphoric consummation or spousal union of masculine mind and feminine nature" that Mary Jacobus identifies as the gender plot of "natural supernaturalism" (*Romanticism, Writing, and Sexual Difference: Essays on* The Prelude [Oxford: Clarendon Press, 1989], 206) and that Bloom himself, in *Blake's Apocalypse: A Study in Poetic Argument* (Ithaca, N.Y.: Cornell University Press, 1963), offers as "anyone's best hint for reading William Blake: every female personage finally relates to, or is, a form of nature; every male at last represents humankind, both male and female" (119). Bloom's work, which began as mythopoeic readings of Shelley and Blake, has always had ready to hand such a symbolic economy; and since nature, in this mythopoesis, is what Man or the Imagination is not, woman figures the imagination's death, whether as the natural world of sensuality and sexuality or as "the genuine obscenity of a vampire will, natural and female" (*Blake's Apocalypse* 292); the "sinister manifestation of Nature-as-temptress" (*The Visionary Company: A Reading of English Romantic Poetry* (Ithaca, N.Y.: Cornell University Press, 1971 [1961]), 144). A naturalizing rhetoric of gender marks the history of modern aesthetics in part because aesthetics constantly confronts the unnatural power of signs: for arguments that seek to back up that assertion, see my *The Politics of Aesthetics*.

37. Cathy Caruth, "Speculative Returns: Bloom's Recent Work," *MLN* 98, no. 5 (1983): 1,286–96, at 1,294, italics in original. So far as I know, this is Caruth's first published article. She has since, of course, become the preeminent theorist of trauma in the field of literary and cultural criticism and theory.

38. As we have seen, Bloom always insists on his memory's auditory rather than visual character, but implicit complications show up when he elaborates on his powers of memory, as in this interesting passage in *The Western Canon* where he is invoking the traditionally visual rhetorical art of memory. "The art of memory, with its rhetorical antecedents and its magical burgeonings, is very much an affair of imaginary places, or of real places transmuted into visual images. Since childhood, I have enjoyed an uncanny memory for literature, but that memory is purely verbal, without anything in the way of a visual component. Only recently, past the age of sixty, have I come to understand that my literary memory has relied upon the Canon as a memory system. If I am a special case, it is only in the sense that my experience is a more extreme version of what I believe to be the principal pragmatic function of the Canon: the remembering and ordering of a lifetime's reading. The greatest authors take over the role of 'places' in the Canon's theater of memory, and their masterworks occupy the position filled by 'images' in the art of memory." Harold Bloom, *The Western Canon: The Book and School of the Ages* (New York: Harcourt Brace, 1994), 39.

39. On incorporation and melancholia, see Nicolas Abraham and Maria Torok, *The*

Shell and the Kernel: Renewals of Psychoanalysis, trans. Richard Rand (Chicago: University of Chicago Press, 1994).

40. Robert O. Preyer, "Voyagers of the Imagination," review of *The Visionary Company*, *The Yale Review* 51 (1961): 316–19, cited by Fite, *Harold Bloom*, 31.

41. On the comedic strain in Bloom, see Roy Sellars, "Harold Bloom, (Comic) Critic," in *The Salt Companion to Harold Bloom*, 255–89.

42. I am referencing here one of Bloom's most interesting books: *The American Religion: The Emergence of the Post-Christian Nation* (New York: Simon & Schuster, 1992), which argues for the Gnostic character of much religious activity in the United States. Bielik-Robson is less sure what to do with the Bloom who, as Roy Sellars and Graham Allen comment in their introduction to *The Salt Companion*, seems to abandon the theme of agon in favor of Shakespeare "inventing" us (Sellars and Allen, xiv). This is a side of Bloom that Bielik-Robson chooses to ignore: "Yes, but this seems to be only one, more serene and 'Pateresque,' of Bloom's later incarnations" (323 n. 27).

43. "Truths are illusions of which we have forgotten that they are illusions, metaphors which have become worn by frequent use and have lost all sensuous vigour, coins which, having lost their stamp, are now regarded as metal and no longer as coins." Friedrich Nietzsche, "On Truth and Lying in a Non-Moral Sense," trans. Ronald Speirs, in *The Birth of Tragedy and Other Writings*, ed. Raymond Geuss (Cambridge: Cambridge University Press, 1999), 141–53, at 146.

44. Harold Bloom, *Agon: Toward a Theory of Revisionism* (Oxford: Oxford University Press, 1982), 107, cited in Bielik-Robson, *The Saving Lie*, 9.

45. And as splendidly repressed elsewhere in Bloom: "Death is the most proper of literal meanings, and literal meaning always participates in death." *Poetry and Repression: Revisionism from Blake to Stevens* (New Haven: Yale University Press, 1976), 10.

46. I discuss the complicated proximity between aesthetics and shock in *The Rhetoric of Terror: Reflections on 9/11 and the War on Terror* (New York: Fordham University Press, 2009), 32–37. Adorno is the great theorist of repressed terror within the beautiful, but the theme of shock is prominent in, e.g., Edmund Burke, who identifies a certain shock experience conditioning the beautiful as well as the sublime, since in both cases an impression "strikes us without any preparation," gripping the senses before the understanding can be mobilized: see *A Philosophical Enquiry into the Origin of Our Ideas of the Sublime and the Beautiful*, ed. James T. Boulton (Notre Dame: University of Notre Dame Press, 1986 [1958]), 107–8.

47. Harold Bloom to Antonio Weiss, *Paris Review*.

48. Bloom, speaking to Imre Salusinszky in Salusinszky, *Criticism in Society: Interviews with Jacques Derrida, Northrop Frye, Harold Bloom, Geoffrey Hartman, Frank Kermode, Edward Said, Barbara Johnson, Frank Lentricchia, and J. Hillis Miller* (New York: Methuen, 1987), 67.

49. For instance, in the preface to the 1997 reissue of *The Anxiety of Influence*: "He insisted that an epistemological stance in regard to a literary work was the only way out of the tropological labyrinth, while I replied that such a stance was no more or less a trope than any other" (xix); then again in 2011 in *The Anatomy of Influence*: "For many years my late friend and colleague Paul de Man would argue as we walked together. More often than not the dispute turned upon de Man's conviction that he had found

the truth about criticism, which was that it must take up an epistemological or ironic stance with regard to literature. I answered that *any* perspective we adopted toward figurations would itself have to be figurative, as his philosophical mode clearly was" (13). The story also shows up in Taylor's "Bloom's Day" (57) and in other interviews and profiles. Bloom has never stopped replaying this wrestling match.

50. Neil Hertz, who knew de Man well, comments: "the notion that Paul de Man ever cupped *any*one's face in his hands (excluding some close family members) seems really unlikely" (personal communication).

5. Professing Theory: Paul de Man and the Institution of Reading

1. Some important work on de Man will be mentioned in subsequent notes. For a sustained meditation on the spirals of "reading" in de Man's work, see Werner Hamacher's remarkable essay "'Lectio': de Man's Imperative," available in several venues, including Hamacher's *Premises: Essays on Philosophy and Literature from Kant to Celan*, trans. Peter Fenves (Stanford: Stanford University Press, 1999), 181–221. My own best effort to provide an overview of de Man's work is my essay "De Man, Schiller, and the Politics of Reception," which now forms part of my book *The Politics of Aesthetics: Nationalism, Gender, Romanticism* (Stanford: Stanford University Press, 2003), 95–124.

2. John Guillory, *Cultural Capital: The Problem of Literary Canon Formation* (Chicago: University of Chicago Press, 1993). References to this book will be given parenthetically in the body of the text.

3. See, e.g., Carlin Romano's invocation of Guillory's "powerful" critique of de Man in Romano's strident "Deconstructing Paul de Man," *The Chronicle Review*, March 3, 2014 (accessed May 20, 2014). This is the article that accompanies the caricature of de Man's defaced face that I discussed briefly in the Introduction.

4. Guillory's book has been extensively discussed, but neither the accuracy of his account of de Man nor the filiations linking that account to his book's broader claims about literary canon formation have been carefully examined. As I note a little later in this chapter, Peggy Kamuf's sharp review of *Cultural Capital* in *Diacritics* has almost nothing to say about the book's chapter on de Man: see Kamuf, "The Division of Literature," *Diacritics* 25, no. 3 (1995): 53–72. I have found Guillory's work a helpful irritant over the years, and the present chapter represents something of an effort to make payments on an overdue account by decompressing the brief critiques of *Cultural Capital* (and especially of its de Man chapter) that I offer in *Phantom Formations: Aesthetic Ideology and the Bildungsroman* (Ithaca, N.Y.: Cornell University Press, 1996) and *The Politics of Aesthetics*.

5. Guillory borrows the notion of cultural capital from Pierre Bourdieu. Of Bourdieu's many writings in this area, see especially *Distinction: A Social Critique of the Judgment of Taste*, trans. Richard Nice (Cambridge, Mass.: Harvard University Press, 1984). The idea of cultural capital goes back at least to Karl Mannheim, *Ideology and Utopia: An Introduction to the Sociology of Knowledge*, trans. Louis Wirth and Edward Shils (New York: Harcourt, Brace, 1936 [1929]).

6. Pierre Machery and Etienne Balibar, "Literature as an Ideological Form: Some Marxist Propositions," trans. James Kavanaugh, *Praxis* 5 (1981): 57; cited in Guillory, 80.

7. Friedrich Schiller, *On the Aesthetic Education of Man, in a Series of Letters*, trans. Elizabeth M. Wilkinson and L. A. Willoughby (Oxford: Clarendon Press, 1967), 219. I discuss Schiller's notion of the Aesthetic State in *Phantom Formations* (via a reading of Goethe's *Wilhelm Meisters Wanderjahre*), 95–133; see also 211–13 for a critique of these closing remarks of Guillory's.

8. John Guillory, "Who's Afraid of Marcel Proust? The Failure of General Education in the American University," in *The Humanities and the Dynamics of Inclusion Since World War II*, ed. David A. Hollinger (Baltimore: Johns Hopkins University Press, 2006), 25–49, at 34.

9. Fredric Jameson, *Postmodernism, or, The Cultural Logic of Late Capitalism* (Durham, N.C.: Duke University Press, 1991), 4. Graduates of elite schools play a substantial role in the culture industry, of course, where the stratifications are different from but not unaffected by the hierarchy of the American school system. The persistence of the humanities major (at about 7 percent of degrees awarded nationally, a figure that has held steady since the 1970s) was noted briefly in the introduction to this book. The retreat of print culture is obvious: according to a National Endowment for the Arts report from 2004, only about 50 percent of Americans read any sort of novel (or play or story, etc.) at all that year (see "Fewer Noses Stuck in Books in America, Survey Finds," *New York Times*, July 8, 2004). The border between "high" and "mass" culture, however, is designed on both sides to be very porous. In "Who's Afraid of Marcel Proust," Guillory notes the successful "massification" of certain high-canonical authors in the United States (Shakespeare, Austen) as opposed to others (Proust). The main point as regards my argument with Guillory's argument in *Cultural Capital*, as will become clear a little later in this chapter, is that the discourse of aesthetics is not simply a "high cultural" phenomenon.

10. Kamuf (who is of course one of the Anglophone world's most prominent translators and interpreters of Derrida), dismisses Guillory's explanation of his focus on de Man with little more than an exclamation of incredulity: "'The equation theory-deconstruction-de Man' is, he claims, 'already present in the professional imaginary' [Guillory 178]. Oh, really? Reading that, one may be relieved, alarmed, or merely amused at the idea that there is someone out there who believes he has his finger on the pulse of the 'professional imaginary.' Or even at the idea that someone would so confidently invoke such a concept, which illustrates too well the violence of conceptual totalization. To escape this violence many, if not most, of Guillory's readers (I include myself) will probably choose to ignore the claim. Which is not to say that this framing device is easy to ignore: on the contrary, it intrudes and insists on almost every page of the [fourth] chapter" (Kamuf, "The Division of Literature," 62–63).

11. Many critics have commented in passing on de Man's spare, antitheatrical charisma (as I have myself in the book chapter mentioned earlier). Samuel Weber has this interesting remark in an interview: "I have long felt that de Man, in his practice as teacher and as writer, was the most Lacanian, or Freudian, or psychoanalytic of literary critics. Not explicitly, of course, but in his use of authority, in his tendency to multiply apodictic statements in a way that undermined the absoluteness of the claims they seemed to be making." Samuel Weber, *Mass Mediauras: Form, Technics, Media* (Stanford: Stanford University Press, 1996), 185.

12. Thomas Pepper, *Singularities: Extremes of Theory in the Twentieth Century* (Cambridge: Cambridge University Press, 1997), 96 n. 9.

13. See my "Introduction" to *Legacies of Paul de Man*, ed. Marc Redfield (New York: Fordham University Press, 2007), for some reflections on the breadth and complexity of de Man's influence in the Anglo-American academy.

14. Jacques Derrida, *La carte postale: De Socrate à Freud et au-delà* (Paris: Flammarion, 1980), 360.

15. A revised version of "Semiology and Rhetoric," originally published in *Diacritics* 3, no. 3 (1973): 27–33, became the first chapter of *Allegories of Reading*. I shall be using conventional acronyms in what follows to refer to works by de Man: *Aesthetic Ideology* (*AI*), ed. Andrzej Warminski (Minneapolis: University of Minnesota Press, 1996); *Allegories of Reading: Figural Language in Rousseau, Nietzsche, Rilke, and Proust* (*AR*) (New Haven: Yale University Press, 1979); *The Resistance to Theory* (*RT*) (Minneapolis: University of Minnesota Press, 1986); *The Rhetoric of Romanticism* (*RR*) (New York: Columbia University Press, 1984); *Romanticism and Contemporary Criticism: The Gauss Seminar and Other Papers* (*RCC*), ed. E. S. Burt, Kevin Newmark, and Andrzej Warminski (Baltimore: Johns Hopkins University Press, 1993). References to these works will be indicated by acronym and page number in the body of the text.

16. On de Man's introduction to *Studies in Romanticism* 18, no. 4 (1979): 495–99, see Sara Guyer, "At the Far End of This Ongoing Enterprise . . ." in *Legacies of Paul de Man*, 77–92.

17. This is a large question—that of error, mistake, and interpretive violence in de Man—and I have tried to address it in "Mistake in Paul de Man: Violent Reading and Theotropic Violence," in *The Political Archive of Paul de Man: Property, Sovereignty, and the Theotropic*, ed. Martin McQuillan (New York and Edinburgh: Columbia University Press and Edinburgh University Press, 2012), 103–17.

18. Marcel Proust, *Le temps retrouvé*, in *A la recherche du temps perdu*, ed. Jean-Yves Tadié et al. (Paris: Gallimard, 1989), 4:468; *Finding Time Again*, trans Ian Patterson (London: Penguin Books, 2002), 198, translation slightly modified. Patterson translates "anneaux nécessaires" somewhat freely as "necessary armature."

19. Gérard Genette, "Métonymie chez Proust," *Figures III* (Paris: Seuil, 1972), 41–63, here 42, 53, my translation, Genette's italics. Genette also establishes that Proust assimilates metaphor to comparison (as opposed to substitution, as in classical rhetoric); this suggests to Genette the utility of the Jakobsonian gesture of assimilating metonymy to contiguity (as opposed, once again to a substitutive trope). Genette is thus able to make the pairing metaphor/metonymy illuminate the fundamental moment of the *Recherche*: involuntary memory is a metaphor (the taste of one tilleul-infused madeleine resembling another) but the miraculous unfolding of the remembered taste into narrative—into "*une chambre, une maison, une ville entière*"—occurs as a massive metonymy (58).

20. One can push the analysis further. The chamber music of the flies is a synecdoche of summer, but its immediate figurative task is more local: the flies' music, like Camus's hammering, conveys to Marcel "the sensation of the light's splendor" in the dark room. The music is a synesthetic substitution for the light, or more precisely for the splendor of the light, a substitution enabled by the fact that both the flies' music

and the light's splendor are synecdoches of summer. The music and light, therefore, are part of a chain of synecdoches linked to each other like terms in a metaphor (they share the proper meaning "summer," just as Achilles and the lion share the proper meaning "ferocity" or "strength"). De Man's assimilation of this synecdoche to metaphor, while certainly a little violent, does not seem sheerly an exercise of his "own discretion" either.

21. I believe one can bring de Man's thought into useful proximity with Derrida's here: the imperative-to theme (which is also to say the imperative-to-language) in de Man may be thought in Derridean terms as the promise and affirmation—the "yes yes"—that opens language as an infinite relation to the other. Derrida's powerful reading of de Man in *Memoires* runs in this direction, as he glosses de Man's pun on Heidegger, "Die Sprache verspricht (sich)" (*AR*, 277; the play is on Heidegger's dictum *Die Sprache spricht*). ("*Die Sprache verspricht*" means "language promises"; "*die Sprache verspricht sich*" means "language misspeaks.") "Everything begins," Derrida suggests, "with this apparently post-originary and performative modalization of Sprache. . . . This is not to say that all of this performativity is of the type of the promise, in the narrow and everyday sense of the term. But this performative thereby reveals a structure or destination of the Sprache. . . . What is essential here is that a pure promise cannot properly take place, even though promising is inevitable as soon as we open our mouths—or rather as soon as there is a text." Jacques Derrida, *Memoires: For Paul de Man*, rev. ed. (New York: Columbia University Press, 1988), 97–98.

22. "Theory of Metaphor" was originally published as an article in *Studies in Romanticism* 12, no. 2 (1973): 475–98. The Proust essay first appeared as "Proust et l'allégorie de la lecture," in a *Festschrift* for Georges Poulet, *Movements premiers* (Paris: Jose Corti, 1972), 231–50; versions of *Allegories of Reading*'s Rilke chapter and one of its Nietzsche chapters also appeared in 1972: see "Introduction," to Rainer Maria Rilke, *Oeuvres* II: *Poesie* (Paris: Seuil, 1972), 7–42; and "Genesis and Genealogy in Nietzsche's *Birth of Tragedy*," *Diacritics* 2, no. 4 (1972): 44–53. The order of composition of these texts is, as far as I know, a moot question.

23. For a collection of essays more or less dedicated to the question of de Manian materialism, see Tom Cohen, Barbara Cohen, J. Hillis Miller, and Andrzej Warminski, eds., *Material Events: Paul de Man and the Afterlife of Theory* (Minneapolis: University of Minnesota Press, 2000).

24. Orrin Wang, *Romantic Sobriety: Sensation, Revolution, Commodification, History* (Baltimore: Johns Hopkins University Press, 2011), 113. For a slightly more extensive consideration of Wang's discussion, see Chapter 2.

25. Jacques Derrida, "Typewriter Ribbon: Limited Ink (2) ("within such limits")," in *Material Events*, 281. Tom Cohen flips Derrida's formula around in his energetic essay, "Toxic Assets: De Man's Remains and the Ecocatastrophic Imaginary (An American Fable)," in Tom Cohen, Claire Colebrook, and J. Hillis Miller, *Theory and the Disappearing Future* (New York: Routledge, 2012), 89–129: "Derrida does not explicate de Man's 'materiality' so much as divert it toward the *spectral* circuitry which he himself would like to keep open—one which maintains the rhetoric of the *to come*. In turn, one could say that the formulation involves a sleight of hand, in so far as de Man's term suggests rather a sort of *matter without 'materiality'* if the latter term retains any concep-

tual or binary form at all" (120). In my view Cohen is right to point to a disruptive blankness that de Man's term is designed to convey (and perform), though a potential problem with Cohen's formulation is that de Man's late essays do not use the term *matter* but rather *materiality*: clearly de Man wanted the *–iter*. Furthermore, Cohen's emphatic troping of materiality as sludge, oil, and toxic waste (92) risks the very hypostatization that he wishes to avoid.

26. Guillory goes so far as literally to naturalize de Manian materiality by way of a rapid jab at "Shelley Disfigured": "The linguistic Atropos cutting the thread of Shelley's text produces the pathos of indetermination (accident) out of the simple determinism of a material causality (in this case, bad weather)" (229). What Guillory himself means by "material" here is unclear (if one's vocabulary is Aristotelian, "bad weather" could be termed the efficient cause of Shelley's death, but hardly the material cause); it would seem that he has assimilated the material to something like "the real" in a precritical sense—the natural world as physical force and phenomenal experience.

27. There is one apparent counterexample to my claim here: a sentence in "Hegel on the Sublime" in which de Man speaks of a moment in Hegel in which "the idea leaves a material trace, accessible to the senses, upon the world" (*AI*, 108). But as even this fragment of a sentence, let alone the rest of the discussion, makes clear, the point is that, although the material trace, like any sign, is accessible to the senses, its status *as* sign causes the phenomenal "presence" of a sensation to be contaminated by the differential structure of the trace.

Guillory's is not an uncommon misprision—it takes even more extreme form in the argument Walter Benn Michaels mounts against de Man. In *The Shape of the Signifier: 1967 to the End of History* (Princeton: Princeton University Press, 2004), Michaels returns to some of the issues he and Stephen Knapp engaged in their famous position paper "Against Theory" (for discussion of that essay, see Chapter 2). Michaels explains de Man's notion of materiality in the terms of its opposite—phenomenality: e.g., "The purely material, in other words, is everything that can be seen by the reader" (6); it is the "idea of the reader's experience" (ibid.). Michaels also assimilates a text's "physical features" to "what Derrida calls its marks" (13). (This is what Derrida explicitly explains he does *not* mean: see, e.g., *Limited Inc* [Evanston, Ill.: Northwestern University Press, 1988], 23.) All of this is being driven by Michaels's interest in constructing a binary opposition according to which we either understand meaning as authorial (the only way in which, according to Michaels, we should conceive of meaning) or are forced to understand meaning as the reader's experience (which, absurdly, would make every detail in the reader's perceptual field count as part of the meaning), and "anyone who thinks the text consists of its physical features (of what Derrida calls its marks) will be required also to think that the meaning of the text is crucially determined by the experience of its readers" (13). For an extensive critique of Michaels, see Wang, *Romantic Sobriety*.

28. I have elsewhere tried to sketch out an interplay among aesthetics, technics, and theory: see *Politics of Aesthetics*, 14–29. For an extremely helpful reading of Heidegger that clarifies how technics may be understood both as a power to fix and control, and as a "movement of unsecuring," see Weber, *Mass Mediauras*, 55–75.

29. Guillory engages in a hardworking and generally respectful argument with Neil

Hertz's essay "Lurid Figures" (see Guillory, 233–35). I leave aside here the extremely interesting topic of pathos in de Man; on this subject, see Hertz's "Lurid Figures," in Lindsay Waters and Wlad Godzich, *Reading de Man Reading* (Minneapolis: University of Minnesota Press, 1989), and his follow-up essay "More Lurid Figures," *Diacritics* 20, no. 3 (1990): 2–49; also my *Politics of Aesthetics*, 95–124; and Rei Terada, *Feeling in Theory: Emotion after the "Death of the Subject"* (Cambridge, Mass.: Harvard University Press, 2001), 48–89 and *passim*.

30. The most important and visible example would be Cathy Caruth's work on trauma, which took initial form as her introductions to two linked issues of *American Imago* 48, nos. 1 and 4 (Spring and Winter 1991).

31. Avital Ronell, *Stupidity* (Urbana: University of Illinois Press, 2002), 97.

32. For a meditation on the political dimension of de Man's thought that is particularly attentive to the violence of formalization, see Cynthia Chase, "Trappings of an Education: Toward that which we do not yet have," in *Responses: On Paul de Man's Wartime Journalism*, ed. Werner Hamacher, Neil Hertz, and Thomas Keenan (Lincoln: University of Nebraska Press, 1989), 44–79.

6. Querying, Quarrying: Mark Tansey's Paintings of Theory's Grand Canyon

1. With one exception: *Constructing the Grand Canyon* (1990), which is one of the paintings I discuss in this chapter, and which uses snippets of text that I, at least, cannot identify. The other works that I am nicknaming "theory paintings" draw identifiably either on the de Man or the Derrida pages. *Derrida Queries de Man, Close Reading, Bridge over the Cartesian Gap, Incursion, a,* and *Reader,* all from 1990, use either page 146 or 147 or the double-page spread 146–47 from *Blindness and Insight* as "texture" in this way. So does the painting *Archive,* from 1991. Although (as we shall see in the case of *Derrida Queries de Man*) these paintings may include lines of print from other pages of *Blindness and Insight* or from pages from other texts altogether (the degree of blur makes it impossible to be sure), one can at least say that the 146–47 page spread dominates and marks—in a sense "signs"—these text-paintings. (Only the painting *a* has clearly incorporated other texts: the female figure who is drawing the graffiti-figure stands on ground striated with text printed in a font different from that of *Blindness and Insight.* The wall, however, on which she draws she is once again page 147 of *Blindness and Insight,* which therefore remains the dominant textual marker.) I shall be discussing the (complicated) significance of the de Man text (these are pages from the essay "Literary History and Literary Modernity") as part of my discussion of *Derrida Queries de Man* in the next section of this chapter.

Two more paintings from 1990, *Under Erasure* and *John the Baptist Discarding His Clothes in the Wilderness (after Domenico Veneziano),* use silkscreened pages from Gayatri Spivak's translation of Jacques Derrida's *Of Grammatology* (Baltimore: Johns Hopkins University Press, 1976). Although Tansey does not reproduce visible page numbers, in *Under Erasure* he gives prominence to the running head "The Violence of the Letter" and offers enough legible fragments of text that one can reconstruct the background as—or at least as dominated by—the page spread 112–13 of *Of Grammatology.* The bottom of page 112 of this text is also identifiable as the text striating the bottom triangle of "foreground" in *John the Baptist*. Readings of these paintings, therefore, would want (carefully) to take their initial cue from this section of *Of Grammatology*, in which Derrida offers his famous critique of Claude Lévi-Strauss's pages on "A Writing Lesson" in *Tristes Tropiques*.

2. Tansey's work has been discussed by scholars interested in theory and philosophy: see especially Mark C. Taylor, *The Picture in Question: Mark Tansey and the Ends of Representation* (Chicago: University of Chicago Press, 2010).

3. Arthur Conan Doyle, "The Adventure of the Empty House," in *The Complete Sherlock Holmes* (New York: Doubleday, 1953), 2 vols., 563. Further citations from the Holmes stories and novels are taken from this edition. Since the two volumes are continuously paginated, only page numbers will be given in parenthetical references in what follows, though I shall also give the name of the story for ease of reference. In describing Holmes's fighting skills, Conan Doyle is referring to "bartitsu," a martial art that had a brief moment of popularity at the end of the nineteenth century.

4. Mark Tansey, in Arthur C. Danto, *Mark Tansey: Visions and Revisions*, ed. Christopher Sweet, notes and comments by Mark Tansey (New York: Abrams, 1992), 128.

5. We can be reasonably sure that Tansey has captured the running head of page 146 here, since below it one can make out words ("and jointly fall") from the first print line of that page. See Paul de Man, *Blindness and Insight: Essays in the Rhetoric of Contemporary Criticism* (New York: Oxford University Press, 1971), 146. (Pagination is the same for the original or the revised version of *Blindness and Insight*.)

6. De Man offers his own translation of Nietzsche's texts in *Blindness and Insight*; the edition that de Man references is Friedrich Nietzsche, "Vom Nutzen und Nachteil der Historie für das Leben," *Unzeitgemäße Betrachtung II*, in Karl Schlecta, ed., *Werke I* (Munich, 1954).

7. I believe I am able to read the following fragments on the path: "plane"—or possibly "plan"—"gr," "that," "in this context." I have searched the text of *Blindness and Insight* (thanks to Abigail De Kosnik for helping me with an electronic search) and have only found the phrase "in this context" on two pages of the book, and neither works as a source (in one case the initial letter is capitalized; in the other the phrase rides over a line break). The typeface does resemble that of *Blindness and Insight*, though: a version of Times typeface with distinctively long ascenders and descenders. (I thank Todd Sample of Oxford University Press for researching the typeface of *Blindness and Insight* for me.) The path toward these figures remains a mystery.

8. My word "typeface" is potentially misleading here, to the extent that it suggests a fully automated printing process. It looks to me as though Tansey has lettered the title of the painting with a Leroy lettering machine or some equivalent.

9. De Man's existential vocabulary here, which opposes biology to ontology, prevents him from dwelling on one of Nietzsche's salient paradoxes, which is that human historical action has something fundamental in common with its conceptual opposite, animal life. On the one hand, as de Man puts it, the "restlessness of human society, in contrast to the placid state of nature of the animal herd, is diagnosed as man's inability to forget the past" (146); on the other hand, when man *is* able to forget the past, he accedes to his true humanity, even though at such moments he seems to coincide with the nonhistoricity of the animal. "Moments of genuine humanity thus are moments at

which all anteriority vanishes, annihilated by the power of an absolute forgetting," as de Man sums up this side of Nietzsche's argument (147).

10. Holmes's method has been studied with particular care by semiologists: see *The Sign of Three: Dupin, Holmes, Peirce*, ed. Umberto Eco and Thomas Sebeok (Bloomington: Indiana University Press, 1983). Most of the contributors reflect on similarities between Holmes's practice of logical inference and what Charles Sanders Peirce calls abduction. For a particularly interesting discussion, see Eco's contribution, "Horns, Hooves, Insteps: Some Hypotheses on Three Types of Abduction" (198–220).

11. Eco, "Horns, Hooves, Insteps," 216; I have corrected what appears to be a typo by substituting "and" for "of." Eco is discussing one of Holmes's most extravagant feats: his reading of Watson's mind in "The Adventure of the Cardboard Box" based on Watson's facial expressions and eye movements. (Because this story ran into publishing difficulties, Conan Doyle later moved its mind-reading scene to another story, "The Resident Patient," so it appears twice in the collected works: see 488–89 and 1,044–46). Holmes creates a narrative for Watson's train of thoughts that, as Eco points out, in the "real" world would soon enter an astronomically low probability zone, since it would require choosing at every point among numerous alternative paths that Watson's thoughts could plausibly have taken.

12. In honor of Wilde, we may note that the Holmes-Watson relationship is granted a late, fleeting bloom in "The Adventure of the Three Garridebs," when Watson is shot in the thigh and Holmes embraces him and cries out in anxiety. Watson comments: "It was worth a wound—it was worth many wounds—to know the depth of loyalty and love which lay behind that cold mask. The clear, hard eyes were dimmed for a moment, and the firm lips were shaking. For the one and only time I caught a glimpse of a great heart as well as of a great brain. All my years of humble but single-minded service culminated then in that moment of revelation" (1241). Holmes then "rip[s] open [Watson's] trousers with his pocket-knife."

13. See, e.g., "The Adventure of the Bruce-Partington Plans," in which Holmes is assured that "the whole force of the State is at your back if you should need it" (1,088). A few of the later stories feature German villains; and in "His Last Bow," Conan Doyle has an elderly Holmes come out of retirement on the eve of the First World War to become a deep-cover counterintelligence agent for Britain. For a glimpse of the stories at their most racist, see "The Adventure of the Three Gables." For a study that locates the Holmes stories within a context of late-nineteenth-century technologies of identification and surveillance, see Carlo Ginzburg, "Morelli, Freud, and Sherlock Holmes: Clues and Scientific Method," in Eco and Sebeok, *The Sign of Three*, 81–118.

14. See my earlier note, and compare, e.g., "The Adventure of the Dancing Men," 593–94.

15. Many more examples of hypersignificant faces and facial signifiers in the Holmes stories could be cited here. Now and then, the hyperlegibility of the face turns into something stranger. "The Yellow Face" is a particularly interesting example, since this story puts pressure on the presumed hyperlegibility of race as well as the face, and is one of the very few cases in which Holmes fails to read the plot's riddle correctly. The plot involves an American woman who has married an Englishman and, unbeknownst to him, has brought over to England her mixed-race child by her deceased African

American first husband. She keeps the child secreted in a neighboring house, and has it wear a mask whenever it looks out a window; her new husband, jealous of her secret visits to this house, consults Holmes, who suspects that a former husband has returned, and is as surprised as the husband and Watson when the secret is revealed. The story has an atypically sweet ending, with the new husband accepting the child. The plot mechanism itself is simplistic, but the figuration of the "face" is striking. Despite the title, no literal "yellow face" appears in the story. The mask worn by the child is "of a livid chalky white" [406–7] and "of the strangest livid tint" [414]; when the mask is removed, she stands revealed as "a little coal-black negress" [414]. An odd mobility or figurative excess marks the stereotyped signs of race in this text. No wonder Holmes has trouble reading it.

16. And before we manage to learn anything of Professor Moriarty, in "The Adventure of the Final Problem," *he* has already generated a brother, Colonel James Moriarty, who doubles Watson in struggling for public control of the story of Holmes and Moriarty.

17. Conan Doyle borrows major motifs from Poe, of course: Dupin and his narrator and Holmes and Watson are close relatives (the brilliant aesthete-detective and the first-person narrator-foil, inhabiting a smoke-saturated room, etc.). The Holmes-Moriarty double repeats, in a somewhat more violent register, Dupin's specular faceoff with the cunning Minister D—in "The Purloined Letter." And there are other significant gestures of homage: at one point Conan Doyle has Holmes echo Dupin's account, in "The Purloined Letter," of the play of identification in the even-odd guessing game: "You know my methods in such cases, Watson. I put myself in the man's place, and having first gauged his intelligence, I try to imagine how I should myself have proceeded under the same circumstances" (455, "Musgrave Ritual"). On the abyssal doublings and archival echoings in the Dupin stories (and their intimacy with high "theory"), see Barbara Johnson's classic essay, "The Frame of Reference: Poe, Lacan, Derrida," *Yale French Studies* 55–56 (1977): 457–505. A convenient anthology collecting Poe's story and texts by Lacan, Derrida, Johnson, and other critics is John P. Mueller, *The Purloined Poe: Lacan, Derrida, and Psychoanalytic Reading* (Baltimore: Johns Hopkins University Press, 1987).

18. Eve Sedgwick's work on the gothic deserves (and has often received) an essay unto itself. Probably the most illuminating reading for anyone wanting to analyze the Holmes-Watson bachelor snuggery in relation to the specular, violent Holmes-Moriarty agon would be the two Dickens chapters in Sedgwick's classic *Between Men: English Literature and Male Homosocial Desire* (New York: Columbia University Press, 1985).

19. The newspapers usually only present fragments of a case, of course, and usually wrongly give credit to Scotland Yard. Only Watson can reliably transform Holmes's cases into public narratives. There is one curious partial exception: "The Stock-Broker's Clerk," in which the solution is revealed at the end of the story by a newspaper.

20. Holmes appears to have other publicity engines at work besides Watson. "You see me now," he tells Watson in "The Musgrave Ritual," "when my name has become known far and wide, and when I am recognized both by the public and by the official

force as being a final court of appeal in doubtful cases. Even when you knew me first, at the time of the affair which you have commemorated in 'A Study in Scarlet,' I had already established a considerable, though not a very lucrative, connection. You can hardly realize, then, how difficult I found it at first, and how long I had to wait before I succeeded in making any headway" (446). Holmes grows more famous as the stories progress: by the time of "The Reigate Puzzle," "Europe was ringing with his name" and "his room was literally ankle-deep with congratulatory telegrams" (458). In the late stories, he and Watson have become media figures—to the point that an admiring police inspector, in the late novel *The Valley of Fear*, remarks, "Come along, Dr. Watson, and when the time comes we'll all hope for a place in your book" (925).

21. It is of interest, in this context, that Holmes rivals in recognizability, if not in overt monstrosity, those other master-avatars of mass culture and mechanical reproducibility, Frankenstein and Dracula.

22. Holmes's brother Mycroft represents the exaggerated limit-case. Like Harold Bloom's or Samuel Johnson's, Mycroft's genius brain inhabits a large, sedentary, and potentially uncontrollable body (though "after the first glance one forgot the gross body and remembered only the dominant mind"; 1077, "The Adventure of the Bruce-Partington Plans"). Mycroft is much more of a central computer than Bloom—more omnivorous in his data consumption, more "tidy and orderly" in his data processing, less programmed to pathetic affect. Both, however, exemplify the genius as cyborg, and Mycroft helps us posit an affinity between geniuses who internalize "the canon" and geniuses who internalize "the nation." Mycroft holds a secret but all-important salaried position in the British government. "Occasionally he *is* the British government," Holmes tells Watson: "His position is unique. He has made it for himself. There has never been anything like it before, nor will be again. He has the tidiest and most orderly brain, with the greatest capacity for storing facts, of any man living. The same great powers which I have turned to the detection of crime he has used for this particular business. The conclusions of every department are passed to him, and he is the central exchange, the clearing-house, which makes out the balance. All other men are specialists, but his specialism is omniscience. We will suppose that a minister needs information as to a point which involves the Navy, India, Canada, and the bimetallic question; he could get his separate advices from various departments upon each, but only Mycroft can focus them all, and say offhand how each factor would affect the other. They began by using him as a short-cut, a convenience; now he has made himself an essential. In that great brain of his everything is pigeon-holed and can be handed out in an instant. Again and again his word has decided the national policy" (1076, "The Adventure of the Bruce-Partington Plans").

23. Tansey's painting plays complexly with the similarities and differences between itself and its archival quasi-double. The differences are dramatic, of course: Tansey's painting is a high-art large-scale canvas, nearly seven feet in height, whereas Paget's pen and ink wash drawing for *The Strand Magazine* is scaled to its purpose (it is 10.5 in. × 6.75 in.), which is to "illustrate" a mechanically reproduced text. Paget's originals, however, have in our day become expensive commodities on the art market, so any full analysis of the allusive gesture linking Tansey's painting to Paget's drawing would need to avoid translating that relationship into a complacent binary opposition. Paget's il-

lustration is the first to include his signature and the first to be used as a frontispiece in *The Strand Magazine*.

24. "An examination by experts leaves little doubt that a personal contest between the two men ended, as it could hardly fail to end in such a situation, in their reeling over, locked in each other's arms" (555). This unexplained replication and multiplication of Holmes into an anonymous collective of "experts" on the final page of "The Final Problem" is one of the odder twists in the Holmes canon, but rhymes with the stories' persistent emphasis on doubling, mechanical reproducibility, newspapers, and so on.

25. As regards that hat (in case anyone cares): it is true that Holmes wears a top hat in the city, and that Conan Doyle never uses the word "deerstalker"; but Molly Ierulli has pointed out to me that, headed for the country, Holmes wears an "ear-flapped traveling cap"—essentially a deerstalker—in the story "Silver Blaze" (383), so the hat is not entirely Paget's intellectual property.

26. When Watson, who has been decoyed away, returns to find Holmes vanished, he shouts back: "it was in vain that I shouted. My only answer was my own voice reverberating in a rolling echo from the cliffs around me . . . I shouted; but only that same half-human cry of the fall was borne back to my ears" (553–54). The pattern continued ten real-time years later: when Doyle finally gave in and brought Holmes out of the waterfall in "The Adventure of the Empty House," he had Holmes tell Watson: "I am not a fanciful person, but I give you my word that I seemed to hear Moriarty's voice screaming at me out of the abyss" (564).

27. Paul de Man, "Shelley Disfigured," *The Rhetoric of Romanticism* (New York: Columbia University Press, 1984), 122.

28. See Neil Hertz, "The Notion of Blockage in the Literature of the Sublime," in *The End of the Line: Essays on Psychoanalysis and the Sublime* (New York: Columbia University Press, 1985), 40–60.

29. Arthur C. Danto, "Mark Tansey: The Picture Within the Picture," in Danto, *Mark Tansey*, 7–29, at 29. Danto's desire to pinpoint this painting's fundamental agon and to name it "Rousseau" may have contributed to his having misidentified the de Man text that Tansey silkscreens into the background of *Close Reading*, a painting that Danto discusses in close proximity to *Derrida Queries de Man*. As noted in an earlier footnote, *Close Reading*, like most of the 1990 "theory" paintings, draw on pages 146–47 from "Literary History and Literary Modernity"; Danto mistakenly identifies the silkscreened text as stemming from another essay from *Blindness and Insight*, "The Rhetoric of Blindness"—de Man's famous essay on Derrida (see Danto, 28–29). One might indeed have expected Tansey to draw on that essay for his textualized landscapes, especially for *Derrida Queries de Man*, but if he did at any point in these paintings, the source has been blurred out of recognizability, at least for this viewer, who, except in the case of *Constructing the Grand Canyon,* has had to work from reproductions.

30. Judi Freeman, "Metaphor and Inquiry in Mark Tansey's 'Chain of Solutions,'" in Judi Freeman, ed., *Mark Tansey/Judi Freeman: With Essays by Alain Robbe-Grillet and Mark Tansey* (San Francisco: Chronicle Books, 1993), 13–68, at 42.

31. It would take a very long footnote to situate the "Heidegger affair" that was created first in the French and then in the broader European and Anglo-American

media, nominally in the wake of Victor Farias's sensationalizing study, *Heidegger et le nazisme* (Paris: Verdier, 1987). The "de Man affair," which I have touched on in the Introduction and Chapter 1, was primarily an Anglo-American phenomenon but registered in a few European media centers.

32. Paul de Man, *Allegories of Reading: Figural Language in Rousseau, Rilke, Nietzsche and Proust* (New Haven: Yale University Press, 1979), 277.

33. Jacques Derrida, *Of Spirit: Heidegger and the Question*, trans. Geoffrey Bennington and Rachel Bowlby (Chicago: University of Chicago Press, 1989 [1987]), 93–94. The italicized phrase "before any question" spurs a huge footnote that a full consideration of Derrida's framing of the "question of the question" would need to read very carefully. See *Of Spirit*, 129–36.

34. Paul de Man, "Dialogue and Dialogism," in *The Resistance to Theory* (Minneapolis: University of Minnesota Press, 1986), 113.

35. Stephen J. Pyne, *How the Canyon Became Grand: A Short History* (New York: Viking, 1998), xiii. Pyne notes that one of the preconditions for aesthetic and cultural processing of the Canyon as "Grand" was the invention of geologic time. "Between the late eighteenth century and the mid twentieth century, the known age of the earth increased a millionfold, from less than 6,000 years to more than 4.6 billion" (51). (The stratigraphy of the Grand Canyon goes into deep time: the lower levels cut into the Proterozoic Vishnu schist.) According to Pyne, the modern tourist experience of the Canyon took shape after the extension of a Santa Fe railroad link to the South Rim in 1901.

36. This was the second monumental canvas of Moran's that Congress had purchased; two years earlier, the government had bought his *Grand Canyon of the Yellowstone* and hung it prominently in the Capitol. Moran's renditions of Yellowstone were particularly famous; reproductions of them circulated in magazines, and they often plausibly receive credit for helping to create the conditions for the establishment of Yellowstone as the first National Park in 1872. *The Chasm of the Colorado* is the first famous painting of the Grand Canyon. Moran painted renditions of the Canyon for the next four decades; he is the landscape artist of the era most strongly associated with the Canyon (and, as noted, with other Western sites, particularly Yellowstone, that were being granted national significance in the post–Civil War era).

37. The identification seems a safe guess, though the face is obscured and we have only the iconic bald dome and the ridge of eyeglasses to rely on (see Danto's key to the painting, 137: Foucault is the only figure whom Danto identifies in the painting, apart from the Yale Critics). One might have expected the figure of the surveyor peering through his instrument right above Foucault to be a famous theorist, but he does not resemble anyone I, at least, can identify.

38. Jacques Derrida, "Some Statements and Truisms about Neologisms, Newisms, Postisms, Parasitisms, and Other Small Seismisms," in *The States of "Theory": History, Art, and Critical Discourse*, ed. David Carroll (New York: Columbia University Press, 1990), 89. See the Introduction for discussion of this text.

Index

Abraham, Nicolas, 236–37n39
Abrams, M. H., 10, 35, 66, 69–74, 84, 104, 218n19, 219n26, 224n6
Adair, Gilbert, 195n32
Adorno, Theodor, 47, 201n83, 237n46
aesthetics: as education, 4–5, 18, 40–41, 56–57, 128–30, 157, 185, 208n71; as locus of excess, linked to romanticism and "theory," 41–42, 159, 168, 207nn62–63; as phenomenalization of signification, 8–9, 58, 185
Allen, Graham, 234n28, 237n42
Alter, Robert, 39
Anderson, Amanda, 50
Arac, Jonathan, 2, 34, 191n1, 202n35
Arendt, Hannah, 33
Arnold, Matthew, 45, 47, 209n73
Auerbach, Erich, 223n2
Avedon, Richard, 109

Bahti, Timothy, 200n27, 216n11
Baker, John, Jr., 221n35
Balibar, Étienne, 238n6
Banville, John, 195n32
Barish, Evelyn, 15–17, 224n6
Bate, Walter Jackson, 84
Bateson, F. W., 68–69, 72, 75, 218nn19,22, 219n24
Beers, Henry A., 206n60
Begley, Adam, 108–9
Bell, Daniel, 47
Bennett, William, 209n74
Bérubé, Michael, 194n22
Bielik-Robson, Agata, 118–21, 234n25
Bloom, Harold, 2, 9–12, 23, 25, 27–37, 39, 43, 62–63, 84–86, 103–24, 180, 184, 193n13, 201n31, 224nn6,9,

225n13, 227n25, 230nn3–5, 230–31n6, 231nn9,10, 231–32n15, 232nn16,18, 232–33n20, 233nn21–23, 236n38, 237n42, 237–38n49, 247n22; *The Anxiety of Influence* and influence theory, 114–21, 233–34n25, 234n26, 234–35n29, 235nn32–34, 236–37n36, 237n45; as personification of the "canon," 11, 103, 107–12, 117
Bonnefoy, Yves, 213n99
Bourdieu, Pierre, 41, 128, 238n5
Bradley, Arthur, 235n32
Brassier, Ray, 214n104
Brenson, Michael, 209n75
Bright, Martin, 213n97
Brisman, Leslie, 193n13, 198n18
Brodsky, Claudia, 200n27
Brooks, Cleanth, 3, 31, 62, 68, 72, 75, 84, 200n24, 218nn19,22, 218–19n23, 230n3
Brooks, Peter, 198n18
Brown, Wendy, 194n23
Bruss, Elizabeth, 115, 118
Buckley, William F., 104, 200n25, 230n3
Burke, Edmund, 47–48, 210n85, 237n46
Burt, E. S., 213n99
Butler, Judith, 212n94

Campbell, Colin, 39, 231n13
canon debate, 12, 40, 106, 126–27
Caraher, Brian, 217n18, 218n19
Caruth, Cathy, 60, 99, 116–17, 200–1n27, 215n108, 226n19, 236n37, 243n30
Chaplin, Tracy, 192n7
Chase, Cynthia, 201n27, 203n41, 204n45, 219n25, 243n32

Cheney, Lynne V., 209n74
Clark, David L., 42, 222n38
Cohen, Tom, 201n27, 241–42n25
Colebrook, Claire, 194–95n29
Connaroe, Joel, 204n46
Culler, A. Dwight, 229n2
Culler, Jonathan, 14, 26, 48, 49, 62–63,
    191n1, 194n25, 198n14, 211n89,
    215n1, 216n11, 216–17n12, 235n29
Currie, Mark, 26–28, 196n4, 198n15
Cusset, François, 20, 196n2

Danto, Arthur C., 172, 248n29, 249n37
Davies, Hugh Sykes, 218n19
de Bolla, Peter, 234nn28,29
deconstruction, 1, 5–6, 8–9, 14, 20–21,
    23, 26, 33, 48, 66, 69–70, 72–73,
    125, 130–32, 158–59, 166, 175, 184,
    204–5n48. *See* "theory"
Deconstruction and Criticism (Bloom, de
    Man, Derrida, Hartman, Miller), 10, 63
de Graef, Ortwin, 3, 38, 195n30
de Man, Paul, 1–18, 22–34, 35–36,
    50–54, 55–61, 63–65, 74–75, 80–81,
    103, 118, 122–24, 125–57, 158–60,
    163–66, 171–75, 180–86, 200–1n27,
    224nn9,11, 237–38n49, 241n21, 243–
    44n1, 244n6, 244–45n9; *Allegories of
    Reading* (Proust reading), 139–44;
    critique of aesthetics, 4, 7–8, 56–61,
    215n106; on figurative language and
    reading, 4, 8, 35–37, 137, 140–48, 150,
    153–54; on linguistic materiality,
    146–48, 157, 207n63, 241–42n25,
    242nn26,27; "Literary History and
    Literary Modernity," 164–65, 225n13;
    "The Resistance to Theory," 4–5,
    55–61, 136, 151; review of Bloom's
    Anxiety of Influence, 112–15, 121,
    235n31; "Semiology and Rhetoric,"
    174; "Structure intentionnelle de
    l'image romantique," 85–87, 90, 102,
    224nn6,10,11, 224–25n12; wartime
    journalism and "de Man affair," 2–4,
    16, 38, 164–65, 172–73, 191–92n2,

194–95n29, 195n32. *See also*
    language; prosopopoeia; rhetorical
    reading; "theory"
DeMaria, Robert, Jr., 232n16
Deresiewicz, William, 192n4
Derrida, Jacques, 1–2, 5–7, 12, 14,
    17–18, 19–28, 30, 32–39, 48, 50–52,
    76, 78–79, 118–19, 121, 135, 147,
    150, 153, 158–60, 164–66, 171–75,
    180–86, 191n1, 191–192n2, 197n8,
    203n43, 207n62, 213nn96,99, 241n21,
    242n27, 243–44n1; on "theory," 6,
    195n35, 196–97n5
Deutsch, Helen, 232n16
Donoghue, Denis, 34
Doyle, Arthur Conan, 159–60, 165,
    172, 244n3, 246n17, 248nn25,26. *See*
    Sherlock Holmes

Eco, Umberto, 167, 245nn10,11
Ehrmann, Jacques, 198n13
Eliot, T. S., 42, 62
Empson, William, 62
Esch, Deborah, 201n27

Farias, Victor, 249n31
Felman, Shoshana, 2, 32, 191n1, 201n28,
    202n35, 204n45
Ferris, David, 201n27
Fish, Stanley, 5, 155, 221n36
Fite, David, 234n28
Fletcher, Angus, 27
Folkenflik, Robert, 232n16
Foucault, Michel, 5, 6, 27, 181, 184–85,
    222n38, 249n37
Freeman, Julie, 172–73
Freud, Sigmund, 16, 117, 120, 221n38,
    226n21
Fry, Paul H., 193n13, 226n22, 234n31
Frye, Northrop, 84

Gasché, Rodolphe, 9, 192n11
Gelley, Alexander, 27
Genette, Gérard, 142–43, 215n1, 240n19
Giamatti, A. Bartlett, 213n99

Ginzburg, Carlo, 245n13
Godzich, Wlad, 2, 34, 191n1, 202n35
Graff, Gerald, 30, 35, 44, 49, 192n3,
   211n89
Gray, Paul, 231n11
Grossvogel, David, 27
Guillory, John, 12–13, 53, 106–7, 124,
   125–57, 194n24, 208n70, 238n4,
   242–43n29
Guyer, Sara, 202n37, 240n16

Hamacher, Werner, 238n1
Hamilton, John, 109
Harpham, Geoffrey Galt, 45
Harris, Thomas, 233n21
Hartman, Geoffrey H., 2, 9–11, 23, 25,
   27–35, 37, 39, 42–43, 61, 62, 84–102,
   104, 112–13, 180, 184, 201n32,
   204n47, 213n99, 218n22, 223nn2,5,
   225n15, 226nn18,19, 229nn36,38,
   230n4; "Romanticism and Anti-Self-
   Consciousness," 87–89, 226nn16,17;
   Unmediated Vision, 87, 224n8, 227n28;
   "Voice of the Shuttle," 96–99,
   227–28n30, 228n34; Wordsworth's
   Poetry, 11, 87, 89–96, 99–102,
   226n24, 227nn25,26
Hegel, G. W. F., 110–11
Heidegger, Martin, 33, 173, 201n30,
   241n21, 248–49n31
Hersey, John, 230n6
Hertz, Neil, 97, 199n19, 228n31, 235n29,
   238n50, 242–43n29
Hilles, Frederick W., 229n2
Hirsch, E. D., 66, 68–69, 72, 74–75, 80,
   218nn19,20,21,22, 221n36
humanities, in the American university,
   3–4, 13–14, 44–47, 106, 129, 157, 185,
   194n22. See also aesthetics: as education; university
Humboldt, Wilhelm von, 43

imagination, romantic: 11, 84–94, 97,
   100–2
Irwin, John T., 198n18

Jacobs, Carol, 37, 137, 219n25
Jakobson, Roman, 35, 217n14
Jackson, Virginia, 64–66, 78–79,
   215n105, 216n7, 221n34, 222n39
Jameson, Fredric, 5, 39, 129, 201n28
Johnson, Barbara, 37, 54–55, 66, 191n1,
   201n27, 204n45, 212nn94,94, 217n15,
   228n33, 246n17
Johnson, Lyndon B., 209n75
Johnson, Samuel, 232n16
Juhl, P. D., 80, 222n42

Kamuf, Peggy, 77–79, 129–31, 133, 149,
   152, 221nn36,37, 238n4, 239n10
Kandell, Jonathan, 213n97
Kant, Immanuel, 46, 147, 221n38
Keenan, Thomas, 201n27
Kelley, Brooks Mathers, 210n79
Kermode, Frank, 84
Khalip, Jacques, 229n41
Kihn, Martin, 233n22
Klein, Richard, 27
Knapp, Stephen, "Against Theory"
   (with Walter Benn Michaels), 10,
   66–67, 74–82, 218n19, 220–21n33,
   221nn36,38, 222nn39,44
Kramer, Hilton, 30, 35, 199n20
Krieger, Murray, 26
Kuiken, Kir, 227n27

Lacan, Jacques, 5, 6, 110
language, 4–5, 7, 12, 17–18, 21–22,
   57–58, 145–46, 150, 157, 158, 173–75
Lehman, David, 15–17, 22, 23, 107
Leitch, Vincent, 35, 203n40, 204–5n48
Lentricchia, Frank, 28, 51–52, 53,
   213n98
Levinson, Marjorie, 219n24
Lewis, Philip, 27
literature, 8, 126–27, 150–53
Lloyd, David, 206n57
Loraux, Nicole, 228n35
Lovejoy, A. O., 207–8n64
lyric, 62–67, 73, 82–83, 215n1, 216n11,
   217n14; "new lyric studies," 64–66

Macaulay, Lord, 232n16
MacFarquhar, Larissa, 109, 117
Machery, Pierre, 238n6
Mack, Maynard, 31, 199n24, 229n2,
    230n3
Mannheim, Karl, 238n5
Martin, Wallace, 2, 34, 191n1, 201n32,
    202n35
Martz, Louis, 31, 199n24, 229n2, 230n3
McGann, Jerome, 207n62, 216n7,
    223n1
McGrath, Brian, 215n107
McGrath, Charles, 233n22
McLaughlin, Kevin, 215n109
Menand, Louis, 42
Michaels, Walter Benn, 72, 242n27;
    "Against Theory" (with Ste-
    phen Knapp), 10, 66–67, 74–82,
    218n19, 220–21n33, 221nn36,38,
    222nn39,43,44
Miekes, David, 230n5
Mill, John Stuart, 47
Miller, J. Hillis, 2, 10, 23, 24–29, 31–35,
    37, 39, 66–67, 69–74, 184, 193n19,
    194n27, 213n99, 214n101, 219n27,
    220n32; debate with M. H. Abrams,
    35, 66–67, 69–74, 219n26; on first
    meeting de Man, 197–98n12; read-
    ing of "A slumber did my spirit seal,"
    69–74, 220n31; on "Yale critics," 23,
    28–29, 33, 198–99n18
Milton, John, 92
Moorman, Mary, 218n18
Moran, Thomas, 179, 249n36
Mueller, John P., 246n17

Naas, Michael, 197n8
Newmark, Kevin, 201n27
Nietzsche, Friedrich, 35, 163–65, 120,
    173, 237n43, 244n6, 244–45n9
Nightingale, Andrea Wilson, 201n84
Nussbaum, Martha, 212n94

Oakley, Francis, 205–6n55
Oren, Dan O., 229n2

Paget, Sidney, *The Death of Sherlock
    Holmes*, 159–60, 167, 170–71,
    247–48n23
Paulhan, Jean, 87
Pepper, Thomas, 133–34
personification, 49–55, 66, 74, 93,
    97–98, 104, 122, 138, 149, 156, 166,
    170. *See also* Bloom, Harold; de Man,
    Paul; prosopopoeia; "theory"
Phelps, William Lyon, 206n60
Plunkert, David, 195n33
Poe, Edgar Allan, 169
Poirier, Richard, 29, 33
Pope, John, 199n24
Pottle, Frederick, 229n2, 230n3
Poulet, Georges, 34
Preyer, Robert O., 237n40
Prins, Yopie, 64–66, 215n105, 221n34
Pritchard, William, 29–30, 33, 35, 52,
    199n19
prosopopoeia, 17, 102, 145–48, 166
Proust, Marcel, 140–44, 240n19,
    240–41n20
Pyle, Forest, 41–42, 207n63, 225n12,
    227n27
Pyne, Stephen J., 178–79, 249n35

Rajan, Tilottama, 224n10
Raleigh, Sir Walter, 206n60
Rancière, Jacques, 9–10, 192n12, 193n15,
    207n62
Redfield, Marc, 193n14, 206n56,
    207n60, 210n82, 214n104, 223n1,
    232n17, 237n46, 238nn1,4, 239n7,
    240n17, 242n28, 242–43n29
rhetorical reading, 7, 12–13, 35–37,
    58–61, 63, 70, 112–14, 128, 132–34,
    137, 139–48, 150, 153–54
Richards, I. A., 62
Riddell, Joseph, 203n39, 220n29
Rieder, John, 206–7n60
Riffaterre, Michael, 147
Romano, Carlin, 16, 238n3
romanticism, 9–11, 41–44, 62–63,
    84–88, 193n13, 206n60, 207n62,

223n1. *See also* aesthetics; imagination, romantic; lyric; "theory"

Ronell, Avital, 154, 212n94

Rorty, Richard, 221n36

Rose, Jacqueline, 195n32

Rossi, Stephano, 154

Rousseau, Jean-Jacques, 36, 80–81, 144–45

Rousset, Jean, 19

Said, Edward, 5, 198n17

Salusinszky, Imre, 122

Schiller, Friedrich, 128

Schlink, Bernhard, 195n32

Schneiderman, Stuart, 27

Searle, John, 202nn32,36

Sedgwick, Eve, 169, 212n94, 246n18

Sellars, Roy, 237nn41,42

Sewell, Richard, 199n24

Shaw, Peter, 205n50

Sherlock Holmes, 16, 159–60, 165, 167–73, 244n3, 245nn10–13, 245–46n15, 246nn16–19, 246–47n20, 247nn21–22, 248nn24–26

Shumway, David R., 49

Siegel, Lee, 212n94

Siegel, Sandra, 27

Shumway, David R., 211n91

Simpson, David, 50, 210–11n86

Smith, Barbara Herrnstein, 128

Spivak, Gayatri, 5, 159, 212n94

Sprinker, Michael, 215n106

Steiner, George, 27

Stephens, Mitchell, 38, 205nn49,50, 212–13n96

Swann, Karen, 229n41

Tansey, Mark, 14, 23, 49, 159–67, 170–73, 175–86, 195n35, 243–44n1, 244n8; *Constructing the Grand Canyon*, 14, 159, 175–85, 249n37; *Derrida Queries de Man*, 14, 159–66, 170–73, 244n8

Taylor, John, 109, 111, 233n23

Taylor, Mark C., 244n2

Terada, Rei, 50–52, 65–66, 212n94, 242–43n29

"theory," 1–18, 20–24, 30–33, 47–57, 61, 62, 66, 74–75, 78, 82–85, 103, 106, 127–28, 131–35, 167, 171, 173, 181, 183, 185; and aesthetics, 1, 5–10, 39–40, 57–58, 185; as deconstruction, 1, 5–9, 20–22, 30, 75, 158, 166, 184; as media event, 1, 14–16, 21–22, 37–39, 148, 158–59; as personified by de Man, 1, 4, 10–17, 23, 35, 51–55, 131–32, 149, 166, 185; as personified by de Man-and-Derrida, 1–2, 4, 10, 14, 23, 28, 30, 33, 37, 50–51, 158, 170; and romanticism, 1, 9–10, 41–42, 83; as self-resistance, 1, 4–5, 8, 22, 55–57, 61

Thomas, Henri, 195n32

Thomas, Paul, 206n57

Thompson, D'Arcy W., 228n35

Tinker, Chauncey Brewster, 229n2

Todorov, Tzvetan, 27

Torok, Maria, 236–37n39

Trilling, Lionel, 104

university: in the United States, 3–4, 13, 43–47, 49, 106, 129, 157, 158, 185, 194n22, 211n89. *See also* aesthetics as education; humanities, in the American university; romanticism; "theory"

Vermeulen, Pieter, 226n19

Veysey, Lawrence, 43

Vickers, Nancy J., 221n34

Waith, Eugene, 199n24

Wang, Orrin N. C., 81, 83, 147, 221n36, 221–22n38, 222n43, 242n27

Warminski, Andrzej, 33, 201n27, 202n36, 203n43, 219n25

Warren, Robert Penn, 230n3

Wasserman, Earl, 84

Weber, Samuel, 239n11, 242n28

Weiskel, Thomas, 193n13, 198n18, 226n21

Weiss, Antonio, 111, 232n20

Wellek, René, 31, 84, 192n5, 193n13,
     200n24, 223nn2,3, 224n6
Whalley, George, 206n60
Williams, Jeffrey, 214n100
Wimsatt, William K., 3, 31, 62, 84,
     200n24, 229n2, 230n3
Winks, Robin, 200n25
Woodward, Kenneth L., 231n10
Wordsworth, William, 89; *The Prelude*,
     90–95; *The Ruined Cottage*, 100–2,
     147; "A slumber did my spirit seal,"
     66–83, 100, 217n17, 217–18n18,

218–19n23, 219n24; "Strange fits of
     passion," 99–100

Yale Critics, 2–3, 5, 9, 15, 23–39, 49,
     62–63, 83, 85, 103, 158–59, 180–84,
     191n1, 198n17, 200n26
Yale School, 3, 181, 212n94. *See also* Yale
     Critics
Yale University, 3–4, 31–33, 104, 193n13,
     199–200n24, 200n25, 209nn76,77,
     210n79, 229n2
Yates, Frances, 233n21

Sara Guyer and Brian McGrath, series editors

Sara Guyer, *Reading with John Clare: Biopoetics, Sovereignty, Romanticism*.

Philippe Lacoue-Labarthe, *Ending and Unending Agony: On Maurice Blanchot*. Translated by Hannes Opelz.

Emily Rohrbach, *Modernity's Mist: British Romanticism and the Poetics of Anticipation*.

Marc Redfield, *Theory at Yale: The Strange Case of Deconstruction in America*.